WINSTON CHURCHILL:
AN INTIMATE PORTRAIT

WINSTON CHURCHILL:

AN INTIMATE PORTRAIT

VIOLET BONHAM CARTER

SMITHMARK

This edition published in 1994 by SMITHMARK Publishers Inc.,
16 East 32nd Street, New York, NY 10016

SMITHMARK books are available for bulk purchase for sales
promotion and premium use. For details write or call the
manager of special sales, SMITHMARK Publishers Inc.,
16 East 32nd Street, New York, NY 10016; (212) 532-6600.

This edition published by special arrangement
with W.S. Konecky Associates, Inc.

ISBN: 0-8317-5868-6

Printed in the United States of America

10 9 8 7 6 5 4 3 2 1

Quotations from *The World Crisis, My Early Life: A Roving Commission,* and
Amid These Storms (Thoughts and Adventures) by Winston Churchill are used by
permission of Charles Scribner's Sons. Copyright, 1923, 1927, 1930, 1932, Charles
Scribner's Sons; renewal copyright 1951, 1955, © 1958, 1960 Winston Churchill.

To Winston Churchill
who in his lifetime took his place among the immortals
and whom I was blessed to call my friend

PREFACE

It may seem an act of rash presumption for one who, like myself, has never written a book to make a first attempt on this tremendous theme.

I feel, therefore, that I should explain the reasons which have given me courage to attempt it.

I have had the supreme good fortune to know Winston Churchill for the best part of my life. I have seen him at close range both in his public and his private life, in war and peace, in good times and in bad. I have had the opportunity to share his thoughts, to watch the workings of his extraordinary mind, to feel the impulse of his indomitable heart, and on occasion to remember and record his words.

While writing this book, I have often been reminded of Gray's remark to Horace Walpole that "any fool may write a most valuable book by chance, if he will only tell us what he heard and saw with veracity."

It has occurred to me that if a witness, however insignificant, had chanced to record their evidence of some of the epic figures of the past—of Julius Caesar—Cromwell—Napoleon—Abraham Lincoln—it might be welcome to posterity whatever its limitations. What I have to offer here is my evidence.

VIOLET BONHAM CARTER

CONTENTS

──────◄┤├►──────

Contents

LIST OF ILLUSTRATIONS

———◄ ►———

WINSTON CHURCHILL:
AN INTIMATE PORTRAIT

———————◄◄ ►►———————

FIRST ENCOUNTER

I FIRST MET Winston Churchill in the early summer of 1906 at a dinner party to which I went as a very young girl. Our hostess was Lady Wemyss and I remember that Arthur Balfour, George Wyndham, Hilaire Belloc and Charles Whibley were among the guests.

The Liberal Party had just been swept back to power on the flood tide of an overwhelming majority. Sir Henry Campbell-Bannerman was Prime Minister, my father, H. H. Asquith, Chancellor of the Exchequer and Winston Churchill was holding his first office as Under-Secretary for the Colonies. With his dramatic South African exploits behind him and a political career in the making, he was already on the highroad to fame. His critics might have called it notoriety. For then as always he had critics. His unabashed confidence, unsquashable re-silience, his push and dash and flair for taking short cuts through life, his contempt for humdrum conformity, always challenged stolid, stick-in-the-mud opinion here and elsewhere. No one knew better how to perform the public service known as putting the cat among the pigeons.

I found myself sitting next to this young man who seemed to me quite different from any other young man I had ever met. For a long time he remained sunk in abstraction. Then he appeared to become suddenly aware of my existence. He turned on me a lowering gaze and asked me abruptly how old I was. I replied that I was nineteen. "And I," he said almost despairingly, "am thirty-two already. Younger than anyone else who *counts,* though," he added, as if to comfort himself. Then savagely: "Curse ruthless time! Curse our mortality. How cruelly short is the allotted span for all we must cram into it!" And he burst forth into an eloquent diatribe on the shortness of human life, the immensity of possible human accomplishment—a theme so well exploited by the poets, prophets and philosophers of all ages that it might seem difficult to invest it with a new and startling significance. Yet for me he did so, in a torrent of magnificent language which appeared to be both effortless and inexhaustible and ended up with the words I shall always remember: "We are all worms. But I do believe that I am a glowworm."

By this time I was convinced of it—and my conviction remained unshaken throughout the years that followed.

Later on he asked me whether I thought that words had a magic and a music quite independent of their meaning. I said I certainly thought so, and I quoted as a classic though familiar instance the first lines that came into my head.

> Charm'd magic casements, opening on the foam
> Of perilous seas, in faery lands forlorn . . .

His eyes blazed with excitement. "Say that again," he said, "say it again—it is marvelous!" "But," I objected, "you know these lines. You know the 'Ode to a Nightingale.'" He had apparently never read it and never heard of it before. (I must, however, add that next time I met him he had learned not merely this but all the odes of Keats by heart—and he recited them quite mercilessly from start to finish, not sparing me a syllable.)

Finding that he liked poetry, I quoted to him from one of my own favorite poets, Blake. He listened avidly, repeating some lines to himself with varying emphases and stresses, then added meditatively: "I never knew that that old Admiral had found time to write so much good poetry." I was astounded that he, with his acute susceptibility to words and power of using them, should have left such tracts of English literature entirely unexplored. But however it had happened he had lost nothing by it. As he himself put it, when he approached books it was "with a hungry, empty mind and with fairly strong jaws, and what I got I bit." And his ear for the beauty of language needed no tuning fork.

Until the end of dinner I listened to him spellbound. I can remember thinking: *This* is what people mean when they talk of seeing stars. That is what I am doing now. I do not to this day know who was on my other side. Good manners, social obligation, duty—all had gone with the wind. I was transfixed, transported into a new element. I knew only that I had seen a great light. I recognized it as the light of genius.

Remembering my callow youth readers may well discount the indelible impression I then received. But young and inexperienced as I was I had even then some standards of comparison. My lot happened to have been cast by Fortune in a context of rare and various minds. From earliest childhood my father had been my closest and most intimate friend. As I grew up I had met and listened with delight to many of his political colleagues and opponents, to Arthur Balfour, to John Morley, to Augustine Birrell, Lord Hugh Cecil and Edward Grey, to name a few. Among my own generation my friends were drawn from the contemporaries of my four Oxford brothers, who all belonged to vintage years. And yet, I knew that I had never met anyone before at all like Winston Churchill. What was it, I asked myself, which marked him out from all the rest? I might, if I had known them at the time, have answered my own question in the words of Dr. Johnson: "We all know what light is. But it is difficult to *tell* what it is."

I cannot attempt to analyze, still less to transmit, the light of genius. But I will try to set down, as I remember them, some of the differences which struck me at the time between him and all the others, young and old, whom I had known.

First and foremost he was incalculable. He ran true to no form. There lurked in every thought and word the ambush of the unexpected. I felt also that the impact of life, ideas and even words upon his mind was not only vivid and immediate, but *direct*. Between him and them there was no shock absorber of vicarious thought or precedent gleaned either from books or other minds. His relationship with all experience was firsthand.

My father and his friends were mostly scholars, steeped in the classical tradition, deeply imbued with academic knowledge, erudition and experience. Their intellectual granaries held the harvests of the past. On many themes they knew most of the arguments and all the answers to them. In certain fields of thought there was to them "nothing new under the sun." But to Winston Churchill everything under the sun was new—seen and appraised as on the first day of Creation. His approach to life was full of ardor and surprise. Even the eternal verities appeared to him to be an exciting personal discovery. (He often seemed annoyed to find that some of them had occurred to other people long ago.) And because they were so new to him he made them shine for me with a new meaning. However familiar his conclusion it had not been reached by any beaten track. His mind had found its own way everywhere.

Again—unlike the scholars—he was intellectually quite uninhibited and unself-conscious. Nothing to him was trite. The whole world of thought was virgin soil. He did not seem to be the least ashamed of uttering truths so simple and eternal that on another's lips they would be truisms. (This was a precious gift he never lost.) Nor was he afraid of using splendid language. Even as I listened, glowing and vibrating to his words, I knew that many of my captious and astringent friends would label them as "bombast," "rhetoric," "heroics." But I also knew with certainty that if they did they would be wrong. There was nothing false, inflated, artificial in his eloquence. It was his natural idiom. His world was built and fashioned in heroic lines. He spoke its language.

One other, paradoxical impression I carried away from this, our first encounter. Although he had the ageless quality of greatness I felt that he was curiously young. In fact, in some pedestrian ways, he made me feel that I was older. I felt that, though armed to the teeth for life's encounter, he was also strangely vulnerable, that he would need protection from, interpretation to, a humdrum world which would not easily apprehend or understand his genius. And in this last fear I was right.

It was my father's invariable habit to sit up reading in his bedroom for an hour or two before going to bed. I always went to say good night to him and share with him the adventures of my day. That night I burst into his room and poured out my experience, assuring him that for the first time in my life I had seen genius. I remember his amused response: "Well, Winston would certainly agree with you there—but I am not sure whether you will find many others of the same mind. Still, I know exactly what you mean. He is not only remarkable but unique. He will now have every chance to extend himself and show his paces."

I remember instinctively omitting from my story the fact that Winston had never read the "Ode to a Nightingale," fearing that it might lower him in my father's estimation. This unusual act of censorship was a proof that I had forged a new loyalty.

When I proclaimed to others my discovery, I found my father's warning fully justified. My estimate of Winston Churchill was not sympathetically received. In fact I was mocked by many. The attitude of the general public toward him at the time was, at best, one of expectant interest, curiosity, and tolerant amusement; at worst, one of mistrust and acid reprobation. In Tory and social circles he had for some years past been a red rag which turned the mildest cows into infuriated bulls. He was an outsider, a pusher, thruster, and self-advertiser. After he crossed the Floor * he became, in addition, a rat, a turncoat, an *arriviste* and (worst crime of all) one who had certainly arrived. To take him down a peg or even several pegs was not only a pleasure but a duty—to society and to the nation.

The Liberals were naturally far more discerning. To their credit they have never regarded intellect as a dangerous factor in a politician. They recognized Winston Churchill's quality and they gloried in their glittering catch. But even among Liberals there were certain reservations and suspicions. He was "sound" on Free Trade, on South Africa and on Retrenchment, but what about Reform—and Peace? He appeared to have found fighting a rather too congenial occupation in the past. Had he got Liberalism in his bones? Would he stay put?

In private life though he inspired devotion in his friends he did not exercise on his contemporaries the fascination of his father, Lord Randolph Churchill. I remember asking my father, who as a young man in his early days in Parliament had known and loved Lord Randolph, which of the two he rated higher, and his reply: "You can't compare them. Randolph was irresistible. He had incomparably more charm, more wit. But—Winston is by far the better fellow of the two."

It is true I think that, though Winston Churchill impressed and often dazzled, he did not charm or try to charm. He was as impervious to atmosphere as a diver in his bell. By a blessed fluke I found my way into the bell and never lost it. To me it was a far more exciting place than the watery elements it excluded. But for those outside it often seemed to be an impenetrable shell. He sometimes made a brilliant sortie, but in conversation he exhaled rather than inhaled and this was occasionally, and not unnaturally, resented by his interlocutor. I remember my stepmother, who enjoyed self-expression and indulged it to the full, complaining that he had "a noisy mind."

Hoping to provide a double treat I placed beside him at a luncheon party one of the rarest and most remarkable women of her generation, Lady Horner, an intimate friend both of my father and of Lord Haldane, and before their day of Burne-Jones, Ruskin and the Pre-Raphaelites. Her conversational resources were unlimited, her human understanding flexible and deep. I noticed with anxiety that hardly a word had passed between them. In answer to my solicitous inquiries she told me that after an aeon of unbroken silence she made a frontal attack

* In the House of Commons the Government and Opposition sit facing each other. A member who changes his party, as Winston Churchill did, crosses the Floor and sits facing his former colleagues.

and said to him: "Do tell me—what on earth *are* you thinking about?"
He replied: "I am thinking of a diagram" and relapsed into complete
absorption. She added: "I don't like people who make me feel as though
I wasn't there." In later years they became fast friends.

When he was staying with us in Scotland the same fate overtook my
young stepcousin Diana Lister (now Lady Westmorland), who was so
outraged by his neglect that she snatched up her plate and knife and
fork and finished her luncheon standing at the sideboard. He did not
even notice her flight till at the very end of luncheon, casually glancing
at her empty chair, he asked me innocently: "What happened to that
jolly little trout?" He was full of compunction when I told him what
had happened and explained the vital matter which had filled his mind
to the exclusion of all else. To me these trivial incidents were illustrations both of his political weakness and his strength. William James once
wrote that men of genius differ from ordinary men not in any innate
quality of the brain, but in the aims and objects on which they concentrate and in the degree of concentration they manage to achieve.
Winston Churchill possessed a power of concentration amounting almost to obsession. It gave his purpose a momentum which often proved
irresistible. But the rock on which that purpose sometimes foundered
was the human element he had failed to take into account. Though he
was the most human of all human beings, he was himself far too extraordinary to know how ordinary people "worked."

I take, as an illustration, the episode which wounded him more
deeply than any other in his whole career. The Dardanelles expedition,
perhaps the most imaginative strategic concept of the First World War,
was first frustrated by a monolithic soldier at the War Office and then
defeated by a megalomaniac sailor at the Admiralty. Winston had failed
to recognize that the essential condition of its success was to secure not
the mere passive acquiescence but the active co-operation of Lord
Kitchener. Again the final breach with Fisher which hurled him from
the Admiralty fell like a thunderbolt. Their association had (in his own
words) been "deep and fiercely intimate." No two men had ever agreed
and disagreed more often and more passionately. No one knew better
than he did just how invaluable and how impossible a colleague Fisher
could be. And yet he seems to have had no inkling that their relations
had reached breaking point.

At the time of the Abdication his championship of Edward VIII was
inspired by a romantic loyalty. He would have been prepared to stand
alone beside his King against a world in arms. But he was also quite

oblivious to the state of mind of the ordinary men and women of this country, who expected from their King a Queen and not a hole-and-corner morganatic marriage.

Ordinary men and women were equally bewildered by his congenital incapacity to be commonplace. The British people like seeing in their statesmen a reflection of themselves, perhaps in slightly sublimated form. Lord Baldwin recognized this taste and assuaged it to the full. He realized that the public loves to hear the tunes it knows and he played them with a masterly dexterity and skill.

I remember the old Duke of Devonshire of that day who suffered from deafness once saying to my father of Lord Spencer: "I always hear *him* because I know exactly what he is going to say." The trouble with Winston Churchill was that no one ever knew what he was going to say—or do. The unpredictable is rarely popular. More often than not it is mistaken for the unreliable. The public likes getting what it expects. It resents surprises and prefers being lulled to being startled.

I am not of course suggesting that in that first summer of our early friendship any of these reflections, forecasts, or analyses crossed my mind. But I knew that politics depends above all else upon the power of persuading others to accept ideas. I was disturbed to find among so many people a blank and blind refusal to recognize Winston Churchill's rare and dazzling quality. And I sometimes felt amazement and alarm at his own seeming unawareness of their reactions to himself. Though he had vision he appeared to lack antennae—to ignore the need to feel his way about other minds. I remembered, with some reassurance, the lines of Blake:

> Does the Eagle know what is in the pit
> Or wilt thou go ask the Mole?

What need was there for him to grope his way among the groundling moles when he could soar above their heads? It was true that he never tempered the wind of his words or his opinions either to shorn or unshorn lambs. But how could he be expected to project himself into the mind or body of a sheep? Yet, as I had even then observed, the world was full of sheep, and sheep had votes.

It was he himself who had once quoted to me the words of one of his great heroes, Napoleon Bonaparte: "I have always marched with the opinions of four or five millions of men." The day would come when he would need the support of millions to realize his aims. In his own words, "great numbers are at least an explanation of great changes."

Armies are just as necessary in politics as in war. And they can only be recruited by persuasion.

Yet every time we met he exorcised in me any misgivings about his future; by the impetus of his mind, by his unerring instinct for the living thought and word, above all by his imagination—"imagination, which, in truth, is but another name for absolute power." Although I knew he did not see the world we lived in as it was, I felt he had the latent power to make his world our own, to impose his shape and pattern on events.

And in spite of his dark moments of impatience and frustration sometimes verging on despair, I was conscious of his own ultimate confidence in himself. He had no doubts about his star. He might have said with Keats: "There is an awful warmth about my heart like a load of immortality." Even in those early days he felt that he was walking with destiny and that he had been preserved from many perils to fulfill its purpose. And in this mystical conviction History has proved him right.

But in another instinctive certainty he proved wrong. He was convinced that he would die young, that he had only a short span of years in which to cover his appointed course, and this strange premonition filled him with a sense of burning urgency. Would he have time to do what Fate required of him? I was distressed and puzzled by this phantasy of early doom which had no root in facts or reason. I knew that he always traveled with cylinders of oxygen which he imbibed before speaking. Yet it was quite impossible to think of him as ill. His zest, vitality, activity and industry were inexhaustible. He seemed to have been endowed by Nature with a double charge of life. I probed for reasons. "Why should you die young? Why shouldn't you live till you are a hundred?" The only answer that I ever wrung from him was: "My father died when he was forty-six." And these words, though I so little understood their implication, held the key both to his entry into politics and to the course he followed throughout his early years. The mainspring of his thought and action was his hero worship of a father he had hardly known.

About his father's death he has written: "All my dreams of comradeship with him, of entering Parliament at his side and in his support were ended. There remained for me only to pursue his aims and vindicate his memory."

Chapter Two

THE CHRYSALIS

IN HIS BIOGRAPHY of Lord Randolph, Winston Churchill
has told the story of the romance between his father and his beautiful
American mother, Jeannette Jerome. They met at Cowes in 1873. At
first sight Lord Randolph fell in love with her and after a lightning
courtship of two days proposed to her and was accepted. The Duke of
Marlborough demanded a probationary period of delay, and Mrs. Jerome, offended by his caution, swept her daughter back to Paris. A
General Election mercifully intervened, and after Lord Randolph's first
and victorious candidature at Woodstock both families agreed to give
their blessing to the marriage. By an appropriate accident their eldest
son was born, before his time, at Blenheim, the Vanbrugh palace built
by the nation for his great ancestor John Churchill, first Duke of
Marlborough.

Winston Churchill has truly described himself as "a child of both
Worlds." The New World and the Old joined hands in him and both
played their part in his making. Blue blood and red were mingled in
his veins. Imbued with a historic sense of tradition he was quite untrammeled by convention. He was at once tough and tender, a romantic
and a realist, an aristocrat and yet our greatest Commoner. The elements
thus fused in him made him a natural citizen of both worlds and the
great interpreter between his father's and his mother's countries.

But the New World had no hand in his upbringing or education.
That task was left to the untender mercies of Victorian England at its
worst. He grew up in the days when in a certain stratum of society
children spent insulated lives immured in nursery wings and floors. Their

11

parents were remote, Olympian beings who must at all costs be protected from noise, intrusion, worry, interruption—in fact from children, in whom all such hazards are inherent. In many large Victorian households children were therefore rarely seen and never heard. Parents gave audiences at certain stated times, and for such occasions their children were suitably prepared, washed, brushed up and admonished. Mothers came up to say good night, tender and gleaming visions dressed for dinner, shimmering in diamond necklaces and radiant clothes. But life in the raw from which all intimacy springs often remained unshared.

The task of "bringing up" their children was in those days delegated by parents to a nannie, an essentially English institution of great permanence and power. No other country in the world produces nannies and there is still a world demand for them at almost any price. A nannie must enter into her kingdom when the baby is a month old, not a day sooner or later. "I had him from the month" is for her equivalent to saying: "He is my own child"—and from that day on he is. From the first moment of "taking over," pride, vigilance, authority, devotion are recklessly lavished upon a succession of children who do not in fact belong to her but whom she makes her own.

The "prostitution of maternity" her function has been called— wrongly, for there is no commerce in it. To be a nannie is not a profession but a vocation. But that it is a substitute for maternity and for much else besides is certainly true. No nannie has ever looked, or felt, like an old maid—and they all rightly bear the prefix "Mrs." Though weatherbeaten, they preserve an ageless freshness and warmth. They prove that if spinsters are starved it is not for want of husbands but for want of children.

Of Winston Churchill's childhood we know only what he has written of it himself. It is clear that both his parents influenced him deeply—at long range. In a sense their glamour was enhanced by their remoteness. Of his mother he has written: "She shone for me like the Evening Star. I loved her dearly—but at a distance. My nurse was my confidante. Mrs. Everest it was who looked after me and tended all my wants. It was to her I poured out my many troubles. . . ." [1] In his solitary childhood and unhappy school days Mrs. Everest was his comforter, his strength and stay, his one source of unfailing human understanding. She was the fireside at which he dried his tears and warmed his heart. She was the night light by his bed. She was security.

His portrait of her is a masterpiece, drawn with emotion and fidelity. Her stories of the virtues and the vices of her last charge, "little Ella, the daughter of a clergyman in Cumberland," her exaltation of her favorite county, Kent—"the garden of England"—her horror of the lethal habit of "sitting in wet feet," her "partiality for Low Church principles" and deep suspicion of Popish practices—all these authentic touches place Mrs. Everest in the great tradition of English nannies.

He has described her death in one of his most moving and self-revealing passages. "As soon as I heard she was seriously ill I travelled up to London to see her. . . . She knew she was in danger, but her only anxiety was for me. There had been a heavy shower of rain. My jacket was wet. When she felt it with her hands she was greatly alarmed for fear I should catch cold. The jacket had to be taken off and thoroughly dried before she was calm again. . . . I had to return to Aldershot by the midnight train for a very early morning parade. As soon as it was over, I returned to her bedside. She still knew me, but she gradually became unconscious. Death came very easily to her. She had lived such an innocent and loving life of service to others and held such a simple faith that she had no fears at all, and did not seem to mind very much. She had been my dearest and most intimate friend during the whole of the twenty years I had lived. . . ." [2] Until the end of his life her photograph hung in his room.

It was characteristic of him that, through the undying gratitude and love he bore her, Mrs. Everest became to him in his political life a symbol of the poor and needy, a class of whom he had known little at first hand. It was her memory which brought home their plight to his imagination in vivid personal terms. "When I think of the fate of poor old women, so many of whom have no one to look after them and nothing to live on at the end of their lives, I am glad to have had a hand in all that structure of pensions and insurance which no other country can rival and which is especially a help to them." [3] Who can doubt that when he wrote these words it was not the anonymous, destitute and deserving millions but Mrs. Everest who was in his heart and mind? He was proud and thankful to have played a part in helping others who were, perhaps, like her.

And is it sheer coincidence that when he came to choose his country home it was in "the garden of England" that he sought and found it? And that when at Bangalore he took to reading, his first literary discoveries were Gibbon and Macaulay? When he embarked upon Macaulay's *History* and "voyaged with full sail in a strong wind" he remembered that Mrs. Everest's brother-in-law, the old prison warder he had made friends with as a child at Ventnor, had possessed a copy of

Macaulay's *History,* purchased in supplements and bound together, and that he used to speak of it with reverence. And of Gibbon's *Autobiography* he wrote: "When I read his reference to his old nurse: 'If there be any, as I trust there are some, who rejoice that I live, to that dear and excellent woman their gratitude is due', I thought of Mrs. Everest; and it shall be her epitaph." [3]

But while Mrs. Everest held his heart and his mother shone for him in evening skies, it was the image of his father which dominated and obsessed his being. It was in truth an image of his own creation that he worshiped. He did not know his father, nor does Lord Randolph appear to have made any attempt to know his son, whose intelligence he rated so low that he considered him unfit to practice at the Bar. He consigned him to the Army after a brief glance at a game of soldiers Winston was playing with his brother on the nursery floor. He seemed to be able to play with soldiers reasonably well. He had better be a soldier. Thus was his fate determined and unquestioningly accepted.[4]

The icy detachment and indifference of Lord Randolph failed to destroy the proud and passionate allegiance of his son. How he explained them to himself one cannot guess. But the image remained upon its pedestal, intact and glorious. Until the end he worshiped at the altar of his Unknown Father.

Of their relationship he has written with a poignancy which is entirely free from all resentment or reproach. "The greatest and most powerful influence in my early life was of course my father. Although I had talked with him so seldom and never for a moment on equal terms, I conceived an intense admiration and affection for him; and, after his early death, for his memory. I read industriously almost every word he had ever spoken and learnt by heart large portions of his speeches. I took my politics almost unquestioningly from him." [5] And again: "He seemed to own the key to everything or almost everything worth having. But if ever I began to show the slightest idea of comradeship, he was immediately offended; and when once I suggested that I might help his private secretary to write some of his letters, he froze me into stone." [6]

Of his school life he wrote: "I would far rather have been apprenticed as a bricklayer's mate, or run errands as a messenger boy, or helped my father to dress the front windows of a grocer's shop. It would have been real; it would have been natural; it would have taught me more; and I should have done it much better. Also I should have got to know my father, which would have been a joy to me." [7]

Though Winston Churchill often talked to me, with glowing pride, about his father, I was quite ignorant of the nature of their relationship.

But I well remember that when, in our political discussions, I quoted to him my father's views—about tactics, issues, the personality of colleagues or opponents—he sometimes asked me with a kind of wistful envy: "Your father told you that? He talks to you about such things quite freely? I wish I could have had such talks with mine." And he sometimes added: "But I should have had them if he had lived. It *must* have come."

School life was certainly neither natural nor real to Winston Churchill nor, with one important exception, did he learn much from it. He explains that "where my reason, imagination or interest were not engaged, I would not or I could not learn"—and of all his teachers only one succeeded in engaging them.

He was sent at the age of seven to a fashionable private school which for sheer brutality equaled any educational establishment to be found in the pages of Dickens. He owed his removal from it only to a breakdown in his health.

Then came Harrow and the "inhospitable regions of examinations." "I should have liked to be asked to say what I knew. They always tried to ask what I did not know." [8] As a result of this procedure, so familiar to examinees, he found himself at the very bottom of the bottom form. But this misfortune gained him one supreme advantage. Together with his fellow dunces he was taught English by a man who "knew how to do it"—Mr. Somervell—and owing to his long sojourn in the lowest class he learned it thoroughly. "Thus I got into my bones the essential structure of the ordinary British sentence—which is a noble thing." [7]

With the one exception of Sir John Milbanke, he does not seem to have made any friends at Harrow. Only two other contacts with his schoolfellows are recorded. One is the well-known push which precipitated Mr. Leo Amery, then a sixth-form swell, into the swimming pool. The other, more significant and interesting, is an alliance formed between himself and another sixth-form boy for their mutual convenience and advantage. To Winston translating Latin was a laborious and futile business. His ally, a distinguished classical scholar, found it just as difficult to write an English essay. They agreed to swap functions. It took the classicist five minutes to construe Winston's elementary Latin tasks. He in his turn delivered to his ally as *quid pro quo* a weekly English essay. He used to "walk up and down the room dictating" while his friend "sat in the corner and wrote it down in long-hand." [9] He was already practicing the exact technique he used in the composition both of his books and of his speeches throughout his later life.

He had to make three attempts before passing into Sandhurst. The third time he succeeded through the desperate expedient of "learning Mathematics in six months," a formidable feat helped out by cramming and a stroke of luck. "There was a question in my third and last examination about these Cosines and Tangents in a highly square-rooted condition which must have been decisive upon the whole of my after life. It was a problem. But luckily I had seen its ugly face only a few days before and recognised it at first sight. I have never met any of these creatures since." [10]

He had qualified for the cavalry, which, being more expensive than the infantry, presented fewer intellectual obstacles. In the Army as in many other walks of life, the richer you were the less intelligent it was necessary to be. But Lord Randolph was by no means rich, and he did not relish the prospect of keeping chargers for his son. He wrote him a long and severe letter "expressing the bleakest view of my educational career, showing a marked lack of appreciation at my success in the examination, which he suggested I had only scraped through, and warning me of the danger in which I plainly lay of becoming a 'social wastrel.'" [11]

But these baleful parental warnings could not quench the joy he felt at the prospect of becoming "a real live cavalry officer" within eighteen months. And Sandhurst realized all his hopes. For now once more he was able to play at soldiers but on a much wider terrain than the nursery floor. Tactics, Fortifications and Military History seemed a thousand times better worth learning than Latin and Mathematics. Constructing breastworks, putting up *chevaux-de-frise* and cutting railway lines with slabs of guncotton was far more fun than playing compulsory cricket and football. Above all there was the ecstasy of riding. . . . All his money was spent in hiring horses. "No hour of life is lost that is spent in the saddle." His life was only shadowed by one regret. The prospect of a full-scale war seemed dim. The world had become too sensible and peace-loving. The only hope lay with the "savages and barbarous peoples"—Zulus, Afghans and Dervishes—who mercifully still existed. These "might, if they were well-disposed, 'put up a show' some day."

He passed out of Sandhurst, in his own words, "into the world. It opened like Aladdin's cave. . . . An endless moving picture in which one was an actor. . . . All the days were good and each day better than the other. . . . Ups and downs, risks and journeys, but always the sense of motion, and the illusion of hope." [12]

The chrysalis had broken. Real life had begun at last.

———◄◄►►——

Chapter Three

THE SWORD AND THE PEN

LORD RANDOLPH CHURCHILL died in January, 1895. For some time it had been clear that he was fatally stricken. In June, 1894, he had set off on a journey around the world. His son never saw him again except as "a swiftly-fading shadow." "Had he lived another four or five years, he could not have done without me. But there were no four or five years! Just as friendly relations were ripening into an Entente, and an alliance or at least a military agreement seemed to my mind not beyond the bounds of reasonable endeavour, he vanished for ever." [1]

Two months after his father's death Winston Churchill received his commission in the 4th Hussars. He was now his own master. He had no money except an allowance from his mother of five hundred pounds a year, an income which ruled out politics and was barely sufficient for a cavalry officer. When his five months' winter leave came around he found that all his money had been spent on polo ponies and, as he could not afford to hunt, he "searched the world for some scene of adventure or excitement." [2]

Alas! The world was still lapped in peace. It is strange to reflect that in those days (and indeed until 1914) the demand for active service was clamant and the supply to meet it nonexistent. The craving for action and adventure was by no means peculiar to Winston Churchill, though his early reputation as a fire-eater was directly responsible for the odious calumny of "warmonger" which stuck to him throughout his life, a cry still heard and still believed in the General Election of 1950. He belonged to a generation who had a thirst for peril, just as today we have a thirst for pensions. The concept of security in any form did not exist for them. Of the First World War it may be said that never has such a gay and brilliant generation been so ardently prepared to meet an early death. The great and terrible opportunity which lay in wait for them was unforeseen, unguessed at by the youth of 1896 who scoured a placid world in search of danger.

In one remote corner of the world a few shots were being fired in anger. In the guerrilla war in Cuba between the Spaniards and the island rebels it was still possible to realize the dream of being under fire. Thither he went accompanied by a brother officer and there he first brought into play the dual functions of his pen and sword—a combination which was to prove both lucrative and glorious in the years to come. Before leaving England he made an arrangement with the *Graphic* to write dispatches from the Cuban front at five pounds each.

He has described his "delicious yet tremulous sensations" when in the early morning light he first saw the shores of Cuba outlined against dark blue horizons. "I felt as if I sailed with Long John Silver and first gazed on Treasure Island. Here was a place where real things were going on. Here was a scene of vital action. Here was a place where anything might happen. Here was a place where something would certainly happen. Here I might leave my bones." [3]

As it turned out he left no bones behind him, but he realized his dream of hearing bullets crack and whine through the air. One of them passed within a foot of his head, another ripped through the thatch of the hut in which he slept. He had been "under fire"—if only for three days.

But he made in Cuba one discovery which was to prove far more important to his future life than any gain in military experience, the life-giving powers of the siesta. There is an essential difference between a nap—a mere brief spell of nodding in a chair—and a siesta, which means going deliberately and properly to bed. He found that "for every purpose of business or pleasure, mental or physical, we ought to break our days and our marches into two." He records that when he was at the Admiralty in the First World War he found that he could add nearly two hours to his working day by going to bed for an hour after luncheon.[4] This habit he practiced throughout the Second World War. It enabled him to work fully extended into the small hours of every morning. It also broke down many of his colleagues and subordinates who were perforce unable to observe a Cuban timetable.

The 4th Hussars sailed for India in the winter of 1896 and took up their quarters at Bangalore where Winston Churchill and two friends lived in "a palatial bungalow, all pink and white . . . wreathed in purple bougainvillia," and devoted themselves to "the serious purpose of life"—i.e., polo. It was in these surroundings and at the age of twenty-two that the desire for learning came upon him and with it his first impulse to educate himself. Words had always been his toys, his tools, the beloved children of his mind. "I had a liking for words and for the feel of words fitting and falling into their places like pennies in the slot. I caught myself using a good many words the meaning of which I could not define precisely. I admired these words, but was afraid to use them for fear of being absurd. One day, before I left England, a friend of mine had said: 'Christ's Gospel was the last word in Ethics.' This sounded good; but what were Ethics? They had never been mentioned to me at Harrow or Sandhurst. . . . I would have paid some scholar £2 at least to give me a lecture of an hour or an hour and a half about Ethics. . . . But here in Bangalore there was no one to tell me about Ethics for love or money. Of tactics I had a grip: on politics I had a view: but a concise compendious outline of Ethics was a novelty not to be locally obtained. . . ." He was no less puzzled by current phrases such as "the Socratic method," "the Grand Remonstrance"— what did they allude to? He wanted to know more about all this. "So," he concluded, "I resolved to read history, philosophy, economics and things like that." [5]

He ordered books from England and, during the long hot afternoons while others slept, he read voraciously—Macaulay, Gibbon, Darwin, Malthus, Plato's *Republic,* the *Politics* of Aristotle, and Bartlett's *Familiar Quotations.* Because he read—as the hungry eat—neither from habit nor from duty, but from need, these books entered into his system and became a part of him. In the course of his reading his religious beliefs came under heavy fire. Up to now he had "dutifully accepted everything he had been told." But he was severely shaken up by Winwood Reade's *Martyrdom of Man* and depressed by his conclusion (with which Gibbon himself appeared to agree) that "we simply go out like candles" —a prospect which did not appeal to him. And when Lecky weighed in with his *Rise and Influence of Rationalism* he was left indignant at the deceptions which had been practiced on him by the pastors and masters of his green youth. He passed through what he describes as a "violent and aggressive anti-religious phase which, had it lasted, might easily have made me a nuisance." But his "poise was restored during the next few years by frequent contact with danger. I found that whatever I might think and argue, I did not hesitate to ask for special protection when about to come under the fire of the enemy: nor to feel sincerely grateful when I got home safe to tea. I even asked for lesser things than not to be killed too soon, and nearly always in these years, and indeed throughout my life, I got what I wanted. This practice seemed perfectly natural, and just as strong and real as the reasoning process which contradicted it so sharply. Moreover the practice was comforting and the reasoning led nowhere. *I therefore acted in accordance with my feelings without troubling to square such conduct with the conclusions of thought"* [6] (my italics).

These last words are profoundly self-revealing. He was once described by an acute observer as "thinking with his heart." It would have been equally true to say of him that he felt with his mind. Throughout his life his feelings always penetrated and often swayed his intellectual processes. There were, no doubt, moments when his emotions vitiated his judgment but far more often his heart acted as his mind's pathfinder and guide. His emotional response to situations and events was nearly always a true one. The right way to his mind was through his heart and his imagination. I have spent hours with him in fruitless argument, battering in vain on a closed door. If by some lucky phrase, some form of words, some vivid image I could find the way to his imagination or emotions all barriers would fall. His intellect was often inaccessible. His heart was an open city.

But to return to Bangalore, metaphysical conundrums, self-education and even polo (which bulked by far the largest of the three) did not provide the stuff of life. That stuff for him was action. He became growingly restive and impatient in his regimental backwater.

In 1897 when back on leave in England he read the news that fighting had broken out on the North-West Frontier. Here at last was a front line and he must get there. The General in command of operations, Sir Bindon Blood, had once at a party promised him that in the event of trouble he might join him. He at once dispatched an urgent telegram to the General and without awaiting a reply embarked for India. At every port of call he hoped and looked, in vain, for the message which would decide his fate. It was not till he reached the end of his voyage that he found it—at Bombay: "Very difficult; no vacancies; come up as a correspondent; will try to fit you in. B.B."

He had meanwhile been commissioned as war correspondent by the *Allahabad Pioneer* and had providently arranged that his dispatches should be simultaneously published in the *Daily Telegraph* at five pounds a column. One last obstacle remained to be surmounted: to obtain leave of absence from the Colonel of his regiment. He cleared this fence and started on his journey of two thousand miles to the North-West Frontier. His arrival "yellow with dust" at Brigade Headquarters, then encamped upon the summit of the Malakand Pass, marked a milestone in his life. From this campaign his first book was to be born—*The Malakand Field Force.*

His letters to the *Daily Telegraph,* written anonymously "From a Young Officer," were widely read and well received. He resolved "to build a small literary house." Back in his garrison at Bangalore he devoted three or four hours of every day to writing his book. It had an immediate success. The reviewers "vied with each other in praise. . . ." When the first published volume reached him, together with a shower of compliments from newspapers and critics, he was "filled with pride and pleasure."

There is a certain pathos in his reminder to his readers that he "had never been praised before." Until this moment (except perhaps at polo) no encouragement had ever come his way. "The only comments which had ever been made upon my work at school had been 'Indifferent,' 'Untidy,' 'Slovenly,' 'Bad,' 'Very Bad,' etc." Buckets of cold water had descended in a steady downpour on his head. Yet they had failed to quench or even to damp his tough, invincible self-confidence. Now it was vindicated, endorsed by public opinion, high and low. "Here was the great world with its leading literary newspapers and vigilant erudite critics, writing whole columns of praise!" He received a charming letter of congratulation from the Prince of Wales which, incidentally, expressed the hope that he would "stick to the Army before adding Member of Parliament to his name." [7]

But he had reached a decision which remained unshaken by this Royal hope. He knew that "if this [book] would pass muster there was lots more where it came from, and I felt a new way of making a living and of asserting myself, opening splendidly out before me. . . . I resolved that as soon as the wars which seemed to have begun again in several parts of the world should be ended, and we had won the Polo Cup, I would free myself from all discipline and authority, and set up in perfect independence in England with nobody to give me orders or arouse me by bell or trumpet."

This plan of action was to be carried out to the letter. The Polo Cup was duly won. The "ending" of the wars, and his (successful) struggles to take part in them were to prove a longer and more arduous business,

The Indian Frontier war had barely closed when the Sudan campaign opened. His keen desire to share in it met with "resistances of a new and formidable character." In military circles, high and low, he found "an adverse and even a hostile attitude." Abusive epithets like "medal-hunter" and "self-advertiser" were freely used about him. Questions were asked: Why should he write for the papers and serve as an officer at the same time? Why should a subaltern praise or criticize his senior officers? All this he could have taken in his stride but the main obstacle to his going was more "powerful and remote." It was nothing less than the disapproval and hostility of the Sirdar of the Egyptian Army, Sir Herbert Kitchener, a disapproval and hostility which smoldered on, and in the years to come were to affect far greater issues.

All efforts foundered on this rock. Even the personal appeal of the Prime Minister, Lord Salisbury, received a dusty answer. "Sir Herbert Kitchener had already all the officers he required, and if any vacancies occurred, there were others whom he would be bound to prefer before the young officer in question." [8]

Anyone would have taken this "no" for an answer, except Winston Churchill. But "no" is an answer he never accepted. His pertinacity was undaunted. He had chanced to hear that at a dinner party the Adjutant-General, Sir Evelyn Wood, had spoken with resentment of Sir Herbert Kitchener's arbitrary choice of officers for the Sudan campaign. While conceding that the Egyptian Army was the Sirdar's own preserve, Sir Evelyn had asserted with some feeling the right of the War Office to determine the composition of the British Expeditionary Force. Winston Churchill at once conveyed to him through a third party the fact that the Prime Minister's personal appeal on his behalf had been rejected. This move was instantly successful. Sir Evelyn Wood became his *deus ex machina.* Within two days he received from the War Office the news that he had been attached as a supernumerary Lieutenant to the 21st Lancers and ordered to report at once in Cairo. He just had time before he caught his train next morning to arrange that he should write a series of letters to the *Morning Post* at fifteen pounds a column.

He records that on the journey out he experienced the emotions of a criminal fleeing from justice. At every stopping place he feared recall. But when he arrived at Atbara Camp, two hundred miles from Omdurman, he "felt entitled like Agag to believe that 'the bitterness of death was past.' " [9]

Chapter Four

―◄ ►―

THE RIVER WAR

The STORY of the Omdurman campaign is recorded in Winston Churchill's second book, *The River War*. Of his sensations in the famous charge of the 21st Lancers, from which he emerged unscathed, he has written a thrilling description in a much later book, *My Early Life*. To this account he adds a reflection based not on his experience of the battlefield but of the political arena. "In one respect a cavalry charge is very like ordinary life. So long as you are all right, firmly in your saddle, your horse in hand, and well armed, lots of enemies will give you a wide berth. But as soon as you have lost a stirrup, have a rein cut, have dropped your weapon, are wounded, then is the moment when from all quarters enemies rush upon you." [1] By the time these words were written Winston Churchill had experienced both situations.

Three weeks after their charge the 21st Lancers had re-embarked for England. It is characteristic of Winston Churchill's industry and immediacy of purpose that he set to work upon his book during the voyage home. He was entranced by every aspect of the task. "It was great fun writing a book. It built an impalpable crystal sphere around one of interests and ideas. In a sense one felt like a goldfish in a bowl; but in this case the goldfish made his own bowl. This came along everywhere with me. . . . I have noticed in my life deep resemblances between many different kinds of things. Writing a book is not unlike building a house or planning a battle or painting a picture. The technique is different, the materials are different, but the principle is the same." [2]

Readers of his books will find in this reflection an explanation, almost a definition, of their quality. In their structure and proportions they are architectural ("the foundations have to be laid, the data assembled and the premises must bear the weight of their conclusions" [3]); color is splashed about their pages with the brush of a master painter; the writing is in itself a kind of action. We are swept forward on its surge and tide like a ship before a following wind. There is never a moment when either he or we ourselves are becalmed in his theme. As words, thoughts, images pour from his pen we feel the impulse of a torrent whose source is inexhaustible. As I read I think often of Blake's proverb: "The cistern contains: the fountain overflows." Winston Churchill is never the cistern, he is always the fountain.

In writing *The River War* he records that he "affected a combination of the styles of Macaulay and Gibbon" and "I stuck in a bit of my own from time to time." He became aware of the vital relationship between sentences and paragraphs—"as sentences should follow one another in harmonious sequence, so the paragraphs must fit on to one another like the automatic couplings of railway carriages. Chapterization also began to dawn on me. . . . I already knew that chronology is the key to easy narrative. I already realised that 'good sense is the foundation of good writing.' . . . And I repeated earnestly one of my best French quotations, 'l'art d'être ennuyeux c'est de tout dire'." [4]

But his recognition of these sound and basic rules would have done little to make him what he is, one of the greatest chroniclers of all time. Two other factors explain his mastery of this art. First, he always played a part, and sometimes a determining part, in the great events which he describes. He sees them with the dual vision of actor and observer. And secondly he is an artist, and as such he knows how to transmit to others the dramatic impact of events upon his own imagination and to project his own impressions, thoughts, emotions into their innermost experience.

I shall never forget reading *The River War* for the first time in 1910. The impression it made on me may well have been enhanced by the fact that I read it on the banks of the Nile near Omdurman, where I was staying with my brother, Arthur Asquith, then a member of the newly formed Sudan Civil Service. I rode with him over the battlefield and looked down upon it from the summit of Mount Kerreri. I also got to know some of the *dramatis personae* still on the spot—Sir Reginald Wingate, then Sirdar, and Slatin Pasha—at once a character and a character part. It was on this visit and in the palace at Khartoum that I first met and made fast friends with Lord Kitchener. But I remember feeling at the time that these living figures and their *mise en scène* served as mere illustrations to Winston Churchill's story. It was not my senses but his words which had transported me among them.

When in *The River War* he describes his first sight of the advancing Dervish host "when the whole side of the hill seemed to move . . . above them waved hundreds of banners, and the sun, glinting on many thousand hostile spearpoints, spread a sparkling cloud . . ." we see through his eyes this "impression of a lifetime" and our pulses race with his. With him we are suddenly committed to the charge, plunge at full gallop into the deep Khor filled with its "great grey mass gleaming with steel," share the prodigious shock of the collision, tear through it "as an iron rake might be drawn through a heap of shingle" and scramble up the farther side. As the smoke clears we are amazed to find ourselves unhurt. . . . We are not spectators, readers, listeners to a tale. We are charging with the Lancers.

Apart from his power of intimate communication with the reader, which it shares with all his works, *The River War* reveals some aspects of his character which were to distinguish him throughout his life. One quality he already possessed and never lost was his unfailing magnanimity toward the defeated foes. Not only does he feel compassion for their sufferings but he shows a degree of understanding, imaginative discernment and even admiration for his Dervish enemy rare in a subaltern of twenty-five. Describing the wild charge of the Baggara horsemen who rode unflinchingly to certain death against MacDonald's brigade he wrote: " 'Mad fanaticism' is the depreciating comment of their conquerors. I hold this to be a cruel injustice. . . . Why should we regard as madness in the savage what would be sublime in civilized men? For I hope that if evil days should come upon our own country, and the last army which a collapsing Empire could interpose between London and the invader were dissolving in rout and ruin, that there would be some—even in these modern days—who would not care to accustom themselves to a new order of things and tamely survive the disaster." [5] Can any doubt that if in 1940 the Battle of Britain had ended in defeat he would have been one of these?

Another of his characteristics is to be found in the dispassionate candor—and the courage—of his assessment of the personality and achievement of the Commander-in-Chief, Sir Herbert Kitchener. It is prefaced by the explanation that "to do justice to a great man, discriminating criticism is necessary. Gush, however quenching, is always insipid." A full measure of praise is awarded to the Sirdar's strategy, foresight, personal force and extraordinary economy, to his flashes of genius (of which the greatest was the construction of the Desert Railway), to his grasp of the whole conditions of Sudan war, revealing "a breadth and strength of intellect which transcend the limitations of the expert."

Having thus given him his just due Winston Churchill adds: "But the meanest historian owes something to truth" and proceeds to expose "the reverse of the medal." He tells us that the General "who never spared himself, cared little for others," treated all men like machines, incontinently flung aside the comrade who had served with him in peace and peril as soon as he had ceased to be of use. "The Sirdar looked only to the soldiers who could march and fight. The wounded Egyptian, and latterly the wounded British soldier, did not excite his interest, and of all the departments of his army the one neglected was that concerned with the care of the sick and injured." [6]

But his harshest condemnation is reserved for the desecration of the Mahdi's tomb. "This place had been for more than ten years the most sacred and holy thing that the people of the Sudan knew. Their miserable lives had perhaps been brightened, perhaps in some way ennobled by the contemplation of something which they did not quite understand, but which they believed asserted a protecting influence. It had gratified that instinctive desire for the mystic which all human creatures possess, and which is perhaps the strongest reason for believing in a progressive destiny and a future state. By Sir Herbert Kitchener's orders the Tomb had been profaned and razed to the ground. The corpse of the Mahdi was dug up. The head was separated from the body. . . . The limbs and trunk were flung into the Nile. Such was the chivalry of the conquerors!" [7] Denouncing this "wicked act, of which the true Christian, no less than the philosopher, must express his abhorrence," Winston Churchill wrote that if in the future the Sudan were administered on such principles "then it would be better if Gordon had never given his life nor Kitchener won his victories." [8]

If uttered today this verdict would be unanimously endorsed by all shades of opinion. But few would have dared to pass such judgment, however deserved, at a moment when Lord Kitchener, the idol of the nation, was enjoying a Roman triumph and being invested amid the acclamation of his fellow countrymen with the Governor-Generalship of the lands he had conquered.

And it is not difficult to imagine what the feelings of the Sirdar must have been at finding himself thus coolly weighed in the balance by a young subaltern in his own Army, who had conveniently doubled his military duties with those of correspondent to the *Morning Post*. One cannot wonder that Winston Churchill was often a thorn in the flesh of his military superiors. In the case of Lord Kitchener the thorn pricked on under the skin for many years to come.

Reading *The River War* should exorcise the widespread misconception of Winston Churchill's attitude toward war. As it reveals, even in those early years, he saw it plain in all its horror, squalor and inhumanity. On hearing of the death of his gallant comrade, Robert Grenfell, cut down in the Lancers' charge, he wrote: "The realization came home to me with awful force that war, disguise it as you may, is but dirty, shoddy business which only a fool would undertake. Nor was it until the night that I again recognized that there are some things that have to be done, no matter what the cost may be." [9]

When three days after the fight he rode over the battlefield of Omdurman, strewn and heaped with the swollen and blood-soaked corpses of the slain, he was appalled and sickened by the sight. "It is difficult to imagine the postures into which man, once created in the image of his Maker, had been twisted. It is not wise to try, for he who succeeds will ask himself with me: 'Can I ever forget?' I have tried to gild war, and to solace myself for the loss of dear and gallant friends, with the thought that a soldier's death for a cause that he believes in will count for much, whatever may be beyond this world. When the soldier of a civilized Power is killed in action . . . his body is borne by friendly arms reverently to the grave. . . . But there was nothing *dulce et decorum* about the Dervish dead; nothing of the dignity of unconquerable manhood; all was filthy corruption. Yet these were as brave men as ever walked the earth . . . destroyed, not conquered, by machinery." [10]

After the dead, the wounded, who had lain for three days under burning skies, racked by the agony of pain and thirst, some trying to crawl with shattered limbs toward the Nile, "the great river of their country without which the invaders could never have come upon them, but which they nevertheless did not reproach. . . ." [11]

Amid these scenes of human torment he reflected that if, as we are told, vengeance is sweet, no one should drain the cup to the bottom. "The dregs are often filthy-tasting." And he ends the chapter with the prophetic words: "The Dervish host was scattered and destroyed. Their end, however, only anticipates that of the victors; for Time, which laughs at science, as science laughs at valour, will in due course contemptuously brush both combatants away." [12]

————◄ ►■—————

Chapter Five

FIRST POLITICAL SKIRMISH

O<small>N HIS RETURN</small> from the Sudan Winston Churchill decided that the time had come to bid farewell to arms, live by his pen and seek the earliest opportunity of getting into Parliament. Politics was his natural and inevitable vocation. It presented a wider and more decisive front than war, and in his own words it was "almost as exciting and quite as dangerous. . . . In war you can only be killed once but in politics many times."

The immediate cause of his decision, however, was neither vocational nor ideological but financial. In the Army he was earning fourteen shillings a day, out of which he was obliged to keep up two horses and several magnificent and expensive uniforms. He computed that the two books he had already written together with his war correspondence with the *Daily Telegraph* had already brought him in five times as much as the Queen had paid him for "three years of assiduous and sometimes dangerous work." His new book, *The River War,* should produce enough to support him for at least two years.

He therefore planned to return to India in the autumn to discharge his last military duty—the winning of the Polo Tournament—and then to send in his papers and leave the Army.

During the summer he met for the first time a group of new Conservative M.P.'s of whom he was to see much more later on—Lord Hugh Cecil, Lord Percy, Lord Balcarres and others. Among these sophisticated young politicians two or three years older than himself, "all born with silver spoons in their mouths, all highly distinguished at Oxford or Cambridge and all ensconced in safe Tory constituencies," he records rather pathetically that he felt like "the earthen pot among the brass." He was bewildered by their agile dialectics and his own "bold broad generalities about liberty, equality and fraternity got seriously knocked about." They all made rings around him, impaling him with their paradoxes like picadors baiting an innocent and bewildered bull.

His inability to defend the righteous and the obvious against their frivolous and ingenious fallacies and his belated discovery that while he was in deadly earnest they were "only teasing" led him to toy with the idea of going up to Oxford when he came back from India. At Oxford he could surely acquire the necessary facts with which to buttress his confident assertions—and also perhaps learn when to take other people seriously. But when his inquiries revealed that access to Oxford was not to be obtained by gate money but only by passing examinations both in Latin and in Greek he recognized an insuperable obstacle and renounced his plan.[1]

Before leaving for India he called at the Conservative Central Office in search of a constituency, and here it appeared that gate money still opened doors. He received the chilling news that the best and safest constituencies expected the largest financial contributions from their members. "Forlorn hopes" alone were cheap. Yet from this otherwise dispiriting visit one dazzling prospect did suddenly emerge. On his way out he chanced to notice a large book lying on a table labeled with the magic words "Speakers Wanted." He "gazed upon this with wonder." "Do you mean to say," he asked, "that there are a lot of meetings which *want* speakers?" He was informed that there were hundreds of such meetings of all sorts, indoor and outdoor, fetes, bazaars and rallies. He "surveyed this prospect with the eye of an urchin looking through a pastrycook's window" [2] and at once snatched at a cream bun.

His maiden speech was delivered ten days later from a tent in a park near Bath to a gathering of the Primrose League. It was learned by heart so thoroughly that he could have "said it backwards" in his sleep. The sentence over which he "licked his chops" was to the effect that "England would gain far more from the rising tide of Tory Democracy than from the dried-up drainpipe of Radicalism." The audience cheered in all the right places and clapped long and loudly at the end. The *Morning Post* reported the speech verbatim and even wrote an "appreciative leaderette." "So I could do it after all! It seemed quite easy too." [3] It was in a warm glow of self-congratulation that he sailed for India.

In the winning of the Polo Cup he played a glorious part. Through an unlucky accident he was obliged to play with his right elbow strapped to within a few inches of his side. In spite of this crippling handicap he scored three goals out of his regiment's winning four and he was given a great send-off when he took his final leave of them.

Soon after his return he received an invitation to fight a by-election at Oldham. It was a double-member constituency and his partner in the fight was Mr. James Mawdsley, a workingman, the Secretary of the Operative Spinners' Association, who proclaimed his belief in a new doctrine, "Tory Socialism." The Conservative Central Office no doubt had high hopes that this strangely assorted pair—"the Scion and the Socialist" as they were called—would make a wide and variegated appeal and win both on the Tory swings and on the Radical roundabouts. Their partnership (to the Scion at least) seemed "a splendid new orientation of politics."

Unfortunately it did not work out that way. The trade-unionists accused Mr. Mawdsley of "deserting his class" and voted Liberal, while many strong Conservative supporters were outraged by the presence of a "wicked Socialist" on their platforms. Nor were the issues of the fight either congenial or even familiar to Winston Churchill. As so often happens at a by-election, the mountain peaks of politics were suddenly obscured by an irrelevant molehill—a Tithes Bill which the Conservative Government was then passing through the House of Commons. Its purpose was to provide relief for the poor clergy of the Church of England from the rates,* and it naturally aroused the fierce opposition of all Radicals and Nonconformists. The great themes of Tory democracy were submerged. In vain he "defended the virtues of the Government, the existing system of society, the Established Church and the unity of the Empire." [4] Compared to the "Clerical Doles Bill," as it was called by its opponents, these major issues cut no ice.

Toward the end of the contest Winston Churchill was entreated by his principal supporters to throw this Jonah overboard. He confessed that as he was "ignorant of the needs which had inspired it and detached from the passions which it aroused" he yielded to the temptation. This action, though acclaimed by his supporters at Oldham, aroused very different feelings among Conservatives elsewhere. In the House of Commons, where the Bill was at that moment being forced through against stiff opposition, the Government was naturally taunted with the fact that its own standard-bearer had been obliged to bow to the storm of public opinion and had disowned and jettisoned the measure.

* This Bill proposed that ratepayers, irrespective of their denomination, should subsidize the Church of England.

Nor was this sacrifice vindicated by results. In spite of the impact of his personality, his brilliant speeches delivered to enthusiastic meetings, the spotlight of publicity which illuminated his campaign, despite even the sensation created on polling day by the appearance of Lady Randolph Churchill "dressed entirely in blue . . . in a landau and pair with gaily ribboned and rosetted postilions," the Scion and the Socialist were defeated by Mr. Emmott and Mr. Runciman—the Scion by 1,300 votes, the Socialist by 30 more.

Many years later Winston Churchill wrote thus of the result: "Everyone threw the blame on me. I have noticed that they nearly always do. I suppose it is because they think I shall be able to bear it best." And he added that he "returned to London with those feelings of deflation which a bottle of champagne or even soda-water represents when it has been half-emptied and left uncorked for a night" [5] and that no one came to see him, either with condolences or congratulations.

Mr. Balfour's comment on the election has been often quoted: "I thought he was a young man of promise but it appears he is a young man of promises." Yet it was from him alone that Winston Churchill received a letter full of sympathy and understanding, begging him not to be discouraged by the result and assuring him that "this small reverse will have no permanent ill effect upon your political fortunes." [6]

He found consolation by reimmersing himself in *The River War,* which had now reached its final stages. While engaged in this task he listened from the gallery to a debate in the House of Commons in which the desecration of the Mahdi's tomb was denounced by John Morley and C. P. Scott, Editor of the *Manchester Guardian.* "All the Liberals were outraged by an act which seemed to them worthy of the Huns and Vandals. All the Tories thought it rather a lark. So here was I already out of step. . . ." [7] He planned to complete his book for publication in the middle of October. But that month when it came held even greater events in store for him and for his fortunes.

On October 9th, after a summer of fruitless negotiation and increasing tension, President Kruger issued his ultimatum, demanding that British troops should be withdrawn from the frontiers of the Transvaal and that reinforcements on the high seas should not be landed at any South African port. Its expiry was limited to three days and it was followed by the invasion of Natal. Contrary to expectation the Orange Free State threw in its lot with the Transvaal Republic. The curtain had gone up on the South African War.

——◄◄ ►►——

Chapter Six

PRISONER OF THE BOERS

Within AN HOUR of the news of the Boer ultimatum Winston Churchill received from the *Morning Post* an invitation to become its principal war correspondent at a salary of £250 a month with all expenses paid and "entire discretion as to movements and opinions," the highest terms ever offered for the job by any British newspaper. He was overjoyed at this new opening on a new front line and at once took his passage on the earliest steamer, the *Dunottar Castle,* which was sailing two days hence.

The last two days at home were spent in fevered preparation and eager expectation in a London "seething with patriotic excitement and fierce party controversy." He resolved to try to see Mr. Joseph Chamberlain before he sailed, was given an appointment, and they spent a quarter of an hour together jogging in a hansom cab on the way from Chamberlain's house in Princes Gardens to the Colonial Office. Mr. Chamberlain, who seems to have shared to the full all the current delusions, spoke with rosy optimism about our immediate military prospects. " 'Buller',* he said, 'may well be too late. He would have been wiser to have gone out earlier. Now if the Boers invade Natal Sir George White with his 16,000 men may easily settle the whole thing.' 'What about Mafeking?' I asked. 'Ah, Mafeking, that may be besieged. But if they cannot hold out for a few weeks, what is one to expect?' " He added that the War Office, in whose opinion he appeared to have a childlike faith, was "confident." [1]

---

* General Sir Redvers Buller, Commander-in-Chief of the British forces in South Africa.

It was with something like relief that Winston Churchill heard later from Mr. George Wyndham, the Under-Secretary of State for War, that there might yet be some difficulties ahead, that the Boers were well prepared and armed and possessed a new form of heavy Maxim gun (known later as the pom-pom). "I thought it very sporting of the Boers to take on the whole British Empire, and I felt quite glad they were not defenceless and had put themselves in the wrong by making preparations"—a characteristic reaction in which pugnacity and chivalry were mingled in equal proportions, with a sop to principle thrown in.

When he sailed on October 11th he could not guess that he was embarking on a voyage which was to shape his whole future. It was to make him within six months a national figure, to instill in him the imaginative sympathy and compassion he never lost for prisoners and captives, and with it the determination to improve their lot whenever he had power to do so. It increased the chivalrous respect he had always felt for gallant enemies. Above all it was to confirm his belief in his own star and the conviction that he was being specially protected and preserved by Fate for the fulfillment of some unknown purpose.

But though the secrets of the future were withheld, the facts of the present were quite sufficiently exciting. Sir Redvers Buller and the entire Headquarters Staff of our one and only organized Army Corps were all on board. The Commander-in-Chief was neither approachable nor communicative but Winston Churchill made the most of his opportunities for observation. "He looked stolid. He said little, and what he said was obscure. He was not the kind of man who could explain things, and he never tried to do so." [2]

Although I never saw him, no face is more indelibly engraved upon my own memory than that of Sir Redvers Buller. For as a child I proudly wore, pinned to my coat, a china button on which his massive and impassive features were depicted against the background of a Union Jack. His name is connected in my mind with Black Weeks, black looks, colossal blunders and disasters but never with words of censure, criticism or blame. The worse he did the more the country seemed to trust him, from Lord Salisbury downward. The public attitude seemed to be one of sympathy toward the victim of an act of God or Nature.

But while Winston Churchill was taking the outward measure of the Commander-in-Chief he was himself being scrutinized and assessed by an acute observer who has left us a perceptive portrait of him as he then was and a prescient forecast of what he might become. The late Mr. J. B. Atkins, who had been sent out by C. P. Scott to report the war for the *Manchester Guardian,* was also sailing on the *Dunottar Castle.* He had not been many hours on board before he became aware of "a most unusual young man" whom he thus describes: "He was slim, slightly reddish-haired, pale, lively, frequently plunging along the deck 'with neck out-thrust' as Browning fancied Napoleon. . . . It was obvious that he was in love with words. He would hesitate sometimes before he chose one or would exchange one for a better. . . . When the prospects of a career like that of his father Lord Randolph excited him, then such a gleam shot from him that he was almost transfigured. I had not before encountered this sort of ambition, unabashed, frankly egotistical, communicating its excitement and extorting sympathy. . . . He had small respect for authority until he had examined it; he had acquired no reverence for his seniors as such, and talked to them as though they were of his own age, or younger. . . . He stood alone and confident and his natural power to be himself had yielded to no man." [3]

There was of course no wireless, and during the journey no news reached the Commander-in-Chief, the Headquarters Staff, or even the correspondent of the *Morning Post.* He has recorded that "the general opinion among the Staff was that it would be all over before they got there. Some of our best officers were on board and they simply could not conceive how 'irregular, amateur' forces like the Boers could make any impression against disciplined professional soldiers." [4]

Toward the end of the voyage a tramp steamer was sighted ahead coming from "the land of knowledge." But for the insistence of the younger passengers she might well have been allowed to pass the *Dunottar Castle* about a mile away. To stop a ship at sea seemed to their seniors a procedure so unusual and irregular as to constitute an almost sacrilegious breach of precedent. They finally consented, however, to a signal being made asking for news. When she steamed past a hundred yards away a blackboard was held up from the tramp steamer's deck bearing the words:

BOERS DEFEATED

THREE BATTLES

PENN SYMONS KILLED

"There had evidently been fighting—actual battles! And a British General had been killed! . . . It was hardly possible the Boers would have any strength left. . . . Deep gloom settled down upon our party. . . ."
"It looks as if it will be all over, sir," said a Staff Officer to the Commander-in-Chief.—"I daresay," he replied, "there will be enough left to

give us a fight outside Pretoria." "His military instinct was sure and true. There was quite enough left!" [5]

By the time they reached Cape Town Winston Churchill and J. B. Atkins had decided to pool their fortunes at least for the Natal campaign. Their goal was Ladysmith. To reach it involved a four days' journey, first by rail to Port Elizabeth and then by a small tug to Durban. They caught the last train which got through and braved the dangers and discomforts of the tug; but when beyond Pietermaritzburg they reached the village of Estcourt they found the line was cut and they could go no farther. Ladysmith was already encircled. They had arrived just too late to be imprisoned in it for many long, tedious, and hungry months of siege. There was now nothing for it but to wait at Estcourt, where a few handfuls of troops were then assembled, expecting to be themselves attacked, surrounded, and cut off at any moment. "Estcourt," wrote Winston Churchill to the *Morning Post,* "now calls itself 'The Front'."

Winston Churchill and J. B. Atkins pitched their bell tent in the railway yard. Atkins recounts that in the evenings they discussed journalism and Winston's political career. "He showed me some articles already published in the *Morning Post* and two in manuscript, and invited my opinion. He was gratified by the wide interest which his work had already aroused. When I had read his articles, he said, 'Now, what do you think of them? Is the interest due to any merit in me or is it only because I am Randolph's son?'—'Do you want a candid answer?'—'Naturally. Any other would be useless'.—'Well,' said I, 'I notice in your articles a sweep and a range of thought, particularly in your philosophical vision of a true Imperialism, which I should not find in articles by other correspondents. But, then, would your articles have excited so much interest if I had written them? I think not.'—'A fair verdict. But how long will my father's memory help me?'—'Curiosity is very keen for a time, but only a short time. I should think it would help you for two or three years, but after that everything will depend on you. But honestly I don't think you will have to rely on your father.' . . . 'The worst of it is,' Winston went on, 'that I am not a good life. My father died too young. I must try to accomplish whatever I can by the time I am forty'." [6]

Winston also liked to talk of strategy and tactics. His belief was that both were " 'just a matter of common sense.' . . . 'Put all the elements of a problem before a civilian of first-rate ability and enough imagination,' he said, 'and he would reach the right solution, and any soldier could afterwards put his solution into military terms.' " [7]

This opinion was a characteristic forecast of a constant future attitude. Throughout his life he was never inhibited by undue respect for experts nor did he ever, except on one occasion when Chancellor of the Exchequer (and then mistakenly), show any hesitation in overruling them if his own "common sense" prescribed it. He was always deeply interested in techniques of all kinds and listened avidly to experts and professionals, imbibing all they told him with a rare accuracy and grasp. But he never fell a victim to the black magic of specialist infallibility. It was the task of specialists and experts to supply the weights and measures; it was for him to assess them and to reach conclusions.

At Estcourt he found some old friends: Leo Amery, now correspondent of the *Times,* whom he met "for the first time . . . on terms of equality and fraternity," [8] and Captain Aylmer Haldane, whom he had known in India, where he had procured him his appointment on Sir William Lockhart's staff and who was now commanding a company of the Dublin Fusiliers. Cavalry reconnaissances were made daily to ascertain the movements of some ten or twelve thousand Boers who might sweep forward at any moment, and Winston Churchill records that "in an unlucky moment it occurred to the general in command on the spot to send his armoured train along the sixteen miles of intact railway line to supplement the efforts of the cavalry." [9] Captain Haldane was put in charge of this operation and on the night of November 14th he invited Winston Churchill to accompany him.

"An armoured train!" wrote Winston Churchill. "The very name sounds strange; a locomotive disguised as a knight-errant; the agent of civilization in the habiliments of chivalry. Mr. Morley attired as Sir Lancelot would seem scarcely more incongruous." He was well aware that "nothing looks more formidable and impressive than an armoured train; but nothing is in fact more vulnerable and helpless." Nevertheless, "out of comradeship, and because I thought it was my duty to gather as much information as I could for the *Morning Post,* also because I was eager for trouble, I accepted the invitation without demur." [10]

Next morning about dawn he woke up J. B. Atkins and asked him whether he would like to join the expedition. Atkins writes: "I said sleepily that I would not go; and a few moments later, as Winston lingered, I explained that my instructions were to follow the war on the British side, and that if after having put my paper to great expense, I got myself on the wrong side, I should be held very much to blame. Winston listened and then said gravely 'That is perfectly true. I can see no fault in your reasoning. But I have a feeling, a sort of intuition, that if I go something will come of it. It's illogical, I know.' He went. I did not see him again until he had escaped from his prison in Pretoria and presented the world with a famous story. *Is this man accompanied by a daemon who tells him things?"* [11]

This is a question which I have often asked myself. Again and again, watching his life and fortunes, it has seemed to me that Winston had a private wire with Fate. His course often appeared to be shaped either by accident or by impulse. It was always unpredictable, sometimes inexplicable in terms of reason. Yet, following it, it is hard not to believe that it was directed by that beam which some call destiny and others instinct, by a power which intervened between him and events and which, not once but many times, preserved his life to serve its purpose. What he called "intuition" was in fact obedience to the beam which shaped his course.

On this occasion, as on many others, the beam proved a true guide. That helpless, vulnerable, and incongruous vehicle—the armored train—turned out to be the iron horse on which he rode to fame.

He has himself described in its dramatic detail the first disastrous lap of that swift journey. General Haldane in his book *A Soldier's Saga* condemns the mission assigned to him as "the height of folly." He adds: "I do not wish to lay blame on anyone but myself, but had I been alone and not had my impetuous young friend Churchill with me, who in many things was prompted by Danton's motto, 'de l'audace et encore de l'audace et toujours de l'audace', I might have thought twice before throwing myself into the lion's jaws by going almost to the Tugela. But I was carried away by his ardour and departed from an attitude of prudence. . . ." [12]

The Boers allowed the train a placid outward run of fourteen miles to Chieveley, posted themselves behind it, and lay in wait for it on its return. First a shell placed on the track exploded, derailing and overturning several trucks which blocked the line between the engine and the rest. Then from the neighboring hillside the Boers poured fire from rifles, Maxims and three field guns on the trapped train and its crew. With bullets whistling overhead which "rang and splattered on the steel plates like a hailstorm" Winston Churchill ran along the line and called for volunteers to free the engine. The driver, his face cut open by a splinter and streaming with blood, vowed that he would not stay another minute and ran for shelter. Winston assured him that no man is ever hit twice on the same day and that a wounded man who continues to do his duty is invariably rewarded for his gallantry. "On this he pulled himself together, wiped the blood off his face, climbed back into the cab of his engine and thereafter obeyed every order which I gave him." [13] Thanks to the coolness, courage and resource of Winston Churchill's leadership the men were rallied and steadied and the engine freed. But after a struggle of seventy minutes amid exploding shells and "the ceaseless hammering of bullets" it proved impossible to raise and re-attach the trucks. It was then decided that the engine should be used to carry back the wounded and that the rest should follow on foot, sheltering themselves behind it. But with the shells bursting around it the engine's pace increased, the infantry could not keep up with it and lagged behind. Winston leaped from the cab and went back along the line to bring Captain Haldane and his men along. He had not gone two hundred yards when two figures in plain clothes appeared upon the line. " 'Platelayers,' I said to myself, and then with a surge of realization, 'Boers!' . . . I turned again and ran back towards the engine, the two Boers firing as I ran between the metals. Their bullets, sucking to right and left, seemed to miss only by inches. . . . I flung myself against the bank of the cutting. It gave no cover. Another glance at the two fig-ures; one was now kneeling to aim. . . . I must get out of the cutting—that damnable corridor! I . . . scrambled up the bank. The earth sprang up beside me. . . . Outside the cutting was a tiny depression. I crouched in this, struggling to get my breath again. . . . Suddenly on the other side of the railway . . . I saw a horseman galloping furiously, a tall, dark figure, holding his rifle in his right hand. He pulled up his horse . . . and shaking the rifle at me shouted a loud command. We were forty yards apart." [14] "I reached down for my Mauser pistol. 'This one at least,' I said . . . but alas! I had left the weapon in the cab of the engine in order to be free to work at the wreckage on the line." [15] "Meanwhile . . . the Boer horseman . . . had covered me with his rifle. I looked towards the river, I looked towards the plate-layer's hut. The Boer continued to look along his sights. . . ." [16] There was nothing for it but to surrender himself a prisoner of war.

Who was the tall dark horseman? When Destiny decided to direct the course of Winston Churchill's life it tried its hand at drama and it proved itself to be a master dramatist. When in the after years of peace the Boer Generals came to England as her friends Winston met their leader, General Botha, at a private luncheon party and told him the story of his capture. After listening in silence Botha said: "Don't you recog-nize me? It was I who took you prisoner. I, myself." [17] And it was Smuts, then Attorney-General of the South African Republic, who interrogated the "defiant young man" who was brought before him, "looking dishevelled and most indignant and claiming immunity as a non-combatant." Here is a drama in which every actor is a star.*

The light of Winston Churchill's star was burning low when with his comrades in misfortune he started on the three days' journey by march and train to prison in Pretoria. The rain streamed down on them from leaden skies and the iron of captivity entered into his soul. "Prisoner of War! . . . You are in the power of your enemy. You owe your life to his humanity, and your daily bread to his compassion. . . ." [18] "All military pride, all independence of spirit must be put aside. These may be carried to the grave but not into captivity." [19] He cursed himself for not having gone off upon the engine which would have borne him back to freedom and "meditated bleakly upon the sour rewards of virtue."

He was, however, surprised and deeply impressed by the humanity and courtesy of his Boer captors, at whose hands he had expected every hardship and indignity. During the long march he engaged in lively argument and discussion with many of them about the origins and outcome of the war. They asked: "Why should you English take this country away from us? Are not our farms our own? Why must we fight for them?" He found them sure that God was on their side and confident of victory.

One conversation with a Boer ticket collector is worth recording, for it reveals that even in those days the racial issue was the main bone of contention between the Boers and ourselves. " 'We are free, you are not free.'—'How do you mean "not free"?'—'Well, is it right that a dirty Kaffir should walk on the pavement—without a pass too? That's what they do in your British Colonies. Brother! Equal! Ugh! Free! Not a bit! We know how to treat Kaffirs.' " Far deeper than political difference lay this sharp antagonism on racial attitudes. "The true and original root of Dutch aversion to British rule," wrote Winston Churchill, is not Majuba Hill nor the Jameson Raid but "the abiding fear and hatred of the movement that seeks to place the native on a level with the white man. . . . The servant is to be raised against the master; the Kaffir is to be declared the brother of the European, to be constituted his legal equal, to be armed with political rights. The dominant race is to be deprived of their

* In his life of his father, J. C. Smuts has written (p. 51): "It appears that my father had developed quite a liking for the high-spirited young man he had interrogated, and so, some days afterwards, he persuaded General Joubert that there was not much point in detaining him, for he was, after all, a newspaper correspondent. . . . His release was, therefore, authorized, but before it could be put into effect he had escaped."

superiority. . . . 'Educate a Kaffir?' said the Boer. 'Ah, that's you English all over. . . . They were put here by the God Almighty to work for us. . . . Insist on their proper treatment will you? Ah, that's what we're going to see about now. We'll settle whether you English are to interfere with us before this war is over.' " [20] What, Winston Churchill wondered, would a Liberal-minded "pro-Boer," like John Morley, say to this?

On arrival in Pretoria the men were led off to their cage while Winston Churchill, Captain Haldane and their two companions were imprisoned in the State Model Schools, where sixty other British officers were already confined.

I often heard Winston Churchill say that he hated every moment of his captivity more bitterly than he had ever hated any other period in his whole life, including even his wretched private-school days. Looking back on it he wrote: "I have always felt the keenest pity for prisoners and captives. . . . Therefore in after years, when I was Home Secretary and had all the prisons of England in my charge, I did my utmost . . . to introduce some sort of variety and indulgence into the life of their inmates, to give to educated minds books to feed on . . . and to mitigate as far as is reasonable the hard lot which, if they have deserved, they must none the less endure." [21]

But though he had books to feed on he found it difficult to read, impossible to write. The hours crawled by "like paralytic centipedes." One flame alone burned steadily in his mind—escape.

———◄◄ ►►———

Chapter Seven

ESCAPE

Winston CHURCHILL had written to General Joubert and to the Secretary for War demanding release as a noncombatant, but he felt little hope that they would accede to his request. He was convinced that the Boer authorities intended to hold him as a kind of hostage to bargain with if necessary. Moreover the Natal papers had reported his exploits in glowing terms, attributing the escape of the wounded entirely to his feat in freeing the engine. On these grounds General Joubert intimated that he would be treated as a prisoner of war. When the news of this decision reached him the die was cast. He must escape.

He cashed a check and bought a suit of tweeds of neutral color. He tried to buy a hat but this boon was refused him. "And yet my taste ran towards a slouch hat. . . ." (He was already preoccupied with hats and had a taste in them.) The hat was finally borrowed from a Dutch fellow prisoner, Adrian Hofmeyer, incarcerated for heresy about the war.

In the meantime Captain Haldane, who was equally determined to escape, had worked out a plan with a Lieutenant Brockie, a South African colonist, who knew the country and spoke both Dutch and Kaffir. They agreed to join forces, though Brockie was reluctant and Captain Haldane confesses in his book to grave anxiety lest his conspicuous and "talkative friend" should compromise their chances of success. On November 11th they made a combined attempt which proved abortive. Impatient and frustrated, Winston determined that nothing should prevent him from taking the plunge on the next day.

In the evening, after his two friends had made another vain attempt, he secreted himself in the lavatory from the roof of which they planned to climb onto the wall beyond. Through a crack in the wall he was able to observe the sentries only fifteen yards away who for a time "remained stolid and obstructive." Then they began to talk to one another and both their backs were turned. "Now or never! I stood on a ledge, seized the top of the wall with my hands, and drew myself up. Twice I let myself down again in sickly hesitation, and then with a third resolve scrambled up and over. . . . I lowered myself lightly down into the adjoining garden and crouched among the shrubs. I was free!" [1]

Here for an hour he lay awaiting the arrival of his friends until he heard the voices of two officers talking to each other behind the prison wall. Amid a flood of gibberish and Latin he heard the words "All up. They cannot get out. The sentry suspects. Can you get back?" To climb back into captivity would have been unthinkable and it was in fact impossible. He replied: "I shall go on alone."

And he walked out alone into the night to cover the three hundred miles which stretched between him and Delagoa Bay. He had in his pocket four slabs of chocolate and seventy-five pounds in notes, but neither map nor compass. He could speak no word either of Dutch or Kaffir. "The town was picketed, the country was patrolled, the trains were searched, the line was guarded . . . how was I to get food or direction? . . . But when hope had departed, fear had gone as well. . . . I looked at the stars. Orion shone brightly. Scarcely a year before he had guided me when lost in the desert to the banks of the Nile. He had given me water. Now he should lead to freedom. I could not endure the want of either." [2]

Orion did not betray his trust. Following his starry guide he struck the railway line and hid in a ditch by the track a few hundred yards beyond a station in the hope of boarding a passing train before it had gathered too much speed. An hour passed. . . . "Suddenly I heard the whistle and the approaching rattle. . . . The flaring head-lights drew swiftly near. The rattle became a roar. The dark mass hung for a second above me. . . . Then I hurled myself on the trucks, clutched at something, missed, clutched again, missed again, grasped some sort of hand hold, was swung off my feet, my toes bumping on the line, and with a struggle seated myself on the couplings of the fifth truck from the front of the train." [3] He was on board a goods train carrying empty coal bags. He burrowed in among the soft sacks, coal-dusty, warm, and comfortable, and thus buried fell asleep.

Waking before dawn he realized that he must not run the risk of being unloaded with the sacks. With a leap he left the train and landed in a ditch, unhurt though shaken. He was very thirsty, searched for water in the darkness, found a clear pool and drank from it. As the dawn broke he saw with infinite relief that the railway line ran straight toward the sunrise. He had taken the right train to freedom! He found a hiding place in a small grove of trees among the hills and here he spent the long hours of daylight—his only food a slab of chocolate, his sole companion a gigantic vulture "who manifested an extravagant interest in my condition." [4]

During these hours his heart "beat so fiercely" that he could not rest. His first elation had evaporated. He faced and recognized the heavy odds against him. He dreaded and abhorred the prospect of being recaptured and dragged back once more to prison in Pretoria. As in his early years at Bangalore he had written that whatever he might think or argue he did not hesitate to ask for divine protection when about to come under fire, so now he "prayed long and earnestly for help and guidance." And as he added then that in those early years "and indeed throughout my life, I got what I wanted," so now he was able to record that "my prayer . . . was swiftly and wonderfully answered."

During the long day he had watched the railway line and seen two or three trains pass along it in both directions. He planned to board one of these at night, leave it before dawn, to repeat the process on successive nights and thus reach Portuguese territory in three laps, subsisting meanwhile on his remaining slabs of chocolate and a pocketful of crumbled biscuit. When darkness fell he hurried to the railway line, took cover and waited. The hours passed but no train came.

His plan now lay in ruins and there was nothing for it but to struggle on on foot, over rough country through high grass and scrub, falling in bogs and swamps, wading through streams. Drenched to the waist, exhausted, weak from want of food and sleep and almost drained of hope he saw the distant lights of what he took to be the fires of a Kaffir kraal. He resolved to use his last reserves of strength to reach them. He would throw himself upon the mercy of the Kaffirs who, it was said, hated the Boers and had friendly feelings for the British. He had bank notes to offer them for help—"a guide, a pony, but, above all, rest, warmth, and food."

He had walked a mile toward the fires when his resolve was shaken by a sudden sense of the imprudence of his plan. He turned and went back wearily upon his tracks toward the railway line and finally sat down "completely baffled, destitute of any idea what to do or where to turn. Suddenly without the slightest reason all my doubts disappeared. It was certainly by no process of logic that they were dispelled. I just felt quite clear that I would go to the Kaffir kraal. I had sometimes in former years held a 'Planchette' pencil and written while others had touched my wrist or hand. I acted in exactly the same unconscious manner now." [5] Fate had intervened.

For hours he walked toward the distant fires, which seemed to recede as he advanced. Toward three o'clock in the morning he drew near enough to see that it was no Kaffir kraal he was approaching but the mouth of a coal mine with some houses grouped around it. The fires by which he had been led were from the furnaces. Among the huts stood a small stone house two stories high.

It was still possible to retrace his steps. But—toward what? Toward "futile wanderings terminated by hunger, fever, discovery, or surrender"? He had heard it said that in the mining district of Middelburg there were a few English residents who had been allowed to remain to keep the mines working. Had he been led to one of these?

He resolved to stake all on this chance. "With faltering and reluctant steps . . . I walked out of the shimmering gloom of the veldt into the light of the furnace fires, advanced towards the silent house, and struck with my fist upon the door. . . . A light sprang up above and an upper window opened. 'Wer ist da?' cried a man's voice. I felt the shock of disappointment and consternation to my fingers. 'I want help . . . I have had an accident,' I replied." The door was opened abruptly and a tall man with a pale face and a dark mustache stood before him. "What do you want?" he said, this time in English. On the spur of the moment Winston improvised: he had fallen from a train, had been unconscious, had dislocated a shoulder. . . .

"The stranger regarded me intently, and after some hesitation said at length 'Well, come in.'" He led the way into a small dark room, struck a light, lit a lamp and laid a revolver down on his end of the table. "'I think,' I said, 'I had better tell you the truth.'—'I think you had,' he said, slowly. . . . 'I am Winston Churchill, war-correspondent of the *Morning Post*. I escaped last night from Pretoria. I am making my way to the frontier. I have plenty of money. Will you help me?' There was a long pause. My companion rose from the table slowly and locked the door. After this act, which struck me as unpromising, and was certainly ambiguous, he advanced upon me and suddenly held out his hand. 'Thank God you have come here! It is the only house for twenty miles where you would not have been handed over. But we are all British here, and we will see you through.'" Describing the "spasm of relief" which swept over him Winston Churchill wrote: "I felt like a drowning man pulled out of the water and informed he has won the Derby!"[6]

His host was Mr. John Howard, manager of the Transvaal Collieries, who had been allowed to remain on the mine with a few others to keep it in working order. As a naturalized citizen of the Transvaal Republic he would have been held guilty of treason in harboring an escaped prisoner and liable to be shot if caught.

Nevertheless he was as good as his word. The hue and cry for Winston Churchill was up and out all over the district and a reward of twenty-five pounds had been offered for his return dead or alive (not a high price for such a catch—even at the 1900 value of the pound). Howard took into his confidence his two Scotch miners and his engineer, a Mr. Dewsnap of Oldham. Not daring to shelter Winston Churchill in his house where there were two Dutch servants, Howard concealed him in a chamber at the bottom of the mine. Here for two days he lived in darkness or by candlelight sustained by chickens, whisky, books and even cigars—his only company a horde of white rats with pink eyes who made constant raids upon his store of candles.

Meanwhile the plans were being laid for the last lap of his flight to freedom. A friendly Dutchman, Burgener by name, was sending three large truckloads of his wool to Delagoa Bay. These trucks were to be loaded at the siding of the mine. It was arranged that Winston Churchill should be hidden among the bales. A tarpaulin would be fixed over each loaded truck and it was thought unlikely, though not impossible, that it would be removed for examination at the frontier. Was he prepared to take this risk?

The prospect gave him more anxiety and misgiving than anything that had so far befallen him in his adventure. But he finally accepted the plan and at two o'clock in the morning of December 19th the signal for departure came. His host appeared and beckoned. "Not a word was spoken on either side. Howard led the way to the siding where three large bogie trucks stood and strolled along to the first truck. . . . As he did so he pointed with his left hand. I nipped on to the buffers and saw before me a hole between the wool-bales . . . just wide enough to squeeze into. From this there led a narrow tunnel formed of wool-bales into the centre of the truck. . . . In this I took up my abode."[7]

And here he found awaiting him a revolver, two roast chickens, a loaf of bread, a melon and three bottles of cold tea—generous rations for the thirty-six-hour journey he expected. (It was in fact to last two and a half days.)

He had learned by heart the names of all the stations on the route and he found a chink through which it was possible to peep and check the various stages of the journey. Late in the afternoon of the second day he reached a large and busy junction which he guessed to be the dreaded frontier town of Komatipoort. Covering himself with sacking he lay, with a beating heart, among the bales. Would they search the trucks? Once indeed he heard the tarpaulin rustle as they tugged at it. Thus eighteen hours passed and still the train made no move. Would it perhaps be shunted to a siding and there forgotten for days, perhaps for weeks? At last it started. But was Komatipoort behind them? Perhaps he had miscounted and the search was still to come. . . .

But when passing the next station he peered through his chink and saw the caps of Portuguese officials on the platform, tension snapped, the long strain was at an end and freedom won. He was flooded with a tide of overwhelming thankfulness and joy. "I pushed my head out of the tarpaulin and sang and shouted and crowed at the top of my voice. Indeed, I was so carried away . . . that I fired my revolver two or three times in the air as a *feu de joie*." [8]

At Lourenço Marques he reached journey's end and crawled forth from his place of refuge "weary, dusty, hungry but free once more." Slipping out of the end of the truck he walked toward the gates where he found Burgener waiting. "We exchanged glances. He turned and walked off into the town, and I followed twenty yards behind. . . . Presently he stopped and stood for a moment gazing up at the roof of the opposite house. I looked . . . and there—blest vision!—I saw floating the gay colours of the Union Jack. It was the British Consulate." [9] He adds that the Consul's secretary was evidently not expecting him and bade him to "be off" and call again next morning. At this his protests were so loud and vehement that they brought the Consul himself to the window and finally to the door.

Neither in his past nor even in his future life can Winston Churchill ever have received a more astounded or enthusiastic welcome. Every resource of hospitality was lavished on him—a hot bath, clean clothes, an excellent dinner "with a real tablecloth and real glasses" and, perhaps most welcome of all, a file of newspapers. He devoured them avidly and learned for the first time of the catastrophic sequence of events since his escape: Magersfontein, Colenso, Stormberg—the Black Week of the British Army.

The news acted on his spirit like a trigger. His inexhaustible reserves of physical and nervous energy were instantly recharged for action. He must rejoin the Army. He decided to embark at once for Durban on a steamer which was leaving the same night. The news of his arrival had spread through the town, which was then full of Boers and their supporters. Fearing his recapture, a body of fully armed Englishmen arrived at the Consulate to escort him and with this bodyguard he marched through the streets to the quay to join his ship.

At Durban he was received with wild enthusiasm. Flags, bands, and crowds awaited him at the harbor. He was carried shoulder-high to the Town Hall where there were insistent demands for a speech "which after a becoming reluctance I was induced to deliver." He was snowed under by an avalanche of telegrams in ecstatic terms. The shortest and the least ecstatic came from London: "Best friends here hope you will not continue making further ass of yourself." [9]

And this was not the only pinch of salt on his well-gilded gingerbread. While the newspapers at home were ringing his praises, extolling his valor in the defense of the armored train and his ingenuity in escaping from his captors, a small section of the press had started a campaign of calumny and denigration. He was accused of abusing his status as a noncombatant and then exploiting it to claim immunity from imprisonment. It was also alleged that in escaping he had broken his parole—a lie which he refuted in four successful libel actions, but which nevertheless I heard repeated as lately as 1947. It was his first baptism of mud, a missile to which he was to become philosophically inured throughout his career.

He got into further trouble with "military and society circles" by a dispatch he sent from Durban to the *Morning Post*. "We must face the facts," he wrote. "The individual Boer, mounted in suitable country, is worth from three to five regular soldiers. The power of modern rifles is so tremendous that frontal attacks must often be repulsed. The extraordinary mobility of the enemy protects his flanks. The only way of treating the problem is either to get men equal in character and intelligence as riflemen, or, failing the individual, huge masses of troops. . . . It is a perilous policy to dribble out reinforcements and to fritter away armies. . . . It would be much cheaper in the end to send more than necessary. There is plenty of work here for a quarter of a million men, and South Africa is well worth the cost in blood and money. More irregular corps are wanted. Are the gentlemen of England all fox-hunting? . . ." [10]

These home truths did not go down well at home. The *Morning Leader* wrote a scathing comment: "We have received no confirmation of the statement that Lord Lansdowne has, pending the arrival of Lord Roberts, appointed Mr. Winston Churchill to command the troops in South Africa, with General Sir Redvers Buller, V.C., as his Chief of Staff."

Meanwhile Sir Redvers Buller sent for him and after hearing all the information he had been able to collect in the course of his adventures he said: "You have done very well. Is there anything we can do for you?" Winston replied at once that he would like a commission. This demand put Buller in an awkward fix. For it was largely as a result of Winston's own embarrassing activities when doubling the roles of fighter and writer that the War Office had laid it down that henceforth no soldier could be a correspondent and no correspondent could be a soldier. But Buller finally capitulated. After taking "two or three tours round the room and eyeing me in a droll manner" he said: "All right. You can have a commission in Bungo's * regiment. You will have to do as much as you can for both jobs. But you will get no pay for ours." [11]

Thus Winston Churchill rejoined the Army as a Lieutenant in the South African Light Horse, christened by him the Cockyollybirds because of their strange headgear (from which he no doubt derived peculiar satisfaction). He wrote: "I stitched my badges of rank to my khaki coat and stuck the long plume of feathers from the tail of the sakabulu bird in my hat, and lived from day to day in perfect happiness."

He fought unscathed through the bloody fiasco of Spion Kop. His brother Jack, who had just arrived, was wounded in his first action as they lay side by side. He rode with the spearhead of the relieving forces into "long-beleaguered, almost starved-out Ladysmith," a memorable and deeply moving experience.

With the arrival of Lord Roberts as Commander-in-Chief and Lord Kitchener as his Chief of Staff the tide of war had changed. (Even the German Emperor in a rare moment of good will had pressed these long-overdue appointments on Queen Victoria in a personal message.) Natal had been evacuated and its loyal colonists were now demanding that retribution should be meted out to the "collaborationists" in their

* Colonel Byng, later Lord Byng of Vimy.

midst who had aided and abetted the enemy. The British Government was inclined to forgive and forget, and an Under-Secretary, Lord Wolverton, had been allowed to make a speech in favor of clemency.

"All my instincts," wrote Winston Churchill, "acclaimed this magnanimity." He telegraphed from Ladysmith a dispatch in which he urged that "a generous and forgiving policy should be followed. . . . The wise and right course is to beat down all who resist, even to the last man, but not to withhold forgiveness or even friendship to those who wish to surrender"—a policy which he preached and practiced consistently throughout his life.

He records that "the message was very ill-received in England . . . where a vindictive spirit ruled. The Government had rallied to the nation . . . and I bore the brunt of Conservative anger." Even the *Morning Post* while printing his message "sorrowfully disagreed" with its content. The Natal papers were "loud-voiced in condemnation." Once more he was out of step with public opinion, and not for the first, or last, time he was right.

On June 5, 1900, Pretoria capitulated. As he rode into the town with his cousin the Duke of Marlborough his first thought was for the prisoners. They found the prison camp surrounded by a dense barbed-wire entanglement. "I raised my hat and cheered. The cry was instantly answered from within. What followed resembled the end of an Adelphi melodrama. We were only two, and before us stood the armed Boer guards with their rifles at the 'ready.' Marlborough . . . called on the Commandant to surrender forthwith. . . . The prisoners rushed out of the house into the yard, some in uniform, some in flannels, hatless or coatless, but all violently excited. The sentries threw down their rifles, the gates were flung open. . . . Someone produced a Union Jack, the Transvaal emblem was torn down, and amidst wild cheers from our captive friends the first British flag was hoisted over Pretoria." [12]

And now, for a variety of good reasons, Winston Churchill decided to leave the Army and to return home. The back of the Boer resistance had been broken and guerrilla warfare stretched ahead. His mother's wedding to George Cornwallis West was to take place in July. A general election though not imminent might well be in the offing. He took the train to Cape Town.

But there was one last adventure still in store for him. After leaving Kopjes Station (about a hundred miles south of Johannesburg) in the first light of early morning the train stopped suddenly with a jerk. He got out on to the line and a small shell from a gun burst almost at his feet. A hundred yards ahead a wooden bridge was in flames. The train was crowded with soldiers, who began to get out of their carriages in confusion. No one was in command. His memories of the armored train had made him "extremely sensitive" about a line of retreat. He ran along the railway line to the engine, climbed into the cab and ordered the engine driver to blow his whistle to make the men re-entrain and steer back immediately to Kopjes Station. The man obeyed. "While I was standing on the footplate . . . I saw, less than a hundred yards away . . . under the burning bridge, a cluster of dark figures. These were the last Boers I was to see as enemies. . . . I thought for many years that the two-inch Creusot shell which had burst so near us . . . was the last projectile I should ever see fired in anger. This expectation, however, proved unfounded." [13]

Chapter Eight

FIRST POLITICAL VICTORY

W HEN Winston Churchill left South Africa it was to exchange one battlefield for another. Within five days of his return to England he visited Oldham, where he was accorded a Roman triumph. The town was gay with flags and banners when he made his entry in a procession of ten landaus, the chariots of those days, which drove through cheering crowds to the music of brass bands playing "See the Conquering Hero Comes." That night he addressed a great meeting in the Theatre Royal and for the first time he was able to tell the whole story of his escape. When he mentioned the name of Mr. Dewsnap, the Oldham engineer who had wound him down the mine, there were cries of "His wife's in the gallery" and wild enthusiasm followed.[1]

Next day he attended a banquet given in his honor at Birmingham by the Midland Conservative Club, of which he was President. He stressed the need for making vigorous efforts to support and reinforce Lord Roberts and his Army if we were to carry through the South African campaign "speedily and triumphantly." He was outspoken in his strictures on the War Office, which had "not altogether escaped criticism during the last few months, nor do I think it enjoys a deep measure of public affection." This was a theme to which he was to return repeatedly in the course of the election. He also spoke of the treatment of prisoners, on which he had views of his own for which he said he had been "very much scolded." "Gentlemen, I am a faithful advocate of clemency to the Dutch rebels. . . . But disenfranchisement and penal taxation do not shock me in the least."[2] He seems to have drawn a sharp distinction between human and political inclemency.

In a subsequent speech at Oldham he protested against the breaking up of pro-Boer meetings by the police and by "some misguided but patriotic Englishmen," and declared that "of all the rights of our glorious Empire there is none more worthy or more noble than the right of free speech." [3]

The stage was now set for the first Khaki Election in our history. The fall of Pretoria and (perhaps even more) the relief of Mafeking with its orgiastic junketings had led most people in England to believe that the war was over and victory won. The Government was far from sharing this illusion but it was determined to exploit it. During its five years of office its popularity had steadily declined and its majority had dwindled from 152 to 128. Here was a heaven-sent opportunity to cash in on victory—supposed or real—to its own electoral advantage. Of the three Khaki Elections in my lifetime the most disreputable—and the most successful—was undoubtedly the so-called Coupon Election which followed the First World War in 1918, fought on the battle cry of "Hang the Kaiser and make Germany pay." The election of 1945, though inspired by the same motive as its predecessors, is the easiest to forgive because it resulted in disastrous self-defeat.

The tone of the General Election of 1900 was set by Mr. Chamberlain with the slogan "Every seat lost to the Government is a seat gained to the Boers," and Winston Churchill records that "Conservatives generally followed in his wake. . . . All the Liberals, even those who had most loyally supported the war measures, including some who had lost their sons, were lapped in a general condemnation as 'Pro-Boers.' " [4] Posters presented pictures of eminent Liberals offering tribute to President Kruger, helping him to shoot British soldiers and haul down the Union Jack. In his life of Sir Henry Campbell-Bannerman, J. A. Spender records that "Lord Roberts and Lord Kitchener were boldly annexed" for electioneering purposes and that "an equestrian portrait of the one and a menacing full figure of the other adorned a poster issued on behalf of Mr. Gerald Balfour at Leeds, which bore the familiar device 'To vote for a Liberal is to vote for the Boer.' " [5] But in Oldham and throughout the country the Liberal electors refused to be browbeaten or stampeded and put up a stubborn fight. The Government gained a mere six seats.

On the day after the dissolution of Parliament Mr. Chamberlain went to Oldham and addressed a packed and enthusiastic meeting in support of Winston Churchill and his quiet colleague, Mr. Crisp. The visit was significant because it was the only speech delivered by Mr. Chamberlain during the whole election outside his own "Midland District" kingdom. He explained that he was there "because one of the candidates was the son of an old friend." The *Daily News* suggested pertinently that if his visit had any motive apart from electioneering tactics it was probably more indicative of remorse. It recalled that after Lord Randolph's resignation of the Exchequer it had been his dearest wish to represent Birmingham. On the death of John Bright the Conservative section of the Unionist Party in Central Birmingham had invited Lord Randolph to stand and he had eagerly accepted when Mr. Chamberlain intervened. He claimed the seat for a Liberal Unionist and insisted on Lord Randolph's withdrawal.[6] It is unlikely that this incident was forgotten by his son even amid "the roar of the multitude" at Oldham. When some fifty years later I once questioned him about it he said: "Yes, it's all true. Joe was determined that there should not be two Kings in Birmingham."

It is nevertheless true that Chamberlain had a genuine affection and admiration for Winston Churchill. My stepmother has recorded in her autobiography an account of her visit to him in his house at Princes Gate after the General Election of 1910. He was then fatally stricken, but though his speech was indistinct his mind was clear and alert. In the course of their conversation he said to her: "Winston is the cleverest of all the young men, and the mistake Arthur * made was letting him go."

The Oldham election was fought at concert pitch and spotlit from start to finish. Charges reflecting on his courage and his honor were hurled at Winston Churchill and passionately rebutted. For the rest he stood on the orthodox ground that the war was just and necessary and must be fought to a victorious conclusion, adding his personal postscript that it should be followed by a generous settlement. He continued to urge the need for Army and War Office reform and to criticize "an unbusinesslike department and ill-conceived system." In his appeals for clemency to rebels and his assertion of the rights of pro-Boers to free speech his latent Liberal instincts occasionally erupted. But in the necessarily sparse and incomplete reports of his campaign I can find no evidence of any active preoccupation with the conditions of the life of the people.

Reading an old letter of my father's, written from Oldham in the early

* Mr. Arthur Balfour.

nineties to a friend, I realize through what different eyes he saw these things. He described the workers streaming out of a large factory when the whistle sounded for the dinner hour. "The great gates opened and there burst out an ocean of men. . . . I watched them closely as they passed me—a long procession of wan-faced, grimy, tired, silent figures. They get an average of 18/- a week, and work, with intervals for meals, from 6 to 6. Civilization and religion have done *something* for them— given them paved streets, water-tight houses, board-schools, Chapels and even (in Oldham) an Art Gallery. But life in its real sense they have never known, and to their dying day will never know." My father was determined that these men should have "life in its real sense" and have it more abundantly. In years to come Winston was to share this determination and to play his full part in implementing it. But in 1900 he was not thinking or feeling in these terms. His imagination had not yet been caught or fired by the challenge of poverty.

In those days an election was spread over nearly six weeks. Writing in later years Winston Churchill praised this procedure as a "wise and prudent law." "Instead of all the electors voting blindly on one day, and only learning next morning what they had done, national issues were really fought out. A rough but earnest and searching national discussion took place in which leading men on both sides played a part. . . . A great speech by an eminent personage would often turn a constituency or even a city. Speeches of well-known and experienced statesmen were fully reported in all the newspapers and studied by wide political classes. Thus by a process of rugged argument the national decision was reached in measured steps." [7]

But what a grueling ordeal for candidates these "measured steps" involved! Those who polled late were obliged to stay the course in their own constituencies for six long weeks while the early elected, hoarse and exhausted, threadbare in thought and speech, were expected to stagger around the country appearing on platforms as "the Victor of X." There were no cars to carry the tired speaker from meeting to meeting, no microphones or loud-speakers to carry his tired voice; he had skilled hecklers and ruthless reporting to contend with, no salary if he won and an enormous bill to pay whether he won or lost.

Apart from its challenge to stamina there is no doubt that the old process of staggering general elections had a very definite effect on their result. The early returns inevitably influenced the later ones. Whether they tended to arrest or to precipitate a landslide is anybody's guess. In my experience triumph and disaster are, like snowballs, apt to gather size and pace as they roll on. The public impulse is to speed both on their way. Voters prefer the band wagon to the burning deck.

The weekly Gallup Polls now published during general elections play the same part as the old staggered polling did, though in a less powerful and dramatic way.

Oldham was among the first constituencies to vote. When the result was declared, though Mr. Emmott still headed the poll, Winston Churchill had succeeded in defeating Mr. Runciman and was elected by 230 votes—a narrow margin in a total of 30,000. But he was in! And he had won a seat for his party. When he arrived with his jubilant supporters at the Conservative Club he found a telegram of "glowing congratulations" from Lord Salisbury already awaiting him. It was followed by "a stream of joyous and laudatory messages." Clamant appeals for his presence and assistance flowed in from all parts of the country. He became, in his own words, the "star turn" of the election.

The stars in their courses competed for him. The day after the poll he was on his way to speak in London with the intention of going thence to Birmingham, where Mr. Chamberlain had demanded his services, when his train was boarded by a messenger from Mr. Balfour asking him to cancel his London engagement and come up at once to Manchester to speak for him. He complied and on his entry the whole audience rose and roared their welcome.

"After this," he wrote, "I never addressed any but the greatest meetings. . . . I had what seemed to me a triumphal progress through the country . . . and quite a lot of victories followed in my train. I was 26. Was it wonderful that I should have thought I had arrived? But luckily life is not so easy as all that: otherwise we should get to the end too quickly." [8]

Parliament was to meet early in December. The great stage on which he knew that he could play his part awaited him. He had only got to take his seat and the curtain would go up. . . . But with a cool, far-sighted prudence he refrained from doing so. In order to be free to concentrate on politics to the exclusion of all else he must not allow himself to be distracted by the need to earn his living. He must somehow accumulate a lump sum on which he could subsist. *The River War* and his salary from the *Morning Post* had brought him in four thousand pounds. He planned to add to this reserve by lecturing during the autumn and winter months at home and in America.

It was during this tour that I had my first glimpse of him—and it was no more than a glimpse. My father, who was then Member for

East Fife, took a house at St. Andrews for a few months every year in order to cultivate his excellent constituency and his indifferent golf. When Winston came to lecture there he spent the night with us. I was then a child and in the throes of infantile paralysis. He was a mere name to me, one of the many I had heard in the political discussions which were the background music of my life. But I can still remember my father's interest, verging almost on excitement, at Winston's arrival and the enthusiasm and amusement with which he described to me his oratorical performance at the Town Hall complete with magic-lantern slides. Remembering his love for Lord Randolph I asked him whether Winston was like his father. He thought a little and then said: "No—not really. He is like no one else. He derives from no one. He is an original and most extraordinary phenomenon." From my bed in a bow window I saw the back of his departing figure when he left the house next morning—the slightly hunched shoulders from which his head jutted forward like the muzzle of a gun about to fire.

After covering more than half Great Britain in a most successful and remunerative tour he crossed the Atlantic on his first visit to his second country, the United States. And here he was innocently surprised to find a very different atmosphere and state of mind from the one he had left in England. Though speaking our own language and "seeming in essentials very like ourselves," some of these "amiable and hospitable" Americans were not particularly excited about the South African War, and, stranger still, many of them thought that the Boers were in the right. Audiences varied sharply both in their size and temperature. Boston blew hot and Baltimore blew cold. In Chicago he had "vociferous opposition" to contend with. The Irish everywhere were hostile. But on the whole he found American audiences "cool and critical, but also urbane and good-natured." They were easy to disarm when he made a few jokes about himself and paid a tribute to the courage and humanity of the Boers.

His opening lecture in New York was presided over by Mark Twain, whose books had been the delight of his early youth. Although they disagreed about the war they got on well together and Mark Twain signed for him every one of the thirty volumes of his works, inscribing in the first the monitory maxim: "To do good is noble; to teach others to do good is nobler, and no trouble."

After ten days in Canada, where he was greeted with tumultuous enthusiasm, he returned to complete his lecture tour in England. By the middle of February he had covered his course. After five months of unceasing travel during which he had spoken once and often twice on every day except Sundays he was (on his own admission) exhausted. But he had achieved his aim. He had earned ten thousand pounds and with it the freedom to give his whole mind to politics without care for any morrow.

Chapter Nine

IN PARLIAMENT

Q UEEN VICTORIA died on January 22nd, two days before the new Parliament was due to reassemble. That morning I remember being sent out with our nurse to buy black clothes. From the hushed house we went into hushed streets where everyone, even the poorest, seemed to be already dressed in black.

A few days later I was taken to see the funeral procession from Devonshire House where the old Duchess still lived and reigned over what, in those days, was called Society. I remember Piccadilly, frozen in silence, lined with soldiers, thronged with patient, waiting crowds as the procession wound its way toward us. The gun carriage which bore the Queen went by. Behind it rode the Captains and the Kings of all the world. The dark skies with a threat of rain had allowed King Edward to wear a cloak, which immensely improved his appearance on horseback. Beside him rode the Kaiser, magnificent in a Wagnerian helmet that gleamed with eagles. I remember the thud of the soldiers' feet, the music of Chopin's "Funeral March," which I had never heard before, the throb of the drums, the deep, still grief of the crowds. It was as though everyone in England had lost his father and his mother. It was also, though I did not know it, and perhaps few guessed it, the beginning of the end of an epoch.

It was in the shadow of this national bereavement that King Edward VII opened his first Parliament with Queen Alexandra at his side, both in deep mourning. This historic ceremony had not taken place since the middle eighties. The King's Speech informed the House that "The war in South Africa has not yet entirely terminated"—an understatement if ever there was one. For though the Khaki Election had been fought to

58

celebrate the victorious conclusion of the war it had refused to conclude. It was in fact to drag on for another eighteen months.

Lord Kitchener, who had been left in command after Lord Roberts' return to England, had the difficult and thankless task of dealing with a mobile and elusive enemy scattered in small groups over the wide spaces of the veldt, an enemy who fought without a uniform, who was a farmer at one moment, a guerrilla fighter the next, and then a farmer again. These guerrilla-farmers needed no commissariat for they could draw upon their farms for horses, food and forage. Faced with this dilemma Kitchener proceeded to strip the country of its farms and stock and in cases where treachery had occurred or communications had been cut to burn the farms. Farm-burning was alternately defended by the Government as a punitive measure and as a military necessity. Meanwhile homeless noncombatants were swept into concentration camps which had been hastily improvised and were often shockingly mismanaged. They were overcrowded, insanitary and ravaged by epidemics, and the mortality among women and children was high. These tactics were later to be branded by Campbell-Bannerman as "methods of barbarism," a phrase which earned him obloquy at home but in the opinion of General Botha helped more than any other in the end to make peace and union in South Africa.

The South African War had aroused an extraordinary clash and confusion of feelings in Britain. It was our first war against a civilized enemy since the Crimea. The horrors of the Crimean campaign, often resulting from gross military incompetence, had been forgotten but its glories were still bright. The pale flag of pacifism therefore had few adherents. Yet there were large numbers of people who had not lost their sense of right or wrong even about a war. They hated the idea that a small and gallant nation should have been provoked into intransigence and would be crushed by overwhelming military superiority. The general feeling was that once in it we must go through with it, but that any ethical flaws in the process must be made good by a magnanimous peace. I do not think there has been any war in which the enemy was less hated, even when he proved much more formidable than we expected. And, of course, our national pride was wounded and tickled in various ways by our defeats, the participation of the Empire, and the German Emperor's ham-handed interventions. When it was learned that he had been kind enough to send us a plan of campaign drawn up by his General Staff, there was an explosion of fury, the echoes of which were still reverberating in 1914.

The Liberal Party, which had been—and still was—deeply divided over the issue of the war, was united in its opposition to the Government's demand for unconditional surrender. It urged that a proclamation should be issued to the Boers announcing that their co-operation as citizens would be sought and that when peace was restored they would have their full share in the rights of self-government.* To this plea Lord Salisbury had returned a barren answer. It was desirable, he said, that these countries should someday attain the position of self-governing colonies of Great Britain, but he "knew not how long the delay might be. It might be years, it might even be generations."

This shelving of self-government for generations provoked a strong protest even from that staunch "Imperialist" Sir Edward Grey.

The election had injected little new blood into the Conservative rank and file or its Front Bench. "The stable remains the same, the horses are the same but every horse is in a new stall" was Sir Henry Campbell-Bannerman's apt comment on the reconstructed Ministry. The Cecil stable still provided most of the best horses. Lord Salisbury, who had broken Lord Randolph Churchill, was still Prime Minister. His nephew, Arthur Balfour, who had been Lord Randolph's comrade in arms in the Fourth Party, was Leader of the House of Commons. Many of its members had watched the rise of that bright star to its brief glory and seen it fall to earth. It is easy to imagine the expectancy, emotion, curiosity with which the House of Commons awaited Randolph's son, whose exploits had already brought him fame in his own right.

What were his feelings as he braced himself for what he then regarded, and not then alone but throughout his life, as "the supreme ordeal"? No statesman in our history has felt a deeper reverence for the House of Commons. He approached it now with "awe as well as eagerness." When should he try his fortunes—on this which was to be his greatest stage, forum and battleground? He took counsel with many well-wishers and friends and received much conflicting advice. "Some said: 'It is too soon; wait for a few months till you know the House.' Others said: 'It

* It is often forgotten that up till the outbreak of war there was no divergence in policy between my father and Sir Henry Campbell-Bannerman. Both agreed that the Boer ultimatum made war inevitable, both joined in voting the Government supplies, both abstained from supporting the Amendment to the Address "disapproving of the conduct of the negotiations which had involved us in hostilities with the South African Republic"—to which 135 of the Opposition, including Mr. Labouchère and Mr. Lloyd George, subscribed. They differed on one point only. Three days after the ultimatum my father pronounced against the ultimate annexation of the Republic. Campbell-Bannerman on the other hand held the view that the future of the Republic must be within the Empire and to this opinion my father was later converted.

is your subject: do not miss the chance.' " [1] South Africa was his subject. Within four days of taking his seat he resolved to take the plunge in the debate on the Address.

He learned that "a rising young Welshman, a pro-Boer, and one of our most important bugbears, named Lloyd George," would probably be called about nine o'clock and that if he wished to do so he could follow him. Lloyd George had put down an amendment framed in moderate terms, but whether he would move it or not was still uncertain. "In those days, and indeed for many years," wrote Winston Churchill, "I was unable to say anything (except a sentence in rejoinder) that I had not written out and committed to memory beforehand. . . . I had to try to foresee the situation and to have a number of variants ready to meet its possibilities. I therefore came with a quiverful of arrows of different patterns and sizes some of which I hoped would hit the target." [2] From this technique he never deviated throughout his long and glorious Parliamentary career. The arrows of his swift retorts which sped like lightning to their mark owed their perfection to prefabrication. By some sixth sense he was able to foresee the bull's-eye before it was presented. It was largely to this gift of inspired and accurate prevision that he owed his mastery of debate. For in spite of his command of words, unequaled in its power, originality and range, he never was a ready speaker. The artist in him forbade slipshod spontaneity. He was too verbally fastidious to leave his words to chance. To him a speech must be, in substance and in form, a work of art. As such it demanded hours of time and toil to fashion. "I need not recount," he wrote of his maiden speech, "the pains I had taken to prepare, nor the efforts I had made to hide the work of preparation." [3]

He sat in the corner seat above the gangway behind the Government front bench, the seat from which Lord Randolph had made his speech of resignation. The hour had come. "Towards nine o'clock the House began to fill. Mr. Lloyd George . . . announced forthwith that he did not intend to move his amendment. . . . Encouraged by the cheers of the 'Celtic fringes' he soon became animated and even violent. I constructed in succession sentence after sentence to hook on with after he should sit down. Each of these poor couplings became in turn obsolete. A sense of alarm and even despair crept across me. I repressed it with an inward gasp." On the bench beside him sat a friendly and experienced Parliamentarian, Mr. Gibson Bowles, who must have been aware of his distress, for he threw him a lifeline. "He whispered: 'You might say "Instead of making his violent speech without moving his moderate amendment, he had better have moved his moderate amendment without making his violent speech." ' Manna in the wilderness was not more welcome! It fell only just in time. . . . I was up before I knew it, and reciting Tommy Bowles's rescuing sentence. It won a general cheer. Courage returned. I got through all right." [4]

This speech was a brilliant Parliamentary performance, for it was not only a fearless expression of his own mind but it was acclaimed alternately by both sides of an acutely divided House of Commons. When he said of Lloyd George's speech, "I do not believe that the Boers would attach particular importance to the utterances of the honourable Member. No people in the world have received so much verbal sympathy and so little practical support as the Boers," he drew cheers from the Government benches. But when he added, "The Boers who are fighting in the field—*and if I were a Boer, I hope I should be fighting in the field*—" he was warmly cheered not only by the Liberal Opposition but even by the Irish Nationalists. At this point in his speech he noticed "a ruffle" on the Treasury bench below him. Mr. Chamberlain was making a comment to his neighbor. George Wyndham told him afterward that Mr. Chamberlain had remarked: "That's the way to throw away seats!" [5]

He went on to rebut the charges of treachery on the one side and barbarity on the other and to express his belief that as compared with other wars the war in South Africa had been carried on with unusual humanity and generosity. He urged the setting up of a civil rather than a military government as soon as possible, and told the House that "The Boer farmer is a curious combination of the squire and peasant, and under the rough coat of the farmer there are very often to be found the instincts of the squire." He had been ashamed to see such men "ordered about by young subalterns as if they were private soldiers." He appealed to the Government to "make it easy and honourable for the Boers to surrender and painful and perilous for them to continue" the fight, and expressed the earnest hope that the Colonial Secretary would "leave nothing undone to bring home to these brave and unhappy men who are fighting in the field that whenever they are prepared to recognize that their small independence must be merged in the larger liberties of the British Empire there will be a full guarantee for the security of their property and religion, an assurance of equal rights, a promise of representative institutions, and last but not least of all, what the British Army would most readily accord to a brave and enduring foe—all the honours of war." At the same time he urged the Government not only to maintain but to increase the strength of the Army by a regular quota of reinforcements. This war was not a war of greed. It had been from beginning to end a war of duty. The House was deeply moved by his closing sentence in which he thanked it for "the kindness and patience . . . which have been extended to me, I well know, not on my own account, but because of a certain splendid memory which many honourable Members still preserve." [6]

When he sat down amid cheers he received tributes from both sides of the House. Sir Robert Reid, who followed him, said that he possessed the same courage which so distinguished Lord Randolph during his short and brilliant career. Speaking next day, my father expressed agreement with his plea for civil government and the hope and belief that "his interesting and eloquent speech . . . was the first step in a Parliamentary career of the highest distinction." The press was attentive—and enthusiastic. Describing the scene, the *Morning Post* wrote that "rarely has a maiden speech been listened to by so crowded a House. The moment the word went round that 'Churchill's up,' every inch of room was occupied; the side galleries filled; the bar was thronged. Mr. Churchill was obviously nervous—who would not be, addressing such an audience and inheriting such a name? But he made an excellent début and in the emptying of the Chamber which followed the conclusion of his speech nearly every member who passed along the gangway stopped to murmur a congratulatory word." [7] But perhaps the most interesting comment came from H. W. Massingham, the finest lobby correspondent of his day, then writing for the *Daily News*. He described the "final interest of the evening" which "took the shape of a kind of duel between two young members in whose careers the House takes an interest—Mr. Lloyd George and Mr. Winston Churchill. Mr. George never speaks now without drawing a house—a sure sign of mastery of his audience and his subject. . . . All these powers Mr. George displayed in his speech last night. . . . For the most part it was a continuous story of what may be called the true horrors of war—the cruelties of farm-burning, the sufferings of the women and children, and all the train of miserable consequences that follow the path of an invading army. . . . It ended on the note that the war was not only cruel but wrong.

"Mr. Winston Churchill's reply was in very striking contrast to the speech to which it was indeed only nominally an answer. The personal contrast was as strong as that of treatment and method. Mr. George has many advantages; Mr. Churchill has many disadvantages. . . . Mr. Churchill does not inherit his father's voice—save for the slight lisp—or his father's manner. Address, accent, appearance do not help him. But he has one quality—intellect. He has an eye—and he can judge and think for himself. Parts of the speech were faulty enough—there was claptrap with the wisdom and the insight. But such remarks as the impossibility of the country returning to prosperity under a military government, the picture of the old Boers—more squires than peasants— ordered about by young subalterns, the appeals for easy and honourable terms of surrender, showed that this young man has kept his critical faculty through the glamour of association with our arms." [8]

What was the maiden speaker's verdict on his own performance when, having reached the shore, he "scrambled up the beach, breathless physically, dripping metaphorically, but safe"? "Everyone," he wrote, "was very kind. The usual restoratives were applied, and I sat in a comfortable coma till I was strong enough to go home. The general verdict was not unfavourable. Although many guessed I had learnt it all by heart, this was pardoned because of the pains I had taken. The House of Commons, though gravely changed, is still an august collective personality. It is always indulgent to those who are proud to be its servants." [9]

It was after this debate that his first meeting with Mr. Lloyd George took place. They were introduced to each other at the bar of the House of Commons. After congratulating him on his speech Mr. Lloyd George said: "Judging from your sentiments, you are standing against the Light." Winston Churchill replied: "You take a singularly detached view of the British Empire." "Thus," he wrote, "began an association which has persisted through many vicissitudes." [10]

Winston Churchill once expounded to me the methods by which a Government back-bencher may make his reputation. "There are two ways," he said. "One is to defend an indefensible action of a Minister on your own side. The other is to attack your own side." This was retrospective wisdom, for though he was to employ both methods during his first two months in Parliament they were not dictated by tactics but by the impulse of genuine conviction.

The occasion on which he used the first method with conspicuous success was in a debate on March 12, 1901, on the case of General Colville, an officer who had been appointed by the War Office to a command at Gibraltar. They subsequently discovered facts about his conduct in some South African action fought nearly a year before and dismissed him from his command. The Opposition condemned this belated punishment, supported the General, and demanded an inquiry. A debate was fixed for the following week. "Here," wrote Winston Churchill, "was a country with which I was familiar, and I had plenty of time to choose the best defensive positions. The debate opened ill for the Government, and criticism was directed upon them from all sides. In those days it was a serious matter for an Administration, even with a large majority, to be notably worsted in debate. . . . I came in well on this, with what everybody thought was a debating speech; but it was only the result of a lucky anticipation of the course of the debate. In fact I defended the Government by arguments which appealed to the Opposition. The Conservatives were pleased and the Liberals complimentary. . . . I really seemed to be finding my footing in the House." [11]

Massingham's comment on the speech is again illuminating and all the more significant in that he was writing for a Liberal newspaper, the *Daily News:* "To their [the Government's] rescue came Mr. Winston Churchill in what was certainly the ablest speech he has made since his entry into the House. I say 'ablest' because it was a pure debating speech" (even Massingham was here deceived!) "conceived on lines of singular breadth, argued with great acuteness and closeness and now and then with little gestures and tricks of manner—such as bent shoulders and eager, nervous action of the hands—which at moments made one catch one's breath with the thought of how his father looked and spoke. I do not yet find in this young man the depth of character, the great political force that lay behind all his most fantastic adventures. But nothing could be more remarkable than the way in which this youth has slipped into the Parliamentary manner and has flung himself as it were straight into the mid-current of the thoughts and prejudices of the House of Commons. He chose on this occasion to act as the 'bonnet' of the Government, the man who should lead them out of a dangerous pass. And he did it to perfection. Mr. Balfour showed his gratitude by vehement and repeated cheering. . . . The speech was a happy stroke for his own Parliamentary reputation and for the Government which he has placed under so deep an obligation. It is not exactly pleasing to hear this young man for there are defects of manner, thought and speech which do not commend themselves to the fastidious taste. But it is clear he is going to arrive as his father arrived before him." [12]

By this skillful and astute performance Winston Churchill rendered signal service to his leaders and earned their gratitude. To wring "vehement cheers" from Arthur Balfour was no mean achievement. Congratulations rained down upon him from the "highest ministerial circles." If he had been, as his detractors have suggested, a cold-blooded careerist, a smart tactician on the make, his course was clear: to march along the road of party orthodoxy into office. This course he found himself unable to pursue because, in his own words, he found himself "in marked reaction from the dominant views of the Conservative Party." He admired "the dauntless resistance of the Boers" and thought farm-burning "a hateful folly. . . . I thought we should finish the war by force and generosity, and then make haste to return to paths of peace, retrenchment and reform." To this Gladstonian goal he must have guessed he was unlikely to travel behind his present leaders.

And he added: "Although I enjoyed the privilege of meeting in pleasant circles most of the Conservative leaders, and was always treated with extraordinary kindness and good-nature by Mr. Balfour; although I often saw Mr. Chamberlain and heard him discuss affairs with the greatest freedom, I drifted steadily to the left. I found that Rosebery, Asquith and Grey and above all John Morley seemed to understand my point of view far better than my own chiefs. I was fascinated by the intellectual stature of these men and their broad and inspiring outlook upon public affairs. . . . I became anxious to make the Conservative Party follow Liberal courses. I was in revolt against 'Jingoism'. . . . I found myself differing from both parties in various ways, and I was so untutored as to suppose that all I had to do was to think out what was right and express it fearlessly. I thought that loyalty in this outweighed all other loyalties. I did not understand the importance of party discipline and unity, and the sacrifices of opinion which may lawfully be made in their cause." [13] The "untutored" state of mind he thus describes remained a constant attitude throughout his life.

On May 13th, two months after his adroit speech for the defense, he passed to the attack. Mr. St. John Brodrick, Secretary of State for War, had announced a costly and ambitious scheme for the reorganization and enlargement of the Army on Continental lines. Winston Churchill challenged these proposals in a speech which revealed for the first time the weight and power of his mind. And it was not his mind alone which was engaged. His theme involved his deepest emotions. For it was on this issue of military expenditure and its relation to social reform in our national economy that, thirty years earlier, Lord Randolph had fallen, to rise no more. After his death his son pledged himself to one purpose, in the words I have already quoted: "There remained for me only to pursue his aims and vindicate his memory." Here was the opportunity.

Winston Churchill knew that, for him at least, emotion was no substitute for preparation. He wrote: "I took six weeks to prepare this

Portrait of Winston Churchill by Sir William Orpen, 1916

Lord Randolph Churchill

The Mansell Collection

Lady Randolph Churchill

*Copyright Radio Times Hulton
Picture Library*

The room at Blenheim Palace in which Churchill was born in 1874

Mrs. Everest

The future Prime Minister at the age of seven

speech, and learnt it so thoroughly off by heart that it hardly mattered where I began it or how I turned it. . . . I was called at eleven o'clock on the first day. I had one hour before a division after midnight was taken on some other subject. The House was therefore crowded in every part, and I was listened to throughout with the closest attention. I delivered what was in effect a general attack, not only upon the policy of the Government, but upon the mood and tendency of the Conservative Party, urging peace, economy and reduction of armaments. The Conservatives treated me with startled consideration, while the Opposition of course cheered generously. As a speech it was certainly successful; but it marked a definite divergence of thought and sympathy from nearly all those who thronged the benches around me." [14]

That speech, delivered at the age of twenty-six, can hold its own with those of his greatest vintage years. In reading it today it is interesting to note that Winston Churchill had already forged and fashioned the distinctive mold of style through which he poured his thought throughout his life.

He opened with a moving vindication of Lord Randolph Churchill. "If I might be allowed to revive a half-forgotten episode . . . I would recall that once upon a time a Conservative and Unionist Administration came into power supported by a majority nearly as powerful and much more cohesive than that which now supports His Majesty's Government. When the time came to consider the Estimates, what used to be the annual struggle took place between the great spending departments and the Treasury. The Government of the day threw their weight on the side of the great spending departments and the Chancellor of the Exchequer resigned. The controversy was bitter, the struggle uncertain, but in the end the Government triumphed and the Chancellor of the Exchequer went down for ever, and with him, as it now seems, there fell also the cause of retrenchment and economy, so that the very memory thereof seems to have perished, and the words themselves have a curiously old-fashioned ring about them. I suppose that was a lesson which Chancellors of the Exchequer are not likely to forget in a hurry." At this point he quoted from Lord Randolph's letter of resignation to Lord Salisbury. "Wise words stand the test of time. I am very glad the House has allowed me, after an interval of fifteen years, to lift again the tattered flag of retrenchment and economy. . . ."

The Chancellor of the Exchequer had then refused to consent to estimates for the two services amounting to £31,000,000. Parliament was now being asked to vote something more than £59,000,000. . . .

"What has happened in the meantime to explain this astonishing increase? Has the wealth of the country doubled? Has the population of the Empire doubled? Have the armies of Europe doubled? Is the commercial competition of foreign nations so much reduced? Are we become the undisputed master in the markets of the world? Is there no poverty at home? Has the English Channel dried up and are we no longer an island? Is the revenue so easily raised that we do not know how to spend it? Are the Treasury buildings pulled down and all our financiers fled? . . . During the weeks I have been a member of the House I have heard honourable Members opposite advocate many causes, but no voice is raised in the cause of economy. . . . I think it is about time that a voice was heard from this side of the House pleading that unpopular cause; that someone not on the bench opposite, but a Conservative by tradition, whose fortunes are linked indissolubly to the Tory Party, who knows something of the majesty and power of Britain beyond the seas, upon whom rests no taint of cosmopolitanism, should stand forward and say what he can to protest against the policy of daily increasing the public burden. If such a one is to stand forward in such a cause, then, I say it humbly, but I hope with becoming pride, no one has a better right than I have, for this is a cause I have inherited and a cause for which the late Lord Randolph Churchill made the greatest sacrifice of any Minister in modern times."

He proceeded to subject the Brodrick scheme to devastating criticism. Three Army corps were to be kept ready for expeditionary purposes. They should be reduced to two. "One is quite enough to fight savages and three are not enough to begin to fight Europeans."

In a prophetic passage he went on to foreshadow the scale and magnitude of total wars to come.

"I have frequently been astonished since I have been in this House to hear with what composure and how glibly Members, and even Ministers, talk of a European war. I will not expatiate on the horrors of war, but there has been a great change which the House should not omit to notice. In former days when wars arose from individual causes, from the policy of a Minister or the passion of a King, when they were fought by small regular armies of professional soldiers, and when their course was retarded by the difficulties of communication and supply, and often suspended by the winter season, it was possible to limit the liabilities of the combatants. But now, when mighty populations are impelled on each other, each individual severally embittered and inflamed—when the resources of science and civilization sweep away everything that might mitigate their fury, a European war can only end in the ruin of the vanquished and the scarcely less fatal dislocation and exhaustion of the conquerors. Democracy is more vindictive than Cabinets. The wars of peoples will be more terrible than those of Kings."

He would not complain if this vast expenditure on the Army were going to make us secure. "But it will do no such thing. The Secretary for War knows . . . that if we went to war with any great Power his three army corps would scarcely serve as a vanguard. If we are hated they will not make us loved. If we are in danger, they will not make us safe. They are enough to irritate; they are not enough to overawe. Yet while they cannot make us invulnerable, they may very likely make us venturesome."

The honor and security of the British Empire must depend on a strong Navy. That is "the only weapon with which we can expect to cope with the great nations. That is what the Chief Secretary to the Lord Lieutenant [Mr. George Wyndham] calls the 'trust to luck and the Navy' policy. I confess I do trust the Navy. This new distrust of the Navy, this kind of shrinking from our natural element, the blue water on which we have ruled so long, is the most painful symptom of the military hydrophobia with which we are afflicted. Without a supreme Navy, whatever military arrangements we may make, whether for foreign expeditions or home defence, must be utterly vain and futile. With such a Navy we may hold any antagonist at arm's length and feed ourselves in the meantime, until, if we find it necessary, we can turn every city in the country into an arsenal and the whole male population into an army." Again a flash of accurate prevision of the course of two world wars to come.

"Why," he asked, "should we sacrifice a game in which we are sure to win to play a game in which we are bound to lose? . . . From the highest sentimental reasons, not less than from the most ordinary practical considerations, we must avoid a servile imitation of the clanking military empires of the European continent, by which we can never obtain the military predominance and security which is desired, but may only impair and vitiate the natural sources of our strength and vigour."

He ended with a fine peroration. "There is a higher reason still. There is a moral force . . . which, as the human race advances, will more and more strengthen and protect those who enjoy it. . . . And we shall make a fatal bargain if we allow the moral force which this country has so long exerted to become diminished, or perhaps even destroyed for the sake of the costly, trumpery, dangerous military playthings on which the Secretary of State for War has set his heart." [15]

By its power and eloquence the speech held the House spellbound for an hour. The Opposition was enthusiastic. The Conservatives, recovering from their "startled consideration," were shocked into sour admonition. Mr. Brodrick confidently expected that "Parliament will not sleep the less soundly because of the financial heroics" of the honorable Member for Oldham and hoped that "the time will come when his judgment will grow up to his ability . . . and when the hereditary qualities he possesses of eloquence and courage may be tempered also by discarding the hereditary desire to run Imperialism on the cheap." Mr. Arthur Lee rebuked him for confusing "filial piety with public duty. . . . This is not the time to parade or pursue family traditions. . . ."

The *Times* delivered its verdict: "Mr. Winston Churchill repeats the most disastrous mistake of his father's career." [16]

The most lyrical tribute came from his faithful troubadour Massingham: ". . . in its elevation of purpose, its broad conception of national policy, and in the noble and delicate movement of its closing sentences, I recall nothing like it since Gladstone died. And I will make two criticisms on it. The first is that it is a speech that should long ago have been delivered from our own benches. The second is that in the years to come its author should be Prime Minister—I hope Liberal Prime Minister—of England." [17]

This prophecy was not calculated to commend Winston Churchill to his disaffected party or its leaders. But even within the ranks of his own party he was not entirely isolated. Among the more independent and adventurous spirits of the rank and file there were many who admired his fearless challenge to authority and turned to him as a focus and exponent of their own doubts and discontents. He gathered around him a small Parliamentary group nicknamed "The Hooligans," after its most distinguished member, Lord Hugh Cecil, which included also Mr. Ian Malcolm and Mr. Arthur Stanley. They acted in concert both on policy and tactics and dined together every Thursday in the House of Commons, always entertaining one distinguished guest. Though less formidable than the Fourth Party they proved lively and effective irritants to the Government and succeeded in making themselves thoroughly unpopular with the faithful and the Front Bench.

From this close working alliance with Lord Hugh Cecil there arose one of the greatest friendships of Winston Churchill's life. He was fascinated by a mind so rare and individual and, both in its attitude and processes, so different from his own. "Here for the first time, and I am afraid almost for the last," he wrote, "I met a real Tory, a being out of the seventeenth century, but equipped with every modern convenience and aptitude." He was at once bewildered and impressed when his friend "leapt into the political arena accoutred with every intellectual weapon . . . to defend causes which nobody then seemed to consider very important and few people now bother about at all." [18] Few bothered about them less than Winston Churchill. Yet so fervid was his admiration and so firm his friendship that he even allowed himself to be dragged into Lord Hugh's "vehement resistance" to a Bill for allowing a man to marry his deceased wife's sister. He confesses that he was himself "at first sight inclined to think this might be a very excusable and often reasonable arrangement" and he tried to point out to Lord Hugh its many practical advantages. "He was scandalized at my ignorance of Ecclesiastical Law. . . . The object of the Christian Church, he explained, was to enlarge the bounds of family affection to the widest possible extent without admitting within those bounds the possibility of sex disturbance. . . . Dethrone the principle of prohibited degrees and in hundreds—nay in thousands—of households the position of these devoted women, hitherto unquestioned, would become a target for comment and calumny." He stressed "our duty to preserve the structure of humane, enlightened, Christian society. Once the downward steps were taken, once one's moral and intellectual feet slipped upon the slope of plausible indulgence, there would be found no halting-place short of a general Paganism and Hedonism, possibly agreeable from time to time in this world of fleeting trials and choices, but fatal hereafter through measureless ages, if not indeed through eternity itself." [19]

It is hard to imagine arguments less calculated to appeal either to Winston Churchill's conscience or his mind, and coming from any other quarter he would have dismissed them with ribald indifference. But to oblige a friend he was always ready to go to almost any length, and he characteristically agreed to assist Lord Hugh in the incongruous, prolonged and grueling task of obstructing the Deceased Wife's Sister Bill of 1901 in Grand Committee. Their joint efforts would have been doomed to defeat but for Lord Hugh's final resort to a Parliamentary stratagem of doubtful character. Being a Private Member's Bill, its fate depended upon the vote being taken before the clock struck four. Lord Hugh loitered in the lobby. "He literally crawled inch by inch across the matting which led to the portals where the votes were counted." Fifteen seconds before the division ended the clock struck and the Bill was dead!

The Radicals and Nonconformists who had supported it were furiously indignant and received Lord Hugh with howls when he re-entered the Chamber. They declared that his maneuver was "not cricket." These hostile demonstrations left him unmoved. "What was all this talk of 'not playing cricket' when the transcendental character of the marriage tie was at stake? . . . We were not playing a game; we were discharging a solemn and indeed awful duty."

Though he discharged his "awful duty" like a man, Winston Churchill admitted that in "the growing tolerances of the age" he was "ultimately induced to acquiesce in the legalizing of a man's marriage with his deceased wife's sister." There must I think have been many issues on which he and his friend and ally did not see eye to eye, but on one at least they found themselves in passionate agreement—on the divine right to disagree.

During his early years as a back-bencher Winston Churchill concentrated his fire on two main targets: Army reform, on which he could speak with knowledge and authority, and economy, the cause he had inherited from his father. I have seen it alleged that because he was at this time engaged upon his biography of Lord Randolph Churchill, his early Parliamentary career was "based on an almost slavish imitation" of his father. This is, in my view, a gross misconception of his habit of mind, which was never, either then or since, one of "slavish imitation." He did not ape his father's views. He accepted them unquestioningly as a faith.

But it is perhaps curious that he should have selected from his father's credo the arid (though vitally important) subject of economy in preference to the more human issues of social problems and conditions with which Lord Randolph was equally concerned. In later life financial problems rarely engaged his attention and certainly never challenged his imagination. Retrenchment made no appeal to his lavish and expansive spirit either in public or in private life. Scraping, pinching and cheese-paring were not congenial to his nature. One cannot imagine him, like Mr. Gladstone, delving into wastepaper baskets to salvage discarded half-sheets of writing paper for the public good. Economy was the graft of filial piety, not the natural fruit of the tree. But whether graft or growth, it was in these early years the mainspring of his political thought and action, the spearhead of his attack upon the Government.

On April 14, 1902, the Chancellor of the Exchequer, Sir Michael

Hicks Beach, introduced a budget which proposed the imposition of a duty on corn. Winston Churchill opposed it in a speech which was then generally regarded as a continuation of his campaign for economy. He arraigned the Government both for extravagance and for the maldistribution of our resources. They were now taking 150 millions a year for domestic purposes and as much again for the Army and Navy. No one would deny that the Navy was much more important than the Army to an island empire, yet we spent an equal proportion of our national resources on both. Everything pointed to a vastly increased cost of government. Education would cost more, the Sinking Fund must be restored. We must reduce income tax, we must be prepared for bad trade.

Then came an astonishing flash of vision of the shape of things to come. "What would it come to? The basis of taxation would have to be broadened, and . . . the Committee should realize that further expenditure meant serious taxation of bread and meat and other necessaries of the food of the people. . . . Two gigantic issues would be raised. In the first place the Fair Trade issue. . . . A tax which in the first instance would be honestly imposed solely for the purpose of revenue would, no doubt . . . become Protective in character. . . . The honourable and gallant Member for Sheffield [Sir Howard Vincent] would say, why not kill three birds with one stone—raise the revenue, support British industries, and consolidate the Empire?" (An exact forecast of the arguments which were to be used by Mr. Chamberlain when he launched his Protectionist Campaign.) "They would stand once more on the old battlefields with all the old broken weapons and amid grass-grown trenches and the neglected graves of heroes who had fallen in former conflicts. Party bitterness would be aroused such as the present generation could furnish no parallel for except in the brief period of 1885-6. He wondered how the advent of such a tremendous issue would affect the existing disposition of political parties." [20]

How indeed? It was to have a revolutionary effect not only upon the disposition of parties but upon that of his own career. The events which he foretold were still undreamed of. More than a year was to elapse before they came to pass. But readers of this prophetic utterance who saw the prophecy fulfilled, almost to the letter, must ask themselves, as J. B. Atkins did at Estcourt: "Has this man a daemon who tells him things?"

Some time afterward the Hooligans entertained Mr. Chamberlain as their distinguished guest at one of their weekly dinners. There had been a lively debate that afternoon on the case of a Mr. Cartwright who had been imprisoned for a year in South Africa for publishing a seditious libel on Lord Kitchener during the war. After serving his sentence he wished to come to England but the military authorities refused to allow him to leave South Africa. The Liberals were indignant at this infringement of personal liberty. All the Opposition leaders spoke in protest and John Morley moved the adjournment. Winston Churchill and a small group of Conservatives supported him.

"I am dining in very bad company," said Mr. Chamberlain to his rebel hosts. They explained "how inept and arrogant the action of the Government had been. 'What is the use,' he replied, 'of supporting your own Government only when it is right? It is just when it is in this sort of pickle that you ought to have come to our aid.' However, as he mellowed he became most gay and captivating. . . . As he rose to leave he paused at the door, and turning said with much deliberation: 'You young gentlemen have entertained me royally, and in return I will give you a priceless secret. Tariffs! There are the politics of the future, and of the near future. Study them closely and make yourselves masters of them, and you will not regret your hospitality to me.' " [21]

The "secret weapon" which was to change the face of British politics was already forged. It was soon to be unsheathed.

Chapter Ten

THE TURNING POINT

W INSTON CHURCHILL has related how in the year 1895, as a young subaltern, he had the privilege of lunching with Sir William Harcourt. "In the course of a conversation in which I took, I fear, none too modest a share I asked the question, 'What will happen then?' 'My dear Winston,' replied the old Victorian statesman, 'the experiences of a long life have convinced me that nothing ever happens.' Since that moment as it seems to me," wrote Winston Churchill, "nothing has ever ceased happening." [1]

Yet during the spring of 1903 there was a brief interlude in which nothing of any importance was happening or indeed seemed likely to happen. The Boer War was over. Lord Salisbury had retired in July, 1902, and been succeeded by his nephew and heir-apparent Arthur Balfour. The new Prime Minister believed that, in the political sphere at least, the less that happened the better. The barometer pointed firmly to "no change."

Out of these cloudless skies Mr. Chamberlain dropped his atom bomb. In a speech at Birmingham on May 15th, just before the Whitsuntide recess, he proclaimed to an astonished nation that the Empire was in danger of dissolution and could only be held together by the bonds of material interest in the shape of imperial preference. This would, of necessity, involve taxing food (though, paradoxically, not raw materials). We must abandon our free-trade system, embrace protection, and use tariffs, not only to protect our decaying British industries but as offensive weapons with which to threaten and, if need be, to retaliate against "the foreigner." He announced his intention of fighting the next election on this issue.

Whether by accident or design the speech was delivered on the very day on which Mr. Balfour was engaged in defending to an indignant deputation of agriculturalists the repeal of the corn duty by his Free Trade Chancellor of the Exchequer, Mr. Ritchie.

Few speeches in our history have produced such profound and lasting effects on the course of British politics. It united the Liberal Party; it brought chaos and confusion to the Conservatives. It led to a realignment of political forces and a dramatic transfer of power from Right to Left.

It also provided Winston Churchill with what he needed most—a cause and a theme.

It was not as a crusader or a missionary that he had entered politics, but rather as a fish takes to the water or a bird to the air, because it was his natural element. He had not thought it necessary to evolve or assume a conscious or coherent political philosophy. Though born and cradled in the purple of the Tory fold he was not of it. His ardent and adventurous mind, forever on the move, could not have been contained within its static bounds. Not only the memory of his father's faith and fate but his own imperious liberal impulses and instincts had ruled out orthodoxy from the start. He called himself a Tory democrat—and a democrat he was. But though never (to my mind) a Tory he saw and judged events in the historic framework of tradition. He revered "the old glories of Church and State, of King and Country." But he wished these ancient institutions to be the bulwarks of the liberties and progress of what he called "the masses." And to him at that time "the masses" were a political abstraction. He had no firsthand experience of the conditions of their daily lives.

He has written truly of his political course that "I have mostly acted in politics as I felt I wanted to act. When I have desired to do or say anything and have refrained therefrom through prudence, slothfulness or being dissuaded by others, I have always felt ashamed of myself at the time. . . . I do not see how it would have been possible for me in the mood I was in after the South African War to have worked enthusiastically with the Conservative Party in the mood they were in at that time. . . . Thus when the Protection issue was raised I was already disposed to view all their actions in the most critical light. . . . Still, I am sure that in those days I acted in accordance with my deepest feeling and with all that recklessness in so doing which belongs to youth and is indeed the glory of youth and its most formidable quality." [2]

I have seen it suggested that his espousal of the Free Trade cause was a tactical move dictated by impatience and ambition, and that Arthur

Balfour could have squared and silenced him by inviting him to join the Government. I am convinced that his own explanation is the true one, that, in his own words, he "acted in accordance with his deepest feeling." His faith in Free Trade was a passionate conviction, perhaps the only economic conviction he ever held, and it was upheld and reinforced by the assurance that his father would have shared it.

He flung himself into the fight. But first, he said to me in after years, "first I had to learn economics. I had to learn economics in eight weeks." "How did you set about it?" "I went to my father's wise and trusted counsellor at the Treasury, Sir Francis Mowatt, and he coached and grounded me with facts and general principles and arguments and gave me half a dozen books to read. He girded on my armor and equipped me for the fight—and then" (with relish) "I found no difficulty in doing the rest myself."

He has drawn a vivid portrait of this great public servant who had served under Gladstone and Disraeli at the Treasury and been private secretary to Mr. Gladstone. "Tall, spare, with a noble brow, a bright eye and strong jaws, this faithful servant of the Crown, self-effacing, but self-respecting, resolute, convinced, sure of himself, sure of his theme . . . Governments, Liberal or Tory, came and went. He served them all with equal fidelity, cherishing his Gladstonian sentiment as a purely private affair." This "Gladstonian sentiment" would have led him to "consign to the uttermost limbo jingoes, Imperialists, bi-metallists, socialists, protectionists and their like." [3]

He had loved to talk about Lord Randolph to Lord Randolph's son. "How quick he had been to learn the sound principles of public finance, how readily he had mown down his fair trade or protectionist wild oats, and how resolutely he had fought for public economy and reduction of armaments! What fun he was to work with and serve! What a tragedy had laid him low!" What emotion Mowatt must have felt as he equipped his old chief's son to carry on his father's fight. And this time there were no Protectionist wild oats to be mown down.

Winston Churchill did not await the completion of his economic education before joining issue with Chamberlain. Within a week of the Birmingham pronouncement my father replied to him at Doncaster. Winston spoke the same night at Hoxton. Of the Protectionists he said: "They are wrong in economics, wrong in political conceptions, wrong most of all in their estimate of public opinion." And of Chamberlain: "It will need all his most weighty arguments . . . all his courage and all his oratory to persuade the English people to abandon that system of Free Trade and cheap food upon which they have thrived for so long and under which they have advanced from the depths of poverty and distress to the first position among the nations of the world." [4]

A week later he challenged the new fiscal policy in the House of Commons and warned the Government that it would mean a change "not only in the historic English parties but in the conditions of our public life. . . . The old Conservative Party with its religious convictions and constitutional principles will disappear and a new party will arise . . . rigid, materialist and secular whose opinions will turn on tariffs and who will cause the lobbies to be crowded with the touts of protected industries." [5]

Meanwhile it was no secret that the Government was a house divided against itself. The only secret was the position of the Prime Minister, and as to this he declined to give any hint or clue. Both sides laid claim to him, "fought over him like dogs over a bone." Winston Churchill described him in the House of Commons as "a great Free Trader out of school-hours!" He was finally driven to "refuse to express a settled conviction where no settled conviction exists." He extracted from his colleagues a Trappist vow of public silence until a Board of Trade inquiry had reported on the relevant facts and in the meantime he refused to allow the matter to be debated in Parliament.

In a letter to the *Times,* under the heading "Unionist Free Traders and the Government," Winston Churchill protested against the gagging of the House of Commons. "The great question of the day may be argued in the Palace and the coal hole. Every Chamber of Commerce may debate it. Every public body may pass a resolution. It is on the agenda of the Eton Debating Society. It is in order in the Parliament of Peckham. There is one place in the British Empire where it is 'taboo'. The House of Commons, most interested, most concerned, most responsible, is to be gagged and smothered by a cynical and ingenious abuse of its own procedure." [6]

But no procedural dodge could impose silence on the thousands throughout the country who (unlike the Prime Minister) had already reached conclusions which they did not hesitate to express with vehemence. The rifts in the Conservative Party were widening into chasms. Arthur Balfour tried to bridge them by publishing an enigmatic paper entitled "Economic Notes on Insular Free Trade" in which it would have been hard to discover a "settled conviction" or even a unifying formula. He had built no bridge for others but had woven for himself a tenuous tightrope on which he was to balance uneasily for the next two years.

Mr. Chamberlain had no use for tightropes or for bridges. On September 9th he wrote a letter to the Prime Minister resigning from the

Government and announcing his intention to conduct a campaign in the country to win support for his proposals. On September 14th a Cabinet was held at which the Prime Minister gave no hint to his colleagues of Chamberlain's resignation, informed them that he was himself in favor of some undefined fiscal change and gave the free-trade Ministers what the Duke of Devonshire described as "notice to quit." Mr. Ritchie, Lord George Hamilton and Lord Balfour of Burleigh thereupon resigned. Had they known that their antagonist-in-chief, Mr. Chamberlain, had left the Cabinet they might well have acted differently. The Duke of Devonshire was persuaded to delay his decision, but when two days later the Prime Minister showed him Chamberlain's letter of resignation and his own reply accepting it, he followed his Free Trade friends and left the Government. He appears to have been the only colleague whose departure Arthur Balfour regretted or whose services he made any effort to retain.

"It seems paradoxical indeed," he wrote to Mr. Chamberlain when accepting his resignation, "that you should leave the Cabinet at the same time that others of my colleagues are leaving it who disagree . . . with us both." [7] It was a paradox he accepted philosophically, perhaps even with relief. Some explanation of both is to be found in a later sentence in his letter: "If Preference involves, as it almost certainly does, taxation, however light, upon food-stuffs, I am convinced with you that public opinion is not yet ripe for such an arrangement. . . ." And he added: "If you think you can best serve the interests of Imperial unity . . . by pressing your views on colonial preference with the freedom that is possible in an independent position but is hardly compatible with office, how can I criticize your determination? The loss to the Government is great indeed: but the gain to the cause you have at heart may be greater still. . . . If so what can I do but acquiesce?" He was prepared to "acquiesce," to await the result of Mr. Chamberlain's efforts to convert the electorate to food taxes. If public opinion ripened he would lend a hand in bringing in the harvest. If not, nothing was lost and well, or ill, could be left alone.

Meanwhile he filled two of the empty places in his Cabinet with two strong Protectionists, Mr. Austen Chamberlain and Mr. Alfred Lyttelton. In Winston Churchill's words: "He was careful to shed Free Trade and Protectionist blood as far as possible in equal quantities. Like Henry VIII, he decapitated Papists and burned Hot Gospellers on the same day for their respective divergencies in opposite directions from his central, personal and artificial compromise." [8]

This mature, seasoned and sensitive politician appears to have remained serenely unaware of the growing alienation of public opinion and of the impending disruption of his own party.

To Winston Churchill, then aged twenty-nine, with only three years of Parliamentary experience, these portents were crystal-clear. "We are on the eve of a gigantic political landslide," he wrote to the Duke of Devonshire. "I don't think Balfour and those about him realize at all how far the degeneration of the forces of Unionism has proceeded and how tremendous the countercurrent is going to be." [9] He was right. During the next two years the "countercurrent" was to grow and swell to that torrential tide which swept the Conservative Party out of power for close on twenty years. The fiscal battle was now joined on every platform throughout the country. Mr. Chamberlain carried the Fiery Cross of his "raging, tearing propaganda" from one great city to another, and my father followed him like his shadow, answering his arguments, exposing his fallacies, challenging his figures. Though I was not yet grown up, he took me with him. It was the first great political campaign I had ever taken part in and it left an indelible impression on my memory.

It was a duel fought with facts and figures and it might therefore have been a dull one, but my father could raise pure argument to an aesthetic level, and I shall never forget the rapt attention with which vast audiences listened to his speeches, closely reasoned as a Bach fugue. How was it, I wondered, that an economic issue without emotional appeal stirred public opinion so profoundly? I think that two elements played their part. First there was the fear of dearer food. The ghosts of the Hungry Forties still walked, the memories of the Corn Laws were not dead. And then there was, among Liberals at least, the belief that free trade was the way to international peace and understanding, the belief in the old saying that "if goods do not cross frontiers armies will."

Again, the Free Traders were not only skillful in the presentation of their case and united in its support but they were also lucky in the timing of the issue. Chamberlain's appeal to save our "decaying industries" from "unfair competition" and "dumping" by retaliation against "the foreigner" might, in a slump, have met with some response; but it fell on deaf ears in a time of great and rising prosperity. The plea that "our agriculture has been practically destroyed; sugar has gone; iron is threatened; wool is threatened; cotton will go" was crushingly refuted by soaring Board of Trade returns which proved all these "threatened" and expiring industries to be in rude and waxing health. With the best will in the world our "workingmen" failed to recognize themselves as "sheep in a field; one by one they allow themselves to be led to the slaughter." [10] Nor was "the curse of cheapness" likely to be a cry with any popular appeal. Again, if protection was not going to raise prices for the consumer why were bacon and maize exempted from protective duties on the ground that "they were the food of the poorest of the poor"? And if (as we were told) "the foreigner" would pay the duty on imported food and goods and thus endow the revenue how would the British manufacturer be protected? If on the other hand foreign goods were kept out how would the revenue benefit from the duty?

Listening as I did, night in night out on platforms and day in day out at every meal, to all the changes rung upon this theme I felt that the Free Trade case was "money for jam." And no one brought to its defense a greater mastery and grasp, more brilliant powers of exposition and combative zest than Winston Churchill.

The battle of the hustings was reinforced by a struggle between rival leagues—the Tariff Reform League, which had been formed to support Mr. Chamberlain, and the Unionist Free Food League, created by the Unionist Free-Traders to oppose him. Its President was the Duke of Devonshire and among the many distinguished Conservatives who gathered around him were Sir Michael Hicks Beach, Mr. Ritchie, Lord George Hamilton, Sir Edgar Vincent, Sir John Gorst, Major Seely, Lord Hugh Cecil and Winston Churchill.

But the whole Conservative press backed Chamberlain and he had captured the party machine. When Chamberlainite candidates were selected to fight two by-elections, the Duke of Devonshire, as President of the Free Food League, published a statement saying that "An elector who sympathises with the objects of the League would be well advised to decline to give his support at any Election to a Unionist candidate who expresses his sympathy with the policy of Mr. Chamberlain and the Tariff Reform League." [11]

This statement marked for many Unionists the parting of the ways. Winston Churchill's way had already been determined by himself. From now on he devoted all his energy, pugnacity and matchless gift of concentration to the defeat of Mr. Chamberlain's proposals. He worked in close alliance with his old friend Lord Hugh Cecil and they often spoke from the same platform. On one occasion (in November, 1903) they bearded Mr. Chamberlain in his den by holding a meeting in the Town Hall, Birmingham, under the auspices of the Free Trade Union. The interest aroused by this meeting was further enhanced by a threat of violence. Sandwich men paraded the streets with bills "Shall Radicals be allowed to oppose our Joe?" But profiting by their experience of Mr. Lloyd George's meeting two years before, the police had drafted three hundred men into the basement of the Town Hall and the meeting passed off peacefully if not quietly.

The speakers were greeted by "a remarkable demonstration, a section of the audience rising and waving hats and handkerchiefs while the other portion hissed and shouted. . . . Outside the hall the voices of an enormous crowd could be heard shouting and cheering." [12] When Winston Churchill expressed his regret that he did not see many of his old friends and added, "But it is part of the price which a politician has to pay if he refuses to jump with the jumping cat," [13] the audience rose and cheered for several minutes.

The *Times* commented justly that the speech was one to which the whole Opposition could subscribe. Such passages as "The happiness of our people is to be found in social reform rather than in fiscal malformations, by increasing temperance rather than tariffs, through the schoolmaster, the scientist and the physician rather than the tax-gatherer and the Custom House official" [14] and "Cheap food might be a parrot-cry to the millionaire proprietor of a score of newspapers but to the worker's wife trying to make the week's wages cover the week's bills, it was a grim fact" [13] give the impression that he is speaking in a new idiom to a new audience. These allusions to temperance, schoolmasters and weekly bills must in his mouth have had a strangely unfamiliar ring.

Yet he was not at that time contemplating a change of political allegiance; it was his aim to win the battle of free trade within the Conservative Party. He was fighting hard to hold his own position at Oldham. His Executive had passed a vote of confidence in him at the end of July, though he had then told his constituents frankly that even the success of Mr. Chamberlain's campaign in the country would not reconcile him to the abandonment of free trade. "I will never accept its results until I am convinced by logic and reason." [15]

But by October there were signs of strain between him and his constituents. They came to a head when in November Sir Gilbert Parker, M.P., attacked him in a speech delivered at Oldham to the local Protectionists and was supported in his strictures by a prominent Conservative Councilor, Joe Hilton, who suggested that Mr. Churchill should seek another constituency at the next election and in the meantime keep silence. When two days later Winston Churchill accompanied by Lord Lytton arrived at the North Chadderton Conservative Club where they were both to speak, they found the hall in darkness and were told that they were not to be allowed to use it. When the reporters present asked Winston Churchill for an interview he replied that all he had to say was "I am in favor of free trade and free speech."

A large crowd had assembled outside the Club, which gave him a great reception, and when he entered his brougham to drive away the heads of the horses were seized and there were loud and insistent cries of "Speech! Speech!" He left his carriage, mounted the box and said: "We are invited to make the most momentous departure in the policy of this country that any nation has ever been asked to make. . . . We are asked to make this great departure—and after the most inadequate inquiry fair and free discussion is refused. I do not intend to accept the decisions of any caucus. I was elected as Member for Oldham and I am not going to depart from those principles of Free Trade on which I was elected. . . . Do not imagine for one moment that I have embarked upon this fight without intending to see it through." [16]

Yet as he drove away through the darkness he must have known that it was not as Member for Oldham that he would see it through. This was the final breach.

On December 19th he sent a message of good wishes to the Liberal candidate in a by-election at Ludlow wishing him success in his contest against a protectionist opponent. "The time has now come," he wrote, "when Free Traders of all parties should form one line of battle against a common foe." [17] A few days later in a speech at Halifax he said: "English Liberalism has been through many wanderings and much tribulation in the last twenty years and it is today confronted by a powerful federation of vested interests. Yet it is a weapon and an instrument which in the hands of Mr. Gladstone would easily smash to pieces these pantomime politics and this cheap Jack Imperialism with which we are inflicted and insulted today." [18] And he ended his speech with the words "Thank God we have a Liberal Party!"

On December 23rd the Oldham Conservative General Purposes Committee passed a unanimous resolution intimating to Mr. Churchill: "That he had forfeited their confidence in him as Unionist Member for Oldham and that in the event of an Election taking place he must no longer rely on the Conservative organisation being used on his behalf."

The battle for the Conservative Party was lost. The battle for the country was still to be fought and won.

Chapter Eleven

CROSSING THE FLOOR

WHEN PARLIAMENT reassembled in February, 1904, Winston Churchill took his seat below the gangway. Although he still sat on the Conservative side he was now, in his own words, a "declared opponent of the present Government." [1]

In the country the credit of the Government was falling steadily and the disintegration of the Conservative Party proceeded apace. Four Ministers had resigned from the Cabinet and in the House of Commons some fifty Conservative or Unionist members gradually withdrew their support.

The opposing forces, though unorganized, were ardent and united in a common aim: to push the Government off the fence and force the issue at a general election. "The very air of Westminster smells of dissolution," said Winston Churchill hopefully at the outset of the session. But dissolution was not yet in the wind. However uneasily he wore his crown Arthur Balfour refused to abdicate.

Of this many-sided man of diverse gifts and tastes it was often said, and innocently believed, that politics was among the lowest and the least of his concerns. He was too civilized for politics and would have infinitely preferred to immerse himself in science, philosophy, music, literature, or even in lawn tennis and golf. What had public life got to offer him? He was indifferent both to its prizes and its causes. Though plausible, this theory was profoundly misconceived. There could be no greater fallacy than to imagine that because he did not believe in causes Arthur Balfour was not deeply involved in politics or that he was devoid of political ambition. Politics was the greatest game of his life and the one he played the best. And it was not as an amateur or dilettante that he played it but as a professional, perfectly equipped and all out to win. And to win for his side, for in spite of his apparent detachment there never was a better party man. To split his party was, in his eyes, the unforgivable sin. To remain its leader was his firm resolve.

Music, philosophy, science, lawn tennis might call and call in vain. The call and pull of power were more imperious. In Winston Churchill's words: "The Prime Minister remained immovable, inexhaustible, imperturbable; and he remained Prime Minister." [2]

Exasperated by this attitude Winston used every weapon in his armory to perturb, exhaust and remove the Government. He was convinced that a dangerous and collusive game was being played by Mr. Balfour and Mr. Chamberlain at the expense of the nation. He was determined to expose and defeat them and to this end he devoted, with ruthless pertinacity, all his dialectical and tactical resources. He became the living embodiment of Lord Randolph's famous maxim that "the business of an Opposition is to oppose."

By his old political associates he was regarded as an upstart renegade, "no gentleman," a traitor to his party and his class. They refused to believe in the sincerity of his convictions and attributed his action to impatient ambition and the restless pursuit of his own "main chance." Mr. MacCallum Scott, a contemporary Liberal Member of Parliament, has written that "the followers of Chamberlain repaid his hostility with a passionate personal hatred over which they vainly endeavoured to throw a mask of contempt. There was no better hated man in the House of Commons—not even Mr. Chamberlain himself." [3]

In this tempestuous session hatreds, passions and enthusiasms were in spate. Liberals were stirred to indignation by the importation of thousands of indentured Chinese laborers to work in the South African gold mines, and to live confined in compounds in conditions akin to slavery. When a Conservative member, Major Seely, a close friend and associate of Winston Churchill, spoke in support of Sir Henry Campbell-Bannerman's motion of censure on this issue he was greeted with such uproar from the Conservative benches that he was unable to make himself heard. Winston Churchill rose to defend his friend and appealed to the Speaker on a point of order: "I am quite unable to hear what my honourable friend is saying owing to the vulgar clamour maintained by the Conservative Party." [4] The Speaker's appeal for order was in vain and when the Prime Minister rose to reply his speech was also drowned in clamor, this time from the Irish benches.

A week later it was Winston Churchill's turn. The Unionist rank and file, led by the Prime Minister, refused to hear him. "The time has come," he said, "when the country ought to be relieved from this shifty policy of equivocal evasion; they have a right to know what public men think on public questions and what political chiefs believe on great political principles." [5]

The scene that followed is described by Massingham. "With the utmost abruptness the Prime Minister without listening even for his opening sentences left the House followed by the other Ministers. No sooner had the Prime Minister left the House than seventy or eighty Tory Members stole out of it one by one leaving Mr. Churchill with an audience of less than a dozen of his own side, most of whom were Free Traders. This leaving of the House was not a mere impulse; it was a concerted business led by Sir Frederick Banbury and other choice spirits. I have seen many gross and ignorant things done by parties in the heat of passion but I have never seen so common a display as this. For the moment the slipping away of the Tories obviously disconcerted the young speaker but he fought hard against embarrassment and as he developed his argument spoke not only with power and persuasiveness but with a certain moral elevation that comes to a man when he feels he is fighting a great cause alone. When his speech, listened to by an audience composed almost entirely of Liberals, came to an end Mr. Herbert Gladstone crossed over to him and offered him public reparation for the slight that had been done him. The Liberals cheered very loudly." [6]

Whatever effect these tactics may have had on the House of Commons they did not impress the country. Major Seely resigned his seat and appealed to his constituents for a vote of confidence on the Chinese labor issue. The Conservatives were unable to find a candidate to contest the by-election and he was returned unopposed. Winston Churchill did not resign his seat. He challenged his constituency association to demand his resignation and assured them that in this event it would be forthcoming and that he would submit himself immediately for re-election. His challenge was not accepted.

And now an event occurred which was to hasten his final break with the Conservative Party. A deputation of Liberals from North-West Manchester invited him to become Free Trade candidate at the next election and pledged him the full support of the Liberal organization. He realized that it would be a bold and hazardous adventure, for the seat was held by a large majority by a popular and influential local employer, Sir

William Houldsworth. But the prospect of fighting in this great Free Trade citadel with its historic traditions fired his imagination—and he had never been afraid of risks. He resolved to accept the invitation. Before being adopted he addressed an all-party meeting of a branch of the Free Trade League which he had founded at Oldham. He said that for some time past he had determined that he would not attempt to contest Oldham at the next General Election and he added: "Until this great Protectionist agitation is laid to rest again, I trust for ever, I have no politics but Free Trade. . . . I will work with and for any Free Trader whatever his politics." [7]

At the end of April he was unanimously adopted by the Liberal Association as Free Trade candidate for North-West Manchester, and on May 13th he addressed a great meeting in the Free Trade Hall in the company of John Morley, who described him prophetically as "a man who will carry the lamp when other hands have let it fall." It was in his speech at this meeting that he used the famous passage of invective: "Corruption at home, aggression abroad, sentiment by the bucketful, patriotism by the Imperial pint, the open hand at the Public Exchequer and the open door at the public-house, dear food for the million, cheap labour for the millionaire. That is the policy of Birmingham and we are going to erect against the policy of Birmingham the policy of Manchester." [8]

When the House met again after the Easter recess a curious incident took place, unique in Winston Churchill's oratorical career. He broke down in the middle of a speech, groped and struggled in vain amid sympathetic cheers to recover the thread of his argument, failed to do so, and was finally compelled to sit down. He was making a fierce attack on the Government for its failure to deal with the legal position of the trade-unions and championing the claims of the working classes to a larger and fairer share in the government of the country. "When they considered," he said, "how vast the labour interest was, how vital, how human, when they considered the gigantic powers which by the consent of both Parties had been given to the working classes, when, on the other hand, they considered the influence in this House of company directors, the learned professions, the service Members, the railway, landed and liquor interests, it would surely be admitted that the influence of labour on the course of legislation was even ludicrously small." [9]

The *Daily Mail* reported the incident in full and vivid detail under the banner headlines:

MR. CHURCHILL BREAKS DOWN
DRAMATIC SCENE IN THE HOUSE OF COMMONS

It described the speech as "Radicalism of the reddest type." It recorded that "he had been speaking with all his wonted force and vigour, brightness of idea and freshness of expression and that courage which leads him to make side thrusts at the Government and Mr. Chamberlain. . . . Mr. Chamberlain was sitting watching him through half-closed eyelids, measuring as it seemed the force of this persistent, able young man. . . . 'It lies with the Government to satisfy the working-classes that there is no justification' . . . he said with accustomed fire and appropriate action and was on the point of clinching his argument with right fist smacking left palm. But the words would not come. He hesitated and began again. 'It lies with them . . .' 'What?' he ejaculated as someone suggested a word which was not the right word. He lifted a slip of paper from the bench but the cue was not there. He searched the deep pockets of his coat and found no help. Major Seely picked torn scraps from the floor and the words were not there. Plucky and determined Mr. Churchill went at the fence again. 'It lies with them to satisfy the electors . . .' was all he could say. . . . Liberals, Nationalists and Unionist Free Traders cheered in warm sympathy as he gave up. He sat down murmuring thanks to the House for its kindness. The Conservative Party looked silently on wondering what had overtaken him so suddenly and dramatically." [10]

Wild rumors and speculations about his state of health ran riot. It was recalled that a short time before his death Lord Randolph had broken down in the same way. Was Winston's bright flame like his father's a "brief candle" soon to flicker into darkness? Was he burning himself out?

The explanation was of course much simpler. He had always memorized his speeches and had never accustomed himself to "thinking on his feet." Thought is an organic and continuous process which, for better for worse, sustains itself, but memory is mechanical and its breakdown, like that of a machine, is absolute. When in later years he described this incident to me he said: "I suddenly had a complete blackout. It was not that I was unable to find the right words to express what I meant— I have usually been able to lay my hands on words in an extremity—but I didn't know *what* I meant—I didn't know what I was talking about."

It was a disagreeable experience but he was in no way unnerved by it. Nor did it lead him to change his methods. He continued to learn his speeches by heart but he learned them (if possible) even more thoroughly than before and armed himself with fuller notes. I have never seen him make a platform speech without a verbatim script before him, though he rarely glanced at it.

On May 16th he made his last speech from the Conservative side of the House on the second reading of the Finance Bill. "Extravagant finance," he said, "would in the long run drag this powerful Government to the ground. Extravagant finance was written on the head of their indictment, and it would be written on the head of their tombstone." There followed an interesting passage revealing the change in his attitude toward the Boer War. He did not deny that a great portion of the expenditure was due to the South African War. He said nothing about that war; he was "tarred with responsibility, in his own small way, as much as anyone on this side of the House for acquiescing in that immense public disaster." He then attacked Chamberlain and the "New Imperialism." "There were two kinds of Imperialism. . . . They ought to distinguish between the amateur Imperialists who gave their lives on the field, and the professional Imperialists who got their living by practising it in politics; they ought to distinguish between the sentiment which united us to our Colonies, and that bastard Imperialism which was ground out by a party machine and was convenient for placing a particular set of gentlemen in power." [11] The *Manchester Guardian* reported that "his neighbours melted away till scarcely a Protectionist was left in the House."

On May 31st Winston Churchill crossed the floor. The scene was undramatic. The few who witnessed it were not sure at the time whether it had any symbolic significance. It was thus described by the *Manchester Guardian:* "Most of the benches were empty from end to end and on this scene of desolation rested the twilight of a rainy afternoon. Presently Mr. Churchill put in an appearance. Standing at the bar he glanced at his accustomed place below the Ministerial gangway, made a rapid survey of the corresponding bench on the Opposition side, marched a few paces up the floor, bowed to the Chair, swerved suddenly to the right and took his place among the Liberals. This might have been a casual choice, but as if to emphasize its significance Mr. Churchill in the course of the evening returned again and yet again to the same place. At length some of his new neighbours began to suspect that an event of some importance had occurred. . . ."

He had secured the coveted corner seat below the Opposition gangway from which in days gone by his father poured the fire of his attacks on Mr. Gladstone and Sir Stafford Northcote. Here, among the great shades of the Fourth Party and with a living host of friends and allies at his side, he was for the first time in his four years of Parliamentary life in tune with his surroundings.

At a great meeting held a week later at the Alexandra Palace to honor the centenary of Cobden's birth he spoke in the company of Mr. Lloyd George and Sir Henry Campbell-Bannerman. "They tell me," Mr. Churchill said, "that I ought to join the Liberal Party. Well—it's not a bad idea." [12]

It turned out to be an excellent idea—both for Winston Churchill and for the Liberal Party.

Chapter Twelve

———————◄ ►————————

BALFOUR RESIGNS

THE CONSERVATIVE GOVERNMENT was on its death-bed, but like King Charles II it was taking "an unconscionable time a'dying." Its end was awaited with equal impatience by the Opposition and by Mr. Chamberlain. Unlike Arthur Balfour he was acutely aware of the temperature of public opinion. He was eager to strike while the iron was hot, and he felt it cooling.

Winston Churchill told the House of Commons that whereas both he and Mr. Chamberlain wanted to see the Government turned out and go to the country, the difference between them was that he was able to express his opinion, and Mr. Chamberlain was for the present dissembling his.[1] His words were too true to be tolerable and during the rest of his speech he was denied a hearing.

Sir William Harcourt died in October and John Morley told my father that at his memorial service Joe had confided to him that he intended to "hurry things."

But Arthur Balfour refused to be hurried. Taunts, jeers, denuncia-tion, the advice of well-wishers, the steady loss of by-elections * left him unmoved. He continued with tireless ingenuity and patience to up-hold a false façade of party unity and to devise, in Winston Churchill's words, "a succession of formulas designed to enable people who dif-fered profoundly, to persuade themselves they were in agreement." [2]

The political atmosphere was reflected in social relations. There was as yet no ostracism but amenities between the wives of leaders of the rival factions were becoming crisp and cool. One night the Duchess of

* The Government majority had been reduced by by-elections from 134 to 68.

91

Devonshire, who was dining with us, said, across my stepmother, to Lady Londonderry: "There is only one thing for this Government to do—suspend the Septennial Act and go on till your majority dies a natural death from by-elections." Lady Londonderry received this advice with an uncomfortable and mirthless laugh.

All through the autumn the platform campaign raged in a steady crescendo, and once more I followed the drum with my father from one great meeting to another. For us the iron was getting hotter.

In those days of the small electorate speeches were not only listened to but reported verbatim and avidly read. When I think of the patience and apparent pleasure with which vast audiences would follow close-knit argument buttressed by hard, dry facts—import and export statistics and Board of Trade returns—I realize how impossible it would be to get the same attention for the same matter nowadays. I remember hearing that the Newcastle Hippodrome, holding some three thousand people, was sold out for several nights in succession while the Free Trade v. protection case was debated by a distinguished but rather dry and academic Liberal, J. M. Robertson, and a Conservative protagonist of tariffs. No hippodrome in this country could be half filled, even for one night, by such a performance today.

Winston Churchill was now delivering his speeches from Liberal platforms and our welkin rang with his praises. He spoke the Liberal language both in idiom and in accent as though it were his native tongue (in fact he spoke it better than most natives!). "Liberalism," he said at Newcastle, "will never die until it has ceased to hope, will never perish until it has ceased to dare." [3] He ignored the small fry of the Conservative Party and struck hard at the two giants. At the National Liberal Club he said of Chamberlain: "The country thought Mr. Chamberlain . . . was a prophet with a message. They have found him a politician groping for a platform."

His attack on Arthur Balfour at Manchester was a thrust which pierced deeper. "I am not surprised that Mr. Balfour has declared that he does not intend to dissolve Parliament. Abdications have often taken place in the history of the world, but if you look back on the course of history you will see that they have usually been made by masculine not by feminine monarchs. Kings have abdicated but never Queens, and it is one of the attractive qualities of Mr. Balfour that his nature displays a certain femininity. No doubt it is that element in his nature which prompts him to cling to office on any terms as long as it is possible to do so." [4]

Subtlety was not one of Winston Churchill's characteristics. It was certainly never apparent in his approach to his fellow men. But in this diagnosis there was a penetrating subtlety which made it deadly. It revealed to many a quality in Arthur Balfour of which they had been subconsciously aware but to which they had never given a name.

Toward the end of February Winston Churchill made a speech in the House of Commons which (in the opinion of the *Manchester Guardian*) "marked yet another milestone in his progressive path." He spoke in support of a motion of Mr. Redmond's on the government of Ireland. "We might," he said, "have a poor thing of a Government, but at least it was our own, and slowly the electoral machinery could change it; but in Ireland there was no change possible, it was an arbitrary authority under the specious guise of representation." [5]

He had become a Home Ruler. He was assimilating one by one the various articles of the Liberal creed. Irish self-government might well have stuck in his throat, for to Lord Randolph Home Rule had been anathema. But he swallowed it, apparently without an effort. His filial piety had ceased to be his sole directing light. He was now charting his own course. This was an important new departure.

He made two other noteworthy speeches in this session. One of them earned him general praise and approval and even elicited from Mr. Chamberlain the rare tribute "that it was in the best Parliamentary tradition." The other aroused bitter resentment and indignation among his opponents and was critically received by at least a section of his friends. The first was delivered on March 8th when he brought in a Private Member's motion: "That in the opinion of this House the permanent unity of the British Empire will not be secured through a system of preferential duties based upon the protective taxation of food." The Prime Minister, Mr. Chamberlain and my father all took part in the debate.

When Winston Churchill rose he was greeted by an outburst of cheering and countercheering "such as can rarely have been heard in honour or in depreciation of so young a politician." [6] "The main argument against these taxes," he said, "is based on a great principle, which is that this country should be free to purchase its supplies of food wherever it chooses and whenever it chooses in the open markets of the world." He spoke of "a vast thriving population living on a soil which could not support in decent comfort a twentieth of their number."

He then passed from the economic to the international aspect of his theme, from the bread of the people to the peace of the world. "The dangers which threaten the tranquillity of the modern world come not from those Powers that have become interdependent upon others, interwoven by commerce with other States; they come from those Powers which are more or less detached, which stand more or less aloof from the general intercourse of mankind and are comparatively independent and self-supporting. Quite apart from the economic argument . . . we do not want to see the British Empire degenerate into a sullen confederacy, walled off, like a mediaeval town, from the surrounding country . . . and containing within the circle of its battlements all that is necessary for war. We want this country and the States associated with it to take their part freely and fairly in the general intercourse of commercial nations." [7]

My father and stepmother had dined at the House of Commons before the debate with a small party, which included among others John Morley, Herbert Gladstone, Harry Cust and Winston Churchill. My stepmother wrote in her diary: "I sat next to Winston. Dinner was slow, hot and noisy and I begged him not to *utter* for fear of tiring himself. . . . I went up to Mrs. Speaker's Gallery at ten to nine as I did not want to perform acrobatic feats to get to my front seat over rows of ladies' backs. . . . Winston got up at nine sharp. He made an admirable speech, moderate, well-reasoned, quick, short and telling—about twenty-five minutes. . . . Joe spoke later—long, dull, pointless I thought—all his old fire gone. He lost his audience who were so anxious to hear Lord Hugh, Henry and Arthur that they shouted 'Time! Time!' I never thought I should live to hear this. Joe's cause is lost."

My stepmother's vivid descriptions of events are often liable to be colored by her own strong personal sympathies and antipathies for the dramatis personae involved in them. But though she recognized Winston's great qualities he was never one of her heroes. He neither dazzled nor disarmed her. There was always something a little prickly in their relationship, perhaps because neither of them liked listening. Her praise on this occasion may therefore be taken as dispassionate.

Although the Government is said to have feared defeat, it survived with a modest majority of forty-four. But three weeks later on a Private Member's motion of censure on "the Prime Minister's policy of Fiscal Retaliation," it was defeated *nemine contradicente*. The Prime Minister was absent from the debate and from the House.

Winston Churchill rose immediately to ask "whether there is anything in the health of the Prime Minister to cause anxiety to his friends as the right honourable Gentleman has not been in his place to defend the policy especially associated with his name. . . . After the passing of such a Resolution, framed deliberately as a vote of censure and supported by the official Opposition, does the Prime Minister consider it consonant with his public duty and personal honour to continue in his present position? The situation will raise a storm of execration and contempt in the country. . . . To keep in office for a few more weeks and months there is no principle which the Government is not prepared to abandon, no friend or colleague that they are not prepared to betray, and no quantity of dirt and filth that they are not prepared to eat." [8]

This was strong meat but not one whit too strong for the palate of the Opposition, who were outraged by the absence of the Prime Minister—and indeed of the whole Front Bench.

When on the following day Arthur Balfour reappeared in the House Winston Churchill repeated his question. Did the Prime Minister propose to expunge the resolution? And if it stood did he consider retention of office consonant with his public duty or personal honor? The Prime Minister's reply revealed a fantastic situation. He regretted that Mr. Churchill had not given him notice of the question as he would then have made himself acquainted with what appeared to have happened the night before. "At present," he said, "my sole knowledge is derived from the Question the honourable member has put to me."

The Prime Minister and Leader of the House of Commons owed his "sole knowledge" of his Government's defeat to a back-bencher's question! When pressed again by Winston Churchill, Sir Henry Campbell-Bannerman and others he said: "I have now read the Resolution. . . . I propose to take no action in the matter. I do not see that any action is required." [9]

In July the Government was again defeated, this time on a motion of Mr. Redmond's. I have a vivid recollection of the sensation caused by this event. I had now crossed the Rubicon called "coming out" and after a dinner party at home we all went on to a ball at Lord Revelstoke's. My father looked in after midnight on his way home from the House of Commons and brought with him the news of the Government's defeat. The ballroom buzzed with excitement, speculation, apprehension, wild surmise. We might have been dancing at Brussels on the eve of Waterloo. And whose Waterloo was it going to be? Would the Government go out? The Liberal Party was underrepresented at balls, so there were more fears than hopes, but the general consensus was that after this second defeat it must.

As we drove home my father expressed his firm conviction that Arthur Balfour would neither dissolve nor resign. And he proved to be right.

But the Government was badly shaken, inside as well as out. Arthur Balfour was to have lunched with us next day but sent a telegram to say that owing to the "political crisis" it was impossible for him to do so.

Within four days the matter was raised in the House of Commons. The Prime Minister, Sir Henry Campbell-Bannerman, my father, Sir Edward Grey, John Redmond and Winston Churchill all spoke—Sir Edward Grey making (I thought) the finest and the most impressive speech in the debate. But its most sensational feature was the ruthless attack on Arthur Balfour delivered by Winston Churchill.

He said they had been told *ad nauseam* of the sacrifices which the Prime Minister had made. . . . The House ought not to underrate or deny those sacrifices. Some of them must have been very galling to a proud man. There were first sacrifices of leisure and then sacrifices of dignity. . . . Then there was the sacrifice of reputation. . . . For some years the right honorable Gentleman led the House by the respect and affection with which he was regarded in all quarters. In the future he would not continue to lead the House by the respect and affection of the Opposition at least.

"It had been written that the Right Hon. Gentleman stood between pride and duty. Pride said 'go'; but duty said 'stay'. The Right Hon. Gentleman always observed the maxim of a modern writer that whenever an Englishman took or kept anything he wanted he did it from a high sense of duty. He was sure that public opinion outside the House would approve and acclaim any action which might be taken by the constitutional Opposition to terminate a situation which was as dangerous as it was disgraceful and to dismiss from unlawful power a Minister who had flouted the traditions of Parliament and dishonoured the service of the Crown." [10]

Arthur Balfour replied to this assault on the same day in a telling and (what many felt to be) a merited rebuke. "As for the junior Member for Oldham, his speech was certainly not remarkable for good taste, and as I have always taken an interest in that Hon. Gentleman's career, I should certainly, if I thought it the least good, offer him some advice on that particular subject. But I take it that good taste is not a thing that can be acquired by industry. . . . I think I may give him some advice which may be useful to him in the course of what I hope will be a long and distinguished career. It is not, on the whole, desirable to come down to this House with invective which is both prepared and violent. The House will tolerate, and very rightly tolerate, almost anything within the rule of order which evidently springs from a genuine indignation aroused by the collision of debate; but to come down with these prepared phrases is not usually successful. . . . If there is preparation there should be more finish and if there is so much violence there should certainly be more obvious veracity of feeling." [11]

It was characteristic of Winston Churchill that, so far from resenting this retort, he thoroughly appreciated the effectiveness of the points which had been scored against him. Lady Frances Balfour, who happened to meet him as he left the House, told us that he had said to her that Arthur's speech had been quite excellent. "He caught me in my weak place—the preparation." Though no one disliked being disagreed with more, either in counsel or in private life, I have often noticed that in the cut and thrust of Parliamentary debate, however fierce the struggle, the artist in him was always able to stand back, to appraise and even to enjoy the fine stroke and the fine phrase of an opponent. Blood might flow but there was no poison in the wounds that he inflicted or received.

Early in August the House rose. The autumn was spent in speculation and suspense. One question obsessed all minds in both parties— the date of the coming General Election. Of its imminence there could be no doubt in any quarter.

In mid-November Winston Churchill's platform campaign was suddenly interrupted by a breakdown in his health. He canceled all his engagements and went abroad. Mr. Lloyd George was also obliged to go abroad to recover from trouble in his throat. These casualties on the eve of battle caused us some anxiety.

On November 14th my father and stepmother spent the night at Windsor Castle, where the King and Queen were entertaining the King of Greece. There was a large party which included among others Sir Henry Campbell-Bannerman, Gerald Balfour, Edward Grey, Alfred Lyttelton, Haldane and Joe Chamberlain. While they were all assembled before dinner to await the King and Queen, Chamberlain said to my father that though we might get in at the election we should not last long and that then his policy would triumph. He added that in the event of our immediate victory we should of course be dependent on the Irish vote. This forecast amazed my father and he was in the act of placing the first bet of his life when the transaction was interrupted by the entry of the King and Queen.

Meanwhile dissension broke out among the Liberal leaders on the issue of Home Rule. After consultation with his colleagues, Sir Henry Campbell-Bannerman made a wise and moderate speech at Stirling in which he made it clear that only "instalments" of self-government for Ireland could be expected in the next Parliament—though these must be consistent with and lead up to the "larger policy." Lord Rosebery spoke two days later at Bodmin accusing him of having "hoisted once more in its most pronounced form the flag of Irish Home Rule" and declaring "emphatically, explicitly and once for all that I cannot serve under that banner." [12]

This speech caused grave embarrassment to his colleagues. It aroused anger and dismay among the Liberal rank and file who were at last united to a man and advancing to a victory which now lay within sight and reach. The Conservative Party hailed it as a godsend.

My father did not take it tragically, but he said: "If Arthur Balfour is a wise man he will resign today. Our little squall is the best we can do for him, and I doubt if any other stroke of luck will come his way between now and January."

The Prime Minister must have shared this view. On December 4th he tendered his resignation to the King.

———◄ ►———

Chapter Thirteen

LIBERAL FLOOD TIDE

ARTHUR BALFOUR'S sudden and dramatic resignation was hailed as a master stroke, nicely calculated to "dish the Whigs" at a moment when their leaders were at loggerheads and confusion prevailed in their ranks. Moreover the Home Rule bogy, which had once more reared its ugly but welcome head, would prove a useful distraction from food taxes and Chinese labor in the coming election. Campbell-Bannerman would be hard put to it to form a Government. Would he even attempt it?

These hopes were soon to be confounded. The King, who had established a friendly and even cozy relationship with Sir Henry in the autumn at Marienbad, at once sent for him. He accepted office without a moment's hesitation (on December 5th), and by midnight on the 7th all the Cabinet offices were filled and a strong and able Government representing all sections of the Liberal Party was formed. Lord Rosebery was the only notable absentee.

The key posts were held by Sir Edward Grey at the Foreign Office, my father at the Exchequer, Mr. Lloyd George at the Board of Trade and Mr. Haldane at the War Office. John Morley went to the India Office and John Burns to the Local Government Board. At my father's request Winston Churchill was offered the post of Financial Secretary to the Treasury—the springboard to the Cabinet. He asked instead to be Under-Secretary for the Colonies. He told me that Campbell-Bannerman, astonished at his choice, exclaimed: "Well, you're the first man who has asked me for something *worse* than I offered him!" I asked him whether it was the prospect of answering for his department in the

House of Commons which had influenced his choice. (His chief, Lord Elgin, the Colonial Secretary, was in the House of Lords.) He said: "A little, perhaps, but not entirely. I was interested in South Africa and I knew something about it. But if I had known that your father had specially asked for me to work with him at the Treasury I should have been so flattered that I should have gone there."

On January 8th Parliament was dissolved and we all plunged into the election.

January, 1906, was a great month in the life of Winston Churchill. On January 1st he issued his election address; on the 2nd his masterly biography of Lord Randolph Churchill was published; on the 3rd he went to Manchester to contest his seat. The 13th was polling day in Manchester and on the 15th the results were announced in the press.

In his election address he pledged himself to (1) Free Trade; (2) religious equality and the public control of Education; (3) reduction of expenditure on armaments; (4) taxation of ground values; (5) amendment of licensing and Trade Union law; (6) reform of the administration of Ireland.

"I am glad," he wrote, "that the Parliament elected in 1900 is about to be dissolved. Few Parliaments in our modern experience have been less worthy of respect. A majority elected under the spell of patriotic emotion, upon a national issue, in the stress of an anxious war, has been perverted to crude and paltry purposes of party. . . . Seven more years of dodge and dole and dawdle. Seven years of tinker, tax and trifle. Seven years of shuffle, shout and sham. Do not be taken in again."

This was the challenge thrown down by Winston Churchill to the Conservatives of North-West Manchester. The former member, Sir William Houldsworth, was no longer there to take it up. He had retired and been replaced by a young solicitor, Joynson-Hicks by name, later to be better known as "Jix."

Like every contest in which Winston Churchill played a part, it was dominated by his personality. The crowds struggling to get into his meetings were so great that he was often obliged to address dense throngs outside the hall and hundreds jammed upon the stairs inside before he could reach the platform. On one occasion the sheer weight of the audience in an overfilled hall threatened to bring down the floor. There were cries of "the floor is giving way," and a panic was feared. "Let us do justice," said Winston coolly, "even though the floor fall" and proceeded with his speech—while the floor, mercifully, held.[1]

Mr. Balfour, who was defending his seat in a neighboring division of

Manchester, was acted off the stage. The press, the public and the limelight were all focused on the fight in the North-West. Winston had "stolen the picture" from the ex-Prime Minister.

Mr. Charles E. Hands, who was covering the election for the *Daily Mail,* gave a vivid impression of his effect on the electors under the headlines:

"WINSTON"

MORE INTERESTING THAN FREE TRADE

MANCHESTER FASCINATED

HIS JU-JITSU

HE SETS A FASHION IN HATS

"There is no question about it; the public interest of Manchester in the General Election is centred and focussed on the personality of Mr. Winston Churchill. You can hardly see the rest of the political landscape for this dominant figure. . . . You hear more talk in Manchester of 'Winston' than of Free Trade. . . . He appeals to their sporting sense. 'It isn't so much his politics, it's his Ju-Jitsu that I like', said a citizen today. . . . They discuss his various attributes; his mammoth posters with 'Winston Churchill' in letters five feet high, his alliterative habit . . . his book, his clothes. He is wearing a new old-fashioned hat, a flat-topped sort of felt hat and already the hatters are having inquiries for articles of that pattern." [2]

He had cast his spell on Manchester and "Jix," though an efficient and experienced solicitor, well versed in all his legal duties, had never yet been called upon to exorcise a spell. How should he set about it? He hit upon the bright idea of exploiting his opponent's (fairly recent) Conservative past and thus exposing him as a turncoat and a deserter.

We read in his biography that "he had been at some pains to enlist the services of the ghost of his rival by compiling a pamphlet consisting of statements made by that Mr. Churchill who was once Conservative member for Oldham. The pamphlet was freely circulated, and the electors were eager to know what answer any man could return to such a damning indictment."

Winston Churchill appeared at a meeting with the pamphlet in his hand. To the cries of "Answer it!" "What about it?" he replied that he denied nothing. He had said all these things. He had said them because he belonged to a stupid party which he had left because he did not want to go on saying stupid things. Amid loud cheers he tore the pamphlet into shreds and "flung it from him with a dramatic gesture, expressing . . .

contempt for the cause he had once espoused." [3] After this incident his past was effectually laid.

One feature of the General Election of 1906 was the launching of a militant campaign by the suffragettes. They went into action in North-West Manchester under two of their most redoubtable leaders, Miss Sylvia Pankhurst and Mrs. Drummond, and they concentrated their fire on Winston Churchill. Night after night they tried to wreck his meetings by their demonstations; banners were unfurled, his speeches were continuously interrupted, ejections took place, confusion and disorder prevailed. On one of these occasions Winston Churchill invited a female interrupter to ascend the platform and put her question before he made his speech. This she did and asked: "Will the Liberal Government give women votes?" Winston replied that having regard to the treatment he had received and the destruction of the great meetings he had witnessed by advocates of woman suffrage nothing would induce him to vote for giving women the franchise, though the only occasion on which he had voted on the question he had supported the proposal. Cheers followed and the questioner was removed from the hall. Mr. Churchill then told his audience that "he was not so hostile to the proposal as he thought it right to say just now but that he was not going to be henpecked." [4]

The phrase caught on. It became a popular catchword throughout Manchester and was used as a gag in the pantomimes. As he passed through the streets people turned around with a laugh and called out to him: "Don't be henpecked, Winston!" This is the way to win elections. But quite apart from personal touches like henpecking and hats he fought a serious and brilliant campaign on the main issue of Free Trade and on this issue the past traditions of Manchester were linked with its present interests. Prosperity and principle went hand in hand.

January 13th was polling day. Charles Hands wrote in the *Daily Mail:* "To the general relief Manchester's frenzied fortnight has come to an end. The excitement has been too great, its expression too exuberant. Serious citizens have viewed with apprehension the unprecedented scenes of electioneering excitement and have been hoping for the end to come quickly before enthusiasm degenerated into frenzy and frenzy expressed itself in tumult and disorder. . . . Never before was Mr. Balfour the object of blatant rowdyism in Manchester. Mr. Joynson-Hicks, who is so pluckily fighting Mr. Churchill, has had his carriage stoned. 'Winston' has had his meetings systematically interrupted. In no remembered contest have meetings been so crowded on both sides or so charged with electrical excitement." [5]

Winston Churchill has recorded the end and the result of this tumultuous fortnight. "My individual fight was part of a vehement national revolt against the Conservative Government. Nothing like it had been seen in the memory of mortal man, and nothing like it was seen till 1931. . . . No one, however, could possibly suppose that the final result would be so sweeping. Even the most ardent Liberal would never have believed it. When we rose up in the morning all the nine seats were held by Conservatives. When we went to bed that night all had been won by Liberals.* Arthur Balfour was out, and with him all his friends. . . .

"Some of us belonging to the victorious party had a supper at the Midland Hotel. . . . There was a gallant little man, a Mr. Charles Hands, on the staff of the *Daily Mail,* who had been a correspondent in the South African War and whom I had known there. . . . He wrote extremely well, but of course on the Conservative side. I invited him to supper. 'What do you think of that?'—'It is', he said, 'a grand slam in doubled no trumps'. It certainly seemed very like it." [6]

Lord James of Hereford had written to Winston Churchill from Sandringham: "You must have thought 'I walked on clouds, I stood on thrones'." Winston was not alone in feeling the sky under his feet. For the country followed suit. As the results flowed in day after day, even the victorious Liberals were dazed by their triumph. They had prayed for rain and been given the deluge. The Government's supporters numbered 513, of whom 377 were Liberals. Of the Conservatives who had gone into battle 400 strong, only a shattered remnant of 157 came back to the House of Commons. An earthquake had occurred which changed the shape of British politics.

It has been truly written by Professor Alfred North Whitehead that "the great convulsions happen when the economic urges on the masses have dovetailed with some simplified ideal end. Intellect and instinct then combine and some ancient social order passes away." This is an exact description of what happened to England in 1906. It is a year which has been justly compared by historians to the year 1833, when the only comparable convulsion in our history followed the passage of the great Reform Bill.

* There were in fact seven Liberal and two Labour victories.

————— ◄┤ ├► —————

Chapter Fourteen

OUR FRIENDSHIP

I HAVE now reached the moment in time which I described in the opening chapter of this book, of my first meeting with Winston Churchill. In the intervening chapters I have tried to give an outline of the experience which had shaped him and made him what he was, of how the young man I met in 1906 had come about.

From this time onward he became my friend. I knew him—both in his public and in his private life—and with him, more than with most men, the line between the two was often blurred. For this reason there were times when I saw more of him and knew more of the inner workings of his mind than at others. When we were ardently aligned on public issues he liked to share his thoughts with me. He poured them out in a molten torrent and we burned and glowed together in passionate agreement. But when we differed our disagreement was all the more distasteful to him because I was his friend. He reproached me with a glowering look: "You are not *on my side*"—and took scant interest in the reasons which had brought me to this pass. Disagreement was, in any form, obnoxious to him, but when combined with personal affection it became a kind of treachery. He demanded partisanship from a friend, or (at the worst) acquiescence.

There were therefore gaps and interludes in our association when the wires fused between us. But estrangement was impossible. And when the wheel of circumstance spun around and we were once more in the fighting line together the very fact that we had differed brought an added edge and zest to our reunion and perhaps to him the certainty that my convictions as well as my emotions were now engaged once more upon his "side."

But in June, 1906, and for many years to come there was only one side for him, for me and for a great host of others throughout the country. We were riding on the crest of the tidal wave which had swept us to victory and we were almost stunned by our triumph and by our opportunity. Yet we had no misgivings. Power had come to us at last and we had no doubt what we should do with it. We knew that we had great needs to meet and great hopes to fulfill. But the wind and the tide and the will of the age were with us. We felt that we were in tune with the hour.

It was a time of ferment when a spirit was moving on the face of the waters and they were stirred. The spirit of change was abroad and it had brought to power men who were not afraid of change. They did not wait for change to take them by the throat; they took it by the hand.

Winston Churchill was one of them. Until this moment he had won his way to fame by words, and some alleged that they were the only weapons in his armory. But now at thirty-two as a member of a Government supported by a vast majority he was for the first time in his life invested with authority and power to act. He did not hesitate to prove that he could use them.

Yet though he never shrank from radical solutions or new departures I think that there were some features of the world of 1906 he would not willingly have changed. It was a stable and a civilized world in which the greatness and authority of Britain and her Empire seemed unassailable and invulnerably secure. In spite of our reverses in the Boer War it was assumed unquestioningly that we should always emerge "victorious, happy and glorious" from any conflict. There were no doubts about the permanence of our "dominion over palm and pine," or of our title to it. Powerful, prosperous, peace-loving, with the seas all around us and the British Navy on the seas, the social, economic, international order seemed to our unseeing eyes as firmly fixed on earth as the signs of the zodiac in the sky.

It was a time of booming trade, of great prosperity and wealth in which the pageant of London society took place year after year in a setting of traditional dignity and beauty. The great houses—Devonshire, Dorchester, Grosvenor, Stafford and Lansdowne House—had not yet been converted into museums, hotels and flats, and there we danced through the long summer nights till dawn. The great country houses still flourished in their glory and on their lawns in the green shade of trees the art of human intercourse was exquisitely practiced by men and women not yet enslaved by household cares and chores who still had time to read, to talk, to listen and to think.

The atmosphere of those days is well given in Maurice Baring's *Puppet Show of Memory:* "I went to the Derby that year and backed Persimmon; to the first performance of Mrs. Campbell's Magda the same night; I saw Duse at Drury Lane and Sarah Bernhardt at Daly's; I went to Ascot; I went to balls; I stayed at Panshanger; and at Wrest, at the end of the summer, where a constellation of beauty moved in muslin and straw hats and yellow roses on the lawns of gardens designed by Lenôtre, delicious with ripe peaches on old brick walls, with the smell of verbena, and sweet geranium; and stately with large avenues, artificial lakes and white temples; and we bicycled" (bicycling was at that time still considered a thrilling adventure), "we bicycled in the warm night past ghostly cornfields by the light of a large full moon."

That is a true picture of the ease and grace of the world in which Winston Churchill had been born and nurtured, the world which belonged to the few. But there was another world with which his party was concerned, the world of the many. For though in those days it was easy to be rich it was also easy to be very poor. Dire, grinding poverty, that cruel ugly ghost, still stalked the streets in that heyday of our prosperity. I can remember as a child being haunted by the beggars in the streets, the crossing sweepers who held out their tattered caps for pennies, the children in rags, fluttering like feathers when the wind blew through them, the down-and-outs sleeping out under the arches or on the benches in the parks with an old newspaper for cover. Those were the days when an agricultural laborer earned and brought up a family on thirteen shillings a week, when a worker in the towns earned eighteen shillings to a pound, to say nothing of the submerged mass of sweated workers down below. There was no insurance against sickness or unemployment, no Old Age pensions with their promise of safety at the end of life, no net stretched beneath the feet of those who fell except that of sporadic charity and the workhouse.

In 1901 B. Seebohm Rowntree had published his memorable work *Poverty, a Study of Town Life,* a house-to-house investigation of living standards and conditions in York. It was followed a year later by Charles Booth's *The Life and Labour of London.* These analyses proved that both in York and East London 30 per cent of the population fell below the standard at which the barest physical needs could be satisfied. Applying these figures to our whole population, Campbell-Bannerman declared that "twelve million of the people were underfed and always on the verge of hunger"—and whether this inference was statistically accurate or not, it was not far from the truth. In *The People of the Abyss*

Jack London describes lodgings in which beds were let on a relay system, three tenants to a bed, each occupying it for eight hours, so that it never grew cold. Small wonder if, according to Rowntree, mortality among the very poor was more than twice as high as among the best-paid section of the working class.

The Liberal Government was determined to lay this ugly specter of poverty, to redress the wrongs of the Industrial Revolution and to spread a net over the abyss.

It is to Winston Churchill's signal credit that he embraced these aims and worked and fought with all his heart and might to realize them. Except over the land taxes in Lloyd George's People's Budget I never knew him hesitate in his support of any social measure. It was not in principle or theory that he differed from the rank and file of his party. It was the soil from which he had sprung, his personal background, context and experience which made him seem a "foreign body" among them, and as such, at times (unjustly) suspect. A mistrustful colleague once said warningly to A. G. Gardiner: "Don't forget that the aristocrat is still there—latent but submerged."

Though he had supported himself by his own tireless industry, he was not acquainted with poverty. As he once said to me, "I have always had to earn every penny I possessed but there has never been a day in my life when I could not order a bottle of champagne for myself and offer another to a friend." I do not think it would ever have occurred to him to travel third-class or on an omnibus in order to save money (though he might well have done so for a lark). I doubt if he had ever packed his own clothes. It was simpler far to ring a bell, and throughout his life the bells he rang were always answered. The late Sir Edward Marsh, his devoted secretary and friend, once told me that until Winston married and his children's nurse (inevitably) demanded seaside visits for their health, he had never heard of the existence of such things as "lodgings." He at once developed a lively interest in the origin and mechanism of "lodgings."

He had faced hardship, danger, battle and sudden death in four campaigns and yet in some respects his life had been a sheltered one. The petty stints, shifts and economies which were the common lot of many of his political associates and followers were to him unexperienced and unthinkable. A leveled world in which such trivial, irksome, sordid cares were universally imposed would have been drab and odious to him.

He loved "the tide of pomp/That beats upon the high shore of this world," the grandeur and the pageantry of English life, its ceremonial symbols and ordered hierarchies. As Sir Isaiah Berlin has written of him: "As much as any King conceived by a Rennaissance dramatist or by a nineteenth century historian or moralist he thinks it a brave thing to ride in triumph through Persepolis; he knows with an unshakeable certainty what he considers to be big, handsome, noble, worthy of pursuit by someone in high station and what on the contrary he abhors being dim, grey, thin, likely to lower or destroy the play of colour and movement in the universe." [1] Such predilections were not the symptoms of "the submerged but latent aristocrat," but an inseparable part of his romantic and artistic vision.

They had no place in the vision of the colleague with whom he was to work in closer alliance than with any other in the years that followed —David Lloyd George—to whom a ride through Persepolis (if he had ever heard of such a place) would have been a ridiculous and meaningless proceeding and for whom those in "high station" existed only to be brought low. Of this association and of its powerful influence on one period of Winston Churchill's life there will be more to tell hereafter.

During this opening year of the new Government's existence, his mind and energies were concentrated, to the exclusion of all else, upon his first great ministerial responsibility. The Liberal Government had decided, in the teeth of fierce Conservative opposition, to make an immediate grant of self-government to South Africa. The task of introducing and piloting the new South African Constitution through the House of Commons was assigned to Winston Churchill.

Many years afterward he told me how astonished—and overjoyed— he had been when he was sent for by the Prime Minister and asked, quite unexpectedly and at a fortnight's notice, to undertake it. He had taken it for granted that Sir Henry Campbell-Bannerman would take charge of the measure himself, and that his own duty would be confined to standing by as a bottle washer to deal with details when required. He leaped at the opportunity of discharging a task in which his convictions, his emotions and his own active experience were so intimately engaged. He had fought against the Boers and had been their prisoner; he had escaped from them and fought them again. Yet all the time he had respected them as brave and chivalrous enemies and pleaded for a generous peace. As so often in his life there was a dramatic and historic fitness in the chance which made him the chosen instrument to implement the act of faith which he had advocated. The soldier of fortune who had once fought only with a pen or a platoon had now become a Minister, for the first time handling nations and institutions.

I did not hear his early skirmishes with Mr. Chamberlain and others on the Chinese labor issue—memorable for the coining of a phrase which has now passed into the language: "terminological inexactitude." *
He had to fight hard, and as usual he ignored the small fry and struck at the great. Mr. Chamberlain was now his main target and opponent. "The right honourable Gentleman," he said on one occasion, "has contracted deep obligations to this country in respect of South Africa. At his bidding . . . this nation and the Empire have made unparalleled sacrifices for that country. No sooner had the war come to an end than the right hon. Gentleman got tired of the South African situation, pushed it away from him as a toy which had ceased to amuse, and embarked at once upon another adventure which was as rash and as uncalculated as the first, and the only difference between the two was that, whereas the first enterprise of the right hon. Gentleman has had the effect of nearly ruining himself, if we desired counsel and guidance in regard to this grave situation in South Africa, it is not to the right hon. Gentleman we should appeal, however great our difficulties might be." [2]

At the end of July I went to hear him introduce the new Transvaal Constitution in the House of Commons. It was the first time I had ever heard him speak and I was full of curiosity and excitement. I remember wondering whether, like so many public performers, he had a separate public personality and being relieved to find that he behaved and spoke exactly like his private self. Yet his speech was in some ways unexpected. There were no flights of rhetoric, there was no party challenge or provocation. There was measured weight and *gravitas*. He was persuasive, temperate and restrained throughout, showing a perfect sense of the occasion. For his command of language I was of course prepared, but what impressed me was his mastery of his subject and the architectural form and balance of his speech.

He announced that there would be manhood suffrage, "one vote one value," throughout the Transvaal; that there would be no proscription of the Dutch language, Members of the Transvaal Parliament would be allowed to address it either in Dutch or in English. In the coming November the arrangements for recruiting Chinese labor would cease. "No law will be assented to which sanctions any condition of service or residence of a servile character." He ended with a fine appeal to the

---

* "The contract . . . may not be a desirable contract, . . . but it cannot in the opinion of His Majesty's Government be classified as 'slavery' in the extreme acceptance of the word without some risk of terminological inexactitude." Hansard, *Parliamentary Debates,* February 22, 1906.

Conservative Opposition. "We are prepared to make this settlement in the name of the Liberal Party. That is sufficient authority for us; but there is a higher authority which we should earnestly desire to obtain. I make no appeal, but I address myself particularly to the right honourable Gentlemen who sit opposite. . . . They are the accepted guides of a Party which, though in a minority in this House, nevertheless embodies nearly half the nation. . . . I will ask them whether . . . they cannot join with us to invest the grant of a free Constitution to the Transvaal with something of a national sanction. With all our majority we can only make it the gift of a Party; they can make it the gift of England." [3]

This appeal went unheeded. The grant of self-government was denounced by Arthur Balfour as "a dangerous, audacious and reckless experiment." The invective of the Opposition was so fierce and prolonged that the Prime Minister was only left one minute in which to reply before the closure. The measure was condemned with equal vehemence both by Lord Lansdowne and by Lord Milner in the House of Lords. The *Times* wailed like Cassandra, and on the day after the speech the *Daily Mail's* banner headlines ran as follows:

ANOTHER MAJUBA

TRANSVAAL GIVEN BACK TO THE BOERS

FRUITLESS SACRIFICES OF THE WAR

22,000 LIVES AND £250,000,000 FOR NOTHING

But this act of courageous statesmanship was triumphantly vindicated. The grant of self-government to the Transvaal and the Orange River colony was followed in 1910 by the federation of all the South African colonies. Within eight years our old enemies were fighting by our side under the generalship of Louis Botha, the first Prime Minister of the Union of South Africa and our true and loyal friend.

As Winston Churchill in later days reminded the Opposition, the House of Lords might well have rejected this great measure of conciliation if it had been within their power to do so. But by a fortunate chance the authority to implement it rested on letters patent issued by the Crown which do not require the statutory assent of Parliament.

The House of Lords was already showing its teeth though few of us then guessed with what mad folly it would use them. Winston was at that time inclined to show a charitable optimism about the political sanity of peers, and he made a hopeful but monitory speech in the country at the end of the session. "I am inclined to think that the House of Lords will be shy of interfering with the present Liberal majority in the House of Commons. I am a man of peace. Nothing would cause me greater pain than that we should have an angry dispute with these lordly people and so I say to them 'go easy'. The Liberal Party did not get their great majority for nothing. We did not sit all through the months of this year working hard passing bills for these bills to be mutilated and cast out by an irresponsible Assembly." [4] But his warnings went unheeded and there were few rational grounds for hope. Had not Arthur Balfour declared in an election speech that it was the duty of voters to ensure that "the great Unionist Party should still control, whether in power or whether in Opposition, the destinies of this great Empire"?

The House of Lords had recognized this duty to the full. In the new Government's first year of office they had started on the massacre and mutilation of all Liberal measures. The Education Bill was so mauled and mangled that its own authors were compelled to disown and drop it. The Plural Voting Bill was rejected outright, and in the following year four Land Reform Bills met with the same fate. The coming constitutional struggle was already casting its shadow over the new Parliament.

Winston Churchill was not slow to recognize it. Though South Africa was his official responsibility and his main preoccupation, he was never either willing or able to confine his energies within departmental bounds. In June, 1907, Sir Henry Campbell-Bannerman moved a resolution in the House of Commons that "in order to give effect to the will of the people as expressed by their elected representatives, . . . the power of the other House . . . should be so restricted by law as to secure that within the limits of a single Parliament the final decision of the Commons shall prevail." Winston made a spirited speech in which he described the House of Lords as a "one-sided, hereditary, unpurged, unrepresentative, irresponsible, absentee." "Has the House of Lords ever been right?" he continued. "Has it ever been right in any of the great settled controversies which are now beyond the reach of Party argument? Was it right in delaying Catholic emancipation and the removal of Jewish disabilities? Was it right in driving this country to the verge of revolution in the effort to secure the passage of reform? Was it right in resisting the Ballot Bill? Was it right in the almost innumerable efforts it made to prevent this House dealing with the purity of its own electoral machinery? Was it right in endeavouring to prevent the abolition of purchase in the Army? Was it right in 1880 when it rejected the Compensation for Disturbance Bill? I defy the Party opposite to produce a single instance of a settled controversy in which the House of Lords was right." [5]

The temper of Government supporters was rising. Here was this vast majority * straining at the leash, eager for action. They were hot from the polls and, justifiably, flushed with victory. Their mandate was beyond challenge. Yet at every turn they found themselves frustrated and condemned to impotence by a body whose authority rested solely on the hereditary principle and in which their opponents possessed a permanent majority.

The new House of Commons was a very different body from its predecessor. My stepmother recorded a characteristic comment when she returned from the opening of Parliament in February. "The new House is sadly unfamiliar to me, fearfully overcrowded and full of strangers." It was indeed "full of strangers." Many familiar and established figures had vanished in the landslide and hundreds of raw, ardent, unknown men had suddenly (and many to their own amazement) been swept into the House. More than three hundred had never sat in Parliament before. They were a variegated lot, including among men of high ability and promise some cranks on hobbyhorses with bonnets full of bees, the bearers of "banners with a strange device." Charles Masterman described some of them as "Smithites," a category based on a story told by Winston Churchill in his life of Lord Randolph about Lord Salisbury and Sir Henry Drummond Wolff, a member of the Fourth Party: " 'I do not understand,' said Lord Salisbury as they walked together one day, 'what your real political position is.' 'Oh, I am a Smithite,' replied Sir Henry reverentially,—'a convinced "Smithite" in politics.' 'And what is your object?' 'To do good, just to do good,' was the reply." [6] There were no doubt many new members whose aims were as wide and undefined as those of any Smithite. But their faith and zeal were positive. They believed that they had been returned to Parliament to build a new heaven and a new earth—and some of them were convinced that they could do so.

One portent of the new House of Commons was the presence of a Labour Party, which the election had brought into being for the first time as a Parliamentary force. Liberals and Labour had co-operated closely throughout the contest and avoided three-cornered fights wherever possible. As a result fifty-three Labour members were returned of whom twenty-four were allies of the Liberal Party ("Lib-Labs") and twenty-nine were Independents nominated by the Labour Representative Committee.

* The Liberals alone were 377 strong, and supported by their Irish and Labour allies they numbered 513 out of a total of 670.

It was a mild and gentle Labour Party, on the whole indifferent to theory and concerned mainly to defend the interests of the working class. Halevy wrote truly that "in the whole of Europe there was no Socialist Party which was so completely representative of a class, . . . there was not one so undoctrinal." [7] The Labour members of those days were for the most part radical workingmen, many of whom owed their seats to Liberals and were supported by them. I remember shortly after the election some French Parliamentarians coming over on a visit to our House of Commons, curious and eager to see our new political phenomenon, a Parliamentary Labour Party. They were bitterly disappointed by its unrevolutionary appearance until Lord Robert Cecil (who, like all his family, was never overdressed) strode into the Chamber. *"Ah, voilà enfin le vrai ouvrier!"* they exclaimed with relief and I had not the heart to undeceive them.

As I got to know our rank and file I often wondered how these earnest, high-thinking and low-living men made head or tail of Winston —and still more what he made of them. There is no doubt that his political performance left them dazzled and blinking, sometimes with a vague mistrust. Turning away from the sun they saw spots. I think that to them he seemed a bird of paradise, of brilliant plumage and incalculable habits. To him they were impersonal units of that indispensable collective entity—a reliable majority. I could not conceive communication between him and them in any code but that of politics. They spoke, felt, thought and lived in such a different idiom from his own. Knowing both languages I realized that though they must become his workmates they could never be his playmates. I remember once telling him as I left the House of Commons that I must hurry home because we had a dinner party of forty that night. *"Forty* to dinner? And who are they?" "Oh, some of our Liberal members—Horridges and Berridges and Mastermen, Runcimen and Hornimen. . . ." He was vicariously aghast at the prospect. "My poor child—you call that a dinner party? And what will happen to *you* in this grim *galère?"* He was amazed when I said I should enjoy it and muttered something about "great causes to whose altar even gleaming youth must bring its sacrifice."

But to do him justice he indulged in very little "play," even when offered in a more congruous and congenial context. He was entirely absorbed in his work and thought of little else. In spite of Tory rancor at his "treachery to his class" (and its reward), he was socially besieged, assailed and pursued by importunate hostesses. Like him or loathe him, no one could deny his *réclame*. He was the most discussed, conspicuous and contentious figure of his day inside the Government or out of it.

But pleasure might beckon, and the sirens sing in vain, they could not coax his nose from the grindstone. Even at week-end parties where I sometimes met him he arrived accompanied by his work and often spent the whole morning toiling at it in his bedroom, appearing at luncheon still in its grip. On such occasions I watched with some amusement the heroic efforts of his female neighbors to derail his train of thought, and their discomfiture. His mind contained no insulating dodges or devices, no fireproof curtains or watertight compartments. Once engaged by a theme it was wholly possessed.

What did he look like in these early years? It is difficult to convey a true impression of his physical appearance. He did not, like Mr. Gladstone, "look the part" of the Great Man as popularly imagined and depicted. There was nothing immediately arresting or impressive either in his stature or in his features. Meeting him casually one might have noted slightly hunched shoulders from which his head jutted at a forward angle, a brooding forehead, blue eyes and sandy hair. His face was rounded like a child's. (He used to say: "All newborn babies look like me.") He was not carved in stone or cast in bronze but rather molded in a lively clay.

Action or speech transformed him. The clay became a mobile and translucent mask through which his inner being shone, transfusing it with light and fire. It then assumed an infinite variety of Protean shapes —in turn that of an orator, a pugilist, a statesman, or a Puckish schoolboy cocking defiant snooks at all authority. Every emotion was faithfully reflected. His was a face that could not keep a secret. His personality thrust its way through so forcibly that his features seemed irrelevant trappings of his intrinsic self.

In those days I was dancing with my generation all night and every night. And not with my own generation alone. Our elders came to talk and eat innumerable suppers and occasionally revolve—more stiffly and more staidly than they did in later years when the one-step lured the oldest and the stiffest to jerk and shuffle around the ballroom floor. Winston never came to a ball except on very rare and grand occasions. He attended the Court Ball *con amore*. But that of course was an official ceremony rather than a bacchanal. He enjoyed its splendid ritual, the Royal Quadrille with which it opened in those days, the glittering tiaras, medals, decorations, the martial uniforms with clanking swords in which even the most civil of civilians were attired, the procession in to supper in which all members of the Government and their female belongings took a part. He also looked in late after the House of Commons at some of the great balls given at the classic houses.

Those were red-letter nights for me. I forsook the floor, threw all engagements to the winds, cut dances right and left, sank deep into a sofa by his side and talked—or rather, listened to him talking. Our conversation, if so it can be called, always revolved around the same themes. Like the ballgoers in the *Young Visiters* we "talked passionately about the laws" and those engaged in making them, and about both we shared at that time the same loves and hates. How infinitely fortunate it was, I often thought, that we had the same addiction to the same kind of "shop." Sometimes he made a full-blown speech to me, which was delivered later to a larger and a worthier audience. But he was not just trying it on the dog. He liked thinking aloud, in sharp contrast to my father, who always thought alone, almost behind locked doors, as though it were a slightly indecent occupation. I never felt, as Queen Victoria did with Mr. Gladstone, that he was "addressing me like a public meeting." Hearing him think was to me an exciting and enthralling occupation. Was he, as people said, inebriated by his own words? I did not care, I only knew that I was.

At balls as elsewhere he was impervious to his surroundings, blind and deaf to the gyrating couples, the band, the jostling, sparkling throng. I remember once in a momentary lull directing his attention to the appearance of a friend of his who crossed our line of vision looking her very best. "Look—there goes X—isn't she looking lovely tonight?" He looked at her, appraised her beauty and replied: "Yes—there goes X. A great woman—sagacious—chaste." This choice of epithets took my breath away. There were a hundred different adjectives which could with truth have been applied to X. But if one had scoured the dictionary with a tooth-comb it would have been impossible to discover three which less described her. She was neither "sagacious," "chaste" nor "great." Did he, I wondered, know any more about the human content of these people who belonged to his own world than about that of the Liberal rank and file?

Yet about the greatest figures in the political field his estimates and judgments were curiously sound. He often gave me in those early days appraisals of his front-rank colleagues and opponents as penetrating and true as those recorded in much later years in his portrait gallery,

Great Contemporaries. I think that for him human beings fell, roughly, into three categories: the great figures whom he weighed, measured and assessed in a historical perspective and about whom his judgment rarely erred; the (so-called) average man and woman who often made no impact on his attention, let alone his mind; and lastly his friends—those who had found their way into his heart.

His friendship was a stronghold against which the gates of Hell could not prevail. There was an absolute quality in his loyalty, known only to those safe within its walls. Their battle was his own. He would concede no inch of ground, no smallest point against them. In a friend he would defend the indefensible, explain away the inexplicable—even forgive the unforgivable.

This inner citadel of the heart held first and foremost his relations, in their widest sense. His strong family feeling embraced not only his mother and his brother Jack, but cousins, uncles, aunts—the whole Guest tribe and "Sunny," Duke of Marlborough. (He confided to me that one of his reasons for preferring the post of Colonial Under-Secretary to that of Financial Secretary to the Treasury was that Sunny had once held it.) I often told him that one quality he shared with his great hero Napoleon was nepotism; that if he had been Napoleon he would have popped all the Guests, his brother Jack and Sunny Marlborough on every throne in Europe and made his mother Empress of Byzantium. He did not deny it and suggested that "it might have been quite a good thing to do. I think Sunny would have done very well in Spain. Jack might have had one of the Scandinavian countries. Then Ivor Wimborne with his lovely Alice—a lustrous pair—might well have shone and ruled in Italy. Freddy [Guest] could have been accommodated with a modest throne in one of the smaller European countries. . . ." He smiled as he distributed these crowns but it was clear that the prospect appealed to him.

His blood relations were accepted without question and *en bloc*. Next came his friends, strangely diverse in character. It would have been difficult to establish any common denominator between, for instance, Lord Hugh Cecil and Jack Seely, one an intellectual of the first water, the other a dashing man of action, of ebullient courage, robust self-confidence and simple mind.

In the summer of 1907 he forged one of the greatest friendships of his life with F. E. Smith. This brilliant star shot suddenly into the political skies, like a meteor in reverse, from earth to heaven, from obscurity to fame. I can recall no reputation more instantaneously established by a maiden speech. I happened by good fortune to be in the Speaker's Gallery when an unknown Mr. Smith was called. According to his son even the members of his own party had for the most part not the slightest idea who he was and "seeing this unknown youth rise at such a moment uttered murmurs of surprise and dissatisfaction. 'Who is this boy?' they asked; 'haven't we got anyone better?' " The speech gave them—and others—a conclusive answer. From start to finish it was a triumph of hard-hitting wit which swept the House with gales of cheers and laughter. The Conservative rank and file shouted and roared in ecstasy, their leaders rolled about on the front bench in convulsions of amusement and delight. The speaker alone remained impassive and unmoved.

When he sat down amid a great ovation he was overwhelmed with congratulations. Perhaps the highest tribute he received was a note passed to him by the Irish Nationalist Tim Healy, a virtuoso in invective, saying: "I am old, and you are young, but you have beaten me at my own game."

The sensation created in the House was reflected by a flutter of excitement in the Ladies' Gallery above. A very famous hostess confided to me her plans to get an instant introduction to him so that she might secure him for a coming week-end party. But how, she whispered, could one set about it? Did *anybody* know him? In less than no time everybody knew him.

Between him and Winston a close and lasting bond was sealed of mutual admiration and affection. Ranged against one another in the fiercest and most ruthless party conflicts in our history, their loyalty to one another was never strained. "Our friendship," Winston wrote, "was perfect. It was one of my most precious possessions. . . . He had all the canine virtues in a remarkable degree—courage, fidelity, vigilance, love of the chase." [8] And paying tribute to his dialectical powers: "For all purposes of discussion, argument, exposition, appeal or altercation F.E. had a complete armoury. The bludgeon for the platform; the rapier for a personal dispute; the entangling net and unexpected trident for the Courts of Law; and a jug of clear spring water for an anxious perplexed conclave." And he adds in a revealing sentence: "He was always great fun." I think that there was no friend in his life with whom he had greater fun, and of the kind he loved the best.

This inner circle of friends contained no women. They had their own place in his life. His approach to women was essentially romantic. He had a lively susceptibility to beauty, glamour, radiance, and those who possessed these qualities were not subjected to analysis. Their possession of all the cardinal virtues was assumed as a matter of course. I remember his taking umbrage when I once commented on the "innocence" of his approach to women. He was affronted by this epithet as applied to himself. Yet he would certainly have applied it to me as a term of praise. Young women should be "innocent"—men, young or old, should not. I think he divided women into two categories: the virginal snow-drops, unsullied by experience, or even knowledge, of the seamy side of life, who should be sheltered and protected from its hazards, and the mature who were at home among the seams, had scrambled in and out of pitfalls and adventures and to whom he could talk without pro-tective inhibitions in his own language. The second class was of course incomparably the most rewarding, and it was among these that he sought—not his romances—but his female friends. I remember the ad-miration with which he used to talk to me about Miss Maxine Elliott. "A great and valiant woman. Like a tigress bearing its cub in its mouth she carried her little sister" (Gertrude Elliott, later Lady Forbes-Robert-son) "through the jungle of life, protecting her from the ferocities and perils she had herself encountered and contended with." I was eager to hear something of the "ferocities and perils" of the jungle and begged him to enlarge upon them. But he refused, saying that the jungle was a territory outside the orbit of my life and would, he trusted, so remain forever. "Not for you the savage claws of predatory beasts . . ." etc.

This was the classic Victorian attitude, except that in him it was devoid of all censoriousness, hypocrisy and cant. He was neither strait-laced nor squeamish. It was not so much a question of morality as of the "rules of the game"—which applied not only between men and women but between two different kinds of women. Each had her proper place and must remain within it. The line of demarcation which divided them must on no account be crossed or blurred.

This attitude remained a constant one, though with the passage of years I graduated into a no man's land between the lines. I remember very vividly a birthday dinner party, given for Winston by Mrs. Edwin Montagu some time in the thirties, at which I sat beside him. There was a large and variegated company and among the female guests there were few, if any, snowdrops. Most of them were thoroughly versed in the life of the jungle. At the end of dinner someone proposed Winston's health and we all drank it with such exuberant affection that he was moved. When he rose to reply in a few sentences he said: "This is the sort of company I should like to find in heaven." I could not help wondering how many of those present he would find there. The same thought may have occurred to him, for when he sat down he said to me reflectively: "Yes—this is the sort of company I should like to find in heaven." Then, as his eye roved around the table, resting on each questionable candidate in turn: "Stained perhaps—stained but *positive*. Not those flaccid sea anemones of virtue who can hardly wobble an antenna in the waters of negativity." And he murmured once again: "Stained perhaps. . . ."

No inventory of Winston Churchill's human relationships would be complete without some mention of the bond between him and those who served him—his private secretaries—and here the word "bond" should be taken in its literal sense. For they were indeed his bond slaves, but in a bondage fraught with such devotion that they hugged their chains, and when political upheavals freed them they felt lost without them. Winston might be—and indeed he was—exacting, arbitrary, often unreasonable and always inexhaustible. Yet he was also always human, and he was their friend. They neither expected nor did they receive "consideration" from him, but they were assured of his affection and tenacious loyalty. He covered those who served him with strong wings—for did they not belong to him? They shared the tempest of his fortunes and its glory and to exchange these for a calmer, freer lot would have been like leaving the ocean for a millpond.

On his first day at the Colonial Office (in December, 1915) he appointed as his private secretary Eddie Marsh, a young civil servant, two years older than himself, who remained an inseparable adjunct of his life, following him from office to office throughout the many vicissitudes of his career. "It was an understood thing," wrote Eddie, "that I was Ruth to his Naomi, and that whither he went, so long as it was not into the actual Wilderness, where I should have no visible means of support, I should go." [9]

To those who knew both intimately as I did the incongruity of their association never palled. At the time it began they hardly shared an inch of common ground. Eddie Marsh was a fine classical scholar with a deep knowledge and love of literature, a passionate addict of the theater and a discoverer and patron of young poets (and later of painters), on whom he lavished help of every kind. His friends and his enthusiasms were legion. To strike a dumb note on his keyboard would have been a *tour de force*. This was achieved only by politics. The sweep and crash of world events left him unmoved, uninterested and almost unaware—until they touched a friend. And then it was particular results not general causes which concerned him. He discharged his Civil Service duties with punctilious perfection, meticulous accuracy and the complete absence of mind we bring to a timetable when we look up trains for other people. The destination was of little consequence although the time was always right. Through Winston's choice he was mercifully translated into private secretaryship, his true vocation, in which his rare gifts for vicarious emotion, personal service and attachment found full scope.

His appearance was so much a part of himself that an attempt to suggest it should be made for those who have not seen him depicted to the life by the immortal pencil of Max Beerbohm. He had a head cocked to attention like a bird's, bristling eyebrows always agog with eagerness, ecstatically expressing every mood, in one eye a monocle which he occasionally removed to wipe away from it a tear, evoked by laughter or a line of poetry or a play (Eddie always cried at the theater), and a falsetto voice which was like a high-pitched chirrup. He used to complain of the "vexatiously frequent" response of "Yes, madam," to his "Hello" on the telephone and often assured his friends that he had "deep organ tones" at his command but could never manage to use them in conversation in what seemed to him to be a natural manner. (I was aware of these only on the rare occasions when he called a dog—in a deep bass.)

The amenities between himself and his chief are well illustrated by a story he used to tell of how, having woken up one morning with an *extinction de voix,* he presented himself to Winston and said in a whisper: "I'm afraid I shan't be much use today as I've lost my voice." "What," thundered Winston, "is that resonant organ extinct?" I remember his repeating to me at the time another characteristic snatch of dialogue between them. Winston had attended a performance of Beerbohm Tree's production of *Antony and Cleopatra,* which had excited and impressed him, but Tree had made one mistake. He had said: "Unarm, Eros; the long day's task is done," which didn't scan. The line should of course begin "Eros, unarm." * This gave Eddie an opportunity for a short disquisition on the beauty which may lie in departing from the norm of a meter. He supported his thesis with Palgrave's note in the *Golden Treasury* on Shelley's line, "And wild roses, and ivy ser-

---

* This story is improved by the astonishing fact pointed out to me by my American publisher that not only Winston but that master of poetic erudition Eddie Marsh were both wrong. Tree had spoken the line as Shakespeare wrote it. *Est ubi nutat Homerus.*

pentine," arguing that a good poet might have written "And roses wild" but it took a great one to write "And wild roses." "Yes," said Winston, "and I suppose it would have taken the greatest poet of all to write 'And wild roses and serpentine ivy.' "

Toward the end of 1907 Winston set out, with Eddie in his train, on a four months' official tour of British East Africa, Uganda, the Sudan and Egypt. In the intervals of inspecting these countries he stalked lions, speared wart hogs, saw crocodiles, hippopotamuses and a white rhinoceros. But it was the butterflies in Uganda which made the deepest and most lasting impression on his mind. He described them to me on his return in words which glowed with all their colors. His lifelong love of butterflies was born of that journey. In his book *My African Journey* he wrote: "Never were seen such flying fairies. They flaunted their splendid liveries in inconceivable varieties of colour and pattern in our faces at every step. Swallow-tails, fritillaries, admirals, tortoise-shells, peacocks, orange-tips . . . flitted in sunshine from flower to flower, glinted in the shadow of great trees, or clustered on the path to suck the moisture from any swampy patch. . . . I found them sometimes so intoxicated with feasting that I could pick them up quite gently in my fingers without the need of any net at all." [10]

Nearly fifty years later I was sitting with him on an August afternoon in the garden at Chartwell. He was bemoaning the fact that the summer had been a bad one for butterflies when suddenly to his delight he saw two red admirals alighting on a clump of buddleia bushes he had planted to attract them. I shall never forget his pleasure. "They are the first I have seen this summer! You know I sometimes think of devoting some part of my Eightieth Birthday Fund to the creation of butterflies." I asked him how he would set about it. "By appealing to people not to capture and destroy them, helping them to live and multiply throughout the world." I thought it so like him, in this sunset moment of his life, to be concerned with the propagation of butterflies in a world which he had always wished to fill with color.

While Winston was in Africa exploring tropical forests, which he described as "glittering Equatorial slums," I was exiled to an Alpine peak in Switzerland with a patch on my lung. I bitterly resented this banishment at a moment when both my own life and the political situation were so exciting. The issue between Lords and Commons was simmering. C-B had declared that "a way must be found and a way will be found . . . by which the will of the people expressed through their elected representatives . . . will be made to prevail," and the Cabinet was engaged in devising and agreeing on the way. Meanwhile Sir Henry Campbell-Bannerman's health began to fail. He was taken ill in February but remained cheerful and confident of his own recovery. King Edward, who visited him in his sickroom before leaving for Biarritz in early March, was however evidently convinced that he could never return to active political life for he sent for my father and discussed with him in general terms the reshuffling of the Cabinet he might desire to make on C-B's resignation. My father recorded that the King "had heard gossip that Winston was anxious to get into the Cabinet, keeping his present office of Under-Secretary. He was opposed to this and said that Queen Victoria had vetoed a similar proposal by Lord Rosebery in favor of Sir Edward Grey when he was Under-Secretary for Foreign Affairs. I said that Winston had every claim to Cabinet rank and that he had behaved very well when twice passed over for Lulu * and Mc-Kenna, both of whom had inferior claims. The King agreed and was quite warm in his praise of Winston, but thought he must wait until some real Cabinet office fell vacant."

My father could not have been accused of impetuosity. But he never played safe. He believed in Winston's genius and consistently supported his claims to opportunity, often in the teeth of opposition from his more cautious colleagues. If there were risks he was prepared to take them, for in his view the stakes immeasurably outweighed them.

During these months my father had a difficult and in some ways an embarrassing part to play. He was carrying the whole burden of government, presiding over the Cabinet and leading the House of Commons, with the Prime Minister unable to deal with urgent decisions and the King abroad. Yet he was anxious to do nothing which could alarm his chief about his own condition. At the end of March C-B sent for him and in a moving interview told him that he was dying. He submitted his resignation to the King, who asked my father to form a Government and summoned him to Biarritz. This last *démarche* evoked outspoken criticism both from politicians and the press. It was felt that the King should have returned from his holiday instead of obliging his future Prime Minister, then engaged in the crucial task of forming a new Government, to leave the country and go to Biarritz. But the King was firm and after a few hectic days of Cabinet making my father left for Biarritz to kiss hands.† In spite of my entreaties I had not been passed fit to come home for these events and many telegrams and letters passed

* Lewis Harcourt, son of Sir William Harcourt.
† "Kissing hands" is a ceremony inherent in receiving office from the King.

between us, in one of which I adjured him to "make the most of Winston." His reply was reassuring. "You need have no fear on W's account. He will be well looked after and provided for in your absence."

Winston was given the Board of Trade but the devious route by which he reached it was (strangely) not revealed to me until many years later, when he told me about it himself. An erroneous story has been published that my father first offered him the Local Government Board and that Winston had replied that he did not wish to be "shut up in a soup-kitchen with Mrs. Sidney Webb." These words may have been uttered on some other occasion but the truth is that my father, divining his real vocation, offered him the Admiralty (later the realization of his highest ambition) and that he refused it, and asked for the Local Government Board instead. My father was naturally astounded by this choice and told Winston that it had never occurred to him that he could possibly want such a post. He added: "I have already told John Burns, who is difficult to place elsewhere, that he can stay on there. But if you prefer a job in the domestic field to one of the fighting departments you had much better take the Board of Trade—from which I am moving Lloyd George to the Exchequer." This Winston gladly accepted.

That afternoon he happened to meet Sir John Fisher (then First Sea Lord), with whom he had already struck up a warm friendship, who asked him what he had got. When Winston told him that he had refused the Admiralty Fisher exploded and overwhelmed him with reproaches. What might they not together have done at the Admiralty! What a heaven-sent opportunity he had thrown away! And he so fired Winston's imagination with his glowing picture of their joint rule of the seas that Winston was persuaded to return to my father and tell him that he had changed his mind and that if the Admiralty was still available he would like to take it. But alas! It was not. My father had already offered it to McKenna, who had accepted it.

I do not think, however, that Winston felt more than a momentary regret, if any. When I next saw him his thoughts were entirely concentrated on the home front. He saw himself as a social reformer of the most radical kind, and for this role the Board of Trade offered ample scope.

We did not meet until nearly two months after my return from abroad. For seven weeks on end he had been through the grueling ordeal of fighting two by-elections in succession and he seemed to me

—for the first and only time in my experience—in a state of physical exhaustion.

In those days promotion to Cabinet office entailed a by-election. Winston, who always welcomed a fight, went up to Manchester full of pugnacity and confidence and received an enthusiastic welcome. Less than half of those who wished to attend his opening meeting could be squeezed into the Grand Theatre and the *Manchester Guardian* prophesied that "a mighty Free Trade victory is in sight." But all the forces hostile to the Government, and in particular to himself, were concentrated against him. By Conservatives he was the best-hated member of the Government and his elevation to Cabinet rank was the last drop of bitterness in their cup. From far and wide they came to speak and work for his defeat. Their efforts were reinforced by the Suffragettes, whose campaign of full-blooded violence was first launched at this election under the generalship of Mrs. Pankhurst herself, aided by her two daughters Christabel and Sylvia.

"Painful scenes were witnessed in the Free Trade Hall," wrote Winston Churchill, "when Miss Christabel Pankhurst, tragical and dishevelled, was finally ejected after having thrown the meeting into pandemonium. This was the beginning of a systematic interruption of public speeches and the breaking up and throwing into confusion of all Liberal meetings. Indeed, it was most provoking to anyone who cared about the style and form of his speech to be assailed by the continued, calculated shrill interruptions. Just as you were reaching the most moving part in your peroration or the most intricate point in your argument, when things were going well and the audience was gripped, a high-pitched voice would ring out 'What about the women?' 'When are you going to give women the vote?' and so on. No sooner was one interrupter removed than another in a different part of the hall took up the task. It became extremely difficult to pursue connected arguments." [11]

Winston went much further in the direction of appeasement than he had done at his last election, when he had firmly refused to be "henpecked," but even his promises of friendship and support in the Cabinet failed to placate the Furies. He was defeated by his old opponent Joynson-Hicks by 429 votes, a Socialist candidate polling 276.

Of his defeat he wrote: "It took only five or six minutes to walk from the City Hall where the poll was declared to the Manchester Reform Club. I was accompanied there by tumultuous crowds. As I entered the club a telegram was handed to me. It was from Dundee and conveyed the unanimous invitation of the Liberals of that city that I should become their candidate in succession to the sitting member . . . who was about to be promoted to the House of Lords. It is no exaggeration to say that only seven minutes at the outside passed between my defeat at Manchester and my invitation to Dundee. . . . Here I found a resting-place for fifteen years." [12]

A howl of triumph and jubilation went up from the whole Tory press at Winston's defeat. The *Pall Mall Gazette* compared him to a "draper's assistant at an after season sale; everyone could find the bargain he wanted at Mr. Churchill's counter. . . ." [13] The *Daily Express,* under the headlines

REJECTED

MANCHESTER'S REPLY TO THE CHAMPION PROMISER

"Another nail in the Government's coffin. In Manchester of all places! . . . the heart of Cobdenism, the 'last ditch' where the foreigner could dump to his heart's content! Mr. Churchill's cyclone of promises has availed him nothing." [14] Even the *Daily Mail* accused him of behaving "as though he were a clown in a sixpenny circus. He put himself and his principles and his colleagues in the Cabinet up to auction." [15]

The chorus of hysterical exultation at the gain of one (traditionally Conservative) seat bears testimony not only to the Opposition's vindictive animosity toward Winston Churchill but to the importance of his personal position in public life.

To what extent if any were the savage strictures of the press on his election tactics merited? I can find no record of inconsistency nor of extravagant promises in his reported speeches. His much criticized statement that the Government would in due course introduce a measure of Home Rule for Ireland was vindicated by events. I heard no criticism of his conduct of the election from my father or his other colleagues. Yet some there must have been in Manchester at least, for John Morley, who had always been a close and appreciative friend, wrote in his *Recollections:*

"The belief among competent observers in the place is that the resounding defeat of Winston at Manchester was due to wrath at rather too naked tactics of making deals with this, that, and the other group, without too severe a scrutiny in his own political conscience of the terms that they were exacting from him. It is believed that he lost 300 or 400 of these honourably fastidious electors. I have a great liking for Winston; for his vitality, his indefatigable industry and attention to business, his remarkable gift of language and skill in argument, and his curious flair for all sorts of political cases as they arise, though even he now and then mistakes a frothy bubble for a great wave. All the same, as I often tell him in a paternal way, a successful politician in this country needs a good deal more than skill in mere computation of other people's opinions, without anxiety about his own."

I must here express my disagreement with Lord Morley's diagnosis of the cause of Winston Churchill's frequent failure to win popular support. So far from concentrating on a "mere computation of other people's opinions without anxiety about his own" his error—if he erred—was in the opposite direction. He was so wholly possessed by his own opinions that he often failed to take those of others into account, even as a practical factor in a situation. He never had his ear to the ground. Nor would he have felt much interest in its message even if he heard it. It was his own message which concerned him and which he was determined to transmit. He possessed neither the sensitive antennae nor the servile flexibility of the demagogue. The late Lord Keynes once compared Mr. Lloyd George to "a prism which collects light and distorts it and is most brilliant if the light comes from many quarters at once." Winston Churchill was never a receptive or reflective prism. He generated his own light—intense, direct and concentrated as a beam. It is for this reason that during long periods of his later life the British public, which is apt to mistrust brilliance and dislike a glare, just blinked and turned aside.

I am not, however, attempting to suggest that it was through Winston's noble failure to be a demagogue that he lost North-West Manchester—or that he held Dundee—an impregnable Liberal seat which had never returned a Conservative since the Reform Bill. But though his victory was there assured he had a rough and lively contest against three opponents, a Conservative, a Socialist and a "quaint and then dim figure in the shape of Mr. Scrimgeour, the Prohibitionist, who pleaded for the kingdom of God upon earth with special references to the evils of alcohol." [16] (Who could then have foretold that this same Mr. Scrimgeour, a freak candidate polling a bare few hundred votes, would be the instrument destined to unseat him in the years to come?)

The Dundee election is memorable for a speech delivered in the Kinnaird Hall a few days before the poll, which Winston described in after years as the most successful election speech he had ever made. As such it deserves quotation. It contains a classic definition of the difference between Liberalism and Socialism. "Socialism seeks to pull down wealth; Liberalism seeks to raise up poverty. Socialism would destroy private interests; Liberalism would preserve private interests in the only way in which they can be safely and justly preserved, namely, by reconciling them with public right. Socialism would kill enterprise; Liberalism would rescue enterprise from the trammels of privilege and preference. Socialism assails the pre-eminence of the individual; Liberalism seeks, and shall seek more in the future, to build up a minimum standard for the mass. Socialism exalts the rule; Liberalism exalts the man. . . . An inconclusive verdict from Dundee, the home of Scottish Radicalism . . . would carry a message of despair to everyone in all parts of our island and in our sister island who is working for the essential influences and truths of Liberalism and progress. . . . We shall step out of the period of adventurous hope in which we have lived for a brief spell; we shall step back to the period of obstinate and prejudiced negations. For Ireland—ten years of resolute government; for England— dear food and cheaper gin; and for Scotland—the superior wisdom of the House of Lords! Is that the work you want to do, men of Dundee? . . .

"We are always changing; like nature, we change a great deal, although we change very slowly. We are always reaching a higher level after each change, but yet with the harmony of our life unbroken and unimpaired. . . . There have always been men of power and position who have sacrificed and exerted themselves in the popular cause; and that is why there is so little class-hatred here, in spite of all the squalor and misery which we see around us. . . . That is how we have preserved the golden thread of historical continuity, when so many other nations have lost it for ever. That is the only way in which your island life as you know it, and love it, can be preserved in all its grace and in all its freedom. . . ." [17]

To have delivered a speech of such quality, both in form and content, in the stress and heat of a by-election after seven weeks on the hustings was a feat of intellectual staying power.

He won by a majority of three thousand. "It was with the greatest relief," he wrote, "that I returned to London, was introduced into the House of Commons by the Prime Minister Mr. Asquith, took my seat as a member of the Cabinet and settled down to enjoy the Board of Trade."

————◄◄ ►►————

Chapter Fifteen

PEERS V. PEOPLE

THE CABINET of which Winston Churchill had now become a member was a constellation of brilliant individualists, whose distinction was often matched by their discords. It would be difficult to imagine men more diverse in mind, character and temperament than Lloyd George, Edward Grey, Winston Churchill, R. B. Haldane, John Morley, Herbert Samuel, Augustine Birrell and John Burns.

It was no mean achievement of my father's to have held such a team together without a single resignation until the outbreak of the First World War. He hated quarrels. No one shrank more from what Lord Keynes has called "the soiled clay of personal issues." Rivalries, jealousies and talebearing filled him with embarrassment and distaste. But he rated quality above all else, and rather than shed a drop of it he was prepared to labor, with massive patience, to compose differences, devise healing formulae, soothe wounded vanity and *amour-propre,* little as he understood such skin troubles.

But in 1908, though there were of course many differing degrees of emphasis and inflection, of personal sympathy and antipathy in the Cabinet, there was no rift in the lute. Listening, as I did most days, to the confidences of colleagues about one another, my impression was one of considerable mutual trust and admiration, peppered here and there with some very natural irritation and amusement. (McKenna was so cocksure, Winston talked too much, Lloyd George told everything to the press, John Burns was as vain as a peacock and a roadblock to reform, etc., etc.)

As happens in most Cabinets birds of a feather flocked together.

Kindred minds converged and personal alliances emerged. Of these the closest, and in some ways the most incongruous, was the alliance now forged between Lloyd George and Winston Churchill. To me the most curious and surprising feature of their partnership was that while it exercised no influence whatsoever on Lloyd George, politically or otherwise, it directed, shaped and colored Winston Churchill's mental attitude and his political course during the next few years. Lloyd George was throughout the dominant partner. His was the only personal leadership I ever knew Winston to accept unquestioningly in his whole political career. He was fascinated by a mind more swift and agile than his own, by its fertility and resource, by its uncanny intuition and gymnastic nimbleness, and by a political sophistication which he lacked.

From Lloyd George he was to learn the language of radicalism. It was Lloyd George's native tongue, but it was not his own, and despite his efforts he spoke it "with a difference." This difference may not have been detected by his audiences, but it was recognized by those who knew both the teacher and his pupil. Charles Masterman wrote to his wife: "Winston is full of the poor whom he has just discovered. He thinks he is called by Providence—to do something for them." [1] For Lloyd George, born and brought up in a small Welsh village by his uncle, the village cobbler, there was no need to discover the poor. He had himself been one of them. To him poverty was not a political concept but a stark fact which had entered into his being, bringing with it an instinctive hatred of the rich. Squires, landowners and even parsons were his hereditary enemies.

Winston knew few, if any, parsons and felt little, if anything, about them. Most of his friends and relations were landowners and squires (though he would never have thought of classifying them as such) and he grudged none of them their broad acres. Lloyd George was saturated with class-consciousness. Winston accepted class distinction without thought.

Again, Winston was an intellectual, who arrived at his conclusions through his mind, though his heart often reinforced it. Intellectually Lloyd George had few convictions. His thought was not rooted or grounded in any consistent or abiding principles. His mind had no anchor. He lived by instinct and it served him well. He was an improviser of genius and an emotional opportunist. The Master of Balliol, A. L. Smith, described him truly as having "religious fervor without moral perception." Yet, until in later years his lights had failed, he was, in one respect, emotionally consistent. He was before all things a man of the people, the champion of the disinherited—dauntless, resourceful, ready to fight their battle against all comers and against any odds.

He did not share Winston's broad historical perspective, nor his sense of the significance of world events. His background and his outlook were at this time relatively parochial. He was a Little Englander and a Great Welshman. He was not an Anglo-Saxon by birth, instinct or tradition. He was as unlike an Englishman as Disraeli, and like Disraeli he succeeded, for a time at least, in dominating the Conservative Party, which for so long had hated and despised him.

Unlike Winston he had an undisciplined mind, refused to read papers and always insisted that his officials should brief him by word of mouth. He shared with Winston a contempt for education and had no use for its overrated product, "the trained mind," in which he saw just another class distinction and often an obstruction to his political aims. I have sometimes wondered whether he himself would have gained or lost by education. On the whole I think he might have lost by it. It would have sharpened his critical faculties but might have hobbled his creative power. He was a great initiator, and it was his strength that he saw the goal and not the obstacles.

In spite of his class-consciousness he was never a snob. He was not dazzled by the social glitter or the tinsel lining of what is called success. Society as such had no glamour or attractions for him. Tradition, whether historic or aesthetic, meant nothing to him. He would have found no pleasure in the country houses described by Maurice Baring, or in their inmates. A luxurious hotel on the Riviera with a few political cronies and journalists to talk shop to was far more to his taste. Unlike Winston he did not seek, nor enjoy, contacts with great minds outside the field of politics. But his insatiable appetite for political discussion in season and out of season was not only shared but, in his own view, surpassed by Winston's. (Lloyd George told Lord Riddell that even at his wedding Winston started talking politics to him in the vestry!) [2] This addiction was a great bond between them.

Lloyd George was a virtuoso in all the arts of political manipulation and I think his lack of scruple must at times have startled Winston, though he was too dazzled to be shocked. There is no doubt that he was influenced by it. Lloyd George was his senior by eleven years, and he saw him as a political "man of the world" who knew what was "done" and "not done." One difference between them was that Winston knew when he was being unscrupulous, whereas Lloyd George did not. Winston was so transparent a deceiver on the rare occasions when he

Churchill at the time of the Oldham election

Colleagues in the Cabinet: Churchill and John Morley

Churchill and his devoted private secretary, Eddie Marsh,
with senior French officers

Attending German Army maneuvers in 1909

Attending army maneuvers with Mrs. Churchill at Aldershot, 1910

attempted to deceive that his ultimate sincerity was beyond doubt, whereas Lloyd George's sincerity was often questioned by those who were not under his spell.

It is told of Aristide Briand that at the close of an impassioned oration a friend asked him: "Were you really sincere in what you said?" Briand replied: "How should I know?" If, instead of being an illusioned Celt, Lloyd George had been a disenchanted Latin he might well have replied with the same question. As it was he had no doubts. He was always absolutely sincere at any given moment. If there was any deception he was his own first dupe. In much later years when he had broken with the Liberal Party and was leading the postwar coalition I remember being reproached by Winston for saying of Lloyd George in a speech that "he never sold his soul—he sometimes pawned it" (a theme elaborated with contemporary illustrations). But when I asked him if he thought it true he only replied gently: "Draw it mild, my dear—draw it mild." And then he added reflectively: "My father would have said it. He would not have hesitated to say it." (I gratefully accepted both comments as a high tribute to my invective!)

But in 1908 though I had watched and admired his public performance I had seen little of Lloyd George in private life. When we moved into Downing Street and he became our next-door neighbor * I saw more of him and I was neither skeptical nor spellbound. Winston, near by at the Board of Trade, often looked in to see my father and came down to talk to me in my little sitting room on the garden on his way out. I began to notice a new political inflection in his attitudes and even in his words. I remember saying to him one day: "You've been talking to Lloyd George." "And why shouldn't I?" he replied defensively. "Of course there's no reason why you shouldn't, but he's 'come off' on you. You are talking like him instead of like yourself." He rebutted this accusation by saying that they saw eye to eye on every subject so of course they spoke alike. He added fervently that Lloyd George was a man of genius, the greatest political genius he had ever met. *"You* like him, don't you? *You* admire him too?" I said that I delighted in his society and was always glad to find myself beside him at a meal. And this was true. He was so quick, so responsive, so amusing and so easy to amuse, and he always wanted to please whoever he was talking to. It was this desire to meet everyone, not halfway but all the way, that made me feel that I had no bearings where he was concerned. I always

* The official house of the Chancellor of the Exchequer is No. 11 Downing Street.

felt that he was saying to me what he guessed I wanted to hear, and in my case he sometimes guessed wrong. When I deliberately steered the talk toward a corner he skidded—and we were back on the fairway. Still I might have found this technique flattering if I had not seen it instantly reapplied to his neighbor on the other side, who often happened to be chalk to my cheese. Which was his real self? Not only great audiences but insignificant individuals seemed to have the power of creating him in their own image, for the moment at least. I once asked Maynard Keynes: "What do you think happens to Mr. Lloyd George when he is alone in the room?" Maynard replied: "When he is alone in the room there is nobody there."

Politically I felt wholehearted agreement with and admiration for him. But somehow the words that rang true in his mouth rang false in Winston's. For the first time in my experience of him I felt that he was— quite unconsciously—wearing fancy dress, that he was not himself.

Another feature of their relationship which I observed was that whereas Winston was staunchly loyal to Lloyd George and would not tolerate the mildest criticism or even discussion of his merits, Lloyd George was quite ready to enjoy and to repeat amusing stories at Winston's expense. He was delighted when someone described Winston as being "frank without being straight." "You've hit the nail on the head! That's exactly what he is!" If anyone suggested in Winston's presence that Lloyd George (a veritable corkscrew) lacked straightness his hand would at once have gone to the hilt of his sword.

When my father went to Biarritz to kiss hands, the four key appointments in his Cabinet were published by the *Daily Chronicle*. This caused dismay among his colleagues because the appointments had not yet been submitted to the King and their publication was a serious breach of constitutional procedure. Moreover the leak could only have come through one of them. My father's principal private secretary, Vaughan Nash, whom he had inherited from Sir Henry Campbell-Bannerman, reported that the Editor of the *Daily Chronicle* had telephoned and asked him in all innocence whether he would add to the information about Cabinet changes which had already been given to him by Mr. Lloyd George. Edward Grey, Haldane, Lord Crewe and even John Morley were furious at these disclosures and raised the matter with my father at dinner on the night of his return from Biarritz. Winston came in after dinner and made a passionate defense of Lloyd George assuring my father that he had indignantly denied having given the names to the press. I am sure that Winston believed in his innocence, and equally sure that no one else did.

But in spite of occasional breezes of this kind the Cabinet was at this time a happy family. The Lloyd George-Winston alliance, though suspect, had not yet become a factious element which threatened its unity.

Winston was doing excellent work at the Board of Trade. His first achievement was the Trade Boards Act. Charles Booth had revealed the scandal of the sweatshops in which the submerged men and women of the slums (and particularly the women) worked in shocking conditions for long hours and low wages without the protection of Trade Unions or Factory Acts. A Royal Commission had been set up as far back as 1889 to examine this evil. Sir Charles Dilke had then proposed the setting up of Trade Boards with powers to impose minimum wages in all the sweated industries. But the Home Office of the day took no action. Winston seized the idea and carried the Trade Boards Act.

He then attacked the problem of unemployment. In 1909 Mr. W. H. Beveridge (later Lord Beveridge) had written a book on unemployment which revealed that the workless were in most cases casual laborers. He advocated the setting up of labor exchanges where those in search of work could find new jobs, a German device, which had been recommended by the Webbs in their minority report of the Poor Law Commission. This was a task which properly belonged to the Local Government Board, but its President, John Burns, was unsusceptible to new ideas and averse to new departures. Winston was neither. He grasped the opportunity and established labor exchanges throughout the country. Though he was not the originator of either of these measures he was the first to translate them into action. He also promised and planned a scheme of insurance against unemployment which became law in 1911 as part of the National Insurance Act. This caused considerable annoyance to Lloyd George, who wanted to be in charge of Unemployment Insurance as well as his own Insurance Bill. "I had a weak moment," he told the Master of Elibank, "when Winston was at the Board of Trade. I told him about my plans. He promptly went off with them to his own Department; and then got permission from Asquith to frame a Bill on the lines I had proposed, and to introduce it himself." [3]

Meanwhile my father, though Prime Minister, had introduced his third and last Budget, which was generally praised and welcomed. Its only controversial feature was the one to which he himself attached the greatest value, the grant of Old Age pensions for which he had been saving assiduously during his years at the Exchequer. Though it gave only five shillings a week to those who had not more than twenty-one pounds a year it was denounced by the Opposition as a dangerous and extravagant measure which would undermine the thrift and self-respect of the working classes. In the House of Lords Lord Lansdowne said that the arguments seemed to him "conclusive against it." He declared that Old Age pensions would cost as much as a war without a war's advantages, since a war has at any rate the effect of strengthening the moral fiber of the nation "whereas this measure, I am much afraid, will weaken the moral fibre and diminish the self-respect of the people." Lord Rosebery went so far as to fear that "a scheme so prodigal of expenditure" would be "dealing a blow at the Empire which might be almost mortal." In spite of these forebodings (which illustrate the political atmosphere of those days) the House of Lords did not dare to reject Old Age pensions. After registering a solemn protest they swallowed the pill. My father made it clear that this was only a "modest and tentative" first step toward dealing with the problem of poverty. The reform of the Poor Law, sickness and unemployment were still to come.

In the autumn the Government's Licensing Bill, which had twice been approved by large majorities in the House of Commons, was thrown out by the House of Lords. King Edward, who was rightly alarmed by the reckless course they were pursuing, had privately interceded with Lord Lansdowne to amend rather than reject it and warned him that "if the attitude of the Peers was such as to suggest the idea that they were obstructing an attempt to deal with the evils of intemperance, the House of Lords would suffer in popularity." His warning went unheeded.

After the rejection, at a dinner given in his honor by Liberal Members of Parliament in recognition of the way in which he had conducted the Bill through the House of Commons, my father said: "The question I want to put to you and to my fellow-Liberals outside is this: 'Is this state of things to continue?' We say that it must be brought to an end, and I invite the Liberal Party tonight to treat the veto of the House of Lords as the dominating issue in politics—the dominating issue because in the long run it overshadows and absorbs every other." This declaration commanded the eager and impatient assent of every member of the party.

But another very different issue was to arise, fraught with far-reaching consequences. On October 5th Austria had proclaimed, without warning or negotiation, the annexation of Bosnia and Herzegovina, two provinces of the Turkish Empire which she had administered since the

Treaty of Berlin. On the following day Bulgaria declared her independence. Turkey protested strongly, Serbia mobilized her army. Both denounced Austria's lawless action and demanded compensation. Russia supported Serbia, Germany backed Austria. Great Britain had no interest in the status of Bosnia and Herzegovina, but Edward Grey and my father felt that we could not ignore the tearing up of a treaty to which all the Great Powers were signatory. Great Britain, supported by Russia and France, therefore proposed a conference of the Powers. Austria, supported by Germany, refused to take part in it. Edward Grey made it clear to Russia that, while giving her full diplomatic support, Great Britain would on no account be drawn into war. Meanwhile he labored unceasingly to restrain Serbia and to pacify Turkey. Austria then threatened to declare war on Serbia unless she recognized the annexations, and Prince Bülow informed Russia that unless Serbia gave way and Russia herself gave the same recognition, without informing Britain or France, Germany "would leave Austria a free hand." Faced by the threat of war with Austria and Germany, Russia collapsed and capitulated. The policy of the mailed fist, which had swept Delcassé from power in France, had triumphed again. Edward Grey, whose only part had been to defend the sanctity of treaties and to work for a peaceful solution, was now accused by Austria and Germany of having fomented trouble and sought to provoke a European war.

My father and Edward Grey were both profoundly disquieted by this affair. As Edward Grey wrote in his memoirs it was recognized in after years as a kind of dress rehearsal for 1914. In that year as in 1909 Russia was challenged to defend Serbia. "In 1909 Russia preferred humiliation; in 1914 she faced war." [4]

Our turn was now to come. Our accepted naval policy was that of the two-power standard, i.e., a preponderance of 10 per cent over the combined strength in capital ships of the next two strongest powers. In April, 1908, the German Government introduced a new Navy Law which increased the German program to four capital ships a year. Tirpitz had also enabled German establishments to expand their capacity and accumulate guns and armor in advance so that ships could be completed before the scheduled time. It was therefore possible that unless we increased our rate of shipbuilding Germany might outbuild us in capital ships by the year 1914.

Mr. McKenna, the First Lord of the Admiralty, backed by his Sea Lords, demanded the immediate construction of six Dreadnoughts. He wished the same number to be laid down in each of the two following years, making eighteen in all. It did not surprise me to hear that this proposal had been fiercely opposed in the Cabinet by Mr. Lloyd George. He had never been much concerned either with defense or with foreign affairs, and as Chancellor of the Exchequer he would be obliged to raise some sixteen millions to pay for the new ships. He needed all the money he could lay hands on for the new social services, more especially for the sickness and unemployment insurance schemes which were now being prepared. His opposition seemed to me to be natural and in character.

But what amazed and bewildered me was to see Winston aligned with him—like Bottom "magically translated" into a little-Navy man. I remembered his great speech in the House of Commons (already quoted) in which he had accused the Army of hydrophobia and gloried in belonging to the "trust the Navy school" which Brodrick ridiculed. I thought of his acute awareness of the shape and trend of world events. Had he not felt the ground tremble under our feet during the Bosnia-Herzegovina crisis? I thought of his pugnacity. First France and then Russia had been browbeaten into submission by Germany. Now she was threatening to outbuild us on the seas. Every reflex in his being would normally have responded to such a challenge. Yet he was now proclaiming to his audiences that Germany had "nothing to fight about, no prize to fight for, no place to fight in." [5] What had happened to him?

My father was equally astounded. For the first time he expressed deep disappointment in Winston. It was a personal wound, because he had set such high hopes on him. He took Lloyd George's opposition for granted, as I had done, but he felt Winston's to be out of keeping with his true character and convictions. He said to me one day with great sadness: "I am afraid that Winston is proving himself to be thoroughly untrustworthy." Press and lobby were reputedly informed and canvassed by both. This was Lloyd George's habitual technique, but it had never before been Winston's practice to fight his Cabinet battles by calling in forces from outside. The proposed Naval estimates and the dissensions among Ministers were discussed in all the newspapers. (Charles Masterman, a member of the Government, records that he got his first information of the situation from Massingham.) The *Times* wrote: "It is well known that not long ago a section of the Cabinet headed by the Chancellor of the Exchequer and the President of the Board of Trade attempted a raid on the financial requirements of the War Office and was defeated. It would surprise no one if this same section of the Cabinet . . . should now seek to cover its retreat by a demonstration in force having for its object a material reduction of the Navy estimates as prepared by the Board of Admiralty. . . . The present Chancellor of the Exchequer is avowedly in search of hen-roosts to rob and the Navy Estimates may well seem to offer a very tempting field for his depredations. The hereditary zeal of the President of the Board of Trade for public economy, especially at the expense of the defensive services of the Crown, is one of the most engaging traits in his political character." [6]

The controversy in the Cabinet was violent. Resignation was threatened by McKenna and hinted at by Lloyd George. Lulu Harcourt, Loreburn and Morley, who at the outset seemed inclined to side with the little Navyites, in the end veered back. Edward Grey stood firm behind the Admiralty from start to finish. On February 20th my father wrote to my stepmother, who was away in Switzerland: "The economists are in a state of wild alarm and Winston and Lloyd George by their combined machinations have got the bulk of the Liberal Press into the same camp. There is no real danger in the Cabinet—both John Morley and Lulu Harcourt for various reasons being very disinclined to make common cause with the other two. They (the two) go about darkly hinting at resignation (which is bluff) and there will in any case be lot of steam let off and at any rate a temporary revival of the old pro-Boer animus. I am able to keep a fairly cool head amidst it all but there are moments when I am disposed summarily to cashier them both. Edward Grey is a great stand-by always sound, temperate and strong."

There are amusing side lights on the controversy to be found in Lord Fisher's published correspondence. The letters reveal that Winston made many exploratory approaches to his friend and ally but got very little change out of him. In a letter dated February 28, 1909, Fisher wrote to McKenna: "After writing to you last night I went to the Athenaeum to read the 'Nation.' Presently Winston came in. I nodded and went on reading. When I went out he followed me out. I told him that I could not discuss the naval situation with him. He was extremely cordial and expressed his anxiety about my future. I told him as a great secret that my future was twenty Dreadnoughts before April 1912! This rather upset him and we parted. This morning I have a huge letter from him. It's marked 'Personal, Secret and Private' so I can't send it you but I send my reply. He indicates an inquiry into the Admiralty administration etc. He knows that would imply want of confidence and would enforce resignation. . . . My idea is we shall come out on top. It is not his!"

The reply to Winston which he enclosed runs as follows:

PRIVATE, PERSONAL AND SECRET
My dear Winston,

I appreciate your kind motive in writing me your long letter of to-day's date. I confess I never expected you to turn against the Navy after all you had said in public and in private. ("Et tu Brute!") I am sure you won't expect me to enter into discussion with you as there can be only one exponent of the Admiralty case—the First Lord. As to want of foresight on the part of the Admiralty, the Sea-Lords expressed their grave anxiety in a memorandum presented to the First Lord in December 1907. The Cabinet ignored that anxiety and cut down the Estimates. You want to do the same again! We can take no risks this year—last year we did. We felt then there would be time to pull up—the margin is now exhausted.

I reciprocate your grief at our separation. I retain the memory of many pleasant duets!

In spite of this cold douche Winston's hopes evidently remained unquenched for he continued to write to Fisher and on March 4th received the following reply:

PRIVATE AND SECRET
My dear Winston,

Thanks for your letter . . . and more especially for its concluding French words of your unaltered feelings towards me. It's kind of you to send me these Cabinet revelations. It's too sad and most deplorable. Let us write the word 'Finis'. The Apostle is right! The tongue is the very devil! (N.B. Yours is slung amidships and wags at both ends!)

Yours till the Angels smile on us! (Four more Dreadnoughts!!!)

J.F.

I told Marsh I had burnt your previous letter. No eye but mine had seen it. I have also burnt this one just come from you for the same reason! *'Amantium irae amoris integratio est!'* Have you got the same cook as at Bolton Street?

I think it would be quite lovely to call the four extra Dreadnoughts

NO 1 'Winston'
NO 2 'Churchill'
NO 3 'Lloyd'
NO 4 'George'

How they would fight! Uncircumventable! Read this out to the Cabinet! [7]

I saw very little of Winston during this crisis, in which he knew beyond a doubt that I was not on his side. At the outset I asked him about the revelations to the press and he denied having made them. We argued about the issue and I told him I would rather hear Lloyd George's views straight from the horse's mouth than at second hand through his own. It was not our disagreement that I minded but the sense that he had forsaken his own lights. I was of course annoyed with him on my father's behalf but far more so on his own. I could not bear to see him in this (to me) unrecognizable and abject state of tutelage. I thought of the line "O! what a noble mind is here o'erthrown"—though I cannot say that in any other respect he resembled Hamlet! He was neither distraught nor mad. On the contrary, he was collected, militant and rather cock-a-hoop. I also minded seeing him lose the confidence of many who had always trusted him, and of some who had just begun to trust him, and rejoicing the hearts of his enemies and detractors. One of these crowed to me: "What have you got to say for him now— your treacherous little gutter genius?" and I found it hard to make an effective defense, although I did my best.

My father, who had never any doubt what we should do, had had to strive by every means to keep his Cabinet together and carry it with him and he succeeded in the end. On February 25th he wrote: "We had our final Cabinet on the Navy yesterday and I was quite prepared for a row and possible disruption. A sudden curve developed itself of which I took immediate advantage with the result that, strangely enough, we came to a conclusion which satisfied McKenna and Grey and also Lloyd George and Winston. The effect will be to make us stronger in 1912 than McKenna's original proposal would have done."

McKenna had demanded six dreadnoughts; Lloyd George and Winston Churchill had insisted that four were enough. My father finally satisfied them all by proposing that four should be laid down immediately and money voted for a contingent four to be laid down in the following year *or earlier if the need was proved*.

The extra four were in fact by general agreement laid down in July, a decision which was probably attributed by many to the success of the popular music hall song "We want eight and we won't wait." And though this slogan was not a decisive factor it was a true expression of the public mind and mood. Five dreadnoughts were laid down in each of the following years, thus giving the Admiralty the total of eighteen they had demanded.

What judgment did Winston pass upon his own performance when he looked back on it in after years? His explanation of his attitude, almost amounting to an apology, can be read in *The World Crisis*. On his association with Lloyd George he wrote that "in general, though from different angles, we leaned to the side of those who would restrain the froward both in foreign policy and in armaments." (It would have been difficult to apply the epithet "froward" to Edward Grey.) On the demand for six Dreadnoughts he wrote: "I was still a sceptic about the danger of the European situation, and not convinced by the Admiralty case. . . . I proceeded at once to canvass this scheme and to examine the reasons by which it was supported. The conclusions which we both reached were that a programme of four ships would sufficiently meet our needs." After a detailed analysis of the reasons on which these conclusions were based he added that "there can be no doubt whatever that, so far as facts and figures were concerned, we were strictly right. . . . In the end a curious and characteristic solution was reached. The Admiralty had demanded six ships: the economists offered four and we finally compromised on eight. . . . But although the Chancellor of the Exchequer and I were right in the narrow sense, we were absolutely wrong in relation to the deep tides of destiny. The greatest credit is due to the first Lord of the Admiralty, Mr. McKenna, for the resolute and courageous manner in which he fought his case and withstood his Party on this occasion. Little did I think, as this dispute proceeded, that when the next Cabinet crisis about the Navy arose our rôles would be reversed; and little did he think that the ships for which he contended so stoutly would eventually, when they arrived, be welcomed with open arms by me." [8]

This is a generous amende, particularly in its eulogy of McKenna, a colleague for whom he felt a dislike which was heartily reciprocated. But that any human influence could have made him insensible to the "deep tides of destiny," of which he had always been so intimately aware, was an unfathomable mystery which continued to haunt me long after the Navy crisis was over. I knew that it was no good asking him to explain the inexplicable. Close friendship and constant interchange went on, but on both sides there were reservations. His relationship with Lloyd George became a buried subject between us. He could not confide in me their joint aims and agreed strategy—and still less the disagreements which were to arise between them later on.

And private disagreements were to arise much sooner than I could have guessed. The Government was faced with the problem of paying for the Dreadnoughts without sacrificing its plans for social reform. Out of this necessity was born the so-called People's Budget.

Chapter Sixteen

THE GADARENE PLUNGE

I HAVE seen it stated by some historians and biographers that the Budget was a strategic ruse deliberately framed to provoke the House of Lords into rejecting it, thus digging their own graves. Mr. Malcolm Thomson in his biography of Mr. Lloyd George even goes so far as to say that *as such* it had my father's approval. I can vouch for the fact that so far as my father was concerned there is not a vestige of truth in this suggestion. He would never have lent himself or his Government to such a tactic. During the controversy he repeatedly expressed his belief, both in private and public, that the House of Lords would never throw out a money bill.

Winston Churchill, who was certainly in Lloyd George's confidence, said (in a speech at Norwich on July 26th): "Opportunity is fickle, opportunity seldom returns; but . . . if, as an act of class warfare, for it would be nothing less, the House of Lords were to destroy the Budget, and thus not only create a Constitutional deadlock of novel and unmeasured gravity, but also plunge the whole finance of the country into unparalleled confusion, then, in my judgement, opportunity, clear, brilliant, and decisive, would return, and we should have the best chance we have ever had of dealing with them once for all. These circumstances may never occur. *I don't believe they will occur. If we only all stand firm together I believe the Budget will be carried.*" [1]

And as late as October 9th in a speech at the National Liberal Club he said: "I have never been able to rank myself among those who believe that the Budget will be rejected by the House of Lords. . . . In common with most of us who are here tonight I hold that the rejection of the Budget by the House of Lords would be a constitutional outrage. I do not think we are entitled to assume that such an outrage will be committed. We cannot credit such intentions even though we read them every day brutally and blatantly affirmed by a powerful Party Press. We do not credit such intentions. I have heard it often said, and I have read it more often still, that there are some members of the Cabinet who want to see the Budget rejected, and I have even been shocked to find myself mentioned as one of these Machiavellian intriguers. To those who say we want to see the Budget rejected I reply 'That is not true'."

Though I cannot presume to vouch for Mr. Lloyd George's motives, I do not believe that when he framed the Budget he had any such idea in his mind. His aim and that of the Government was to salvage their schemes of social reform (1) by raising the means to finance them and (2) by including some of these measures in the Budget to insure them against rejection by the House of Lords. On Lord Lansdowne's own admission it was to its connection with the Budget that old-age pensions owed their escape.*

It is true that as the battle proceeded and rejection hung in the balance Lloyd George may well have hoped for it. He is quoted by Charles Masterman as saying: "I'm not sure we ought not to hope for its rejection. It would give us such a chance as we shall never have again." [2] I myself remember an explosion of anger from Edward Grey (who was not often angry) when it was reported that in the course of the General Election which followed Lloyd George had boasted of having set a trap to catch the Lords, and adding that he was proud that this idea had come from Wales. "If it is true that he said *that* I shall certainly call attention to it and see that it is denied. It isn't *his* Budget —we never laid a trap—it's monstrous!" But these hopes and boasts of Lloyd George's came only as afterthoughts, when the battleground had shifted from the merits of the Budget itself to the constitutional issue raised by rejection. They were *esprit d'escalier* which did not represent his original purpose.

What was this Budget, regarded both by its opponents and by its supporters as a sensational and revolutionary measure? Reading its provisions today it is difficult to understand either the fury it provoked or the enthusiasm it aroused. It seems a flea bite now and it was not much more in 1909. Income tax raised from one shilling to one shilling and two pence, the yield of death duties increased from two millions to four, supertax introduced for the first time but at so low a rate that on the

* Because the Lords (by age-long tradition) could not reject a money bill.

highest incomes it amounted to one shilling and nine pence. This was the most important new departure it contained but by no means the most controversial. Children's allowances of ten pounds were granted on incomes under five hundred pounds. Taxes on tobacco, spirits and license duties were raised. Petrol and motor licenses were taxed to finance the improvement of the roads, now exposed to the wear and tear of the new motor traffic. What could be milder or more reasonable?

But the teeth of the Budget lay in the Land Taxes. There were taxes on undeveloped land and on the increase in its value, on its so-called "unearned increment." Even more bitterly resented was a plan for the valuation of all land throughout the country. These were the clauses which inflamed the Tory peers and landowners who saw in them a predatory onslaught on their property and perhaps even more upon their status. It was not only the purse but the power of the landlord which was at stake.

The furious reaction of the ruling classes played a great part in aligning popular support behind the Budget. It was felt that if the rich hated it so bitterly it must be a good thing for the poor. And it was thus that it was presented by Lloyd George in a series of speeches of which one of the most characteristic, delivered at Limehouse in the East End of London, is famous for having given that name to this particular brand of oratory. Here is a sample: "A few months ago a meeting was held not far from this hall demanding that the Government should launch out and run into an enormous expenditure on the Navy and they promised support for the Government in this undertaking. What has happened since then to alter their tone? Simply that we have sent in the bill. Well somebody has got to pay but these gentlemen say they would rather it was somebody else. We sent it among the workers and they all brought their coppers. We sent it round Belgravia but they raised such a howl that we have been completely deafened by it.

"They say 'It's not the Dreadnoughts we object to; we object to the Pensions'. But if they object to the Pensions why did they promise them? They won Elections in the past on the strength of these promises but they never carried them out. . . . Provision for the aged poor—it is time it was done. It's a shame for a rich country like ours that it should allow those who have toiled all their days to end in starvation. It's rather hard that an old workman should have to find his way to the tomb, bleeding and footsore through the brambles and thorns of poverty. We cut a new path through them, an easier one, a pleasanter one through fields of waving corn."

Such appeals may have had little bearing on the merits of the Land Taxes but they were all the more effective on that account. Lord Milner said truly that if my father had been in charge of the People's Budget it would have been much less popular—and unpopular. Looking back on the chain reaction of events it set in motion, it was perhaps fortunate that it was in other hands. My father was, however, a wholehearted supporter of the land taxes, though always (and, as it proved, rightly) skeptical about their financial yield. But there were dissentients in the Government and Winston was one of them. He did not oppose Lloyd George in the Cabinet but pleaded with him in private.

An interesting note by Charles Masterman is published in his life. "Mr. Lloyd George's proposals had few friends then. I remember a prolonged walk one evening in St. James's Park in the light of a gorgeous sunset over Buckingham Palace, Mr. Churchill trying to persuade Mr. Lloyd George and myself to permit him to announce at a meeting to be held, I think, at Edinburgh next day, that we had dropped one of the most controversial of these small imposts. He departed exceeding sorrowful. . . . The taxes were saved, as Mr. Lloyd George recently announced, by the action of Mr. Asquith when a vote in the Cabinet would have rejected them by an overwhelming majority.

"The critical debate was on the clause authorizing the valuation of all the land of England. The Opposition had assembled to laugh it out of court. The Chancellor of the Exchequer was called away by a domestic bereavement. Mr. Asquith undertook to defend a proposition perhaps as unpopular on the Liberal as on the Conservative side. . . ." [3]

I think that Mr. Masterman greatly exaggerates the Liberal opposition to the land taxes both in the Cabinet and among the rank and file of the party. In the long struggle both showed complete solidarity in their support of the Budget from start to finish.

There are other passages in this book which throw light on the ups and downs of Winston's relations with Lloyd George. Lloyd George is quoted as commenting with contempt on the idea that Winston was the author of the Budget. "Winston," he said, "is opposed to pretty nearly every item in the Budget except the 'Brat'.* . . . But all the same he said he had been doing very well in the country." Winston was President of the Budget League, a retort to the Budget Protest League which had been formed under the Presidency of Mr. Walter Long.

---

* An allusion to a provision in the Budget for Children's Allowances in the form of a rebate of £10 in income tax for every child under sixteen, applying to incomes under £500.

Mrs. Masterman gives an account of a luncheon she attended with her husband at No. 11 Downing Street, at which Lloyd George entertained them with a description of a dinner with Winston a few nights before. Both he and Masterman were in high spirits and began "talking wildly, absolutely in fun, of the revolutionary measures they were proposing next: the guillotine in Trafalgar Square and nominating for the first tumbril. Winston . . . became more and more indignant and alarmed, until they suggested that this would give him a splendid opportunity of figuring as the second Napoleon of the revolutionary forces, when, still perfectly serious, Winston, as George put it, seemed to think there was something in it. 'It is extraordinary,' said George, 'I had no idea anyone could have so little sense of humour'." Masterman then reported how Winston, as they walked home together after the dinner, had said "with great solemnity: 'If this is what it leads to, you must be prepared for me to leave you.' "

At a much later date Mrs. Masterman describes a breakfast at No. 11 at which the relative merits of reform of the House of Lords and the abolition of the veto were discussed. Winston was strongly pro-reform and anti-veto. Lloyd George had coquetted with reform but now, feeling the way the wind was blowing in the party, had slid back to veto.

"Somebody mentioned Winston again. George got a little indignant. It is very difficult to say whether a tiny element of jealousy does not enter in. Certain it is that at that moment he was not in George's good graces. 'Winston was up here last night and he got just as he did that time in the spring. You remember, Masterman, he began to fume and kick up the hearth-rug, and became very offensive, saying: "You can go to Hell your own way—I won't interfere. I'll have nothing to do with your —— policy," and was almost threatening, until at last I had to deal very faithfully with him, and remind him that no man can rat twice. The question is how long he takes about it and how much harm he does in the meantime. If he begins going to Asquith and Grey and Haldane' . . . George shook his head partly in anxiety, and partly, I fancy, a little in threat." Mrs. Masterman adds: "Winston, of course, is not a democrat, or at least, he is a Tory democrat. He cursed Charlie one night when they dined together à deux, swearing that he would resign sooner than accept the Veto policy and again spend four years with Sir Ernest Cassel, getting rich: then again and again repeating 'No, no, no: I *won't* follow George if he goes back to that damned Veto'. Three weeks afterwards he was making passionate speeches in favour of the Veto policy. He became cantankerous and very difficult, and, said

George, 'for three weeks while he is at a thing, he is very persistent, but he always comes to heel in the end', which is a very true description of him."

These stories describe Winston Churchill as I did not know him. But they explain and justify the uneasiness I felt about him during this period of his life, an anxiety which was not so much political as personal. Whether right or wrong he had always taken his stand on the rock of his own convictions. He seemed now to be slithering in a quicksand, an element quite alien to his nature. But within a year he began to regain his foothold and in the meantime in his public utterances to speak again in his own accents.

I shall not attempt to record here the long and hard-fought battle for the Budget. Its introduction was admittedly a flop. I went to the House of Commons, agog to hear it, and I failed to sit it out. For four and a half hours the Chancellor read his speech, and it was read so badly that to some he gave the impression that he did not himself understand it. So little was it understood by others that the *Times* described it on the following day as "unadventurous."

When its implications became clear to the Opposition the storm broke and raged both in the House of Commons and in the country for the next seven months. The House sat without intermission all through the summer. On October 8th it adjourned for one week, reassembled, carried the Bill by 230 votes and sent it to the Lords. During these months a fast and furious campaign was waged throughout the country, memorable for the exchanges between the Chancellor of the Exchequer and the Dukes: Mr. Lloyd George was at his best—and worst. He poured a devastating fire of wit, invective, eloquence and ridicule upon the great landowners of the peerage, and in particular upon the Dukes, whom he arraigned as enemies of the people. "A fully equipped Duke," he said, "costs as much to keep up as two Dreadnoughts; and Dukes are just as great a terror and they last longer." His description of the eldest sons of peers as "the first of the litter," though it delighted his audiences and outraged his opponents, caused some of his more squeamish colleagues and supporters (including—surprisingly —John Burns) to wince and squirm. King Edward was gravely displeased by the tone of these speeches and begged my father to restrain the language of the Chancellor of the Exchequer, which he described as "Billingsgate." Whatever my father's own reaction to the idiom of his colleague may have been, he must have put up a stout and loyal defense, for Lord Knollys wrote to him begging him not to "pretend to the King that he liked Mr. Lloyd George's speeches, for the King would not believe it and it only irritated him."

The peers at bay engaged in a counteroffensive which did nothing but good to their opponents. My stepmother remarked truly that "the speeches of our Dukes have given us a very unfair advantage." The Duke of Rutland described the whole Liberal Party as "a crew of piratical tatterdemalions"; words which hardly conjure up the image of Lord Crewe or of Sir Edward Grey. The Duke of Beaufort said he would like to see Winston Churchill and Lloyd George "in the middle of twenty couple of dog-hounds." The Duke of Somerset threatened reprisals for his impending ruin by sacking his estate hands and cutting off his gifts to charity. The Duke of Buccleuch withdrew his subscription of one guinea to the Dumfriesshire Football Club because of the dire need to which the Budget might reduce him. In spite of Lord Rosebery's plea that the Dukes belonged to "a poor but honest class" the public heart was unwrung by their hardships.

If Lloyd George was Enemy No. 1 to the Opposition Winston Churchill was certainly Enemy No. 2. Though he bore no more responsibility for the Budget than any of his Cabinet colleagues, it was felt that as the grandson of a Duke he ought to have "known better." He was a blueblooded blackleg who had once more "betrayed his class" and again from the lowest motives of self-advancement. As President of the Budget League he took an eloquent and active part in the campaign and his speeches aroused almost as much fury as those of Lloyd George. But they were wholly different in character. Both his defense of the Budget and his indictment of the House of Lords were fair, reasoned and statesmanlike, free from vulgarity, cheap sentiment or class catcalls.

On the House of Lords he said at Norwich (on July 26th): "Is it not an extraordinary thing that upon the Budget we should be discussing at all the action of the House of Lords? The House of Lords is an institution absolutely foreign to the spirit of the age and to the whole movement of society. It is not perhaps surprising in a country so fond of tradition, so proud of continuity as ourselves that a feudal assembly of titled persons with so long a history and so many famous names should have survived to exert an influence upon public affairs at the present time. We see how often in England the old forms are reverently preserved after the forces by which they are sustained and the dangers against which they were designed have passed away. A state of gradual decline was what the average Englishman had come to associate with the House of Lords. . . . Year by year it would have faded more completely into the past to which it belongs, until like Jack-in-the-Green and Punch and Judy, only a picturesque and fitfully lingering memory would have remained. And during the last ten years of Conservative Government this was actually the case.

"But now we see the House of Lords flushed with the wealth of the modern age, armed with a party caucus, fortified, revived, resuscitated, asserting its claims in the harshest and crudest manner, claiming to veto or destroy, even without discussion, any legislation however important, sent to them by any majority, however large, from any House of Commons however newly elected. . . . We see the House of Lords using the power which they should not hold at all, which if they hold at all they should hold in trust for all, to play a shrewd, fierce aggressive Party game of electioneering and casting their votes according to the interest of the particular party to which, body and soul, they belong."

In his second Budget my father had established the new principle of differentiation between earned and unearned income for purposes of taxation. At Leicester on September 5th Winston played relevant variations on this theme. "Formerly the only question asked by the tax-gatherer was: 'How much have you got?' . . . But now a new question has arisen. We do not only ask today 'How much have you got?' we also ask 'How did you get it? Did you get it by yourself, or has it just been left to you by others? Was it gained by processes which are in themselves beneficial to the community in general or was it gained by processes which have done no good to anyone, but only harm? . . .' That is the new question which has been postulated and which is vibrating in penetrating repetition through the land."

At the outset of this closely reasoned speech Winston indulged in a little Duke-baiting which incensed the Opposition and its press. He spoke of the "small fry of the Tory Party splashing actively about in their proper puddles," he complained of the dearth of speakers in the Tory party who could attempt to meet the Liberal arguments and of the fact that, *faute de mieux,* it had been obliged to fall back upon the Dukes. "These unfortunate individuals who ought to lead quiet, delicate, sheltered lives, far from the madding crowd's ignoble strife have been dragged into the football scrimmage, and they have got rather roughly mauled in the process. . . . Do not let us be too hard on them. It is poor sport—almost like teasing goldfish. These ornamental creatures blunder on every hook they see, and there is no sport whatever in trying to catch them. It would be barbarous to leave them gasping upon the bank of public ridicule upon which they have landed themselves. Let us put them back gently, tenderly in their fountains; and if a few bright scales have been rubbed off in what the Prime Minister calls the variegated handling they have received, they will soon get over it. They have got plenty more."

I remember asking Winston how this tickling of goldfish had been received at Blenheim by his ornamental cousin Sunny. Were his scales feeling sore? He replied loyally that though Sunny did not like the Budget he had kept out of the scrum. He had kept his hair on and his scales on.

By mid-September my father's faith in the ultimate sanity of the peers was shaken. In a speech at Birmingham he felt it necessary to warn them of the consequences of rejection. "Amendment by the House of Lords," he said, "is out of the question. Rejection by the House of Lords is equally out of the question. . . . Is this issue to be raised? If it is, it carries with it in its train consequences which he would be a bold man to forecast or foresee. That way revolution lies." *

He was summoned to Balmoral by the King early in October and found him gravely disturbed at the prospect of a head-on collision between the two Houses. The King asked him whether he would be acting within his constitutional rights in seeing the Tory leaders and seeking to advise and if necessary to put pressure on them at this juncture. My father replied that he thought it would be perfectly correct from a constitutional point of view and cited the analogy of William IV at the time of the Reform Bill. Within a week the King saw Lord Lansdowne and Mr. Balfour, who told him that they had not yet decided what action the House of Lords should be advised to take. There is, however, strong evidence that the die was in fact already cast.

Among the Unionist peers a wise majority strongly opposed rejection, arguing that such a course would not only be wrong itself but also an invitation to catastrophe. But they were overborne by the tariff reformers, the brewers and the panic-stricken men of property. Insane counsels prevailed. The Budget was rejected by the House of Lords on November 30th—an act without a precedent in the last two hundred and fifty years. My father moved a resolution in the House of Commons: "That the action of the House of Lords in refusing to pass into law the financial provision made by this House for the service of the year is a breach of the Constitution and a usurpation of the rights of the Commons." Parliament was dissolved and a general election followed.

* Birmingham, September 17, 1909.

The King intimated privately to my father that he felt he would not be justified in creating peers until a second general election had taken place. He regarded the Government's policy as tantamount to the destruction of the House of Lords and he thought that before a large creation of peers was embarked upon the country should be acquainted with the particular project for such destruction. My father was thus placed in a delicate and difficult position. He was unable to reveal the King's conditions to his party, for it was his paramount aim to protect the Crown from being involved in a political struggle. He entered the election with the knowledge that he would probably have to fight another before the King would be willing to use his prerogative in creating peers.

He opened the campaign at a great meeting at the Albert Hall (on December 10th) at which he thus defined the issue: "The people in future when they elect a new House of Commons must be able to feel that they are sending to Westminster men who will have the power, not merely of proposing and debating but of making laws." He also claimed freedom for a Liberal Government in the new House of Commons to deal with Home Rule.

The result of the election was a disappointment to all parties. The Conservatives, who had counted on victory, were again defeated; Labour representation was slightly diminished and the Government though returned to power lost 104 seats. Though they still had a clear majority of 63 in Great Britain they would be in a minority if the 82 Irish members voted against them. The only cheerful comment I heard was that of John Burns, who remarked philosophically: "Well, we've got rid of all the accentuated freaks this time!"

My father was very tired after the election and he and I went to the south of France for a few weeks' rest. Edward Grey, Lord Crewe and Jack Pease (a Liberal whip) came in to see us before we left. Discussing the election results, my father told us with amusement that Lloyd George had propounded a fantastic theory to account for the south going against us. "He said that we had won wherever there was Celtic blood, that it was the Anglo-Saxon races who had gone against us. I pointed to Yorkshire and Lancashire where we had gained seats. He stuck to the latter having Celtic blood, but he couldn't make much of a case!" Crewe, Grey and Pease alleged that it was not Anglo-Saxon blood but Lloyd George's own speeches which had lost us votes—at least in the Home Counties. My father then gave high praise to Winston and to his "change of tone." He said that the close reasoning of his speeches was that of a

real statesman. I was amazed to hear him compare Winston's Lancashire campaign to that of Gladstone in Midlothian, for Gladstone was my
father's idol. He had asked some of those who had listened to Winston's
speeches whether he had repeated himself at all and the answer was
"Never."

When I handed on this praise to Winston he glowed and purred with
pleasure. I asked him whether he thought Lloyd George had lost us
seats and he replied, quite truly, that he probably won us as many as
he lost, but added that he certainly said "a good many cheap things. At
any rate I was not going to compete in the same line of business." I
hailed this as a symptom of enfranchisement.

We discussed his impending promotion to the Home Office, a prospect which filled him with excitement and exhilaration. He was always
eager to move on and break new ground and he was already busily exploring the possibilities of his new kingdom. He would have a fine army
to command, the Police Force, but he was mainly preoccupied with the
fate of their quarry, the criminals. His own experience of captivity had
made him the prisoners' friend and his mind was seething with plans
for lightening their lot by earned remissions of sentence and, while "in
durance vile," by libraries and entertainment. "They must have food for
thought—plenty of books—that's what I missed most—except of course
the chance of breaking bounds and getting out of the damned place—
and I suppose I mustn't give them *that*!" I asked what books he thought
they would enjoy and he trotted out several old favorites from his first
days of self-education at Bangalore, headed by Gibbon and Macaulay.
I expressed some doubts about the popularity of his list. "If you had
just committed murder would you feel inclined to read Gibbon?" "Well,
the stern and speedy process of the law might place a noose around my
neck and string me up before I had had time to launch myself on that
broad stream. But for robbery with violence, arson, rape . . ." Here
followed a long inventory of crimes well fitted to whet the appetite of
their authors for Gibbon. I said that I would rather be hanged than endure a life sentence. He vehemently disagreed. "Never abandon life.
There is a way out of everything—except death." He was obviously confident of finding his way out of a life sentence and I daresay he was
right. I quoted Dickens: "Life is given us on the understanding that we
defend it to the last." He liked that and repeated it to himself. " 'Defend
it to the last'—I'd do it. So would you."

To say or quote a form of words which caught his fancy was like giving a sweet to a child. He sucked it, rolling it around his palate and ex-

tracting its full flavor. And it was astonishing how he remembered it. Often after a lapse of years he has quoted back to me words of which I had no recollection and when I asked: "Where does that come from?" he replied: "You said it" or "You quoted it to me"—sometimes remembering the time and place. He could not forget what he had liked, except occasionally on purpose, when his own past utterances conflicted with his present attitudes.

We returned from the Riviera to a difficult and perplexing situation. The morale of the party was low and when my father informed the House of Commons that he had neither received nor asked for guarantees from the King there was a gasp of disappointment from our backbenchers. There was also trouble with the Irish who wanted the Government to drop the whisky duties from the Budget and who threatened to vote against it unless they were assured that the passing of a bill dealing with the veto of the House of Lords was guaranteed during the present year. My father was unmoved by these threats and instructed the Chief Whip to tell Mr. Redmond (in other words, of course) that he could go to blazes.

But the most serious problem to be faced was the disunity in the Cabinet between those Ministers who regarded the reform of the House of Lords as the most urgent and important task and others who gave priority to dealing with its powers, by limiting the right of veto. Edward Grey felt strongly that reform and veto should be dealt with simultaneously. He was supported by Haldane, Winston and (surprisingly) for a short time by Lloyd George. My father disagreed. His view has been accurately recorded by his biographer, J. A. Spender: "In his own mind Veto and Reform were always in separate compartments. With or without Reform the curtailment of the Veto was essential, and no Reform which he ever contemplated was to entail the restoration of the Veto." On the question of reform his mind was clear: that "a Liberal Government would be extremely ill-advised to touch the composition of the Second Chamber until it had settled its powers." [4]

In this view he had the support of the majority of his colleagues and of the Liberal rank and file in Parliament and throughout the country. It is interesting that on this issue he should have given expression to the radical mind of the party while Lloyd George was, for a time at least, in line with its right wing.

A compromise was finally reached by attaching a preamble to the Parliament Bill which expressed the intention "to substitute for the House of Lords as it at present exists a Second Chamber constituted on a popular instead of hereditary basis," but recognized that "such a substitution cannot immediately be brought into operation." The words "cannot immediately" proved to be a wild understatement. The task of reforming the House of Lords is one to which subsequent Governments have paid lip service but from which each in turn has so far shied away.

The Government now laid before the House of Commons three Resolutions embodying the gist of the Parliament Bill. (1) The Lords could neither amend nor reject a money bill. (2) Their power of veto over ordinary legislation was restricted to two years and one month. (3) The duration of Parliaments was to be reduced from seven years to five. The Budget was reintroduced, passed by the House of Commons and accepted without a division by the House of Lords. I shall never forget the tension of the final debate on the Parliament Bill Resolutions in which my father gave this warning: "If the Lords fail to accept our policy . . . we shall feel it our duty immediately to tender advice to the Crown as to the steps which will have to be taken. . . . If we do not find ourselves in a position to ensure that statutory effect shall be given to that policy in this Parliament, we shall then either resign our offices or recommend the dissolution of Parliament. Let me add this, that in no case will we recommend a dissolution except under such conditions as will secure that in the new Parliament the judgement of the people as expressed at the Elections will be carried into law." [5]

The House of Commons now adjourned for a short holiday and my father went on a cruise to Gibraltar on the Admiralty yacht *Enchantress* with Mr. McKenna, Admiral Jellicoe and others. At the King's request they put in at Lisbon to pay their respects to King Manoel of Portugal and the Queen Mother. On May 5th my father reported on this visit to the King and received a telegram from him in reply: "Very glad you liked your stay at Lisbon and that the King was so pleasant. Edward R."

This was the last communication he was to receive from King Edward. He has recorded the events which followed: "We had passed Cadiz and were nearing Gibraltar when the First Lord and I received by wireless our first intimation of the King's illness. Lord Knollys's message to me was of a disquieting kind: 'Deeply regret to say the King's condition is now most critical'. On our arrival a few hours later at Gibraltar I at once gave instructions for our immediate return and on Friday May 6th I telegraphed to Lord Knollys as follows: 'Your telegram received. Am starting at once for home. Please convey my most fervent sympathy and hopes to the Queen and Prince of Wales. We shall be in constant telegraph contact by wireless throughout. Please keep me constantly informed'.

"At three o'clock in the morning of the following day . . . I received by wireless the terrible news of the King's death: 'I am deeply grieved to inform you that my beloved father the King passed away peacefully at a quarter to twelve to-night (the 6th). George'.

"I went up on deck, and I remember well that the first sight that met my eyes in the twilight before dawn was Halley's Comet blazing in the sky. It was the only time . . . that any of us saw it during our voyage. I felt bewildered and indeed stunned. At a most anxious moment in the fortunes of the State, we had lost, without warning or preparation, the Sovereign whose ripe experience, trained sagacity, equitable judgement and unvarying consideration, counted for so much. For two years I had been his Chief Minister, and I am thankful to remember that from first to last I never concealed anything from him. He soon got to know this, and in return he treated me with a gracious frankness which made our relationship in very trying and exacting times one, not always of complete agreement, but of unbroken confidence. It was this that lightened a load which I should otherwise have found almost intolerably oppressive: the prospect that, in the near future, I might find it my duty to give him advice which I knew would be in a high degree unpalatable.

"Now he had gone. His successor, with all his fine and engaging qualities, was without political experience. We were nearing the verge of a crisis almost without example in our constitutional history. What was the right thing to do? This was the question which absorbed my thoughts as we made our way . . . through the Bay of Biscay until we landed at Plymouth on the evening of May 9th." [6]

The political atmosphere was transformed by the King's death. Its dramatic suddenness had shocked the nation. When he returned only nine days before, from Biarritz, to all appearance in good health and spirits, he had attended a performance of *Rigoletto* at Covent Garden the same night. He visited the Royal Academy, and spent a week end at Sandringham, he gave audiences and transacted business until the very morning of his death.

King Edward, the gay Prince who became a wise King, was dearly loved by all sorts and conditions of men—partly because, unlike most kings, he had lived and moved among them. The fact that in his youth he had sought his friends outside Court circles and conventional compounds had given him a wide (though not perhaps a deep) experience of his fellow men. Though unfastidious he was shrewd, intensely human in his warmth of heart, his love of pleasure and his loyalty to friends, gregarious, tolerant, cosmopolitan, a seasoned citizen of the world. His successor, King George V, had had a very different background. As a second son he had not been born or brought up to be a king. His life in the Navy had been remote both from high politics and "high" society. He lacked the ease and the assurance of King Edward and above all his experience.

My father was deeply moved by his first audience with the new King and impressed by "his modesty and common sense." Queen Alexandra led him into the death chamber. Thence he went straight to the House of Commons to move the vote of condolence and make his tribute to King Edward. The funeral ceremonies followed and for a time all discords were hushed.

When a week later he had his second private audience with the King he felt a profound human reluctance to confront him at the outset of his reign with a constitutional decision which, on his own admission, he would have found it difficult, though imperative, to demand from his father. In his *Life and Reign of King George V* Sir Harold Nicolson has quoted the King's entry in his diary on that evening (May 18th): "I gave an audience to the Prime Minister. We had a long talk. He said he would endeavour to come to some understanding with the Opposition to prevent a General Election and he would not pay attention to what Redmond said." [7]

The last of these undertakings my father had already carried out. The first presented greater difficulty and involved political sacrifice of no mean order. But his deep, protective sympathy for the King and his personal revulsion from plunging the country back into violent controversy in the shadow of death and national mourning steeled him to do his best.

He approached Mr. Balfour and proposed a conference. The Opposition accepted eagerly. The King approved with wholehearted relief. The Government's supporters and allies were naturally less enthusiastic. There was suspicion and some resentment among the Irish, in the Labour Party and in a section of the Liberal rank and file. But my father had given his promise to the King and he was clear in his own mind that he had made the right decision. An armistice was declared.

The conference met for the first time on June 17th in the Prime Minister's room in the House of Commons. The Government was represented by the Prime Minister, Mr. Lloyd George, Lord Crewe and Mr. Birrell, the Opposition by Mr. Balfour, Lord Lansdowne, Mr. Austen

Chamberlain and Lord Cawdor. The proceedings were wrapped in secrecy. No progress reports were made to either party and there were genuine fears in both that principles and positions were being bargained away behind closed doors. My father, who genuinely desired agreement, was optimistic at the start, but after five months of what he described as "an honest and continuous effort" to reach a settlement he was obliged (on November 8th) to warn the King that on the subject of Home Rule there was "an apparently irreconcilable divergence of view." After two more meetings the conference broke down.

On the parts played by its members my father described Arthur Balfour as being "head and shoulders above his colleagues." It was at once his weakness and his strength that he saw, with almost crippling clarity, all sides of a case, and not least that of his opponents. Unfortunately his chief colleague, Lord Lansdowne, was by common consent the most obstinate and rigid of the negotiators—a pessimist from the outset, prepared to sacrifice a settlement of all other issues rather than yield an inch on Home Rule. Of all the eight the one who was prepared to go to the furthest lengths in compromise and concession was Mr. Lloyd George.

He harbored a design far more ambitious and far-reaching than that of settling the limited issues submitted to the conference. His aim, known only to a few, was nothing less than the formation of a coalition Government. This plan was outlined in a memorandum written at Criccieth on August 17th in which he urged that "joint action would make it possible to settle these urgent questions without paying undue regard to the formulae and projects of rival faddists." The inducements offered to the Conservative Party included (incredible as it may seem) military service on the Swiss model and an inquiry into tariff reform with an undertaking to act upon its findings. Winston was of course an ardent supporter of this project, although, to his credit, he approached it with more realism and greater reservations.

There is no doubt that Arthur Balfour and Lloyd George were, for the first time, strongly attracted to one another during the conference. Both were consummate artists in the exercise of charm and each proved susceptible to the other's mastery of this instrument. Although their mental processes and methods could not have differed more, both had an element of flexibility almost amounting to fluidity. Arthur Balfour might well have described the passionate differences of his own party in the fiscal controversy as "the formulae and projects of rival faddists." Lloyd George's sensitive intuition was quick to recognize this kinship. It is to Arthur Balfour that he would naturally have taken a proposal which treated principles as fads.

How was it in fact received by Arthur Balfour? Here again there is a wide conflict of evidence. The *Times* in its obituary speaks of his "declining participation in the intrigue." [8] Mr. Lloyd George in his *War Memoirs* writes that he "was by no means hostile; in fact, he went a long way towards indicating that personally he regarded the proposal with a considerable measure of approval. He was not, however, certain of the reception which would be accorded to it by his party." [9] Yet his biographer, Mrs. Dugdale, records that in answer to her question he said that he was never greatly attracted by the plan and remarked: "Now isn't that like Lloyd George. Principles mean nothing to him—never have. . . . He says to himself at any given moment: 'Come on now—we've all been squabbling too long, let's find a reasonable way out of the difficulty'—but such solutions are quite impossible for people who don't share his outlook on political principles—the great things." [10]

This sudden reversion to "the great things" was certainly precipitated, if not caused, by the intimation from the Conservative Chief Whip, Akers-Douglas, that the party would not tolerate so cynical a deal in principles and policies nor a sudden fraternization with men whom they had been taught to regard as robbers, revolutionaries and traitors. The coalition plan broke down.

On my father's part in the proceedings his biographer has written that "it may be stated with confidence that Asquith believed himself to have been fully informed of all that was going on" (the word "believed" is here significant) "and he was certainly aware that Mr. Lloyd George was conferring with Mr. Balfour. He was wholly sceptical about the possibility of a Coalition which could have agreed either on the question of the House of Lords or on Home Rule." [11] Those who imagined that either he or the party he led would have been willing to pay the price of compulsory military service or tariff reform must have been living in Cloud Cuckoo Land. His attitude is I think well described by Mr. Spender as watching "the progress of the business to its inevitable conclusion with a certain detached amusement." [12] I can remember only one comment from him, uttered with a sniff and a shrug: "I knew it would never come to anything."

The only Liberal mourners at the funeral were Winston and Lloyd George. And this time Winston was the one I understood the best. I did not mention the plan to him until it was all over and then only to comment on its inherent impossibility.

I could not guess at this time that except for "the first fine careless rapture" of these early years in the Liberal Party he would only be really happy and at ease in coalition Governments. Though a natural partisan he was never a party politician. In order to extend himself he needed a national or, better still, an international setting. Throughout his life he was never the orthodox mouthpiece of the voice of any party. He could not squeeze himself into the strait jacket of any ready-made doctrine. They were all misfits. The Tory Party would have seemed to be his natural home. But despite his historic sense of tradition he was untrammeled by convention. Despite his romantic feeling for the aristocracy his broad humanity transcended the boundaries of class. His intensely individual and adventurous mind, forever on the move, could never be contained by the Conservatives and its questing, restless brilliance often filled them with an unconcealed disquiet. The Liberals in their great days gave him more scope and a better run. To their credit they have never been afraid of quality, or even genius. But though a democrat to the bone, imbued with a deep reverence for Parliament and a strong sense of human rights, he was never quite a liberal. He never shared the reluctance which inhibits liberals from invoking force to solve a problem. And though he reveled in discussion he was by temperament an intellectual autocrat. He never liked having other people's way. He infinitely preferred his own.

With the breakdown of the conference on November 10th the truce was ended and the dream dissolved. On the same day the Cabinet met and decided to ask the King for an early dissolution, to be followed by an immediate General Election. King Edward had demanded a second election before using his prerogative and my father had naturally assumed that if he complied with this condition and the Government was returned with a decisive majority the King would, if necessary, consent to a creation of peers. It now became his duty to ascertain whether his successor King George V was prepared to take the same action.

If the King proved unwilling to do so the Government must resign.

It is not my purpose here to recount in detail the course of the difficult and delicate negotiations which followed. They have already been recorded by my father's biographers and by Sir Harold Nicolson in his *Life and Reign of King George V*. For the King the situation was complicated by the fact that his two private secretaries and closest advisers, Lord Knollys and Sir Arthur Bigge (later Lord Stamfordham), were giving him directly conflicting advice. The Cabinet had informed the King in a minute that "His Majesty's Ministers cannot take the responsibility of advising a dissolution unless they may understand that, in the event of the policy of the Government being approved by an adequate majority in the new House of Commons, His Majesty will be ready to exercise his constitutional powers (which may involve the prerogative of creating peers) if needed to secure that effect should be given to the decision of the country." The minute added that "it would be inadvisable . . . that any communication of the intentions of the Crown should be made public unless and until the occasion should arise."

Lord Knollys wrote to the King: "I feel certain that you can safely and constitutionally accept what the Cabinet propose and I venture to urge you strongly to do so." Sir Arthur Bigge was equally strongly opposed to the Cabinet's proposals and urged the King to refuse them. He was particularly indignant at hearing that when the King had asked Lord Knollys: "Is this the advice you would have given my father?" Lord Knollys had replied: "Yes, Sir, and he would have taken it."

The advice of Lord Knollys undoubtedly carried great weight with the King. The other factor which must have weighed with him was the insuperable difficulty of pursuing any other course. When, on November 16th, he received my father and Lord Crewe at Buckingham Palace he gave his consent. "I disliked having to do this very much," he wrote, "but agreed that this was the only alternative to the Cabinet resigning, which at this moment would be disastrous." [13] "I have never seen the King to better advantage," wrote my father. "He argued well and showed no obstinacy."

The King demanded that the Parliament Bill should be submitted to the House of Lords before the election and to this my father readily agreed. When, however, the Bill was presented to the peers Lord Lansdowne postponed its discussion and proceeded to bring forward proposals of his own for a "reduced and reconstituted" House of Lords. In the event of a difference between the two Houses on "a matter of great gravity which had not been adequately submitted to the judgement of the people" it should be put to a referendum. This was a far more revolutionary expedient than the limitation of the veto, for as my father said, it substituted a plebiscite for parliamentary government. It was said that many peers would have preferred the Parliament Bill.

One member of the Cabinet alone was shaken, not by the merits, but by the potential popular appeal of these proposals. Mr. Lloyd George, whose nerve and instinct rarely failed him, suffered a momentary loss of both over the referendum. I remember him rushing distraught and panic-stricken into my father's room at No. 10 and saying to him: "We're done! The referendum has killed us!" My father was amazed. He did not pride himself on any flair for "mass appeal" but he was quite sure that the referendum would have none. He applied first aid and Lloyd George left him looking better. "What did you do to restore his morale?" I asked. "I tried a little argument which didn't work and then I said to him: 'Why, its very *name* is against it!' Oddly enough that worked like magic."

In spite of doubts and misgivings in some quarters my father, advised and supported by his able and courageous Chief Whip, the Master of Elibank, decided on an immediate General Election. Never since the days of the first Reform Bill had there been two General Elections in one year. The prospect aroused fury in Conservative circles and charges of maneuvering and sharp practice were flung at the Government. To us these seemed unreasonable, for the breakdown of the conference had clearly demonstrated that what could not be settled in private must be settled in public.

The Liberals fought on the Parliament Bill, Home Rule and National Insurance. Against this the Conservatives proposed to deal with the House of Lords (neither they nor anyone else knew how) and offered Tariff Reform for the third time in succession—and the referendum.

Mr. Lloyd George reverted with apparent ease from his coalition cooings to his best Limehouse form. In a speech at Mile End at the outset of the campaign he arraigned the peers as the descendants of "plunderers," some of whom came over with William the Conqueror, while others had "plundered the poor at the Reformation." "An aristocracy," he said, "is like cheese; the older it is the higher it becomes." This fruity comparison brought us violent letters of protest in which some Liberals joined. Even Winston was critical and feared the effect upon our electoral fortunes. Nor was he placated by the passage which followed and which I thoroughly enjoyed—a retort to the Unionist accusation that the Irish were financing the election on American dollars. This charge related to a tour made by John Redmond and some Nationalist Members of Parliament in Canada and the United States to collect funds for the Home Rule cause, from which they had brought back forty thousand pounds. The subscribers, who included Sir Wilfrid Laurier, were eminently respectable. Yet Arthur Balfour himself had joined in the press outcry against the "dollar fund" by declaring (at Nottingham on November 17th) that "the Government were going to destroy the constitution at the will of American subscribers." Lloyd George punctured this nonsense with the question: "But since when has the British aristocracy despised American dollars? They have underpinned many a tottering noble house." This home truth drove the Duke of Marlborough, who had entertained the Chancellor in his "tottering" house at Blenheim, "publicly to denounce his reference to American heiresses."

A dramatic challenge was made by Bonar Law to Winston to fight him in North-West Manchester—Winston's old seat, which had rejected him in 1908 and been won back by a Liberal in 1910. A condition of the contest was that the loser should remain out of the next Parliament. Winston—uncharacteristically—refused, reflecting perhaps on past electoral hazards, on the bitterness of exile and the cast-iron safety of his fastness in Dundee. His acceptance would have deprived the Tory party of their future leader and might have changed the course of our political history. For Bonar Law was defeated, and if he had kept his bargain, he would have been out of Parliament until 1918.

Historians describe the election as a dull one. For me it was charged with tension and excitement, for everything depended upon its outcome.

It is agreed by judges more dispassionate than myself that my father dominated the campaign. He spoke in all parts of the country and, as Mr. Roy Jenkins has written, "he rained a series of hammer-blows on to the Opposition case." [14] I went with him to all his great meetings and I wondered at the freshness and the zest with which he fought. He seemed impervious to staleness or fatigue. His staying power and his unshaken purpose armed him for this, the final stage, in a long haul.

His constant preoccupation was the position of the King. He often said to me: "If we get in with a working majority the peers will give way without the King coming in at all—and if we don't have an adequate majority the contingency will never arise." "And shall we win?" "I am hopeful." (This I knew meant that he thought we should.) "I have staked everything on this and I shall see it through."

One day we all made guesses about the election figures. My stepmother and I (understating our hopes) plumped for twelve up on our present majority. My father put it at five. He was out by only one seat. When in December the results were declared the Government's total majority, including Labour and the Irish, was 126—just four more than it had been in January. No one could question its sufficiency. Well might Augustine Birrell speak of "the emergency of a certainty."

But there was still some way to go. The Parliament Bill started on its journey through the House of Commons. Meanwhile what my father had called the "deathbed repentance" of the peers was resumed in the House of Lords. Lord Lansdowne introduced a bill for its reform by which its numbers were limited to 350 of whom 220 were to be elected by various methods and 100 appointed by the Crown. One feature of the Bill was its infringement of the Royal prerogative by restricting the number of new peers to be created in any given year to five—thus destroying the power of creation as a solution for a deadlock between the two Houses. Lord Lansdowne frankly described this measure as "a death-blow to the House of Lords as we have known it for so long" and it was received by his supporters in icy silence. For the majority of these it meant, not a mere limitation of their powers as proposed by their enemies, but extinction at the hands of their friends.

Winding up for the Government in the House of Commons on the third reading of the Parliament Bill, Winston expressed his compassion for the fate of "those ordinary Peers, men as good and intelligent as any class of men in the country, but perhaps not better. . . . When they have done all they were told to do, the party they have served so faithfully, the leaders they have followed with such trustful docility, turn upon them in their discredit and cast them on the dust-heap." In the same speech he said that he was "almost aghast" at the Government's moderation. "The powers retained by the House of Lords . . . will not merely be effectual, . . . they will be formidable and even menacing. . . . We regard this measure as territory conquered by the masses from the classes." [15] With these words, amid a roar of acclamation and dissent the Parliament Bill was dispatched to the House of Lords.

And now the Coronation intervened and its festivities imposed a lull. It was a summer of burning heat and hectic gaiety. My father gave a party for the King and Queen, and for the first time in its existence 10 Downing Street was turned into a theater. *The Twelve Pound Look* by J. M. Barrie and the third act of *John Bull's Other Island* by Bernard Shaw were produced by Granville Barker. With Home Rule in the air *John Bull* was hotly topical, and I had one moment of panic when I overheard our eminent guest asking my father whether "this very appropriate play" had been "written for the occasion"—and observed that Bernard Shaw was within earshot! Mercifully the shot missed. The brilliant rebel behaved with exemplary loyalty throughout the evening.

F. E. Smith and Lord Winterton gave a fancy-dress ball at Claridge's attended by members of both parties including Arthur Balfour and my father—though neither of these wore, or needed, fancy dress to cloak their feelings. Both had the power of insulating private life from public life and their personal friendship remained unruffled by their political encounters.

In July the battle was resumed, but it was now complicated by a new development. It was no longer a straight fight between Government and Opposition. An internecine conflict had broken out within the ranks of the Conservative Party. Lord Lansdowne's "reform" bill had died a natural death. Within a week of its demise the Parliament Bill succeeded it in the House of Lords, confronting him with a final challenge to statesmanship and common sense. He failed to rise to it. An extremist group known later as the Die-Hards, led by a hunting peer, Lord Willoughby de Broke, and by an ex-Lord Chancellor, Lord Halsbury, aged eighty-seven, urged him to desperate courses. Yielding to their pressure he allowed the Bill to be amended beyond all recognition. It was, in my father's words, "as completely transformed as if no General Election had been held."

The Cabinet immediately advised the King that the Lords' amendments which destroyed "the principle and purpose" of the Bill would be rejected by the House of Commons and that a complete deadlock between the two Houses would be created. "Hence it would be the duty of Ministers to advise the Crown to exercise its Prerogative so as to get rid of the deadlock and secure the passing of the Bill." Within three days the King intimated that he was prepared to accept this advice. He asked, however, that the Lords should be given the chance of considering the reasons of the House of Commons for rejecting their amendments before he resorted to a creation. To this my father willingly agreed.

The secret of the King's pledge had been so well kept that the Die-Hard group was not alone in believing that the Government was bluffing. Many more responsible figures were equally deluded. Lord Curzon, at a private luncheon of Unionist Members of Parliament, derided the possibility of a creation of peers and advised his audience to "fight in the last ditch and let them make their peers if they dared." [16] (What Lord Lansdowne thought we do not know. But if he guessed at the truth his action in "tearing up the Bill" is impossible to explain.) It therefore became necessary to inform the Opposition leaders of the facts before they entrenched themselves in positions from which they would find it impossible to withdraw. Mr. Lloyd George, on my father's behalf, communicated with Mr. Balfour, and Lord Knollys informed Lord Lansdowne. A meeting of the Unionist "shadow" Cabinet was called at which, according to Mr. Balfour's biographer, "for the first time surrender by the House of Lords was discussed as practical politics." Mrs. Dugdale adds that "there was a distinct division of opinion among those present, but the majority decided that it would be imprudent to resist the menace of the creation of peers." [17]

Lord Lansdowne now demanded from the Government a written statement defining the position and their intentions. The Parliament Bill was due for its third reading in the House of Lords on July 20th and he had summoned his supporters to a meeting on the following day at Lansdowne House. It would then be his duty to undeceive them and, if possible, to restrain them. My father therefore addressed two letters to the two Unionist leaders in the following terms:

Dear Mr. Balfour,
     Lord Lansdowne,
     I think it is courteous and right, before any public decisions are announced to let you know how we regard the political situation.
     When the Parliament Bill in the form which it has now assumed returns to the House of Commons we shall be compelled to ask that House to disagree with the Lords' Amendments.
     In the circumstances should the necessity arise, the Government will advise the King to exercise his Prerogative to secure the passing of the Bill in substantially the same form in which it left the House of Commons; and His Majesty has been pleased to signify that he will consider it his duty to accept, and act on, that advice.

Yours sincerely,
H. H. ASQUITH.

Armed with this document Lord Lansdowne met the Unionist peers, numbering about two hundred. After telling them the facts he indicated that it would be more prudent to allow the Bill to pass, but he asked for no decision and took no vote. The only positive advice he gave his followers was to await the Prime Minister's statement in the House of Commons. Though Lord Lansdowne had the tepid support of the majority his weak and nerveless leadership made no impression on the Die-Hards, who were inspired by real enthusiasm and conviction and to whom death in the last ditch appeared as a heroic enterprise. The only notable result of the meeting was the conversion of Lord Curzon, who, once convinced of the danger of a creation, became a wholehearted advocate of moderate courses.

Mr. Balfour remained passive and aloof, refusing to address his supporters in the House of Commons, on the grounds that such meetings did more harm than good. More harm than good was certainly done by the intensely characteristic paper he circulated to the members of his "shadow" Cabinet from which I cannot resist quoting the following extracts: "I regard the policy which its advocates call 'fighting to the last' as essentially theatrical. . . . It does nothing, it can do nothing; it is not even intended to do anything, except advertise the situation. . . . Their policy may be a wise one, but there is nothing heroic about it; and all the military metaphors which liken the action of the 'fighting' Peers to Leonidas at Thermopylae seem to me purely for Music-Hall consumption. I grant that the Music-Hall attitude of mind is too widespread to be negligible. By all means play up to it, if the performance is not too expensive. If the creation of X Peers pleases the multitude, and conveys the impression that the Lords are 'game to the end', I raise no objection to it, *provided it does not swamp the House of Lords.* . . ." [18]

This devastating essay in deflation was received by his colleagues with dismay, and at their request he agreed to suppress it and to publish a letter of advice to a (supposedly) "perplexed peer" in which he committed himself to support Lord Lansdowne.

On Monday, July 24th, my father was to make his statement to the House of Commons on the Lords' amendments and the Government's intentions. I had never looked forward to a debate with more tense excitement. Although I knew from intimate experience my father's powers of concentration and detachment, he surprised even me by deciding to keep an old engagement made with Winston to meet the King of Portugal at luncheon a bare hour or two before this most crucial Parliamentary occasion. At three fifteen Downing Street was thronged with waiting crowds, the Master of Elibank was champing and chafing with us in the hall, secretaries were telephoning frantically right and left, when at last he and Winston arrived together. We drove to the House of Commons in an open car and were cheered all the way down Whitehall and in Parliament Square.

The Speaker's Gallery was packed to suffocation with female friends and foes, those in the back rows standing upon their chairs. Below, the House was more densely crowded than I had ever seen it and my father got a tremendous reception as he walked up the floor, members on our side waving hats and handkerchiefs. But through the deafening cheers I began to hear shouts of "traitor" and when he rose to speak he was greeted by an organized uproar. For half an hour he stood at the box while insults and abuse were hurled at him by a group of Tory members led by Lord Hugh Cecil and Mr. F. E. Smith. There was a background chorus of "Divide, divide" against which articulate shouts and yells rang out—"Traitor," "Redmond," "Who killed the King?" I could not take my eyes off Lord Hugh Cecil, who screamed: "The King is in duress" and in his frenzied writhings seemed like one possessed. His transformation, and that of many other personal friends, was terrifying. They looked, and behaved, like mad baboons.

The scene was well described by Augustine Birrell as "an orgy of stupidity and ruffianism." Arthur Balfour remained passive throughout, making no attempt to restrain his followers. The Speaker, who did his best, was disregarded and finally adjourned the House. In making his report to the King, Winston wrote truly that: "The ugliest feature was the absence of any real passion or spontaneous feeling. It was a squalid, frigid, organized attempt to insult the Prime Minister." My father's undelivered speech was published in the press on the following day.

The incident naturally caused fierce resentment among Government supporters and some shame among their opponents. My father received a letter of apology and regret signed by Sir Alfred Cripps,* Colonel Lockwood † and other Unionist members. The *Times* rebuked Lord Hugh Cecil, the representative of a university seat, for proving himself "a ring-leader of Parliamentary rowdyism." [19] The *Daily Telegraph* described "the sheer brutality of the long-continued stream of insults and interruptions" as "simply disgusting." [20] The *Evening Standard* even paid tribute to my father: "It is impossible not to remark the wonderful self-control which he exhibited during the great scene. Amid all the turbulence and pandemonium he was easily the calmest man in the House, ignoring with supreme sangfroid the personal epithets hurled at him by his incensed opponents. . . ." [21]

It was suggested in some quarters that the Die-Hards had staged a double-barreled demonstration directed not only against my father but against their own spineless leaders who were counseling surrender. There were rumors of plots to dethrone Arthur Balfour and install F. E. Smith in his place. It was easier to believe in the first aim than the second, but like the prophet Habakkuk the Die-Hards were *capable de tout*.

The next move of the distracted Opposition leaders was an attempt to unite their warring factions by setting down votes of censure on the Government in both Houses. My father replied to Arthur Balfour in a masterly speech, which on this occasion was listened to in silence by a somewhat shamefaced Opposition. He ended with the words: "I am accustomed, as Lord Grey in his day was accustomed, to be accused of breach of the Constitution and even of treachery to the Crown. I confess . . . that I am not in the least sensitive to this cheap and ill-in-

* Later Lord Parmoor.
† Later Lord Lambourne.

formed vituperation. It has been my privilege, almost now I think unique, to serve in close and confidential relations three successive British sovereigns. My conscience tells me that in that capacity, many and great as have been my failures and shortcomings, I have consistently striven to uphold the dignity and just privileges of the Crown. But I hold my office not only by favour of the Crown but by the confidence of the people, and I should be guilty indeed of treason if in this supreme moment of a great struggle I were to betray their trust." 22

I find an entry in my diary: "F. made the finest speech of his life." My judgment may well have been loaded by emotion, but that emotion was shared by others for I have never witnessed a greater Parliamentary ovation than that which he received when he sat down.

My father had asked Winston to wind up for the Government and I remember that this choice was the subject of some private murmurings and cavilings among colleagues who believed that they themselves or others would have done the job better. In this they were mistaken. His speech was one of studied moderation and solid argument enlivened by some brilliant fun directed at George Wyndham and at his old archfriend and enemy F. E. Smith (who during the debate had turned on his own leaders and attacked them for their pusillanimity in yielding to the Government's bluff). "One right honourable Gentleman has told us that the spirit of King Henry V is surging in his breast and the other that he stands with Clive confronting the deadly pistol of the duellist. We may admire their courage all the more because if it has any effect it is an effect which will inure considerably to our advantage. All forms of courage are praiseworthy. But there are two features about the courage of these right honourable Gentlemen which deserve the momentary passing notice of this House. First, it is that kind of courage which enables men to stand up unflinchingly and do a foolish thing, although they know it is popular. Second, it is that kind of courage which cannot only be maintained in the face of danger, but can even shine brightly in its total absence. Mr. Jorrocks has described fox-hunting as providing all the glory of war with only 35 per cent of its danger." (Here George Wyndham interjected "25 per cent.") Winston continued: "Twenty five per cent. The right honourable Gentleman has arrived at a much higher economy, and I think no one has succeeded in manufacturing a greater amount of heroism with a smaller consumption of the raw material of danger than his right honourable and learned Friend" 23 (F. E. Smith).

On the following day when the Commons dealt with the Lords' amendments my father had lost his voice and Winston was in charge.

Lord Hugh Cecil opened with a violent speech in which he accused my father of being guilty of high treason and said that he would "gladly see him punished by the criminal law." The stage was now set for the final clash in this long-fought struggle.

The result of a Parliamentary battle, depending as it does on votes, can usually be assessed within rough limits. But on this occasion no prophet, Whip or crystal-gazer could possibly foresee the outcome. Too many factors were incalculable. On the eve of the debate it was only known with certainty that 80 Government peers would vote for the Bill and that Lord Lansdowne had a list of 320 Unionists who were prepared to abstain. The number of Die-Hards, who were determined to vote against the Bill at all costs, was not known, nor were the numbers, whereabouts or intentions of that cryptic, unseen force the "backwoodsmen." It was believed that a small number of Unionist peers might, in the last resort, be ready to make the supreme sacrifice of voting for the Government and that some of the Lords Spiritual might do so. But these calculations were based on sheer hypothesis and speculation. When the debate opened no one could have forecast the result.

Wednesday, August 9th, was the hottest day of that burning summer. It was said that the temperature (registering 100 degrees) was the highest ever recorded in Great Britain. Arthur Balfour, who found the situation and the climate unendurable, had already left for Paris. My father, still stricken with laryngitis, went down that day to Ewelme for two nights to recover his voice. The King remained in London and watched events. He was not unnaturally disturbed by the course of the first day's debate. The Die-Hards, who were throughout in the ascendant, persisted in their belief that the Government was bluffing. Lord Halsbury, in a speech described by Sir Almeric Fitzroy as "a blunt appeal to blind passion, couched in terms of turgid rhetoric and senile violence," still spoke of "the bogey of the creation of peers." [24] Lord Willoughby de Broke dismissed the result of two General Elections with the words: "You may claim majorities if you like in favour of the Parliament Bill at a dozen General Elections, but that will not alter my view and I do not think it will alter the view of Lord Halsbury or those acting with us in this matter." [25] This claim to impose their "views" in the teeth of a dozen General Elections reveals their grasp of the Constitution they were out to defend.

When after midnight the debate was adjourned until the following day, the King was alarmed by the "fixed and obstinate belief" of the Die-Hards that the creation was an empty threat and that they could safely "call the Government's bluff." Sir Harold Nicolson records that the King's alarm was shared by Lord Stamfordham and that on the morning of Thursday the tenth he wrote to Lord Morley that it was imperative to dispel these illusions. Lord Morley at once submitted a formula to the King which was returned with his "entire approval."

I sat through the whole debate and I shall never forget the tension, the excitement and the stifling heat of the packed Chamber. After two or three opening speeches Lord Rosebery appealed to the Government to reply. Lord Morley then rose and drew from his pocket a sheet of paper from which he read the agreed statement very slowly and distinctly to the House: "If the Bill should be defeated to-night His Majesty will assent to the creation of peers sufficient in number to guard against any possible combination of the different parties in opposition by which the Parliament Bill might be exposed a second time to defeat." There was a moment of intense silence which seemed to me unending. Then a peer rose and asked Lord Morley to repeat his statement. He did so and added: "Every vote given against my motion will be a vote for a large and prompt creation of peers."

That seemed plain enough. But whether the Die-Hards were still unconvinced or whether they had committed themselves too deeply to the last ditch to scramble out of it they remained there, defiant and undeterred. The last thing I remember as I left the Chamber was the tense anxiety on the face of Lord Stamfordham as he sat watching in the gallery, fearing the news he might have to bring back to the King.

I find in my diary: "We were hustled into a lobby to wait for the division figures and there we stood wedged like figs among Salisburys, Selbornes, Lytteltons, etc.—not knowing what eye we dared to catch (though they were in a worse quandary because for once they were all angrier with each other than with us!) Wedgwood Benn came past and said to me: 'I'm afraid the Government are beaten—they've got 111'. My heart sank—I didn't see how we could possibly get as many. Then five minutes later the doors opened and a man rushed through with the news that the Government had won—and all our friends streamed in out of the lobbies delirious with joy. We had won by 17 votes. The Archbishop and twelve Bishops voted for us and thirty-seven Lansdownites— (with whom I hear Lord Knollys had done good work). I saw Winston for a moment and we exulted together. Then I walked back to Downing Street with Edwin Montagu and others. The night was breathless. There was wild uproar and cheering in the streets.

"I feel a load off my heart. A creation would have stripped victory of half its glory. . . ."

Thus the curtain fell on the great constitutional struggle. For the King it was, as Lord Stamfordham wrote next day, "a relief greater than one can describe." My father too, in spite of his invulnerable temperament, must have felt the long strain, particularly in the final stages during which a grave international crisis was brewing.

Now that the issue was decided his scarlet sins seemed, for the moment at least, forgotten. The vilification and abuse to which he had been subjected was now diverted to the "traitors" in the Unionist party who, with the Bishops, had sold the pass and saved the Bill by voting with the Government.

For me, who lived through them, these years are not history but experience. Yet as I reread their history now I rub my eyes with wondering incredulity. If it is true that "Whom the Gods would destroy they first make mad" there can surely never have been an occasion when the gods did their job more thoroughly. For the Gadarene rush to destruction was led, not only by the lunatic fringe (which exists in every party), but by men of the temperate mind of Lord Lansdowne, the cool, ironic detachment of Mr. Balfour and the rare intellectual distinction of the Cecil family. When at the eleventh hour Balfour and Lansdowne turned and tried to stem the rush, the herd was already over the edge.

There was certainly no method in this madness. A *mystique* alone could impose such suicidal strategy. Reading the evidence, it is hard to avoid the conclusion that in those days the Conservative Party did not believe in ballot boxes. They believed (in Mr. Balfour's words) that "whether in power or in Opposition the Unionist Party should control the destinies of this Empire." It was a doctrine of divine right to permanent control of the Empire, Parliament—and ultimately the King. When divine right was successfully challenged, the sanction of force was invoked as a substitute.

I may be justly criticized for allowing the central theme of my narrative to be submerged in the drama of the constitutional struggle. But during two years that struggle was not only the back cloth of Winston Churchill's political life; it was the stage on which he played an active part. On its outcome depended not only the fortunes of the Government of which he was a member but the supremacy of the House of Commons, which throughout his life had been the cornerstone of his political faith. By the victory of 1911 that supremacy was finally established and it has never since been challenged.

Chapter Seventeen

---◄─◆─►---

THUNDER IN THE AIR

In SEPTEMBER, 1908, a great event in Winston Churchill's life took place. He married, and as he himself has truly recorded "lived happily ever after."

His wife was already my friend. I shall always remember our first meeting, two years before their marriage, on the night of my own "coming out" party. "Coming out" was in those days an event which happened suddenly. Overnight, in the twinkling of an eye, one was magically translated from a child into a grown-up person. The process by which this transformation was as a rule accomplished was a large dinner party followed by a ball. Eager as I was to be grown up, I found the preparation for the rite bewildering and painful. For the first time in my life the hair that dangled down my back was put up in a disfiguring pile, I was *laced* into a white satin dress by Worth and, feeling rather breathless and a little cold, I went downstairs to face the forty strangers who had come to dinner. I had never seen one of them before, and the twenty young men, all dressed like waiters (only a little better), looked as anonymous as supers. But the girls were individual and various. Among them one face of classical perfection caught my eye, a profile like the prow of a Greek ship. "Who is she?" I whispered to a brother, and was told that her name was Clementine Hozier. He added: "She is like the 'racing cutter' in *Beauchamp's Career.*" * She had come out a few years before me and, as I gazed upon her finished, flawless beauty and reflected on her wide experience of the world I was just stumbling into,

---

* A novel by George Meredith.

171

I felt an awe-struck admiration. Awe vanished, admiration stayed and with it began a friendship which no vicissitude has ever shaken.

We often met at parties and in country houses and talked of people, clothes, friends—everything except politics. I was conditioned to living in two separate worlds and I never thought of her in a political context but always as a Queen of Beauty on the ballroom floor. Until she married Winston I did not know that she had had a Liberal family background and tradition and—what mattered more—possessed strong Liberal instincts of her own. I soon discovered that she was in fact a better natural Liberal than Winston, and this discovery brought me much relief on her behalf. For in their early married life she shared the rough of his political fortunes to the full.

The ferocity of party politics had overflowed absurdly into the most innocent amenities of social life. During the veto battle and the Home Rule controversy which followed it the political frustration of some of our opponents sought compensation in social ostracism, and Winston headed the list of "untouchables." No epithet was too opprobrious to hurl at him and the doors of many houses were closed against him. Clemmie met these affronts with cool defiance and never wavered in her militant loyalty. His cause was her cause, his enemies were her enemies, though (to her credit) his friends were not invariably her friends. Her appraisal of people was often more discriminating than his own. I asked her once in later years how much she had minded those early days, and she replied: "I didn't mind a bit. It was so exciting—it made me feel heroic and proud!"

I could not go to their wedding, as we were all away in Scotland at the time. My father had taken a house in Aberdeenshire for the summer holidays, Slains Castle, standing on the very edge of rocky cliffs on which tempestuous seas broke night and day. Winston came up to stay with us a few weeks before his marriage. I had imagined that "being engaged" would make him different in all sorts of ways, but he was quite unchanged. I remember that directly he arrived he described to me the various stations through which his train had passed between King's Cross and Aberdeen and made me help him to affix an appropriate and alliterative label to each. (The only one I can remember supplying was "the whirring gouffre of Grantham.") Thence we went north through Doncaster—York—Newcastle and Edinburgh, scraping the barrel of our joint vocabularies for adjectives. He flung himself with zest into our favorite and most perilous pastime of rock climbing, reveling in the scramble up crags and cliffs, the precarious transition from ledge to ledge, with slippery seaweed underfoot and roaring seas below. Though we considered ourselves salted climbers of four weeks' experience and he was a raw novice, he always took command of every operation, decreeing strategy and tactics and even dictating the correct position of our arms and legs. He brought to every ploy the excitement of a child and, like a child, he made it seem not only exciting but serious and important. Every activity shared with him became an enterprise of "pith and moment."

During our calmer walks and talks I tried to elicit his views upon the state of marriage in the abstract. But for once he was not forthcoming, only adjuring me on no account to marry rashly, hastily or unadvisedly nor for many years to come, and above all not to marry X, Y or Z.

Next time I saw him he was married and they both came to a small dinner party at Downing Street. I find an entry in my diary: "I sat between Edward Grey and John Simon and talked to Winston for hours after dinner—or rather he talked to me. He was in glorious form and quite unchanged. Clemmie looked lovely. She complained to me that Winston was trying to educate her and shut her up for hours with 'The Life of a Bee' by Maeterlinck, and that she was not interested in bees." I agreed with her that bees were bores—like most mathematicians. I remember that she also told me that Winston was most extravagant about his underclothes. These were made of very finely woven silk (pale pink) and came from the Army and Navy Stores and cost the eyes out of the head. This year, according to her calculations, he had spent something like eighty pounds on them. When I taxed him with this curious form of self-indulgence, he replied: "It is essential to my well-being. I have a very delicate and sensitive cuticle which demands the finest covering. Look at the texture of my cuticle—*feel* it" (uncovering his forearm by rolling up his sleeve). "I have a cuticle without a blemish— except on one small portion of my anatomy where I sacrificed a piece of my skin to accommodate a wounded brother officer on my way back from the Sudan campaign." He then told me in detail the story of this sacrifice, which he has described in *The River War*.

During the first two years of his marriage Winston was in calm waters at the Board of Trade. He had a stormier passage at the Home Office, where he had to deal with squalls of industrial unrest. His main purpose when he went there was to lighten the lot of prisoners and, despite the strictures passed, alternately by Right and Left, upon his handling of the strikes which broke out during his term of office, he will always be remembered as one of the most humane and human Home Secretaries in our history.

One of his first actions was to telegraph for Wilfrid Blunt's memorandum on prison reform. He told Blunt, as he had often told me, that "it had become a nightmare to him to have to exercise his power of life and death in the case of condemned criminals, on an average of one case a fortnight." [1] Just before leaving office he ordered a number of remissions of sentences, in spite of the protests of the judges. One case of remission which was constantly brought up against him, and in the end became a good-humored stick to beat him with, was that of the Dartmoor Shepherd, an old man who specialized in robbing church boxes, which as a rule contained very small sums of money. The Dartmoor Shepherd was very old and very poor. He had been in and out of prison many times for stealing sums of two shillings or thereabouts. Winston's heart was wrung by his plight and in the teeth of official protests he let him out. There were shocked comments on this irregular and unjustifiable act of clemency, which turned to whoops of triumph and some merriment when the Shepherd, within a few weeks of his release, proceeded to raid another church box.

He was deeply moved by the lot of the boy prisoners whom he visited in Pentonville, many of whom were in prison for sleeping out because they had no homes. I remember his firm refusal in the House of Commons to prohibit roller-skating by children on the London pavements. What matter if a few old women were knocked down? It was far more important that little boys should have their fling of fun.

But though in many quarters he was mocked for his pains, he did a great work in mitigating the lot of prisoners by the imaginative schemes he had confided to me a few days after his appointment. The entertainments, libraries and lectures he had then planned became established facts, from which other reforms have grown. Sir Edward Troup, the Permanent Secretary, wrote that "Once a week or oftener Mr. Churchill came to the office bringing with him some adventurous or impossible projects; but after half an hour's discussion something was evolved which was still adventurous but not impossible."

As Home Secretary he also had the less congenial task of maintaining law and order at a time when both were threatened by a series of strikes in the coal fields, the docks and the railways. In the autumn of

1910 a coal strike of great bitterness and violence broke out in the Rhondda Valley. The cry of "Tonypandy" was as often and as unjustly flung at Winston Churchill as that of "Featherstone" * was against my father. For forty years he was accused at general elections of sending soldiers to attack the miners.

In fact he behaved with exemplary wisdom and restraint. Rioting had broken out in the Rhondda Valley, the mines were being flooded and the Chief Constable of Glamorgan appealed to the military authorities for troops as the local police were unable to maintain order. Winston decided to send instead a contingent of five hundred Metropolitan Police. Meanwhile he promised an immediate Board of Trade inquiry and made an appeal to the miners: "Their best friends here are greatly distressed at the trouble which has broken out and will do their best to help them get fair treatment. . . . But rioting must cease at once so that the inquiry shall not be prejudiced and to prevent the credit of the Rhondda Valley being injured. Confiding in the good sense of the Cambrian workmen we are holding back the soldiers for the present and sending police instead." [2]

Later, after consultation with Lord Haldane, he consented to send a limited number of troops under the command of General Macready as a precautionary measure in case of emergency. General Macready had strict instructions to keep the troops in the background, to use them only for the protection of the mines and not to intervene unless the police had exhausted all their resources. These orders were rigorously observed. On one or two occasions the troops were obliged to intervene when the police were being heavily stoned and had suffered casualties. But there was no bloodshed and for this General Macready in his book gives the whole credit to Winston Churchill: "It was entirely due to Mr. Churchill's forethought in sending a strong force of Metropolitan Police directly he was made aware of the state of affairs in the valleys that

* At Featherstone in Yorkshire a long and bitter coal strike took place in 1893, marked by outbreaks of violence and disorder. Collieries were wrecked, buildings burned and onlookers held to ransom. In response to an appeal from the local authority my father, who was then Home Secretary, sent four hundred members of the Metropolitan Police to assist the local force. When their efforts to restore order and protect the collieries proved unavailing the local authority demanded, on their own responsibility, the intervention of troops. Thirty soldiers were dispatched by the military authorities and when these were in danger of being surrounded and overcome the civil authority (after the Riot Act had been read) had no choice but to direct the troops to fire. They did so and two men on the edge of the crowd were unfortunately killed.

bloodshed was avoided, for had the police not been in strength sufficient to cope with the rioters there would have been no alternative but to bring the military into action." [3]

This just and dispassionate verdict was not endorsed by Winston's political opponents. As so often happened to him, he found himself between two fires. While Keir Hardie was attacking him for "letting loose troops upon the people to shoot down if need be whilst they are fighting for their legitimate rights," the Conservatives and their press were accusing him of vacillation and shilly-shally in withholding the troops for a week and thus endangering lives and property. The *Times* arraigned him and the *Daily Express* wrote that "Nothing was ever more contemptible in childish and vicious folly than Mr. Churchill's message to the miners. . . . It is the last word in a policy of shameful neglect and poltroonery which may cost the country very dear." [4]

Winston made a fine defense of his action in the House of Commons. "Law and order must be preserved," he said, "but I am confident that the House will agree with me that it is a great object of public policy to avoid a collision between soldiers and crowds of persons engaged in industrial disputes. . . . For soldiers to fire on the people would be a catastrophe in our national life. Alone among the nations, or almost alone, we have avoided for a great many years that melancholy and unnatural experience. And it is well worth while, I venture to think, for the Minister who is responsible to run some risk of broken heads or broken windows . . . to accept direct responsibility in order that the shedding of British blood by British soldiers may be averted as, thank God, it has been successfully averted in South Wales." [5] The "melancholy and unnatural experience" of which he spoke was not, alas, to be averted during the railway strike which followed in August.

But between these two events Winston provided the public with an interlude of melodrama which stole the headlines of every newspaper in Europe, caused amusement and some mild anxiety to his friends and rejoiced the hearts of his critics—the "Siege of Sidney Street."

The full story of this incident is told, as only he could tell it, in his collection of miscellanies, *Thoughts and Adventures*. It should be read by all who seek to know him, for despite its relative triviality it is one of the most characteristic and revealing episodes of his life. The bones of the story are as follows. The curtain rises on a January morning. Winston is in his bath, whence he is summoned to the telephone by an urgent message from the Home Office. "Dripping wet and shrouded in a towel" he receives the news that a gang of foreign anarchists led by one

"Peter the Painter," who had already shot four policemen, have been surrounded in a house in Whitechapel, No. 100 Sidney Street, and are firing on the police with automatic pistols. Authority is asked to send for troops to arrest or kill them. Authority is duly given. But—"in these circumstances I thought it my duty to see what was going on myself. . . . I must, however, admit that convictions of duty were supported by a strong sense of curiosity which perhaps it would have been well to keep in check."

Within an hour he was on the field of battle. "Scots Guardsmen and spectators were crouching behind the projecting corners of the buildings; and from both sides of the street . . . and from numerous windows, policemen and other persons were firing rifles, pistols and shotguns . . . at the house which harboured the desperadoes. . . . Some of the police officers were anxious to storm the building at once with their pistols. . . . It was not for me to interfere with those who were in charge on the spot. Yet . . . my position of authority, far above them all, attracted inevitably to itself direct responsibility. I saw now that I should have done much better to have remained quietly in my office. On the other hand, it was impossible to get into one's car and drive away while matters stood in such great uncertainty, and moreover were extremely interesting."

As the fight progressed his interventionist impulse became stronger. When plans were made to storm the house, rush the front door and charge the stairs, smash in the roof and leap down on the assassins from above he confesses that his "own instincts turned at once to a direct advance up the staircase behind a steel plate or shield, and search was made in the foundries of the neighbourhood for one of a suitable size." [6] Fortunately these tactical problems were solved by the house catching fire. Its inmates were now doomed either to burn, surrender, or face "a hundred rifles, revolvers, and shotguns" leveled at the doorway.

But suddenly "with a stir and a clatter" the London fire brigade arrived and, though the police forbade them to advance, insisted that wherever fire was raging it was their bounden duty to put it out. They were not concerned with anarchists or automatic pistols but with fire and water. "Orders were orders." Winston was now given his chance to prove that his presence had its uses. He gave orders that the house should be allowed to burn—and for nearly an hour the conflagration blazed. "Then at last" (according to the *Daily News*) "Mr. Churchill stepped to the middle of the street and waved his arms . . . firemen appeared and regardless of possible bullets poured water on the burning house

. . . and firemen and policemen led by Mr. Churchill rushed forward to the door." [7] The two charred bodies found among the ruins were identified as members of "Peter the Painter's" gang of anarchists. But of Peter himself no trace was ever found, though legend claimed him in the years to come as a "liberator" of the Bolshevik Revolution.

The "Siege of Sidney Street" provided a field day for Winston's critics. Conservatives accused him of exhibitionism, play-acting, forgetting his own "place" and interfering in other people's. In the House of Commons Arthur Balfour remarked with some acidity: "We are concerned to observe photographs in the Illustrated papers of the Home Secretary in the danger zone. I understand what the photographer was doing, but why the Home Secretary?" Many Liberals were disturbed, not for the first or last time, by his zest for planning and directing military operations, by his tendency to overdramatize a situation and himself and to use a steam hammer to crack a nut. A. G. Gardiner wrote that "in the theatre of his mind it is always the hour of fate and the crack of doom." [8] Both these were nearer than his critics dreamed. Meanwhile their charge of dramatizing events was not unfair but the motives they ascribed to him were, in my view, wholly misconceived.

It was not the pursuit of limelight nor the lure of blood and thunder which had drawn him to the Siege of Sidney Street—and to many other scenes of action to which, in the eyes of purists, he did not belong. A deeper impulse was at work to which we find a clue in his own words. "After all," he once wrote regretfully, "a man's life must be nailed to a cross either of thought or action." But though he admitted this necessity he never accepted it. The realm of thought alone always seemed to him to be an insufficient kingdom, cramping and cold. Where his imagination led his body needs must follow. If his mind was busy with war he must command troops, if he argued with the bricklayers he himself must build a wall. It was this imperious need to combine thought and action which led him to board the armored train at Estcourt, to take a personal part in the defense of Antwerp and (most astonishing of all) to desire to exchange the supreme command of our sea power for that of a division in France. Only the King's command prevented him from taking part in the D-Day operations, and had he done so from a ship he might well have followed his heart onto the beaches. Throughout his life he refused to accept the ruling of the modern world that we must either plan or perform, conceive or execute. I always thought, and often told him, that he had been born out of due season, that he should rightly have belonged to an age in which thought and action were a combined operation and not alternative functions each allotted to specialists in their own sphere. But with the Second World War when every decision was a deed he entered into his double heritage.

Meanwhile he considered the game well worth the candle. He had enjoyed every moment of the street fighting in Whitechapel and he made us enjoy it too, for with him no adventure ever lost in the telling. He described the adverse comments on his action as "Sour grapes—they only wish they had been there to see the fun!" I questioned this in Arthur Balfour's case, suggesting that these particular grapes would not have been his cup of tea. He agreed: "No, Arthur would not have enjoyed it—but I *did* enjoy his comment." My father's reaction to the incident was one of helpless amusement. It was "Winston through and through." He knew better than to try to make his colleagues other than they were, and he liked Winston as he was.

Sidney Street was a storm in a teacup, but real and menacing storms were soon to gather in the skies. Mr. J. A. Spender, a man of sober judgment and expression, has written that: "Never in the memory of men living had a Ministry been beset with so many and great dangers as Asquith's Government" [9] during the months of July and August, 1911. The final stages of the struggle between Lords and Commons were taking place; the Kaiser had set "all the alarm-bells throughout Europe" ringing by the dispatch of the gunboat *Panther* to Agadir, and at this grave moment of international danger the first great railway strike broke out. At twenty-four hours' notice the whole railway service of the country was threatened with paralysis. It was an event without a precedent. The motor transport and other measures devised to meet the general strike in 1926 did not exist in 1911. In a few days the strike must have produced a failure of food supplies and raw materials and a complete stoppage of industry with rioting and disorder. Meanwhile, though the public did not know it, there was a possibility that we might be involved in war. Sir Edward Grey had warned the Admiralty that "the Fleet might be attacked at any moment" and it remained in a state of preparedness until the end of September.

The Government was faced with the duty of providing and protecting a transport service and at the same time of trying to bring the parties together. The first part of this task inevitably devolved on Winston Churchill as Home Secretary and he did not hesitate to discharge it by using troops to garrison the stations and protect the line. Where necessary they were employed to deal with rioting and at Llanelly two men were killed when troops repelled an attack upon a train.

For these measures he was violently attacked by Labour members in the House of Commons. Ramsay MacDonald said: "The Department which has played the most diabolical part in all this unrest was the Home Office. . . . This is not a mediaeval State, and it is not Russia. It is not even Germany. . . . If the Home Secretary had just a little bit more knowledge of how to handle masses of men in these critical times, if he had a somewhat better instinct of what civil liberty does mean . . . we should have had much less difficulty during the last four or five days in facing and finally settling the . . . problem." Keir Hardie went further. The Home Secretary, he said, did not seem to understand the gravamen of the charge against him. It was that he and his confreres had violated and overridden the law and superseded settled government without the sanction of Parliament and substituted military rule. . . . Talk about revolution! The law of England had been broken in the interests of the railway companies. . . . A new regime began with the present Home Secretary. Instead of bringing pressure to bear on the railway directors to settle the present dispute the Government had used all the forces of the Crown to intimidate the men. . . . The men who had been shot down in this dispute had been murdered by the Government in the interest of the capitalist system.[10]

Keir Hardie even accused my father of declaring that "if there was a strike the whole forces of the Crown would be used to keep the railways open, and . . . that meant shooting down the strikers if necessary." When cross-examined by Mr. Lloyd George he was obliged to admit that the words he had attributed to the Prime Minister were his own version of the very different statement that "he would employ all the forces of the Crown to keep the railways open."

On the merits of the case my father's sympathy was largely with the men, many of whom he thought underpaid and overworked. On the first day of the strike he met them, asked what their grievance was and offered to set up a Royal Commission to examine it immediately. This offer was at first refused, but later Mr. Lloyd George brought to the task of peacemaking his genius for negotiation. The strike was called off after two days, a Royal Commission was set up and all differences settled.

The Conservative press, which had assailed Winston so bitterly for his handling of the Welsh coal strike, was now loud in his praise. But once again the Liberals were critical and uneasy. They recognized, no doubt, that his action was both right and necessary but they could not forgive the apparent gusto with which he performed it. He was accused by Charles Masterman of a "whiff-of-grapeshot attitude" and even of "longing for 'blood' " [11]—in my view quite unfairly. He did nothing by halves. I have seen him fling himself into the tasks of peace with the same zest and concentration. On this occasion there is no doubt that the international situation had first place in his mind.

Earlier in the year a French force had occupied Fez, to the serious annoyance of Germany, who was already dissatisfied with the situation in Morocco. Negotiations went on throughout June about the compensation Germany was to receive for "disinteresting herself politically" in this French sphere of influence. In the midst of these negotiations, on July 1st, it was suddenly announced that a gunboat, the *Panther,* had been sent to Agadir to maintain and protect German interests. It was said that German merchants had appealed for protection, but as there were no German merchants or residents in the neighborhood this pretext was suspicious. The sudden dispatch of a warship to Agadir was interpreted as an ominous and threatening act. France was alarmed and our own Admiralty did not welcome the prospect of a German naval base on the Atlantic. On July 5th Sir Edward Grey warned the German Ambassador, Count Metternich, that our attitude "could not be a disinterested one." This communication was followed by three weeks of unbroken silence from the German Government. On July 21st, when pressed by Sir Edward Grey for a reply, the German Ambassador was still without instructions.

Then unexpectedly and providentially Mr. Lloyd George entered the field of foreign policy, with decisive results. He was to address the bankers at a Mansion House dinner that evening, and he confided to Winston that he intended to "make it clear that if Germany meant war she would find Britain against her." He said that he was going to show a draft of his speech to the Prime Minister and Sir Edward Grey after the Cabinet. "What would they say?" "I said that of course they would be very much relieved: and so they were and so was I." [12]

In his famous speech that evening Mr. Lloyd George shed all the trappings of a Little Englander. He spoke in a new idiom which was all the more effective because he had never used it before. "If a situation were to be forced upon us in which peace could only be preserved . . . by allowing Britain to be treated where her interests were vitally affected as if she were of no account in the Cabinet of nations, then I say emphatically that peace at that price would be a humiliation intolerable for a great country like ours to endure."

His City audience, according to Winston Churchill, "took it as one of the ordinary platitudes of ministerial pronouncements on foreign affairs. But the Chancelleries of Europe bounded together." [12]

The German Government was thunderstruck. They had assumed that British action would be ruled out by the Peace Party, led by Lloyd George. They were furious with poor Count Metternich for having so grossly misled them about the attitude of Ministers in the country to which he was accredited and he was recalled at the earliest opportunity. Yet, in Winston Churchill's words, "how could he know what Mr. Lloyd George was going to do? Until a few hours before his colleagues did not know. Working with him in close association, I did not know. No one knew. Until his mind was definitely made up, he did not know himself." [13]

The German Government could now have no doubt where Great Britain stood, nor how she would act if they forced war on France. Germany paused on the brink—but was she receding? We did not know. During the next two anxious months the danger of war was always with us. Negotiations dragged on between France and Germany and often seemed near breaking point. There were moments when both their Ambassadors in London thought the situation hopeless and failure inevitable. Edward Grey continued to urge that no precautions should be relaxed. The fleet remained in war preparedness. The tunnels and bridges of the South Eastern Railway were being patrolled day and night. Meanwhile in profound secrecy military conversations were going on between the British and French General Staffs and preparations for landing four to six divisions on the Continent were being made. I remember Lord Haldane telling us with pride that the timetable had been planned in such minute detail that the French had even allowed for *"dix minutes d'arrêt pour café"* at one stage of the proceedings.

And still the battle for the Parliament Act raged on and still the sun blazed down upon us from cloudless skies as one burning day followed another. Too many great events were happening at once. . . . Looking back now I realize that it was during these days that Winston Churchill began to "walk with Destiny" and to know the purpose he had been born to serve. It was in these days that the man of 1914 and 1939 came into being.

As Home Secretary, defense and foreign policy were not part of his departmental business. They concerned him only as a member of the Cabinet. Yet for him nothing else mattered. They dominated every other interest and emotion. "For seven years I was to think of little else. Liberal politics, the People's Budget, Free Trade, Peace, Retrenchment and Reform—all the war cries of our election struggles began to seem unreal in the presence of this new preoccupation. Only Ireland held her place among the grim realities which came one after another into view." [14] And Ireland was relevant to these "grim realities."

One rare and characteristic feature of his greatness was always his power to go on growing. At no moment of his life could anyone have said with certainty: "This is the whole man." He was never finished, to the very end. There was always more to come, and that "more" was incalculable. But the change I watched in him during these months was not growth but a transition sudden and cataclysmic like the struggle of a new birth.

One small incident which he has recorded and which I remember vividly reveals his constant preoccupation with the German menace to Europe and ourselves. On July 27th we were giving our last garden party of the summer. The Downing Street garden was thronged with Ambassadors, Civil Servants, M.P.'s of all persuasions, artists, writers, friends old and new, with all their wives. I was able to snatch a few minutes with Winston and he poured out his anxieties about the immediate situation with its uncertainties and perils and about the long-term prospect which lay beyond this crisis, even if we managed to weather it. Sir Edward Henry, the Chief Commissioner of Police, joined us and I left them together. Winston learned from him that the Home Office was responsible for guarding the magazines in which all our reserves of naval cordite were stored. For some odd reason these magazines had for many years been protected by a few constables. "I asked what would happen if twenty determined Germans . . . arrived well armed upon the scene one night. He said they would be able to do what they liked. I quitted the garden-party." A few minutes later he was telephoning to the Admiralty to demand Marines to guard the magazines immediately. The Admiral in charge treated this demand as the intrusion of "an alarmist civilian Minister" and when pressed he replied: "I refuse." Winston then rang up the War Office and asked Lord Haldane for a company of infantry for each magazine. "In a few minutes the orders were given: in a few hours the troops had moved." [15] The incident illustrates the contrasting attitudes of the War Office and the Admiralty to the emergency, though it is perhaps fair to take into account that on this occasion the Admiralty was represented by a fortuitous Admiral and the War Office by Lord Haldane.

But deeper divergencies between the two fighting departments were soon to be revealed. On August 23rd, after Parliament had risen, my father called a special and secret meeting of the Committee of Imperial Defence. He summoned the Ministers representing the fighting services and their principal officers of the Army and Navy, Sir Edward Grey and Mr. Lloyd George. He also asked Winston Churchill to attend, although the Home Office was not concerned.

My father had been deeply impressed by a remarkable memorandum he had received from Winston giving his own views of the initial stages of a war in which Great Britain, France and Russia were attacked by Germany and Austria. The accuracy of his forecast is uncanny in its exactitude. "It was, of course," wrote Winston, "only an attempt to pierce the veil of the future; . . . to balance the incalculable, to weigh the imponderable. It will be seen that I named the *twentieth* day of mobilization as the date by which 'the French armies will have been driven from the line of the Meuse and will be falling back on Paris and the South,' and the *fortieth* day as that by which 'Germany should be extended at full strain both internally and on her war fronts. . . .' I am quite free to admit that these were not intended to be precise dates, but as guides to show what would probably happen. In fact, however, both these forecasts were almost literally verified three years later by the event." [16] Once again Winston's daemon was "telling him things."

Though my father could not have guessed at the prophetic nature of this memorandum, he was filled with admiration by its grasp, close reasoning and presentation. I remember his praising it to me as a tour de force and adding, not for the first time: "Winston is always admirable on paper. I often wish he used the same economy in speech as in writing." I said that I did not share this wish. "I am not denigrating his conversational powers which give you so much pleasure, but—it's a question of *time*." Economy in talking time was one of the few bones of contention in their relationship. My father liked thinking alone. Winston liked thinking aloud. How often he came down to my little room on the garden after an exiguous interview, gnashing his teeth. "Had a good talk?" "Far too short. Your father has such a six-and-eightpenny view of business!" But when he put his views in writing my father was always deeply impressed by his masterly powers of exposition.

There is no doubt that the memorandum was in his mind when the Committee of Imperial Defence met on August 23rd. They sat all day. An acute difference of opinion was immediately revealed between the War Office, represented by Sir William Nicholson, Chief of the Imperial Staff, and General Wilson, Director of Military Operations, and the Admiralty, represented by the First Sea Lord, Sir Arthur Wilson.

General Wilson maintained that the dispatch of an expeditionary force at the earliest moment was an essential part of the plan which had been agreed on with the French General Staff. He was convinced that the Germans would attack through Belgium and that the six British divisions would play a vital part in supporting the French left and that their presence would stiffen French morale and confidence. He asked for an assurance from the Admiralty that these forces could be transported if need arose. The Admiralty refused to give this assurance. In their view the enemy's fleet must be defeated before troops were transported. We should concentrate our efforts on sea warfare and a close blockade of enemy ports and then land detachments of the expeditionary force on the Baltic coast and the northern shores of Prussia. Mr. McKenna backed his Admirals; Lord Haldane supported his General Staff and urged that the Admiralty should set up a General Staff corresponding to that of the War Office. This suggestion was flatly rejected by the Admiralty. The committee broke up, leaving these differences unresolved.

Lord Haldane then took my father aside and told him that he could not continue to be responsible for the War Office unless the Admiralty would work in harmony with his General Staff and provide itself with a War Staff of its own. This situation added to my father's already grave anxieties. We still had several critical weeks to live through and the collision between our soldiers and our sailors increased our danger. His judgment was on the side of the War Office and against the Admiralty view, but the immediate necessity was to resolve the discord between them.

Haldane was his oldest and dearest friend. He had performed miracles of reorganization at the War Office and had inspired the respect and confidence of all the soldiers. His task there was now accomplished and he was beginning to feel the need of a new opportunity which would satisfy his voracious appetite and limitless capacity for work. He records in his *Autobiography:* "In 1911 I had begun to feel that the back of the necessary work had been broken and to fear that I was becoming stale." [17] Although he has written that he had no desire to be First Lord, he admits that he was almost the only person available to cope with the problem of the Naval War Staff. He believed himself to be the *homme nécessaire* to put the Admiralty into the same apple-pie order as the War Office. My father was aware of Haldane's eager readiness to undertake the task and felt no doubt about his ability to do so. Yet he hesitated, for reasons which he confided to me later.

Meanwhile he said nothing to his colleagues about impending changes and Winston remained in ignorance of Haldane's intimation.

In the middle of August Winston went to stay for a few days with Lady Horner, now a close friend in whose company he no longer thought of diagrams, at Mells in Somersetshire—a place of magical beauty, stillness and peace. But there was no peace or stillness in his mind. Of these days he has written: "I could not think of anything else but the peril of war. I did my other work as it came along, but there was only one field of interest fiercely illuminated in my mind. Sitting on a hilltop in the smiling country which stretches round Mells the lines I have copied . . . kept running through my mind. Whenever I recall them they bring back to me the anxieties of those Agadir days." [18] The lines which haunted him were from A. E. Housman's *Shropshire Lad:*

> On the idle hill of summer,
>   Sleepy with the sound of streams,*
> Far I hear the steady drummer
>   Drumming like a noise in dreams.
>
> Far and near and low and louder
>   On the roads of earth go by,
> Dear to friends and food for powder,
>   Soldiers marching, all to die.

The crisis of Agadir ended peacefully. Germany suffered a diplomatic rebuff. She had receded from the brink, but the British Government, though not the British people, had for the first time faced the immediate threat of war.

In September we were able to get away to Scotland—to Archerfield, a house on the East Lothian coast lent to us by my stepmother's brother, Frank Tennant, in which we spent many happy autumns. My father was often able to use it for week ends, sleeping on Friday and Sunday nights in the train. It was a lovely Adam house looking down an avenue of lime trees, with a fine library and a large and beautiful room with brilliant Pompeian decorations known as the Saloon. But what made it paradise for my father was the possession of a perfect private golf links stretching down to the sea.

I knew that his mind was preoccupied with the change at the Admiralty and I sometimes asked him which way it was moving. I realized that he had hesitations about Haldane, not from any misgivings about

---

* This is how Winston quotes it, though in fact Housman wrote *"flow* of streams."

his capacity to do the job magnificently but because he thought it would be wounding to the *amour-propre* of the Admiralty to send it the same new broom which had already cleaned up the War Office. Another difficulty was that Haldane was in the House of Lords. But it was the first consideration which weighed with him most heavily. I felt sure that the alternative candidate in his mind was my own and he admitted it. "Why don't you ask my advice about it?" I asked him teasingly. He teased back: "Because though in many situations I rate your judicial faculties high I know that in this particular instance they are in abeyance and I could not expect a cool, dispassionate verdict. Between Haldane and Winston you are not a judge—you are a barefaced partisan. Your scales are loaded by gross favoritism and emotion. You are not thinking of the chances of a Naval War Staff being born" (this with a sniff and a twinkle), "or of the reactions of the sensitive Admirals. You are thinking how much Winston would enjoy it!" I admitted that this factor had some weight with me but I added that the Admirals would welcome Winston a jolly sight more warmly than Haldane, thus touching what I knew to be his Achilles' heel. Looking back, I think his mind was probably as good as made up at the time but he was naturally torn by the knowledge that Haldane longed for the task, that by his achievements at the War Office he had deserved it and that there was no one who could do it better. I certainly felt that his choice between the two was still wavering in the balance. And I longed for Winston to go to the Admiralty not only because it would give him his heart's desire but because I felt sure that it was there that he would find his true vocation and his greatest self.

On September 27th he came to stay with us. We played a lot of golf together in golden autumn sunshine with sea gulls circling overhead. I find a note in my diary that "Winston is very pleased with my swing—'complete abandonment, absolute self-surrender' . . . he repeats approvingly as my driver lifts me off my feet and I slice the ball to Kingdom come." I remember a very amusing three-ball match I played with him and my father. We were all three equally indifferent and ecstatic performers. When at the ninth hole we reached the sea, Winston's eye was caught by a thicket of buckthorn, a silvery shrub with orange berries which grows upon the bents along the coast. He asked me what its name was. I said that it was buckthorn and sometimes known as "the olive of the north," a current tag of purest journalese. He rose like a trout to the fly of any phrase and his attention was immediately arrested and deflected from the game. "The olive of the north—that's good. The buckthorn of the south—that's not so good"—and during the remaining holes he rang the changes on every possible combination and permutation of this meager theme, which took his mind and eye completely off the ball. My father was intensely amused and gratified. He crowed in triumph at luncheon: "Winston was four up at the turn but once he heard about the 'olive of the north' he never hit another ball and lost the game." I felt that things were going well, and I was right.

But I had some uneasy moments. Haldane drove over from Cloan on two successive days. He too was uneasy at finding Winston there. "As I entered the approach * I saw Winston Churchill standing at the door. I divined that he had heard of possible changes and had come down at once to see the Prime Minister." This suspicion was, I think, unjustified. Winston always spent some days with us in the holidays and he had come at my father's invitation. There was a great deal of confabulation between the three of them and I remember that on one of Haldane's visits he and Winston were closeted alone together. (Haldane writes that "the Prime Minister shut me up in a room with him." [19])

Winston left us for a night, I think to go to Dundee, and on the day after his return he and my father played golf together in the afternoon. I was just finishing tea when they came in. Looking up, I saw in Winston's face a radiance like the sun. "Will you come out for a walk with me—at once?" he asked. "You don't want tea?" "No, I don't want tea." We were hardly out of the house when he said to me with grave but shining eyes: "I don't want tea—I don't want anything—anything in the world. Your father has just offered me the Admiralty."

I shall always remember our walk through darkening woods down to the sea, where Fidra's lighthouse was already flashing out its signals and, in his words, "the fading light of evening disclosed in the far distance the silhouettes of two battleships steaming slowly out of the Firth of Forth. They seemed invested with a new significance to me." [20]

His whole life was invested with a new significance. He was tasting fulfillment. Never, before or since, did I see him more completely and profoundly happy. The tide of happiness and realization was too deep even for exuberance, though at one moment, in the middle of a purple passage about the scope and range of his new powers, he interjected: "Look at the people I have had to deal with so far—Judges and convicts! This is a big thing—the biggest thing that has ever come my way —the chance I should have chosen before all others. I shall pour into it everything I've got."

It seemed like journey's end. It was in fact the beginning of a journey

---

* "Approach" is the Scottish word for what in England we call a "drive."

which did not end for him till 1945. I was struck by the two characteristic attitudes in which he faced this new, tremendous opportunity: first,
the sense of dedication to a task which Fate had designed him to fulfill
and secondly his unquestioning confidence in his power to fulfill it. These
attitudes remained constant throughout his life.

In *The World Crisis* he has described the end of this great day: "That
night when I went to bed I saw a large Bible lying on a table in my
bedroom. My mind was dominated by the news I had received of the
complete change in my station and of the task entrusted to me. I thought
of the peril of Britain, peace-loving, unthinking, little prepared, of her
power and virtue, and of her mission of good sense and fair play. I
thought of mighty Germany, towering up in the splendour of her Imperial State and delving down in her profound, cold, patient, ruthless
calculations. . . . I opened the Book at random and in the 9th Chapter
of Deuteronomy I read:

" 'Hear, O Israel: Thou art to pass over Jordan this day, to go in to
possess nations greater and mightier than thyself, cities great and fenced
up to heaven.

"2. A people great and tall, the children of the Anakims, whom
thou knowest, and of whom thou hast heard say, "Who can stand before the children of Anak!"

"3. Understand therefore this day, that the Lord thy God is he which
goeth over before thee; as a consuming fire he shall destroy them, and
he shall bring them down before thy face; so shalt thou drive them out,
and destroy them quickly, as the Lord hath said unto thee. . . .'

"It seemed a message full of reassurance." [21]

He needed no reassurance. He was sure of his mission and himself.

—◄ ►—

Chapter Eighteen

THE ADMIRALTY

WINSTON CHURCHILL has described his term of office at the Admiralty as "the four most memorable years" of his life.[1] I think that they were also the happiest. Anxiety, frustration, the distraction of duties which had become irrelevant to the main stream of his thought and purpose, were at an end. The theme which possessed his whole mind and being had now become his official business. It could at last be expressed in action.

He felt to the quick the traditional glamour of his new office, the romance of sea power, the part that it had played in our island history, the conviction that it was today the keystone of our safety and survival. He reveled in its technology and enjoyed its symbols—white ensigns, anchors, even the turtles which had now become his perquisite and gave a new significance to turtle soup! Outside the Admiralty in Whitehall two dolphins carved in stone guarded its entrance; within, the furniture adorned with golden dolphins dated from Nelson's day. And Winston's delights, like Antony's, were "dolphin-like."

He had now become our nearest neighbor. Only the width of the Horse Guards Parade separated the Admiralty from the garden door of No. 10 and it was often crossed hot-foot. It was a joy to see him buoyantly engaged in his new context, tasting complete fulfillment. I remember telling him that even his brooding had assumed a different quality. He travailed almost with serenity. "That is because I can now lay eggs instead of scratching around in the dust and clucking. It is a far more satisfactory occupation. I am at present in process of laying a great number of eggs—'good eggs,' every one of them. And there will be many more clutches to follow." He then enumerated the various tasks which faced him: the creation of a Naval War Staff; the framing of a joint strategy for the Navy in close unison with the Army; the urgent need to increase the gun-power and the speed of the new ships and to prepare against a sudden attack by Germany as though it might come next day. Then there were new appointments to be made—some Admirals to be "poached" and "scrambled" and other to be "buttered," etc., etc.

The impact of his personality vibrated through the Admiralty. He decreed that naval officers as well as resident clerks should be on duty night and day on weekdays, Sundays and holidays, so that in the event of a surprise attack no moment should be lost in giving the alarm. He also ordered a large chart of the North Sea to be hung up upon the wall behind his chair. On this chart a staff officer marked the position of the German Fleet with flags. "I made a rule to look at my chart once every day when I first entered my room. I did this less to keep myself informed . . . than in order to inculcate in myself and those working with me a sense of ever-present danger. In this spirit we all worked." [2] Instancy was his watchword.

Winston's first act on assuming office was to send for his old friend Lord Fisher, then living in retirement by the placid Lake of Lucerne. There had already been many ups and downs in their tempestuous relationship and there were more to come! They had not spoken to each other since the storm over the Navy Estimates in 1909, when Winston with Lloyd George had opposed the building of the eight Dreadnoughts. Apart from this breach Fisher felt inhibited by his loyalty to McKenna, whom he believed to have been ousted from the Admiralty by a "dirty trick." But when assured that Winston had played no part in the exchange of offices between them, and that he had (in Fisher's words) "boxed the compass" and was no longer a little-Navy man, he responded to his summons with alacrity. Despite their conflicts and head-on collisions there was a strange affinity between these two dynamic beings. I think they recognized each other as fellow sparks from the same fire.

Winston found in Fisher "a veritable volcano of knowledge and of inspiration; and as soon as he learnt what my main purpose was, he passed into a state of vehement eruption. . . . Once he began, he could hardly stop. I plied him with questions, and he poured out ideas. It was always a joy to me to talk to him on these great matters, but most of all was he stimulating in all that related to the design of ships. He also talked brilliantly about Admirals, but here one had to make a heavy discount on account of the feuds. . . ." [3]

Heavy indeed. Fisher was an innovator of genius. He had joined the service in the days when ships had sails, when many had no steam and when none had armor. He had transformed and modernized the Navy, reorganized its educational system, he had introduced the submarine, replaced the 12-inch by the 13.5-inch gun, scrapped quantities of obsolescent ships, and built the *Dreadnought,* the first all-big-gun battleship. He had also, amid howls of protest, shifted the pivot of our naval strategy from the Mediterranean to the North Sea, invoking Nelson's axiom: "Your drill ground must be your battleground."

He had achieved a revolution and, like all revolutionaries and most reformers, Fisher had aroused violent opposition both to his policies and to himself within the Royal Navy. The figurehead and leader of the opposing forces was Lord Charles Beresford, the Commander-in-Chief of the Channel Fleet, a popular and genial sailor. The Navy was thus publicly and fiercely split into two rival and contending factions. In the press, in Parliament, in every drawing room and, more serious still, "in every squadron and in every ship" there were "Fisher's men" and "Beresford's men."

The far-reaching changes Fisher fought for and achieved have been triumphantly vindicated by events. But the methods he used to achieve them were often indefensible. Winston has written that "he made it known . . . that officers . . . who opposed his policies would have their professional careers ruined. As for traitors, i.e., those who struck at him openly or secretly, 'their wives should be widows, their children fatherless, their homes a dunghill. . . .' 'Ruthless, relentless and remorseless' were words always on his lips, and many grisly examples of Admirals and Captains eating their hearts out 'on the beach' showed that he meant what he said. 'Favouritism,' he wrote in the log of Dartmouth College, 'is the secret of efficiency.' . . ." Favored officers were said to be "in the fish-pond." [4]

No wonder that Winston, though sorely tempted, hesitated to recall him. He was resolved "to hold the balance even and while adopting in the main the Fisher policy, to insist upon an absolute cessation of the vendetta." Yet he confesses that when after their first conclave they traveled up to London together, he was constantly on the brink of saying: "Come and help me," and had Fisher "by a word seemed to wish to return, I would surely have spoken. But he maintained a proper dignity, and in an hour we were in London. . . . I wonder whether I was right or wrong." [5]

Yet Fisher continued to be his trusted counselor and friend, his oracle and his most constant and prolific correspondent. He poured out letters to his pupil in which "naval conceptions and doctrines" are interspersed with "felicitous and sometimes recondite quotations, with flashing phrases and images, with mordant jokes and corrosive personalities. . . . I was regaled with eight or ten closely written double pages fastened together with a little pearl pin or a scrap of silken ribbon, and containing every kind of news and counsel, varying from blistering reproach to the highest forms of inspiration and encouragement. . . . 'My beloved Winston', they began, ending usually with a variation of 'Yours to a cinder', 'Yours till Hell freezes', or 'Till charcoal sprouts'. . . . Alas, there was a day when Hell froze and charcoal sprouted and friendship was reduced to cinders; when 'My beloved Winston' had given place to 'First Lord: I can no longer be your colleague'." [6]

Meanwhile Winston kept faith with Haldane and worked with him in the closest harmony. Sir Arthur Wilson, the First Sea Lord, was resolutely opposed both to the creation of a Naval War Staff and to the War Office plans for sending an expeditionary force to France in the event of war. These were the very tasks that Winston had been appointed to perform. He therefore waited a few months until Sir Arthur's term of office was due to expire, and in the meantime he and Haldane laid their plans together. In his daily letter to his mother Haldane wrote: "Winston and Lloyd George dined with me last night and we had a very useful talk. This is now a very harmonious Cabinet. It is odd to think that three years ago I had to fight those two for every penny for my Army reforms. Winston is full of enthusiasm about the Admiralty and just as keen as I am on the War Staff. It is delightful to work with him. Ll. G. too has quite changed his attitude and is now very friendly to your bear,* whom he used to call 'the Minister for Slaughter'." [7]

But Winston had to face stiff opposition in the creation of his Naval War Staff. The professional sailors saw in it a move to undermine the authority of the First Sea Lord and believed that collisions must inevitably occur between him and his subordinate, the Chief of the Naval War Staff. Lord Fisher advised that both these offices should be vested in the First Sea Lord, and this proved ultimately to be the right solution. Unfortunately Winston did not accept it at the time.

He made a clean sweep of his Board. Sir Francis Bridgeman succeeded Sir Arthur Wilson as First Sea Lord, and Prince Louis of Battenberg became Second Sea Lord. He chose Admiral Beatty as his Naval Secretary, remembering perhaps with gratitude their first meeting

* "Bear"—Mrs. Haldane's pet name for her son.

in the River War, when from a gunboat on the Nile a young naval officer had tossed a welcome bottle of champagne to a young Lancer standing on the bank. On Lord Fisher's advice he appointed Sir John Jellicoe, over the heads of several of his senior Admirals, to be Second in Command of the Home Fleet, thus designating him for the supreme command in the future. Of this appointment Fisher wrote in an exultant letter to a friend: "My two private visits to Winston were fruitful. I'll tell you . . . the whole secret of the changes! *To get Jellicoe Commander-in-Chief of the Home Fleet prior to October 21, 1914*—which is the date of the Battle of Armageddon. . . . *Nunc dimittis. Everything revolves round Jellicoe!*" [8] Lord Fisher's forecast was only two months out. Like Winston, he had a daemon which "told him things."

He was so delighted with these dispositions and with the general trend of Winston's policy that two months later he was writing to another friend: "So far every step he contemplates is good, *and he is brave, which is everything! Napoleonic in audacity, Cromwellian in thoroughness.*" [9]

For his "Cromwellian thoroughness" I can vouch. All his prodigious powers of energy and concentration were dedicated to learning his new job. Never, even in the two world wars, did I see him more completely immersed in his work. And his work was his life. Leisure or relaxation would have been a punishment. "From dawn to midnight day after day one's whole mind was absorbed by the fascination and novelty of the problems which came crowding forward. And all the time there was the sense of power to act, to form, to organise. . . ." Saturdays, Sundays and every spare day were spent with the fleets at Portsmouth, Portland, Devonport or visiting dockyards and shipyards throughout the British Isles and Mediterranean. He spent eight months afloat on the *Enchantress* during the years before the war (a few of these I had the good fortune to share with him). It became, as he has written, "largely my office, almost my home. . . . I got to know what everything looked like and where everything was and how one thing fitted into another. In the end I could put my hand on anything that was wanted and knew thoroughly the current state of our naval affairs."

His imagination was fired and stirred by the great ships that had now been entrusted to his keeping. And beyond the ships he saw the decisive part they had to play in the world's destiny. There is a fine passage in *The World Crisis* describing his first voyage from Portsmouth to Portland, where the fleet lay. "As I saw the Fleet for the first time drawing out of the haze, a friend reminded me of 'that far-off line of storm-

beaten ships on which the eyes of the Grand Army had never looked',
but which had in their day 'stood between Napoleon and the dominion of the world.' . . . In Portland Harbour the yacht lay surrounded
by the great ships; the whole harbour was alive with the goings and
comings of launches and small craft of every kind, and as night fell ten
thousand lights from sea and shore sprang into being and every mast-
head twinkled as the ships and squadrons conversed with one another.
Who could fail to work for such a service? Who could fail when the
very darkness seemed loaded with the menace of approaching war?

"For consider these ships, so vast in themselves, yet so small, so
easily lost to sight on the surface of the waters. . . . They were all we
had. On them, as we conceived, floated the might, majesty, dominion
and power of the British Empire. All our long history built up century
after century, all our great affairs in every part of the globe, all the means
of livelihood and safety of our faithful, industrious, active population
depended upon them. Open the sea-cocks and let them sink beneath the
surface . . . and in a few minutes—half an hour at the most—the
whole outlook of the world would be changed. The British Empire
would dissolve like a dream; each isolated community struggling forward
by itself; the central power of union broken; mighty provinces, whole
Empires in themselves drifting hopelessly out of control and falling a
prey to strangers; and Europe after one sudden convulsion passing into
the iron grip and rule of the Teuton and of all that the Teutonic system
meant." [10]

As his eyes scanned these vast horizons, it is small wonder that domestic issues dwindled and faded into the background of his mind.

Despite his innate pugnacity Winston Churchill had no desire to
embark on a ruinous arms race with Germany if a way out, consonant
with safety and with honor, could be found. He was in favor of any
attempt to reach agreement and he foresaw that if it failed, the fact that
it had been made would strengthen his hand in Parliament when he
asked for an increase in his Navy Estimates. A new German Navy law
was pending, and in January, 1912, it was conveyed to my father that
the German Government was ready for a discussion about naval plans.
The terms we were prepared to offer were: acceptance of British superiority at sea, no increase in the German naval program, no inter-
ference on our part with German colonial expansion, and an agreement
that neither nation would take part in aggressive plans against the other.
King Edward's old friend Sir Ernest Cassel was sent to Berlin to make
unofficial soundings on these lines. He was well received and the Em-

peror suggested that the Cabinet should send a Minister to Berlin for a full discussion. There is no doubt that Sir Edward Grey would have been preferred to any other, but at that moment he had, at my father's request, taken charge of the negotiations between the miners and the owners in the great coal strike, which had reached a critical position. Moreover, as nothing had been said about policy, the Cabinet was unanimous that it would be premature for him to go. Grey suggested that Haldane should be sent on a private, unofficial visit, and carry out informal negotiations. As Chairman of the Royal Commission on the University of London he went in academic guise but with diplomatic intent.

Winston had planned to reinforce Haldane's mission by a statement of our intentions in a speech at Glasgow, where he was going to inspect shipbuilding works along the Clyde. While waiting at the station for his train, he read in a late edition of the evening papers a report of the German Emperor's speech at the opening of the Reichstag, announcing increases both in the Army and the Navy. One sentence struck him as a challenge, almost as a threat: "It is my constant duty and care to maintain and strengthen on land and water the power of defence of the German people *which has no lack of young men fit to bear arms.*" He resolved to take up the challenge in his speech at Glasgow. "This island," he said, "has never been and never will be lacking in trained and hardy mariners bred from their boyhood up in the service of the sea. . . . The purposes of British naval power are essentially defensive. We have no thoughts . . . of aggression and we attribute no such thoughts to other great Powers. There is however this difference between the British naval power and the naval power of the great and friendly Empire . . . of Germany. The British Navy is to us a necessity and from some points of view the German Navy is to them more in the nature of a luxury. Our naval power involves British existence. It is existence for us; it is expansion to them." [11]

This speech produced an explosion of indignation in Germany which it is difficult to explain. (It has been suggested that the word *"Luxus"* has implications which our English "luxury" has not.) The Emperor denounced it as a piece of arrogance demanding an apology and (as Winston wrote) "the luxus Flotte became an expression passed angrily from lip to lip." The outcry was echoed in some sections of our Liberal press. Winston was attacked by the *Daily News,* which had always been among his strongest supporters. "It is difficult to reconcile Lord Haldane's mission with Mr. Churchill's speech at Glasgow. . . . Lord Haldane is on a mission to cultivate good feeling between the

Governments and peoples of England and Germany. . . . Mr. Churchill's speech has already become the excuse for demonstrations by the
anti-German press on this side of the North Sea and the German armour-
plated press which is owned or subsidised by the armament firms. . . .
Of course that is a consequence which Mr. Churchill cannot have desired
though he ought to have foreseen it. . . . Mr. Churchill will pass and
be forgotten. What we trust will remain and work is Lord Haldane's
mission and the determination to come to an understanding with Germany which doubtless it represents." [12]

Many of Winston's Liberal colleagues were critical and the Tories
were delighted that he had dropped another brick. True, the *Times*
welcomed the speech, but in terms hardly calculated to commend him
to Liberal or moderate opinion. "In short his text was 'We've got the
ships, we've got the men, we've got the money, too'. A more faithful
expansion of the old saying could not be imagined and it will be difficult
in future for Liberals to use the word Jingo any longer as a term of
contempt." [13]

My father did not join in this hue and cry. On the contrary, he considered that Winston had made "a plain statement of an obvious truth,"
even though the word "luxury" might not have been happily chosen.
But the strongest vindication came from Haldane himself, who, on his
return two days later from Berlin, declared that so far from being a
hindrance to him in his negotiations Winston's Glasgow speech had
been the greatest possible help. He had in fact himself used the same
arguments to Bethmann-Hollweg the day before.

Unfortunately these arguments had borne no fruit. The only sheaf
that Haldane brought back with him from Germany was the text of
the new German Navy law, which provided for large and progressive
increases in her naval strength, not for the present year alone but for
the five coming years. All hopes of an agreed reduction were for the
time being at an end.

In introducing his first Navy Estimates in March Winston could not
reveal to the House of Commons the Government's knowledge of the
text of the new German Navy law. He was therefore obliged to submit
hypothetical estimates, contingent on there being no further increases
in the German Fleet. He announced that for the next five years we must
maintain a 60 per cent superiority in Dreadnoughts over Germany, and
two keels to one for every additional ship laid down by her. This meant
abandoning the two-power standard and substituting for it a 60 per
cent superiority over the next-strongest naval power. He coupled this

decision with one more attempt at conciliation—an appeal for a naval holiday in 1913. "Supposing we were both to take a holiday for that year. Supposing we both introduced a blank page in the book of misunderstanding. . . ." He spoke of "results immeasurable in their hope and brightness." [14] But the appeal met with no response. The Emperor sent him a courteous message through Sir Ernest Cassel saying that such arrangements would only be possible between allies. The German aim was to detach us from the Entente, and they demanded from us a formula of neutrality which we refused.

Within a few weeks a new situation was created by the passage of the new Navy law in Germany. Its most sinister feature was not the construction of new ships it authorized but the fact that four fifths of the entire German Navy would be kept in full permanent commission and instant readiness for war. It was in fact "a mobilization order." [15] Winston acted immediately. He submitted a Supplementary Estimate for £990,000. (I called it his 19/11¾d. Estimate, because it avoided the million mark by a hairsbreadth.) There was a further concentration of the Fleet in home waters. Ships were withdrawn from China and even from the Mediterranean. There, as our Battle Fleet moved out, the French heavy ships moved in. In Winston's words "a sense of mutual reliance grew swiftly between our Navies." Thus blindly by his policy Von Tirpitz forged new bonds in the Entente and soldered us together. Mutual reliance became mutual dependence. Indeed Winston was alarmed lest by this dependence we might be forfeiting freedom of choice if it came to a decision between war and peace. "That freedom," he wrote to my father and Sir Edward Grey, "will be sensibly impaired if the French can say that they have denuded their Atlantic sea-board, and concentrated in the Mediterranean on the faith of naval arrangements made with us. This will not be true. If we did not exist, the French could not make better dispositions than at present. . . . If France did not exist, we should make no other disposition of our forces. . . . Nothing in naval and military arrangements ought to have the effect of exposing us to such a charge if, when the time comes, we decide to stand out." [16]

The truth of these words was borne out by the naval conversations which followed between the French and British Admiralties. As in the military talks which had preceded them, they could only be conducted on the hypothesis that we should be fighting in partnership and in this case it would of course fall to us to defend the northern and western coasts of France. We refused, however, to allow these naval arrangements to bind us politically. It was agreed that in the event of a threat of war the two Governments should consult together and concert what common action they should take.

The new Estimates enabled us to increase our submarine and air defenses. Winston was intensely and actively air-minded. The transfer of the Battle Fleet to the North Sea increased our safety. Negotiations with the Empire resulted in the gift to the Royal Navy of a Super-Dreadnought from Malaya.* All this was to the good but it was not enough. The new challenge demanded more drastic and far-reaching measures.

Winston's audacity and vision linked with Fisher's original and inventive genius made an inspired combination. They were agreed that their common aim—the invincibility of the Royal Navy—depended on two factors: firing power and speed. In both we had already stolen a march on Germany. The Dreadnought fired shells weighing 850 pounds, the Super-Dreadnought fired a shell weighing 1,400 pounds. Characteristically, Winston sought immediately to "go one better." When consulted on this project, Fisher "hurled himself into its advocacy with tremendous passion. 'Nothing less than the 15-inch gun. . . . What was it that enabled Jack Johnson to knock out his opponents? It was the big punch.' " [17] But no 15-inch gun existed or had ever been made. Could it be made? The experts were full of confidence, but there could be no absolute certainty. The stresses that might develop in the new 15-inch model were unpredictable. One of Winston's first actions at the Admiralty had been to order the building of the *Queen Elizabeth* and her four sister ships. The orthodox procedure would have been to make a trial gun and test it before giving orders for all the guns of these five ships. But a whole year would be lost and "five great vessels would go into the line of battle carrying an inferior weapon to that which we had it in our power to give them." [18] Some of the authorities consulted thought it would be more prudent to lose the year. It was a fateful and hazardous decision to take and Winston was torn with anxiety. He went back to Lord Fisher, who was "steadfast and even violent" and counseled: "Plunge." "So I hardened my heart and took the plunge. The whole outfit of guns was ordered forthwith." But he was racked and haunted by the possibility of failure. "Fancy if they failed. What a disaster. What an exposure. No excuse would be accepted. It would all be brought home to me—'rash, inexperienced', 'before he had been there a

* The offer of three new battleships from the Canadian Government was, alas, rescinded when Mr. Borden was succeeded by Sir Wilfrid Laurier.

month', 'altering all the plans of his predecessors' and producing 'this ghastly fiasco', 'the mutilation of all the ships of the year'." All this would undoubtedly have been said and more besides. But it was not said. Everything turned out all right. "It proved a brilliant success . . . but when I saw the gun fired for the first time a year later and knew that all was well, I felt as if I had been delivered from a great peril."

I have told this story in detail because I think it is a characteristic instance of Winston's courage—comparable with his action in the Second World War when, at a moment in which invasion threatened, he sent our only armored division out to Egypt. And courage alone was not enough to fill the bill in either case, for courage can be blind, even pigheaded. But his was linked with an unerring recognition of the moment when the stake is such that great risks must be faced and taken. And if, as some sour denigrators then described it, it was a lucky gambler's throw, it must be admitted that throughout his life Winston had been a guided gambler.

I remember in the House of Commons two years later hearing him describe the impact of a shell upon a ship. "If you want to make a true picture in your mind of a battle between great modern iron-clad ships you must not think of it as if it were two men in armour striking at each other with heavy swords. It is more like a battle between two egg-shells striking each other with hammers. . . . The importance of hitting first, and hitting hardest and keeping on hitting . . . really needs no clearer proof." [19] Unlike Lloyd George, who complained that Winston "was getting more and more absorbed in boilers," I delighted in his talk of "boilers." The technique of naval design was quite outside my range of understanding (I have never wanted to know *how* anything was done) but he invested it, like everything he touched, with drama and romance.

The 15-inch gun had solved the problem of firing power. The next essential to be tackled was speed. On this need also Fisher was insistent—and clamant. He wrote to Winston (on January 14, 1912): "I yesterday had an illuminating letter from Jellicoe. . . . He has all the Nelsonic attributes. He writes to me of new designs. His *one, one, one* cry is SPEED! *Do lay that to heart!* Do remember the receipt for jugged hare in Mrs. Glasse's Cookery Book! *First catch your hare!*" [20]

Winston has written a fascinating dissertation on the decisive role of speed in naval strategy. Its gist, though not its subtleties, can be given in a few sentences. "Smashing up the tail of an enemy's Fleet is a poor way of preventing him from achieving his objective, i.e., going where he wants to go. It is not comparable to smashing up his head. . . . If the speeds of the Fleets are equal . . . the heads of both lines will be abreast and the fire will only be given and returned ship for ship. But suppose you have a division of ships in your Fleet which go much faster than any of your other ships or of your enemy's ships. These ships will be certainly able to draw ahead and curl round the head of the enemy's line." [21]

A fast division of greyhound ships, outstripping the enemy in speed and yet as strong in gun power and in armor as any battleship, such was the dream of Fisher, Winston and the Sea Lords. Could such a dream be realized in terms of construction and design? Only by the use of oil fuel instead of coal. Oil gave far greater speed than coal; it occupied less space; it more than halved the man power used for stoking; above all it enabled ships to be refueled at sea by tankers. But alas, while Britain produced the best coal in the world, Britain produced no oil. Where should we get it from? How should we bring it here? Where should we store it? Could we protect it? How should we pay for it? All these questions presented formidable problems. "To commit the Navy irrevocably to oil was indeed 'to take arms against a sea of troubles'," wrote Winston. . . . "Should we drive out into the teeth of the gale, or should we bide contented where we were? Yet beyond the breakers was a great hope. . . . Mastery itself was the prize of the venture. . . . Forward, then!" [22] And once more Lord Fisher, who had been the pioneer of oil fuel in the Navy and who, as long ago as 1886, was known as the "Oil Maniac," propelled him to the plunge.

But now, out of blue skies, an untoward event disturbed their harmony. Winston had hitherto accepted Fisher's advice both in appointing and in scrapping Admirals. (And Fisher enjoyed scrapping Admirals even more than he enjoyed appointing them.) In April Winston had the temerity to appoint three Admirals to high commands without consulting Fisher. And though he wrote to him to explain his reasons, he received a furious letter of reproach and malediction. "I fear this must be my last communication with you on any matter at all. I am sorry for it, but I consider you have betrayed the Navy in these three appointments, and what the pressure could have been to induce you to betray your trust is beyond my comprehension." [23] Winston wrote him a conciliatory reply and tried to soothe and reason with him but he refused to be placated.

By a lucky chance Winston had planned to embark at Genoa for a Mediterranean cruise on the *Enchantress* a few weeks later. My father and I went with him and there was much discussion between us about the Fisher imbroglio. It was very worrying for Winston to be deserted by his fellow plunger at the outset of this crucial venture in which he needed all the inner as well as outward support that he could get. Fisher happened to be in Naples and it seemed a heaven-sent opportunity for lassoing him there and roping him in again. Winston therefore sent him a telegram asking him to stay in Naples until he and my father arrived on May 23rd and to keep a few days absolutely free for them.

I find the following entry in my diary: *"Friday 24th May 1912.* We reached Naples this morning and anchored in the harbour; under grey skies, Vesuvius hidden in the clouds, no sun or colour anywhere. In many ways it looked rather like a Scotch shipping town—(I hope all this is not an omen?). Some of us went on shore in a pinnace—straight to the Museum where we saw the most wonderful treasures. . . ." (Ecstatic enumeration follows.) "Back to the Yacht for luncheon—and *there was Lord Fisher!* in the flesh (but not yet in the bag). I examined him minutely and tried to diagnose his mood and his potential placability. His eyes, as always, were like smouldering charcoals—lighting up at his own jokes. He was very friendly to Father and Prince Louis * but glowered a bit, I thought, at Winston. To me he retailed a stock of anecdotes, puns, chestnuts and riddles which might have come out of crackers. (I expect that all 'great men' of *action* talk like this—at least to women?) After luncheon he dragged us off à contre coeur on a long expedition to a most hideous modern Pompeian villa belonging to some friends of his called X. Poor Father bled—aching to get back to the Museum. Winston *endured* for oil's sake, but behaved as though he were barely conscious. I played up for all I was worth and perjured myself in praise of the most monstrous objects. . . . As the day wore on I noticed signs of mellowing in Lord F. which I feel will turn to melting before long. I whispered at tea to Winston: 'He's melting.' His mind was far away. He gazed at me blankly and said in a hard, loud voice: *'What's* melting?' Distracted I replied: 'The butter', which brought me an 'old-fashioned look' from our hostess, who eyed the bread and butter anxiously. When we got back to the Enchantress Lord F. and W. were locked together in naval conclave. . . . I'm sure they can't resist each other for long at close range."

My next day's entry opens: "Danced on deck with Lord Fisher for a very long time before breakfast." This became a daily routine. I note that his "staying-power is formidable and as he never reverses I reel

* Prince Louis of Battenberg, First Sea Lord.

giddily in his arms and lurch against his heart of oak." He spent the whole of our Neapolitan visit with us and I felt sure, long before Sunday morning, that his anger had evaporated, that oil beckoned irresistibly and that he would come back.

I have since read that he attributed his decision to the sermon of the naval chaplain at morning service on the *Enchantress*. In a letter to his son he wrote: "He fixed his eyes steadfastly on me and said: 'No man still possessing all his powers and full of vitality has any right to say "I am now going to rest, as I have had a hard life", for he owes a duty to his country and fellow men.' It was an arrow shot at a venture like the one that killed Ahab." [24] The chaplain must have been verbally inspired but it was not by any human agency. I cannot help believing that his words were the pretext rather than the cause of Lord Fisher's return. It is always comforting to be told that it is one's duty to one's country to follow a course dictated by one's inclination. I am ashamed to say that though I attended the service I have no recollection of the sermon and was quite unaware of the miracle it had wrought.

Oil was once more poured upon the waters and peace returned to the Admiralty. The Winston-Fisher axis was re-established, and the fateful plunge was taken. It was decided to create the Fast Division; the vital and irrevocable decision to base the future existence of the Royal Navy on oil was made. The problem of supply bristled with difficulties, and Winston's first step was to set up a Royal Commission on oil supply, over which he asked Lord Fisher to preside as chairman. The outcome was the Anglo-Persian Oil Convention which, apart from securing a large proportion of the Navy's oil supplies, proved a most remunerative investment. The British Government, by investing two million, to be spent on developing the Persian oil fields, secured a controlling interest in the company. In *The World Crisis* (published in 1923) Winston estimates the return on this sum as amounting to forty million. In 1928 Lord Greenway wrote that, owing to the much enhanced value of the shares, another twenty million could be added to this figure. He described the transaction as "the only measure of defence (with the exception of the Suez Canal Shares) ever entered upon by the British Government which instead of costing tax-payers a large sum of money has given them an enormous profit"! He added that "The credit of carrying through these extraordinarily favourable contracts is of course entirely due to Mr. Churchill. . . . From the point of view of the Navy it was a great feat of statesmanship for which the country should always be grateful." [25]

Within the Admiralty, Winston had won the battle of speed and power. Another and a harder struggle lay ahead of him, that of wresting from the Cabinet and from the House of Commons the wherewithal to pay for them. His colleagues were becoming increasingly alarmed and indignant at the rising tide of naval expenditure and he admits that they had some cause for complaint. Battleships were assumed to cost $2\frac{1}{4}$ millions each. But the *Queen Elizabeth* class of the Fast Division cost over 3 millions each. The expense of the change-over from coal to oil, involving as it did the creation of a vast oil reserve, was enormous. All this had to be provided out of current estimates. "On more than one occasion," he records, "I thought I should succumb. I had however the unfailing support of the Prime Minister."

And it was not only in the Cabinet that he faced opposition. He was again arousing suspicion and mistrust among the rank and file of his own party. Once more they feared that he was reverting to type—i.e., to his native Toryism—that he was wholly concerned with building up vast armaments and that his interest in reform had waned.

It is true that his mind had become detached from domestic politics. Throughout his life he always found it difficult to think (in his own sense of that word) of two things at once. Confronted with what he saw as a dire threat to our very existence, it is not unnatural that questions like Welsh disestablishment should have failed to arrest his attention. But the National Insurance Act was another matter. Here was an issue by which he had once been fired and in which he had played an active and important part. Had he not once proclaimed that the word "Insure" should be written over the door of every cottage and upon the blotting book of every public man? That Act was now being passed through Parliament in the teeth of furious opposition. Enraged employers were meeting in their thousands at the Albert Hall to vow that Britons never, never, never would lick stamps. Some Duchesses (according to *Punch*) had even threatened to emigrate. It was Lloyd George's prize pigeon, his supreme achievement and his finest hour. Yet Winston seemed oblivious both to its hazards and its glories. Small wonder that Lloyd George felt some annoyance, and complained that Winston was "taking less and less part in home politics," and that he "declaimed about his blasted ships" for a whole morning.[26] According to Lord Riddell, he reproached Winston for having "become a water creature. You think we all live in the sea, and all your thoughts are devoted to sea-life, fishes and other aquatic creatures. You forget that most of us live on land." [27] There was some truth in Lloyd George's accusation. Yet there was one land which still aroused Winston's passions—Ireland. Among domestic issues Ireland alone held its own, and throughout the fierce and bitter Home Rule controversy he fought in the front line.

With the Tories he was chronically suspect, and though they welcomed and supported his strong-Navy policy their personal hostility was in no way allayed. His sincerity was again suspect because his past record of naval and military retrenchment was still fresh in the public mind. The "tattered flag" had now been hauled down, the "stricken field" deserted. Lord Charles Beresford reminded him in the House of Commons that "he had been just as violent against expenditure on the Navy as he is now in favour of it." But he continued to give as good as he got—in fact much better. It was in reply to one of Lord Charles's sallies that Winston once described him as "one of those orators who before they get up, do not know what they are going to say, when they are speaking do not know what they are saying, and when they have sat down do not know what they have said." [28]

Throughout 1913 he fought a hard and lone fight for his Navy estimates. He has recorded that they formed "the main and often the sole topic of conversation at no less than fourteen full and prolonged meetings of the Cabinet. At the outset I found myself almost in a minority of one. . . . By the middle of December it seemed to me certain that I should have to resign. . . . The Prime Minister, however, . . . so handled matters that no actual breach occurred. On several occasions when it seemed that disagreement was total and final, he prevented a decision adverse to the Admiralty by terminating the discussion; and in the middle of December when this process could go on no longer, he adjourned the whole matter till the middle of January." [29]

My poor father's philosophy, patience and ingenuity were strained to their uttermost limits. He was undergoing a repetition of the crisis over the naval estimates of 1909. Once more he was faced with rival threats of resignation from two colleagues. But this time Winston's role was reversed. In 1909 he and Lloyd George were allies, fighting McKenna side by side. Now they were fighting each other. My father was convinced that Winston's demands were justified both by the standard accepted by the Cabinet and by the increasing threat of German sea power. As was his habit in a deadlock, he worked for time. His task was not made easier by an interview given by Mr. Lloyd George to the *Daily Chronicle* (on January 3, 1914), in which he urged the necessity of reducing our expenditure on armaments and insisted that this was "the most favourable moment which had presented itself during the last twenty years" for doing so. (Here his "prophetic soul" for once misled him.) He then made a direct thrust at Winston by recalling that Lord Randolph Churchill had resigned the Chancellorship of the Exchequer in 1887 because he considered the expenditure on armaments in the estimates of that year "bloated and profligate." The total expenditure on the Army and Navy which Lord Randolph had opposed in 1887 was 32 million. His son was preparing an estimate of 51 million for the Navy alone. This open indictment from a Cabinet colleague (and that colleague the Chancellor of the Exchequer) acted as a rallying cry to Winston's critics in the press and in the House of Commons.

I was alone with my father in Downing Street during these crucial weeks, and there were moments when I felt like assassinating several of his colleagues. The following extracts from his letters to my stepmother (then in the south of France) give some idea of his difficulties. *"Jan. 6th, 1914.* Illingworth, Grey, Samuel, Seely etc. full of maledictions of Ll. G. and his heedless interview which had set all Europe by the ears, not to mention the party here. Winston is still in Paris and maintains a dignified and moody silence. *Jan. 20th.* I find political affairs very much embrangled as Ll. G. and Winston are still poles apart over the Navy and it looks as if it might come to breaking-point. If this were plainly inevitable sooner than have a smash-up and resignation I should probably dissolve Parliament and run the risk of the election. I had a long talk with Grey this morning and he inclines to that view. But it is too soon to come to decisions and as the expected rarely happens the clouds may blow over. *Jan. 21st.* Our Navy situation has been developing today and not in a pacific fashion. I had a long talk with Crewe who stayed to luncheon and was as usual wise and far-seeing. This afternoon I have been at a conclave of the malcontents, Ll. G. was there, but Simon, Samuel and of all people Beauchamp are far the most aggressive and most anti-Winston. I doubt increasingly whether the thing can be patched up; it is curious what personal hostility Winston excites even in the most unexpected quarters. *Jan. 23rd.* I think we shall get over our little troubles over the Navy without much more ado—Ll. G. squeezing in one direction and Winston in the other. Neither of them wants to go and in an odd sort of way they are really fond of one another. *Jan. 25th.* Our little crisis seems to be melting away, for the moment at any rate and the alternative of an election is not likely to present itself, if at all, just now. One cannot say for certain till after the Cabinet on Tuesday but both Ll. G. and Winston are anxious for an accommodation. *Jan. 27th.* Haldane, Ll. G., Winston and other visitors, and all the afternoon the Cabinet when we had a long discussion about the Navy without coming to any conclusion. We go on tomorrow when we ought to decide something one way or another. . . . So far I hold my tongue and listen but I expect I shall have to take a fairly strong line in the end. *Jan. 29th.* We had another Cabinet today about the Navy. The leaders of the malcontents (Simon and Beauchamp) came to see me beforehand, to assure me of their loyalty etc.—I having made a strong appeal yesterday to the whole pack not to split at such a time on such a point. There is no doubt that Winston tries them rather high; to use his own phrase today he 'gyrates around the facts'; and in the House we shall have a devil of a time with our own people."

The deadlock continued unbroken throughout February and part of March. The Home Rule controversy was then at its height. Had Winston resigned, Prince Louis of Battenberg, the whole Board of Admiralty, and his Under-Secretaries would have gone with him. "No one," he wrote, "expected me to pass away in sweet silence." Ardent Home Rulers were well aware of the effect this would have had upon the fortunes of their cause. "At last, thanks to the unwearying patience of the Prime Minister, and to his solid, silent support, the Naval Estimates were accepted practically as they stood." [30]

Winston had won hands down, though a few concessions were made which saved Lloyd George's face. As the price of victory Winston agreed to promise a substantial reduction in the estimates of the following year. "But when the time came," he wrote, "I was not pressed to redeem that undertaking."

One economy was, quite fortuitously, to prove providential for the future. A trial mobilization was substituted for the usual naval maneuvers with the result that the fleet, instead of being scattered on maneuvers, was at its stations and instantly ready when war threatened in July.

I felt intense relief at the outcome of this struggle, in which I had been with Winston heart and soul throughout—relief too for my father who, as so often happened, was faced with several simultaneous crises at home and abroad. The final stages of the Parliament Act had coincided with Agadir and its threat to the peace of Europe. Now, while the Home Rule conflict was raging in the country and the House of Commons and the naval controversy was splitting the Cabinet, two Balkan wars broke out which threatened to set the world on fire.

It was hard to watch at such close range the strain and stress endured by those one loved, powerless to lighten their burden by a straw. Only a little human first aid could be given. To Winston it was a help to talk about the load which weighed upon his mind; to my father it was a help to talk of something else.

To both throughout these difficult and stormy years there was one respite from all care, one sure escape to happiness unalloyed—a cruise on the *Enchantress*. These voyages were interludes of pure delight and as such deserve a chapter to themselves.

Chapter Nineteen

INTERLUDES OF DELIGHT

IN the month of May we turned our backs upon a sea of troubles to sail on bluer seas and under brighter skies toward a Mediterranean goal. For this, our treat of treats and lark of larks, was sanctified by high official business.

The Admiralty yacht was (for alas, it is no longer) the sweetest of all the sweets of office. It was the official perquisite of the First Lord and his Board in which they had the right and duty to sail the seas on their official errands. It was a traditional institution dating back to 1664 when the Lord High Admiral, who combined the functions of First Lord and First Sea Lord, sailed in her with his Board on their lawful occasions. The *Enchantress* that I knew and loved was built nearly three centuries later in 1903. She was a ship of 3,800 tons with a crew of between 80 and 100. As a lucky stowaway who had the good fortune to sail from time to time upon her cruises of inspection, I can testify that no official duty was ever laced with a more exquisite and memorable delight.

There is no greater luxury than to be afloat without a timetable on board a ship whose destination can be decreed at will and whim from day to day, almost from hour to hour. The only hazard, except weather, is to be mewed up inescapably with the same companions—and those the wrong ones. But the human elements on the *Enchantress* could not have been more harmonious and exciting. First and foremost there was the First Lord himself, sometimes the First Sea Lord, Prince Louis of Battenberg, tall and blue-bearded, with a simple, natural dignity, and always what Her Majesty the Queen has called "a foam of Admirals" which often included the gay and dashing Admiral Beatty and Admiral Moore. The First Lord's private secretary, Eddie Marsh, was a constant passenger, indispensable alike to work and play, and he had now been joined by a gifted colleague from the Admiralty, James Masterton-Smith, who became Winston's highly prized and devoted friend and thrall and followed him later to the Ministry of Munitions, the War Office and the Colonial Office. The First Lord's guests apart from Clemmie were often his lovely and beloved sister-in-law Lady Gwende-line Churchill, Clemmie's gay and sparkling sister Nellie Hozier, my father and myself. Our tastes and habits varied but they never clashed. My father was a voracious sight-seer, lapping up Baedeker like Hippocrene, scouring museums and lingering in ruined temples. Winston showed some impatience with his absorption in the classical past. "Those Greeks and Romans," he protested, "they are so overrated. They only said everything *first*. I've said just as good things myself. But they got in before me." It was in vain that my father pointed out that the world had been going on for quite a long time before the Greeks and Romans appeared upon the scene. It was impossible to shake Winston's conviction that they had stolen a march on him by unfair means. My father had a staunch ally in his fellow classicist Eddie Marsh—an equally ardent sight-seer. Eddie opened his heart *à deux battants* to every impression, reacting with impartial susceptibility to past and present, ruins, sunsets, fauna, flora, jokes and games. Only the naval aspects of the journey left him cold and it was precisely these problems which obsessed his chief. I find a note in my diary: "W. in glorious form though slightly over-concentrated on instruments of destruction. Blasting and shattering are now his idées fixes. As we leaned side by side against the taffrail, gliding past the lovely, smiling coast-line of the Adriatic, bathed in sun, and I remarked 'How perfect!' he startled me by his reply: 'Yes—range perfect—visibility perfect'—and details followed, showing how effectively we could lay waste the landscape and blow the nestling towns sky-high." He was enthralled by the technology of naval warfare and his sense of its results in human terms was for the time being in abeyance. He also hungered for the newspapers and pouches we should pick up at our next port of call, whereas my father felt intense relief at their absence.

A few rough notes from my diary scribbled in hot haste at the time may possibly convey the daily life and atmosphere of our voyages more vividly than the "emotion recollected in tranquillity" with which I now remember them.

"*Enchantress, May 22nd 1912*. We all left London Tuesday morning. Amusing station send-off scene—Margot, Mrs. West,* Lady Blanche Hozier, Edwin Montagu, Venetia,† Master of Elibank,‡ Bongie,§ Micky,§ etc. We rumbled off to Dover in a Pullman Car full of Cabinet boxes, newspapers, letters, flowers. Calm crossing in bright sunshine. I read 'Imaginary Speeches' with Winston all the way to Calais (we both especially enjoyed the very good one by Lord Rosebery). The train-de-luxe to Paris where we all turned out and had delicious hot baths at the Ritz and an ambrosial banquet at Voisin's before re-embarking in our train. Clemmie not very well, poor darling. Next day long luncheon with Father, W., Goonie and the delightful Bluebeard Admiral [Prince Louis]. Much talk between him and Winston about Napoleonic strategy when we emerged from the Mont Cenis tunnel. Final arrival at Genoa in pouring rain. We found the Enchantress lying, slimy-decked, in the beautiful harbour and steamed off happily under brightening skies. To-day we reached Elba in sunshine and some of us went on shore with W. in the pinnace and drove through flowery fields and vineyards to Napoleon's house—a little villa on a height stymied by a gigantic horror of a Fish museum, erected in his honour by one Demidoff. (Why *fish*?) It was a disappointing shrine for W.'s pilgrim heart but we saw a moving death-mask of him in a church." Naples followed, largely devoted to the recapture of Lord Fisher, though we had one wonderful day at Pompeii, "wandering down the long lovely silent streets among the little courts and houses of the dead where grass and flowers grow. One ought to go there quite alone and hear one's own footsteps echo—not as we did, with a crowd of Vice-Consuls, Naval Attachés and photographers. Goonie and I were carried in palanquins! I'm not sure how much W. enjoyed it but he did notice that the decorations on the walls were exactly like those in the Saloon at Archerfield and that their colours were just as vivid.

"*May 26th*. We went ashore again at Paestum—the most beautiful 'sight' we've seen since we started. Temples of golden stone standing by the sea amongst fields of poppy, marigold, love-in-a-mist and giant *crimson* cornflowers. The great temple of Zeus has double rows of Doric columns and through the colonnades the sea beyond shines like

* Winston's mother, Mrs. George Cornwallis West.
† Venetia Stanley, later Mrs. Edwin Montagu.
‡ Government Chief Whip.
§ Sir Maurice Bonham Carter and Sir Roderick Meiklejohn, my father's private secretaries.

a sheet of silver. Winston was quite unaffected by its symmetry. He concentrated all his powers on trying to catch the little green-backed lizards which darted in and out of the crevices and crannies of the stone with lightning speed and agility. They were very elusive and defeated all his efforts. He then pressed Admiral Beatty and Masterton into the service as beaters to make a drive, adjuring them 'We must be more scientific about our strategy. There is a science in catching lizards and we must master it.' We picnicked and drove back in little tooth-rattling gigs and dog-carts, two in each. I drove with him and we got out and picked armfuls of flowers.

"*Syracuse Harbour May 28th.* We are lying at anchor in the great harbour where the Athenians fought 2,000 years ago. I have just been bathing in it before breakfast with Winston and Clemmie—splashing in fathoms of chrysoprase in a life-belt of enormous size through which I was threaded, like silk through a bodkin, and from which I felt that one unwary wriggle would dislodge me. W. is never so happy as in the water.

"Father, who has been deep in his Thucydides, has been expounding to us on the spot the strategic course of the Sicilian expedition and this engaged W.'s interest—even though it had all happened to the Greeks! (He had, however, all sorts of good ideas about how they could have done it better.) We had a wonderful picnic yesterday on the Epipolae— a high plain above the town—among the ruins of an old Greek fortress— Fort Euryalus. We lunched amongst its fallen walls, great blocks of stone all overgrown with rosemary, wild lavender and candytuft. Admiral Beatty's eyes gleamed when he saw a pot of foie-gras in the basket and he rejected all other food proffered to him with the firm formula 'I think I'll stick to the pâté'—which caused mild anxiety to others who were plodding through their sandwiches. . . . We went up to the Greek theatre towards sunset and lay there among wild thyme and humming bees and watched the sea changing from blue to flame and then to cool jade green as the sun dropped into it and the stars came out. The theatre is a vast stone amphiteatre which used to hold I-forget-how-many thousand people. W. and F. were interested to test its acoustics and *Eddie* was (appropriately) selected to speak to us from the stage. There to our delight he recited A. E. Housman's parody of a Greek tragedy, beginning:

> 'Oh suitably attired in leather boots
> Head of a Traveller . . .'

in his highest falsetto and every word was clearly audible. He said afterwards that he was afraid that the 'offended shade of Aeschylus should dispatch an eagle to drop a tortoise on his head'.

"Little boat-loads of Syracusan musicians came and sang to us round the Yacht in the dark as we played Auction after dinner."

Our nightly bridge on the *Enchantress* deserves a word to itself. My father was an eager and execrable player. Winston was even more dangerous, for he played a romantic game untrammeled by conventions, codes or rules. When playing in partnership they made a happy, care-free and catastrophic combination. But to cut with Winston was to both his private secretaries a severe ordeal. Masterton was a really good bridge player and treated the game with respect. Moreover, though the stakes were low he could not afford to lose overmuch. He used to sit in agony while Winston declared, doubled and redoubled with wild reck-lessness, watching his every discard and building reasonable conjectures on his play, only to be disillusioned and dumfounded again and again. "But, First Lord—you discarded the knave . . ." "The cards I throw away are not worthy of observation or I should not discard them. It is the cards I *play* on which you should concentrate your attention."

Eddie, though an indifferent player, had a passion for cards and all card games transformed him. Over the "green baize" he sat erect with a square jaw and glittering eyes, holding his cards in trembling hands and breathing heavily. He took his own performance very seriously. In bridge he tasted rapture, a rapture which was bittersweet when playing with Winston as his partner. I can still hear his shrill cry of pain when Winston, having led up to and sacrificed his king, declared: "Nothing is here for tears. The king cannot fall unworthily if he falls to the sword of the ace"—a dictum which left Eddie's tears over his fallen king un-dried.

To Eddie, Masterton's word was law at bridge. He revered him as a master, opened his heart to him as to a confessor. The bathrooms in the *Enchantress* were all assembled together side by side, and divided by partitions which did not reach the ceiling, so that one could converse agreeably with one's neighbor. Lying lapped in hot salt water in my bath I often heard Eddie next door pouring out his bridge confessions to Masterton and asking to be guided or shriven. "Masterton," he piped pathetically, "you have always told me that in No Trumps it's right to lead the *fourth* highest of my *longest* suit. Well, I had four dia-monds to the nine, so I led my two which was fourth highest and Winston returned my lead and when he found I only had the nine he was *furious* with me. Was I right, Masterton? And was he wrong?" A long pause—and then very gravely in a deep bass voice from Masterton: "What else had you in your hand, Eddie?" "Well, I had two aces and a King, Queen," etc., etc. Absolution was sometimes withheld and sometimes given. But I felt that master and pupil, penitent and Pope were united by the bond of a common misfortune—that of being Winston's partner —and that they felt deeply for one another and themselves.

Games were the order of the day after dinner, but during the long days at sea there were often occasions when, like the Walrus, Winston felt that the time had come

> To talk of many things:
> Of shoes—and ships—and sealing-wax—
> Of cabbages—and kings—

and I happened to be the lucky Carpenter at hand. We had long talks about everything under the sun. (Would that I had kept a record of them, though it would have been as difficult as bottling Niagara.) There is one which is indelibly engraved on my memory. One night after the fun and games were over, before going to bed we went out and paced the deck together, dark seas below us and bright stars above. For a time there was silence, then he murmured over to himself a text he had always had a fancy for: "Thou shalt not muzzle the ox that treadeth out the corn." After repeating it once or twice, he said to me: "How would you interpret that text? What do you think it means?" I had never read into it any meaning but the obvious one—that it was silly to hamper an ox which was doing its duty. But I realized that this would not fill the bill; to "interpret" I must dig deeper. So I said: "I suppose it may mean that if anyone—ox or man—is performing a unique and essential service—a service which only he can render—he should be exempt from the rules and restraints applying to the ordinary run of human beings. I think it means that genius should be given a special license." This interpretation obviously pleased him. He chewed it over for a time in silence. Then he asked: "And would you accord to *me* this special license?" I replied quite truthfully that I would. His next question was, "And would you accord it to your father?" I said that I did not think that he would ever feel the need of it. It would never occur to him to demand a special license for himself for any activity. He could operate quite freely and comfortably within the rules and regulations laid down for ordinary human beings. "Yet you would give it to me?" "Yes, I would. I think that you *need* more rope. I think there are some things which should be forgiven you which would, rightly, not be forgiven to my father—and for which, incidentally, he would never need forgiveness."

He was obviously deeply interested, and gratified, by this distinction that I drew between them, because he understood that it was a difference in *kind,* not in degree. In degree I would never have put anyone higher than my father. But Winston belonged to a different species. It was impossible to measure him against others. He demanded a yardstick all his own. He was compounded of imponderables—heady impulses, blind spots about the obvious—and with them those flashes of divination which at our first meeting I had recognized as the light of genius as certainly and as irrationally as the water diviner knows when the rod leaps in his hand that he is near a spring. He too had that irrational certainty about himself. What could it matter that he knew I shared it? A world in arms could not have shaken it. And yet he seemed as happy as a child to hear me say that if he were an ox I would not have him muzzled.

"Malta 30th May—2nd June. On Wednesday morning I was just finishing dressing when I received an order from the First Lord to come on deck immediately and see the approach to Malta Harbour. I rushed up to join him. The Island we were approaching looked like one vast fortress, a great heap of battlemented stone built between sky and sea. We sailed into the most wonderful harbour I could have imagined or dreamt of—'harbour of harbours'—strongholds and fortresses piled up on every side, Men of War hoisting their colours with bugle calls from every deck. Grandees of all sorts began to arrive in pinnaces—all the Admirals in the first, followed by their Flag-Lieutenants, then Ian Hamilton * with a military contingent and finally Lord Kitchener looking quite splendid, treble life-size—but alas! dressed as a civilian in a Homburg hat. (He has come over from Cairo to confer with F. and W.) I was enchanted to see him again. He has a strange charm for me which I can't quite account for. Unlike most people I feel wholly at ease with him— (except that I never know *which* eye he is looking at me with). We sat about and talked to these great men and their suites till luncheon time, when we all went off (dressed up as near to the nines as we could possibly manage) to a gigantic official banquet with Admiral Poe, who commands the Mediterranean Fleet. I sat between two Admirals who groused terribly at the removal of their ships to the North Sea. I glibly

* General Sir Ian Hamilton, Governor of Malta and Commander-in-Chief of the Mediterranean Forces.

produced all the arguments I had picked up from W. en route—such as 'much better none than too few', etc."

A list of functions follows—a dinner at the Palace "where we found all the guests (numbering hundreds) arranged in a vast circle as they are at a King-and-Queen or Connaught dinner at home. We all shook hands with them all. I sat between Admiral Poe and a General. Bands playing. After the King's health we danced with myriads of young men all looking exactly alike but fortunately all dressed differently in glittering uniforms. Ian Hamilton, gay as a grig, was never off the floor. I found his paces difficult (he hops like the little hills in the Psalms and often lands upon one's toes). . . .

"Thursday 31st May. Captain Ruck-Keene * (a stern and pessimistic character) gave us ten minutes to leave the ship as the mystic rites of coaling were impending (another argument for oil, as W. did not fail to emphasize!). We drove to San Antonio, Ian Hamilton's country-house, in a procession of flies—just like four-poster beds (with little flannelette valances round the top)—called carrozze. We spent the day there in a steamy, fragrant, Kubla-Khanish garden full of bougainvillaea, flowering pomegranates and blossoming trees of every colour. Jean † endured us and cared for us with grace and rare kindness (even letting us read books if we wanted to). Sir Ian gay, galant and gallant and still very good-looking. He and W. are very old cronies and happy together. Dinner-party. I sat between H. E. the Governor and an Admiral. (All the *Captains* are full of brilliant promise which all the Admirals seem to break. Why is this? I must ask Winston.) We danced afterwards and sat out in the Paradisal garden, the air laden with strange heavy fragrances, Japanese lanterns aglow on trees, stars pricked into the black velvet sky—'On such a night' . . . But I have never known one like it.

"Friday 1st June. The best day of all. We went out on the Cornwallis, Captain Ryan's ship, for battle practice. Father, Lord K., Winston, Prince Louis and Admiral Beatty joined us on board after a little tour in the Destroyer Kennet and we sailed off in this huge iron-grey monster into the open sea in pursuit of the Suffolk which was towing the target. Five minutes before the firing started we were told to put cotton-wool in our ears (or little glass stoppers with *anchors*—so like the Navy!). The Suffolk was four miles off. The minutes were counted—three—two—one. . . . Then it began. . . . I held my hands over my ears. It was

* Captain of the *Enchantress.*
† Lady Hamilton.

less like a sound than a thrilling shock to one's whole being. Every inch of one's body was shaken and vibrating from the soles of one's feet upwards. Then again—and again and again till every thought was driven from one's head. Great bursts of flame flashing out of the side of the ship. Then far away, where the shell struck, a fountain rose out of the sea—higher than Nelson's Column or St. Paul's. I dimly realized for the first time what war would be—and wondered how anyone could *think* in the middle of a battle. After it was all over we went down and washed our faces, pitch-black with 'smokeless powder'.

"Torpedo practice with submarines followed. It is almost impossible to spot the periscope which looks about the size of an umbrella-handle in the waves—but the sea above a submarine looks a lighter green and I should think an aeroplane could easily mark one down in the Mediterranean—though in the North Sea it might be more difficult. W. is very air-minded and wants a service of Naval Air Scouts to watch the coasts and defend dockyards." (This he brought into being and developed during his term of office.)

"There was a sinister postscript—post-mortem would be a truer description—to the battle-practice. Winston was itching with impatience to know how many 'hits' had been scored. I shall never forget his face when Admiral Poe broke to him that there had been—*none!*—'Not one? *All* misses? How can you explain it?'—The Admiral's reply did not have a soothing effect: 'Well—you see, First Lord, the shells seem to have either fallen *just* short of the target or else gone just a *little* beyond it.' I will not describe what followed. . . .

"*Saturday 2nd June.* Our last day. An early morning review of soldiers and Marines on the Marsa—a large arid strip of ground where polo, golf and all other manly pastimes happen. The Bluejackets looked charming and the little Midshipmen with daggers drawn—but I thought it must have been 'small beer' to Lord K. when I remembered the review at Khartoum when the Cavalry and Camel Corps galloped past him in clouds of sun-irradiated sand. He and W. have seemed to get on *very* well together this time—which relieved me, as their relationship has always been a prickly one and Lord K. can't like the prospect of the Mediterranean ships going north. . . . Gigantic reception of 120 Maltese on board the Yacht. Then 28 Flag-Lieutenants came to dinner and we danced afterwards to the 'Russells' band—very amusing and exciting—far too few women but we started off with Sir Roger which is a good ice-breaker. The performance of the eminent was watched by the less eminent and much fun was had by all. The Flag-Lieutenants were all quite delightful—unblasé, amusing, easily amused and wonderfully courteous and keen. I had a very good talk with one Fitzgerald—an A.D.C. of Lord K.'s—about Egypt and the Sudan. We said goodbye to Lord K. who went off to board the 'Hampshire',* which had brought him here from Alexandria, and we sailed away at eleven, as the last pinnace laden with guests disappeared.

"*Bizerta June 3rd.* After a calm and heavenly journey over blue seas past rocky capes and islands we sailed into Bizerta harbour about four. The coast is disappointingly un-African—as Goonie said, 'not unlike the environs of Bournemouth'—on a parched day. No sand or palms or blacks or camels or lions or tigers. The harbour itself is magnificent but not a patch on Malta. Seventeen guns were fired as we steamed in and the 'Suffolk' which had come with us replied and ran up the French flag. Soon afterwards French grandees began to arrive on board—and most ludicrous rites of reception took place. Winston had somehow scraped up out of the depths of the ship ten Marines, none of whom, as their Sergeant confessed, had presented arms for ten years. These were dressed up in scarlet uniforms and placed in a row at the head of the companion ladder and made to bugle and salute and present arms when the man we conjectured to be the Commander-in-Chief set foot on board. He unfortunately turned out to be the Mayor! However, nothing loath they went through it all (perhaps rather better!) a second time.

"The Enchantress was soon flooded with French of all ranks, ages and callings—all hyper-courteous and welcoming but a little non-plussed by their complete inability to make themselves understood by the *men* of our party. French Admiral to the First Lord: 'Vous avez fait une bonne traversée?'—Winston (rather loud): 'Yes, yes, very fine fortifications.' Admiral: 'A la bonne heure—enchanté de vous voir.' Winston (louder still): 'How many torpedoes have you got?' Then, with a great effort: 'Où sont vos sous-marins?'

"We embarked in a Destroyer and went ten miles across the great salt lake which forms the inner harbour. Champagne was served and everyone drank each other's health with low bows. The amount of bowing that went on was phenomenal—and infectious, I found myself joining in—though I suppose women ought to do something else? (But what? Curtseying in a Destroyer would be contre nature.) We disembarked into several motors tightly packed and drove round docks, repairing works, etc., back round the lake by land and home to the

* The *Hampshire* was the ship in which only four years later he was to meet his death. His faithful and devoted Fitzgerald died with him.

Enchantress. Vast official dinner followed. Then a party from the crew of the Suffolk came on board and we wandered about the deck and talked till all hours.

"Next morning at ten we all started for Tunis (except poor darling Clemmie who wasn't well), accompanied by the President, the General, the English Consul, etc. The day was dazzling and beauty indescribable; we drove by blue lakes with green shallows and purple fringes, jagged mountain-ranges—passing on the road strange crabbed brown Old Testament figures jogging on donkeys, hobbled camels feeding. The heat consumed us and it was a relief to plunge into the ice-cool shade of a Museum just outside Tunis. We lunched at an hôtel called Belvedere where a gigantic meal was served with an ice between every course— then into Tunis which is just as I imagined it—a snow-white town under a blue sky, encircled by a wall. The Sukhs very like those of Cairo and Omdurman—cool brown shade—drowsy brown figures asleep upon their counters or squatting at their doors. . . . We drove on to the site of Carthage on the edge of a fabulously blue sea. Tea at the Resident's where everybody wore their grandest clothes—high collars and hats trimmed with ostrich feathers. I had just caught a tortoise which I wanted to take home and stumbled in—tortoise in hand. . . .

"Then came the climax of the day. We arrived at a large open sandy plain where about 4000 troops were drawn up—Infantry, Cavalry, Zouaves, Chasseurs D'Afrique, native troops, the Bodyguard of the Bey. A march past took place. The Cavalry mounted on wonderful Arab horses went past most beautifully at a canter. They then retreated into the distance and at a signal given the whole cohort came straight at us at full gallop with drawn swords flashing in the sun—all shouting a wild cry. It was the most moving and exciting thing I've ever seen. The old French General said to me: 'Vous n'avez qu'à lever votre éventail, Mademoiselle, et ils s'arrêteront.' But of course I didn't—and they charged full-tilt at us to what seemed to be within a yard or two. One felt the ground trembling under one and heard and almost felt the hot breath of the panting horses. I shan't ever forget it.

"Father, to the joy of all of us, made up his mind not to go home in spite of the Master's * alarmist telegrams about the Transport Workers' strike—so the Suffolk which had followed us to take him if it were necessary went back to Malta.

"*6th June*. Heavenly calm and sunshine. I have been watching porpoises playing round the ship. There have been flying fish and dolphins

---

* The Master of Elibank.

too. I wanted to show them to Winston but he is in the stoke hole! Not only does he leave no stone unturned but he insists on turning it with his own hand. But *what* fun for the stokers!

"*7th June. Rounding Cape St. Vincent.* The Lord Chancellor * has resigned, which means a big Cabinet General Post. Haldane will at last have his heart's desire—the Woolsack, which but for Loreburn he would have had in 1906. How lucky both for him and for the War Office and our defences that he didn't. Winston is very excited and is chafing impatiently to discuss all the possible permutations all the time with Father—who as usual is disappointing W. by keeping his thoughts to himself.† I am personally not enthusiastic about X as a successor to Haldane, as I don't feel he will bring a very invigorating dash of new flavour into the Cabinet pudding. But Z is not a very inspiring figure-head for the Army either? It concerns W. more intimately than anyone and he has strong views which he is pouring out to me (faute de mieux) and will no doubt press on F. when he can break through his defences. Now nearing Gibraltar—our last port of call. . . ."

I find records of another lovely cruise the following year (1913), when we embarked at Venice and sailed down the Adriatic.

My most vivid memories of that journey are of our first stop at Spalato (now Split), where we went ashore to see the glorious remains of the palace of the Emperor Diocletian, who apparently retired there after a gay life of Christian baiting. I remember saying to Winston that there was something to be said for being a *retired* Roman Emperor. "Why retired?" he replied sharply. "There's nothing to be said for retiring from anything." We went on to Ragusa (now Dubrovnik), "a most beautiful town in Bosnia, inhabited by Croats—fierce-looking people with Turkish trousers and fiery eyes and red sashes with daggers stuck through them."

The Balkan War had just come to an end. Fighting had taken place within one hundred miles of where we lay and we met many of the troops which were being hastily disbanded. "We motored to Trebinje and longed to go on to Cettinje which was quite near. Admiral Burney who was in charge of the International Brigade came over to see us in a Destroyer. He was to march into Scutari the next day with 1000 troops, two or three hundred from each Power, and establish martial law there —a very exciting mission. I never saw a wilder, more desolate and

* Lord Loreburn.
† See *Great Contemporaries* (Asquith), by Winston Spencer Churchill, p. 104.

brigand-haunted-looking country." Our next stop was at the (then) Austrian naval base of Cattaro—well named the Bocche (Mouths) di Cattaro—a string of bays, one opening out of the other like Russian toys, the town standing on the edge of the innermost of all. On to Valona— a lovely strip of solitary Albanian coast where we spent "a glorious Robinson Crusoe day on the shore and in the woods, bathing in a tepid sea of lapis lazuli, picnicking near a trout stream from which three brown and inarticulate 'natives' extracted fish—then dozing with books on burning shingle—the sun filtering through one's closed eye-lids.

"W. was incapable of lotus-eating even for a few hours. It went against his grain. He first tried 'stunning' fish—i.e. dropping depth charges from a small boat. They exploded under water and shoals of 'stunned' and silvery fish ascended to the surface, where they were duly netted. This occupation palled after a time; the tactics were repetitive, the victims unresisting. He then conducted a far more ambitious seining operation involving strategy and man-power—i.e. dragging the bay for fish with a huge net—W. directing operations from a boat, gesticulating, orating, enlarging on first principles—while some fifty wading sailors at each end dragged at the net, drawing it in with all their might and main—with meagre-ish results, though a few huge silver wrigglers were netted. The sailors were delightful—happy as children— catching tortoises and playing football on the sands.

"When we sailed Winston, still thirsty for adventure, stayed behind for a wild pig hunt at three o'clock in the morning and caught us up next day at Corfu in a Destroyer. We had a marvellous reception from the Greeks, with whom we are apparently very popular. 'Rule Britannia' and 'God save the King' were played again and again and our musty old landaus were surrounded and pursued by large cheering crowds. I talked to many soldiers recovering from their wounds in the old fortress. . . . I drove to the very spot where Ulysses swam ashore and met Nausicaa— and where Neptune turned his ship into an island. . . ."

Greece was the climax of that journey, the country of my dreams which I had always longed to see above all others. We owed our visit there to the insistence of my father. It had lived so long in my imagination that I was almost afraid of reality, but reality surpassed anything I could have imagined. "We passed Parnassus and sailed in the early morning into the Bay of Corinth and drove up to the site of old Corinth where only a few pillars of the Temple of Apollo are still standing. We went to Athens by train running along the edge of the sea past Megara and Eleusis—Aegina and Salamis two large islands lying in the sun. The Acropolis was the first thing we saw—standing high up above us—and we drove there straightaway through a disappointingly modern town. It is a blow to find *trams* running in Athens but it's fun to see the names written over the most squalid little shops in this cultured and precious calligraphy—i.e. 'Σωκρατης και Ἑταιρια' ('Socrates & Co.')! After dining at the Embassy we drove up to the Acropolis again by moonlight—which made the light and shade more dramatic though one lost the golden yellowness of the stone. There are no words to describe the wonder and beauty of the Parthenon. It is the wisest, most serene, most *final* thing I have ever seen. . . . The First Lord, though impressed by what remained erect, was distressed at seeing so many splendid pillars lying prone upon the ground. He felt quite sure that a party of British Bluejackets could hoist them up into position again in no time and regretted that he did not possess the requisite authority to put the work immediately in hand." This impulse was at the time laughed off by some as a characteristic sign of Philistinism and lack of reverence for the past. In fact it proved his prescience, for the work has since been done.

It was sad to weigh anchor and sail away next day from Greece, past sleeping islands in the blue Aegean to the grayer seas and skies of home. The memory of these golden journeys and those I shared them with in our enchanted ship can never fade. Here if ever were Browning's three unities—"the time and the place and the loved ones all together." The time? May, 1913. How little we guessed that in a year or little more the curtain would fall upon the world we knew forever. For though in Winston's mind and in my father's, as I knew, the possibility of war was ever present, its imminence had not yet reached our hearts or our imaginations.

Chapter Twenty

HOME RULE FOR IRELAND

A MONTH before we sailed on our *Enchantress* cruise in May, 1912, my father had introduced the Home Rule Bill in the House of Commons and Winston had moved its second reading in a brilliant speech. They now returned to face the arduous task of carrying it through Parliament against resistance just as fierce and obdurate as that which met the Parliament Act.

The Conservative Party had a new leader. They had lost three General Elections and suffered humiliation and defeat over the rejection of the Budget and the abolition of the veto of the House of Lords. Arthur Balfour was dethroned by the authors of these catastrophes—the Die-Hards whom he had failed to control. They were bored and baffled by his subtleties, bewildered by his metaphysical approach to the plain facts of political life, and outraged by his Laodicean view of Tariff Reform. So he was swept away by a movement called "B.M.G."—Balfour must go. Balfour did go—observing with all his customary detachment and serenity that he had been told that with advancing years there was a danger of petrifaction of the faculties and that although he had not yet noticed these symptoms in himself it might well be that they existed.

The two claimants for the succession were Austen Chamberlain, a "whole-hogger" on tariff reform by lineage and conviction, and Walter Long, a Tory squire with a rosy, bucolic face whom everyone liked and against whom not even the most rabid Die-Hard could have brought the charge of being "too clever by half." He had held various offices and his greatest legislative achievement was the compulsory muzzlement of dogs which extirpated rabies in this country. In the end both candidates retired in favor of Mr. Bonar Law, of whom it was said by some contemporary wag or wit that "he rose between two stools."

If a change from Arthur Balfour was what the Conservative Party wanted they had certainly got it. The contrast between the two leaders was perfectly drawn by Max Beerbohm in a cartoon which depicted Arthur Balfour, a tall figure leaning back with languid grace, his violin in hand, to gaze with puzzled wonder at Bonar Law—banging with all his might upon a drum—and murmuring as he gazed: "What verve! what brio! and *what* an instrument!" The Conservatives undoubtedly preferred the drum, though I can remember one blue-blooded heretic deploring that the great Torty party should be led by "a damned, dissenting Scotch ironmonger." And the Liberals irreverently added a supplication to the Litany for the use of Conservatives who felt the need of it: "Lord, have mercy upon us and incline our hearts to Bonar Law."

Bonar Law was by birth and occupation a Scottish-Canadian iron merchant and—most unfortunately for the fate of Home Rule—the son of an Ulster Presbyterian minister. He is as difficult to describe as to assess. He knew that he was expected by his party to be a "fighting leader," and by crude insults, wild accusations and bad manners he did his best to realize their hopes. Yet I could never persuade myself that there was any zest or passion in his violence. I always felt that he was trying (in the words of the Catechism) to do his duty in that state of life to which it had pleased God to call him. My father once described him as "a conscientious fire-eater" and said that at times he could be almost disarmingly ingenuous. As they walked for the first time side by side in the annual procession of the Commons to hear the King's Speech in the House of Lords, Bonar Law said to him on the way back: "I am afraid I shall have to show myself very vicious, Mr. Asquith, this session. I hope you will understand." My father added, characteristically: "I had no hesitation in reassuring him on that point."

He was an easy man to underrate. Entirely devoid of eloquence or glamour he was yet an astonishingly effective debater. Sir John Simon once said to me that debating with him was like having handfuls of fine, stinging gravel thrown in one's face. There was never a big stone one could fling back. He had a freakishly good memory and never used notes. On the rare occasions when he made use of a quotation he would take a small, black notebook out of his breast pocket and read from it. I remember being intensely amused when he used this device to read to the House of Commons the well-known line "a rose by any other name would smell as sweet" after attempting unsuccessfully to paraphrase it, to the effect that "the odor would have been no less agreeable." On the rare occasions when I met him in private life I thought him a sad and lonely man who found little pleasure in anything and I could not find it in my heart to feel any grudge against him for the insults he hurled nightly at my father during the Irish controversy. I was, however, always conscious that he was deeply hostile to Winston.

For twenty-six years Home Rule had been the declared policy of the Liberal Party and this was the third Bill proposed by a Liberal Government. Throughout these years the Conservative attitude had been one of blank negation and it had not changed. Mr. Balfour, from whom one might have expected more imagination, had declared in his last speech before laying down the leadership that all schemes of Irish Home Rule were the "dreams of political idiots." Mr. Bonar Law had all the political passions and theological prejudices of Ulster in his blood. It was in vain that my father asked the Opposition: "What do you propose to put in its place? Have you any answer to the demand of Ireland—beyond the naked veto of an irreconcilable minority?" [1] In vain Winston Churchill appealed to them to look upon the Irish problem with "a modern eye." [2]

My father had fought and won his first election in 1886 in support of Gladstone on the issue of Home Rule and had lived in the heart of the Irish controversy throughout his political life. It was in that year that Gladstone had introduced his first Home Rule Bill which split the Liberal Party. Chamberlain denounced it as a first step to complete separation and Hartington supported him. The Whigs and a section of the Radicals seceded and adopted the label of Liberal Unionists. The Bill was savagely opposed by the Orangemen in Belfast and by the Conservatives and their new allies in the House of Commons. Lord Randolph Churchill coined the ominous slogan "Ulster will fight and Ulster will be right." The Bill was defeated on its second reading after one of the greatest debates in Parliament. The House rejected the Bill, Gladstone dissolved Parliament and in the election that followed the Liberals were overwhelmingly defeated. During the next six years Ireland was governed by coercion, the split in the Liberal Party proved final and the cause of Home Rule was further tarnished by the Parnell divorce.

Yet Gladstone refused to abandon the struggle to give justice to Ireland. When in 1892 he was returned by a small majority he remained undaunted and at the age of eighty-four he presented a second Home Rule Bill to Parliament. It was passed by the Commons but rejected by the House of Lords. This was for him the end. Though he wished to challenge the Lords by an appeal to the country his colleagues refused to follow him and in March, 1894, he resigned.

The third Home Rule Bill followed Gladstonian lines. It transferred all domestic affairs to the Irish Parliament and left the Imperial Parliament in control of foreign affairs, peace and war, the Army, Navy and taxation and it provided iron safeguards for religious and political minorities. Today it seems incredible that the measure which produced such convulsions of fury, apprehension and violence forty-odd years ago amounted to no more than the establishment of local government with the same limited authority as that which now exists in Northern Ireland.*

Yet it fulfilled the dreams and aspirations of the Irish party and people at that time. I remember John Redmond saying to the House of Commons with deep emotion: "If I may say so reverently, I personally thank God that I have lived to see this day. I believe this Bill will pass into law. I believe it will result in the greater unity and strength of the Empire. . . . I believe it will have the effect of turning Ireland in time . . . into a happy and prosperous country, with a united, loyal, and contented people." [3] Poor Redmond! "Vain hope and promise vain."

The Bill differed in two respects from its predecessor. It was presented by my father as the first step in a federal scheme of devolution which would eventually give to other parts of the United Kingdom the same freedom to deal with their own affairs—and thus lighten the load of the Imperial Parliament and free it to fulfill its duties to the whole country and to the Empire. "There has been reserved for this Parliament," he said, "the double honour of reconciling Ireland and emancipating itself." [4]

It differed also from its predecessors in this vital respect—that the House of Lords no longer had the power to prevent its passage into law. The Conservative leaders, thus deprived of their sovereign weapon, sought a substitute in direct action. They determined to defeat the Bill if necessary by force of arms. In the autumn of 1911 the Ulster Unionist Council announced that Ulster would refuse to obey a Dublin Parliament and would set up a provisional Government of her own headed by Sir Edward Carson, a Dublin man and an ex-law officer of the Crown. It was an irony that his irresistible brogue, his violence and sentimentality made him seem so much more of an Irishman than John

* In fact the Act of 1920 which set up the present Ulster Parliament contains a textual reproduction of the main provisions of the Home Rule Bill of 1912.

The First Lord crossing the Horse Guards with Prince Louis Battenberg

On board the Admiralty Yacht *Enchantress*

Mr. Winston Churchill: 'Any home news?'
Mr. Asquith: 'How can there be with you here?'

On board the *Enchantress* in the
Firth of Forth

A cartoon from *Punch*,
May 21, 1913

Churchill and Lord Fisher, 1913

With Lloyd George in Whitehall, 1915

Speaking at Enfield in 1915

Redmond! Volunteers were raised and drilled with the permission of complaisant magistrates. These measures received the active encouragement and support of Mr. Bonar Law and his colleagues and on the eve of the introduction of the Home Rule Bill a review of eighty thousand Ulster Volunteers was held, at which he and three of his leading colleagues, Sir Edward Carson, Lord Londonderry and Mr. Walter Long, took the salute under a vast Union Jack.

Winston knew the Ulster case by heart. He had been reared on his father's famous slogan. When he was two years old Lord Randolph had become embroiled through his elder brother in a quarrel with the Prince of Wales which led to his ostracism by London society. He went to Dublin as secretary to his father, the Duke of Marlborough, who had been appointed Lord Lieutenant by Disraeli. Though Winston left Ireland before he was five a few vivid memories made an indelible impression on his mind.

He remembered the exciting prospect of going to a pantomime, the drive to the castle where other children were to be picked up, a wait in the rain in its cobbled courtyard, where there seemed to be "much stir." Then people came out of the castle to tell them that they could not go to the pantomime because the theater had been burned down. "All that was found of the manager was the keys that had been in his pocket." As a consolation they were promised to go next day to see the ruins of the building. "I wanted very much to see the keys, but this request does not seem to have been well received." On another occasion he was shown a tall white stone tower which he was told had been blown up by Oliver Cromwell. He understood that Oliver Cromwell had "blown up all sorts of things and was therefore a very great man."

Finally Mrs. Everest, the supreme influence in his early life, was nervous about the Fenians. "I gathered these were wicked people and there was no end to what they would do if they had their way." [5] One day when he was out riding on his donkey Mrs. Everest and he mistook the Rifle Brigade in their dark uniforms for Fenians. Their fear communicated itself to the donkey, who kicked him off and he had concussion of the brain. "This was my first introduction to Irish politics."

It is remarkable that Winston's robust Home Rule convictions should have emerged unscathed from these hazards of his youth and childhood. To both his oracles—Mrs. Everest and Lord Randolph—it was anathema. Even his donkey kicked against it! Yet he defied them all and in the prewar years, when the German menace to our sea power absorbed his mind to the exclusion of domestic issues, Ireland alone held its own. Throughout the fierce and bitter Home Rule battle he fought in the front line.

The front line was Belfast and the announcement (in January, 1912) of his intention to hold a meeting in the Ulster Hall was greeted by a roar of fury. "What a man to select!" thundered Sir Edward Carson. "The most provocative speaker in the whole party, going under the most provocative circumstances to a place where the words of his own father are still ringing in the ear. . . ." [6] The press seethed with reports of the violence that awaited him if he dared to violate this Orange sanctuary.

The Ulster Unionist Council resolved to "take steps" to prevent the meeting being held "in the centre of the loyal City of Belfast." A posse of armed Ulstermen entrenched themselves in the hall and refused to leave it. Winston said that it would have cost the lives of some six policemen to turn them out. The Master of Elibank, who had originally suggested that he should go, began to have second thoughts about it, but Winston remained undeterred. He was not the man to retreat before threats and he could never resist a hornet's nest. A huge marquee was procured. (How well I remember the detailed discussion of its exact measurements, capacity and probable stability!) It was sent on to Ulster in advance and erected on a football ground at Celtic Park on the outskirts of Belfast.

The Master of Elibank suggested that Clemmie should not, as arranged, accompany Winston, but she replied with characteristic gallantry and wisdom that her presence might act as a deterrent to violence. She told me that Winston's cousin Freddy Guest who went with them insisted on taking a loaded revolver which she feared might go off at any moment and wound one of them in the leg.

They had a hostile reception at Stranraer and a sleepless crossing, as they were disturbed all night by Suffragettes who ran like maenads around and around the deck shrieking "Votes for women" into their cabin windows. On their arrival in Belfast they were told that the glass had been taken out of the windows of their car because the dockers had armed themselves with bolts which might be flung at them. At one moment the crowd tried to overturn the car but the police ingeniously defeated them by rapping the hands on the splashboards, bonnet and elsewhere with canes.

When they arrived at the hotel they found it full of furious businessmen who shook their fists at Winston in the passages. The windows of their rooms were draped with thick lace curtains and whenever Winston tried to peep out and have a look at the crowds below he was greeted with a furious booing, curses and imprecations. Sticks were brandished, flags were waved, effigies borne aloft by processions were burned. (Winston was no doubt the most popular of these but Carson and Londonderry had their turn in the Catholic quarter.) Some four thousand troops had been sent to maintain law and order but most of these were concentrated at Celtic Park and those in Belfast wisely remained invisible.

The meeting was at two o'clock. Winston and Clemmie drove with a police escort to the football ground through milling crowds in pouring rain. The marquee was crammed with standing people. There were no chairs. The platform was high and rickety. The audience was composed of red-hot supporters and some equally red-hot opponents and lively and at times threatening amenities were exchanged between them. In the midst of these the rainwater which had accumulated in a deep pool on the canvas roof of the tent poured through in a torrential shower, soaking the just and the unjust alike.

In his speech Winston made a moving plea for justice to Ireland: "The Irish claim has never been treated fairly by the statesmen of Great Britain. . . . And yet why should not Ireland have her chance? . . . History and policy, justice and good sense alike demand for this race, gifted, virtuous and brave, which has lived so long and endured so much, that it should not in view of its most passionate desire be left out of the family of nations. . . ." In his peroration he took the bull by the horns and played a brilliant variation in counterpoint on his father's famous slogan. "It is in a different sense that I adopt and repeat Lord Randolph's words 'Ulster will fight and Ulster will be right.' Let Ulster fight for the dignity and honour of Ireland; let her fight for the reconciliation of races and for the forgiveness of ancient wrongs; let her fight for the unity and consolidation of the British Empire; let her fight for the spreading of charity, tolerance and enlightenment among men. Then indeed Ulster will fight and Ulster will be right." *

The journey home was accomplished without disturbance, even from Suffragettes. We were told afterward that Sir Edward Carson had felt grave anxiety that Winston might be killed and had come over secretly to Belfast to attempt to save him!

Civil war was now openly threatened both in Ulster and by the Conservative leaders at home. In July there was a great Unionist demon-

* February 8, 1912.

stration at Blenheim at which Mr. Bonar Law declared: "I can imagine no length of resistance to which Ulster will go in which I shall not be ready to support them." *

On August 12th Winston indicted the Unionist leaders in a formidable letter addressed to Sir George Ritchie, the Liberal chairman of his constituency, Dundee, a correspondent to whom he often turned when other means of self-expression were for the moment unavailable. He accused Mr. Bonar Law and "his lieutenant Sir Edward Carson of having for some months past incited the Orangemen to wage Civil War upon their fellow-countrymen and if necessary upon the forces of the Crown; and the former has even suggested that this process in Ireland should be accompanied by the lynching of His Majesty's Ministers. . . ." He then gave a warning that incitements to defy the law might well be heard and heeded elsewhere than in Ireland, that there were "many millions of very poor people in this Island . . . crowded into the back streets of cities, forced to toil for a scanty reward through their whole span of existence . . . to whom these counsels of violence and mutiny may not be unattractive and who may be lured to their own and to the public disaster by listening to them. The doctrines of Mr. Bonar Law at Blenheim are the doctrines of Mr. Ben Tillett on Tower Hill. But Tillett's men were starving. . . . No public man Liberal or Nationalist has threatened the Orangemen with force. We seek to liberate not to enthrall, to conciliate, not to coerce. . . . All this talk of violence, of bayonets, bullets, of rebellion and Civil War has come from one side alone. . . .

"The time may well come when the direction of national policy should pass to others. But a transference of power will not be effected by violent means. It will not come till our work is done. It will not come until the leader of the Conservative party has divested himself of doctrines which disqualify him from the discharge of official responsibilities . . . and from which every street bully with a brick-bat and every crazy fanatic who is fumbling with a pistol may derive inspiration."

Winston followed up this powerful salvo with a speech at Dundee in September in which he underlined my father's point that the Government advocated Home Rule not only as a solution to the quarrel with Ireland, but as a first step toward the establishment of a federal system of government in this country. Scotland and Wales would benefit from self-government. He went on to suggest that it might also be extended to areas like Lancashire, Yorkshire, the Midlands and Greater London.

* Blenheim, July 28, 1912.

This proposal was greeted with derisive laughter by the Opposition press. Even the *Manchester Guardian* had reservations and expressed them. Yet it felt constrained to add that "Mr. Churchill's idea, frail and uncertain though it may seem, is a fascinating one." Alas, it fascinated few.

The next act in the Irish drama was the signing of the "Covenant," a declaration which pledged its signatories "to use all means which may be found necessary to defeat the present conspiracy to set up a Home Rule Parliament in Dublin." The ceremony was dramatically staged in Ulster with torchlight processions, bands, Union Jacks and solemn religious services. Sir Edward Carson, who was the first to sign, had announced a few months earlier in a speech at the Criterion Restaurant that he intended when he went over to Ireland to "break every law that is possible," * while Mr. F. E. Smith, a high light of the English Bar, declared that "he would not shrink from the consequences of his convictions, not though the whole fabric of the Commonwealth be convulsed." †

Small wonder that rioting broke out in Belfast and the Chief Secretary Mr. Birrell reported that two thousand Catholics and five hundred Protestants had been obliged to leave the shipyards "upon the friendly advice of their fellow workmen who assured them that their lives would not be safe if they remained."

The House of Commons, through which the Bill was being forced under the guillotine, reflected the passions which raged outside. On November 12th the Government was defeated in a snap division on an amendment to a financial resolution. My father announced the Government's intention to rescind the vote as it did not represent the considered view of the House. Pandemonium broke out. Insults were hurled at the Government and returned, my father was assailed with cries of "Traitor" and the Speaker after suspending the sitting for an hour was obliged to adjourn it. The Opposition cheered wildly, waving their hats and order papers, the Government Front Bench who were also loudly cheered by their supporters began to file out of the House and I was just about to leave the Gallery when I saw Winston and Jack Seely ‡ going out together and heard loud cries of "Rats." Winston, who looked in high good humor, took out his handkerchief and waved it to the cheering Liberals and then before putting it back in his pocket he turned and waved it at the Opposition. I suddenly saw an object traveling

* Criterion Restaurant, June 24, 1912.
† Belfast, July 8, 1912.
‡ Colonel John Seely, then Secretary of State for War.

rapidly through the air in his direction. . . . An Ulster member, Mr. Ronald McNeill, had picked up the only missile ready to hand, which happened to be a book (a copy of the Standing Orders), from the ledge of the Speaker's chair and hurled it at Winston, hitting him on the head. Winston wheeled around toward him and for a moment I feared that a free fight might take place when Will Crooks * struck up "Should auld acquaintance be forgot?" and for a moment anger dissolved in laughter—a moment long enough for Jack Seely and other friends to shepherd Winston out of the House.

Next day Mr. Ronald McNeill, perhaps feeling a little foolish, made what is always described as a "handsome" apology which Winston generously accepted. Mr. Bonar Law, less handsomely, boasted the same night at the Albert Hall that "he had not tried to interfere with these proceedings on the part of his colleagues and would never in similar circumstances think it his duty to do so." [7]

This was an understatement of the course he was to pursue. Not merely did he from the start encourage and support the preparations for armed rebellion in Ulster but in the later stages of the controversy he was uttering incitements to mutiny in the Army. In a speech in Dublin he said, referring to the "precedent" of James II: "In order to carry out his despotic intention the King had the largest paid Army which had ever been seen in England. What happened? There was a Revolution and the King disappeared. Why? Because his own Army refused to fight for him." †

The veto of the House of Lords was to be replaced by the veto of the Army. No wonder that my father described these doctrines as "the complete Grammar of Anarchy."

Why was this anarchy tolerated by the Government? The question must occur to every reader of this violent and irrational patch of English history. No Liberal Government could have contemplated the coercion of Ulster. Why then was it not excluded by a clean cut from the very beginning? The right and obvious course would surely have been to give both parts of Ireland what they wanted—to let Southern Ireland have Home Rule and to allow Ulster to remain within the Union. The answer, incredible as it may seem, is that this was not in fact what either of them wanted. Mr. D. C. Somervell has written truly that "the partition of Ireland, so obvious and inevitable to us today (though not to the present rulers of the Irish Republic), was repulsive to all parties in

* A Labour member.
† Dublin, November 28, 1913.

both islands in 1912. . . . The avowed object of Carson and many of his supporters was not to rescue Ulster but to defeat Home Rule." [8]

Another obstacle to the "clean cut" was that the cut, however and wherever you made it, could not be a clean one. Ulster was not a homogeneous unit. Nationalists and Unionists, Protestants and Catholics were inextricably intermingled within it. Four of its counties (Antrim, Armagh, Down and Derry) were predominantly Orange but contained strong Nationalist minorities, and two others, Fermanagh and Tyrone, were almost evenly divided with the balance slightly tipped in favor of the Nationalists.

One last question must be asked and answered. Why did the Government not bring Sir Edward Carson to trial under the Criminal Law? My father has given his own reply in his book *Fifty Years of Parliament:* "The charge or charges could have been framed so as to be technically water-tight and they could have been proved up to the hilt by clear, and indeed, uncontroverted evidence. But the guilt or innocence of the accused would have ultimately had to be determined by a Jury, and, as the days of jury-packing were happily over, it was as certain as any of the sequences of nature that no Irish Jury would convict." This was in itself a fatal objection but my father added to it "a further argument which carried even greater weight. It was obviously of capital importance that, if it were possible, the birth of the new State should be under the star of Peace. . . ." [9]

But the star of Peace did not rise. Large consignments of arms began to arrive in Ulster; and the Ulster Volunteers were able to discard their dummy rifles and shoulder real arms when Sir Edward Carson and his aide-de-camp and galloper, Mr. F. E. Smith, reviewed them. In the House of Commons, where the Home Rule Bill was on its way to its first rejection by the House of Lords, Mr. Bonar Law asserted that Ulster would prefer foreign to Nationalist rule to which Winston retorted gaily: "This then is the latest Tory threat; Ulster will secede to Germany." *

Meanwhile the comedy of ostracism was being re-enacted on the social stage. Once more, as in the days of the Parliament Act, we became pariahs, traitors and untouchables. Mrs. Dugdale in her biography of Lord Balfour recounts how Sir Edward Carson lunching with him "banged the table till the glasses rang" and declared that any social relations with Home Rulers had become quite impossible—an opinion from which Mr. Balfour did not dissent. Lord Londonderry refused an

* January 1, 1913.

invitation to a dinner party to meet the King because Lord Crewe would also have been present. Lord Templewood in a broadcast (January, 1959) recalled that when two Conservative M.P.'s accepted an invitation to have luncheon with the Asquiths it was regarded as an act of treachery. Our dear friend Mr. Page, the American Ambassador, records that a certain Duchess told him that she and her husband had been invited to dine at the French Embassy. "If the Duke," said she, "went into any house where there was any member of this Government he'd turn and walk out again." So she took the precaution of sending the Duke's secretary on an exploratory mission to the Ambassador's secretary to make sure that there was no chance of such contamination. The same great lady complained that she had positively had to sit in the Peeresses' Gallery "in plain sight of the wives of two members of the Cabinet!" "Somehow," wrote Mr. Page, "it reminds me of the tense days of the slavery controversy just before the Civil War." [10]

We had become inured to excommunication by Society and we took it in our stride with equanimity. Sir Edward Grey despised it, Winston defied it, my father ignored it. It is impossible to be lonely at No. 10 Downing Street and in our day it was a humming hive of interesting and exciting people from every walk of life. I remember saying to my father and Winston: "Aren't we lucky to be cut by all the dullest people in London?" The "grand," not only in those days, were very often dull.

Meanwhile the Home Rule Bill had returned to the House of Commons and passed for the second time through all its stages and once more it was rejected by the House of Lords. After one more passage through the Commons it was bound under the Parliament Act to become law by the summer of 1914—unless? Unless the King refused it the Royal Assent, or forced a dissolution by the dismissal of his Ministers. This was the last wild hope of the Conservative leaders, and some were still so deluded that they believed it could be realized.

A more disastrous course for the Monarchy could hardly have been imagined. As my father pointed out in a memorandum which he submitted to the King, no sovereign had attempted to withhold assent from a Bill sanctioned by Parliament since the days of Queen Anne. If the King were to intervene he would be "dragged into the arena of party politics"; and at a dissolution following a dismissal of Ministers "the Crown would become the football of contending factions. This is a Constitutional catastrophe which it is the duty of every wise statesman to do the utmost in his power to avert." [11]

My father had an audience with the King on August 11th and assured him that he was ready to consider any practical scheme which would enable Ulster to "contract out" of the Home Rule Bill and to encourage a settlement by consent. After the experience of 1910 he was not hopeful about the results of a conference between leaders. Such a meeting would he thought be "either a tea party or a bear garden."

The King, harried by "advice, exhortations and reproaches" from all quarters, continued with admirable patience and pertinacity to try to break the deadlock. He invited leaders of both parties to meet each other as his guests at Balmoral during September. In this atmosphere they relaxed and disarmed and free and friendly talks took place between them. Mr. Bonar Law no longer felt obliged to be "vicious" when golfing with Lord Crewe. But he drew a lurid picture of what might be expected to happen in Ulster which Lord Crewe reported to my father. When the Home Rule Bill became law Sir Edward Carson would set up his provisional Government, usurp the function of the police and courts and thus compel the intervention of the Army. The Opposition would go to all lengths and ultimately be driven out of the House of Commons. They believed that the Army would refuse to obey and thus a dissolution would be forced. But while he contemplated these dire possibilities "at the worst" Mr. Bonar Law recognized that they would be catastrophic, and he favored a conference between the leaders of parties on the basis of excluding Ulster and giving Home Rule to the rest of Ireland. This was the first official suggestion that the Conservative Party might accept Home Rule if Ulster were left out. When my father arrived at Balmoral in early October he wrote confidentially to Bonar Law suggesting a meeting.

The invitation was accepted and my father thus described the meeting: "I remember well that my first 'heart to heart' conversation with Mr. Bonar Law took place in a country house not far from London to which I drove on a November afternoon to find him playing a game of double dummy with his host.* If we did not make much progress it was certainly from no lack on his part of courtesy or of honest endeavour to understand and appreciate an opponent's point of view." [12] These conversations continued intermittently but though they might conceivably have reached agreement with one another Bonar Law was doubtful whether he could carry Lord Lansdowne with him (let alone Sir Edward Carson) and my father was obliged to explain his difficulties with the Irish party. Mr. Bonar Law said that "he was not sure that his were not even

* Sir Max Aitken, later Lord Beaverbrook.

greater; he had to reckon not only with Carsonism (as distinguished from Carson himself) but with the probable revival of a Die-Hard movement among the English Unionists." [13]

Meanwhile Winston, who had always been in favor of excluding Ulster, made a conciliatory speech at Dundee in which he appealed for co-operation to solve the Irish problem: "Our party alone can carry Home Rule into being, but it will take more than one party to make it a lasting success. A settlement by agreement . . . would offer advantages far beyond anything now in sight. Peace is better than triumph provided it is peace with honour. . . . Only one thing would make it worth while or even possible to recast a measure on which so much depends. It is a very simple thing—good will." * No good will was, alas, apparent in the response to this appeal either from Dublin or Belfast. Both rejected partition. In a speech at Limerick Redmond denounced the "two-nation theory" as "an abomination and a blasphemy." One voice alone was raised in praise of Winston—that of his collusive enemy and friend Galloper F. E. Smith, who said that he had "shown a grasp of those facts which are fundamental which none of his colleagues, at least in public, has displayed." † He wished Godspeed to any settlement. But his leader Mr. Bonar Law though he may have desired a settlement did nothing publicly to speed one. Although his private conclaves with my father were already under way he made a speech in Dublin (on November 28th) in which he appealed to the Army (in the words I have already quoted) to disobey orders when the time came.

A few days earlier a sinister development had taken place of which John Redmond and his law-abiding followers had throughout foreseen and feared the possibility. A meeting was held in Dublin sponsored by Padhraic Pearse, a Gaelic teacher, and Professor John MacNeill, one of the founders of the Gaelic movement, to launch a campaign for the enrolment of Irish Volunteers. They would teach Ulster and the Government as well that two could play at that game and that the South could play it better. John Redmond believed in constitutional methods and had steadfastly adhered to them. He was opposed to the movement and he distrusted its leaders. But he was powerless to stop it. His authority was undermined and his power to compromise was thereby weakened. He feared, not without reason, that if he made further concessions he and his Parliamentary followers and the Bill itself might be repudiated by the Irish people.

* Dundee, October 8, 1913.
† West Bromwich, October 11, 1913.

Nevertheless after the private talks had failed he was reluctantly persuaded to agree to the Government's plan of giving the Ulster counties the right to vote themselves out of the Home Rule Bill for six years— that is until two successive General Elections had taken place. These proposals were announced by my father when he presented the Bill to the House of Commons for the third and last time on March 9, 1914. They were (in Winston's words) "rejected with contumely" by the Opposition. Sir Edward Carson described them as "sentence of death with a stay of execution for six years." The Ulstermen were not prepared to submit their case to the electors of the United Kingdom and refused to accept their verdict. Nevertheless the amendment was embodied in the text of the Bill and Redmond gave a reluctant consent to it.

This amendment was a great relief to Winston. "We now felt," he wrote, "that we could go forward with a clear conscience and enforce the law against all who challenged it. My own personal view had always been that I would never coerce Ulster to make her come under a Dublin Parliament, but I would do all that was necessary to prevent her stopping the rest of Ireland having the Parliament they desired. I believe this was sound and right and in support of it I was certainly prepared to maintain the authority of Crown and Parliament under the Constitution by whatever means were necessary." [14]

A few days later (on March 14th) he made a speech at Bradford which provoked violent and contrary reactions.* "If Ulster seeks peace and fair play . . . she knows where to find it. If Ulstermen extend the hand of friendship, it will be clasped by Liberals and by their Nationalist countrymen, in all good faith and in all good will; but if there is no wish for peace; if every concession that is made is spurned and exploited; if every effort to meet their views is only to be used as a means of breaking down Home Rule, and of barring the way to the rest of Ireland; if Ulster is to become a tool in party calculations; if the civil and parliamentary systems under which we have dwelt so long, and our fathers before us, are to be brought to the rude challenge of force; if the Government and the Parliament of this great country and greater Empire are to be exposed to menace and brutality; if all the loose, wanton, and reckless chatter we have been forced to listen to these many months is in the end to disclose a sinister and revolutionary purpose; then I can only say to you: Let us go forward together and put these grave matters

* My father's admiration of its rhetorical quality led him to include a long quotation from it in *Fifty Years of Parliament* "as proof that the Twentieth Century can hold its own in an oratorical competition." (Vol. II, pp. 147-48.)

to the proof!" The speech was denounced by the Conservative press as a provocation to civil war.

The spirit of compromise seemed to have deserted British public life. Concessions were condemned as betrayals. The language of reason could only be used by politicians behind closed doors. In public they were forced to feed the passions they had aroused. In Ulster one hundred thousand men were drilling and possessed large quantities of arms, many of which had been imported from Germany. The South was now competing with the North in enrolling volunteers in thousands and in trying to arm them.

In 1913 Unionists hopes had turned to intervention by the King. In 1914 the Unionists had one last card left to play which, as they made clear in their speeches, might decide the issue—the Army. Of this the Army inevitably became aware. Soldiers all over the country began to ask themselves "to whom they owed allegiance—to the King, to Parliament, to the Government, or to their own conscience and judgement on the merits of the policy which the Government was proposing". [15]

The War Office had received some disturbing reports about discipline, but neither the Army Council nor the Secretary of State was aware that this unrest was being actively fomented and encouraged by Sir Henry Wilson, the Director of Military Operations, from within the War Office itself. His own diary [16] reveals that he was in close and constant touch both with the Ulster leaders and those of the Conservative Party and that he kept them regularly supplied with information.

He received reports from Ulster about the "plans for the north of the 25,000 armed men to act as citadel and the 100,000 to act as constables and the arrangements for the banks, railways, etc., elections, provisional Government and so on" and all this he found "very sensible." He visited Ulster and was delighted to find the arrangements of the Ulster Army "well advanced," adding that he "must come over later and see the troops at work."

It is not surprising that this subversive force working from within the War Office in close alliance with the Opposition leaders and their press outside should have produced a distracting situation both for the War Office and the Army.

In December, 1913, Colonel Seely, Secretary for War, summoned G.O.C.'s in England, Scotland and Ireland to a conference at the War Office and tried to reassure them about the Government's intentions.

Reading the words he addressed to them, one cannot blame the soldiers for leaving the War Office more confused than reassured. His statement bristled with (no doubt unintentional) ambiguities. On the one hand he told them that "a soldier is entitled to obey an order to shoot only if that order is reasonable in the circumstances" and on the other he denied the "claim that officers can pick and choose between lawful and reasonable orders saying that they will obey in one case and not the other." They were finally directed to "make clear to all concerned" a position which was by no means clear to any one of them.

In early March my father received and communicated to the Cabinet police reports from Ireland that depots of arms and ammunition, police and military barracks might be seized by the Ulster Volunteers. A Cabinet committee consisting of Lord Crewe, Mr. Birrell, Winston, and Colonel Seely was appointed to examine and report on the situation. They came to the conclusion that certain depots might easily be seized and that instructions should be given to the War Office to have them adequately protected by armed guards. In *The World Crisis* Winston writes of the "small reinforcements" sent to protect military stores at Carrickfergus and elsewhere that "as it was expected that the Great Northern Railway of Ireland would refuse to carry the troops preparations were made to send them by sea." [17] What in fact he did was to order the Third Battle Squadron of eight battleships to concentrate at Lamlash in the Isle of Arran, station a cruiser near Carrickfergus and send two or three destroyers to the South of Ireland. My father knew nothing of these orders, given to the fleet on March 19th, until the morning of the 21st when he promptly countermanded them. But the Admiralty had already announced them in a statement and the fat was in the fire.

And now London began to buzz and hum with wild rumors of a "plot" hatched by the Government to use the armed forces of the Crown to provoke the loyal Ulster Volunteers to violence and then shoot them down—to attack them by land and sea and capture their headquarters. Some called it the "Ulster Pogrom." Winston was, as usual, the villain of the piece.

As a "precautionary measure" his naval dispositions were certainly open to the charge of being unnecessarily melodramatic and even provocative. But he was wholly guiltless of the sinister intent ascribed to him. From childhood onward he had always had a strong taste for moving soldiers. Now he could move ships. These congenial occupations at times went to his head and often got him into trouble (as in the past at Sidney Street and later, with some, at Antwerp).

Meanwhile Sir Arthur Paget, who was thoroughly rattled and alarmed

WINSTON CHURCHILL: An Intimate Portrait   *240*

by the situation which seemed to be unfolding, came over to London on March 18th to get further briefing from the War Office. And here a crowning blunder was committed. He obtained from Colonel Seely permission for officers domiciled in Ulster to "disappear" if the Army were called upon to deal with a disturbance by the Ulster Volunteers. This was an unwise concession since it seemed to imply the possibility of something like civil war.

But the ham-handed clumsiness with which it was used by Paget directly provoked the fateful "Mutiny at the Curragh." Instead of sounding the few officers concerned in private, individually, he assembled all his officers together and informed them that those domiciled in Ulster would be allowed to "disappear" from Ireland during the period of operations without prejudice to their future, but that those without such domicile who were not prepared to carry out their duties would at once be dismissed from the service. The result of this ultimatum was that Brigadier-General Hubert Gough and fifty-seven cavalry officers out of seventy chose to send in their papers.

Gough and three of his brother officers were immediately summoned to the War Office. They were told that all that was demanded by the Army Council was that they should be ready to do the duty which lay upon all those in the military service of the Crown. They expressed their willingness to discharge this duty and were allowed to rejoin their units in Ireland. A memorandum was drawn up by the Cabinet in three paragraphs, the second of which stated that: "An officer or soldier is forbidden in future to ask for assurances as to orders he may be required to obey." Gough and his officers (who were being advised by Sir Henry Wilson) persisted in asking for a written assurance that they would not be called upon "to enforce the present Home Rule Bill against Ulster." Seely weakly yielded to them and added to the Cabinet memorandum two paragraphs of his own which stated that the Government had no intention of using the forces of the Crown "to crush political opposition to the policy or principles of the Home Rule Bill." These paragraphs were initialed by Sir John French, the Chief of the Imperial General Staff, and Sir Spencer Ewart, the Adjutant-General. When later in the day the document was brought to my father, he at once struck out the added paragraphs and General Gough was immediately informed that they were not be be "considered as operative."

Parliament met on the same day and I shall never forget the debates that followed. The Government's supporters were burning with indignation. The idea that officers had bargained with the Government about their return to duty offended and outraged not only Liberals and Radicals but many good Parliamentarians of all parties.

The country too was aroused and seething with indignation at the action of the officers. In the opinion of R. C. K. Ensor, the historian, "there was reason to believe that, had Asquith then dissolved the Unionist Party would have been swept away." He adds: "But a Government cannot be so irresponsible as the Opposition under Bonar Law had become; and the Prime Minister had the foreign situation in his eye." [18]

Mr. Ensor was right. The cry of "the Army against the people" was raised both in and outside Parliament. Even if there had been no foreign situation my father would never have used so dangerous an issue as an election battleground however great the victory it promised. He accepted the resignations of Colonel Seely, Sir John French and Sir Spencer Ewart * and himself assumed the War Office. "The Army," he said, "will hear nothing of politics from me and in return I expect to hear nothing of politics from the Army."

But though his prompt and decisive action restored confidence to the Army and order in the War Office it did nothing to still the ferment in Ireland. On the night of April 24th a ship, the *Fanny*, succeeded in landing at Larne a cargo of thirty-five thousand rifles and three million cartridges, purchased in Hamburg for the use of the Ulster Volunteers. The naval patrol was skillfully dodged, police and customs officers were held up. This example of triumphant lawlessness naturally spurred on the South to emulation and recruits to the National Volunteers flowed in at the rate of fifteen thousand a week. John Redmond, who had always dissociated himself from unconstitutional methods, was now forced to give the movement his blessing. On June 9th he issued a statement explaining that the Ulster gunrunning had vitally altered the position and that the Irish party now thought it desirable to support the Volunteer movement "with the result that within the last six weeks the movement has spread like a prairie fire and all the Nationalists of Ireland will shortly be enrolled." †

This was the situation which my father had always feared and tried by every means to avert. As he told the King, a general election offered no remedy. Either he would be returned to face the same situation in

---

* His error in failing to dismiss Sir Henry Wilson can only be explained by the fact that Sir Henry's diary, though written, had not yet been published. But even so Sir Henry's retention in office appears indefensible.

† Limerick, June 9, 1913.

Ulster or a Conservative Government would be confronted with an even more dangerous one by the South.

Meanwhile on April 28th and 29th an oratorical battle took place in the House of Commons.

The Opposition had put down a motion demanding an inquiry into the nature of the naval and military movements contemplated by the Government against Ulster and Austen Chamberlain who opened directed his fire at Winston accusing him of having deliberately attempted to provoke violence and disorder.

There was nothing defensive about Winston's reply. He went into the attack with all guns blazing and blowing the target into smithereens. "What we are now witnessing in the House," he said, "is uncommonly like a vote of censure by the criminal classes on the police." "You have not arrested them," interjected a member. "Is that the complaint— that we have been too lenient?" Winston replied. He went on to accuse the Conservative Party, "the party of the comfortable, the wealthy . . . who have most to gain by the continuance of the existing social order," of being "committed to a policy of armed violence and utter defiance of lawfully constituted authority . . . to tampering with the discipline of the Army and the Navy . . . to overpowering police, coastguards and Customs officials . . . to smuggling in arms by moonlight . . . to the piratical seizure of ships and to the unlawful imprisonment of the King's servants. . . . The Conservative Party is committed to that. That is their position." He then reminded them of the millions who "are forced to live their lives . . . stripped of all but the barest necessities, who are repeatedly urged to be patient under their misfortunes, . . . to wait year after year . . . until, in the due workings of the Constitution, some satisfaction is given to their clamant needs. . . . All the time this great audience is watching and is learning from you, from those who have hitherto called themselves 'the party of law and order', how much they care for law, how much they value order when it stands in the way of anything they like! If that great audience is watching here at home, what of the great audiences that watch in India? Think of the devastating doctrines of the Leader of the Opposition. The right honourable Gentleman may laugh in a brief leadership of the Conservative Party, but he has shattered treasure which greater men than he have guarded for generations." He went on to accuse the Conservatives of teaching the Irish Nationalists the truth of John Bright's saying that Ireland never gained anything except by force. The object of the Orange Army was to show that if the veto of the Lords were gone there still remained the veto of force. "It was no longer a question of our coercing Ulster, it was a question of our preventing Ulster from coercing us. . . . All this talk of civil war has not come from us; it has come from you. For the last two years we have been forced to listen to a drone of threats of civil war with the most blood-curdling accompaniments and consequences. Did they really think that if a civil war came it was to be a war in which only one side was to take action? . . . I wish to make it perfectly clear that if rebellion comes we shall put it down, and if it comes to civil war, we shall do our best to conquer in the civil war. But there will be neither rebellion nor civil war unless it is of your making."

Winston closed his speech with a sudden and dramatic change of tone. He reminded the House of the dangers which our difficulties and quarrels might create at home. "Anxiety is caused in every friendly country by the belief that for the time being Great Britain cannot act. The high mission of this country is thought to be in abeyance and the balance of Europe appears in many quarters . . . to be deranged. Of course, foreign countries never really understand us in these islands. They do not know what we know, that at a touch of external difficulties or menace all these fierce internal controversies would disappear . . . and we should be brought into line and into tune. But why is it that men are so constituted that they can only lay aside their own domestic quarrels under the impulse of what I will call a higher principle of hatred?"

He now turned to make a direct appeal to Carson: "The right honourable Gentleman . . . is running great risks in strife. Why will he not run some risk for peace? The key is in his hands now. Why cannot the right honourable and learned Gentleman say boldly: 'Give me the Amendments to this Home Rule Bill which I ask for, to safeguard the dignity and the interests of Protestant Ulster, and I in return will use all my influence and good will to make Ireland an integral unit in a federal system?' " [19]

In *The World Crisis* Winston claims that these words "gave the debate an entirely new turn." [20] But though for a time it stilled the angry clamor of the House a good deal of sound and fury was still to come on that day and the next. Yet Arthur Balfour, while describing Winston's speech as "an outburst of demogogic rhetoric," declared himself as being "heartily in sympathy with the First Lord's proposal" and Carson even went as far as saying that he was "not very far from the First Lord."

Throughout May and June the party battle raged in public while private negotiations for a settlement went steadily on behind the scenes.

On May 26th the Home Rule Bill was passed through the House of Commons for the third and last time and on June 23rd the Government introduced an Amending Bill which proposed that any Ulster county should be entitled to vote itself out of Home Rule for six years. The Lords transformed it into a shape which the Commons could not accept by excluding the whole of Ulster. Nevertheless by the end of June it seemed that an understanding could be reached provided that the two parties could agree on the area to be excluded. The issue was narrowed down to the fate of the two counties of Fermanagh and Tyrone, both racially and religiously intermixed. Both Nationalists and Ulstermen claimed them, both feared their own followers and neither dared give way. In a note in his diary (July 8th) my father records: "Carson is quite anxious to settle, but makes much, honestly I am sure, of his difficulties with his own friends."

My father now made the last move, which he had held in reserve. The King had repeatedly expressed his willingness to help and on July 17th my father advised that he should intervene by summoning a conference of the representatives of all parties concerned, both Irish and British, to meet at Buckingham Palace. "I found the King in a tent in the garden," my father wrote in his diary. "He was full of interest about the Conference and he made the really good suggestion that the Speaker should preside."

The conference held four meetings. "Nothing," wrote my father, "could have been more amicable in tone or more desperately futile in result." In spite of the genuine desire of the two English parties to reach agreement neither Mr. Redmond nor Sir Edward Carson could be persuaded to compromise on the two counties. The conference broke down on the question of Fermanagh and Tyrone.

At three fifteen that afternoon a Cabinet was held at which, in Winston Churchill's words, "turning this way and that in search of an exit from a deadlock Ministers toiled around the muddy by-ways of Fermanagh and Tyrone. . . . The discussion had reached its inconclusive end, and the Cabinet was about to separate, when the quiet grave tones of Sir Edward Grey's voice were heard reading a document which had just been brought to him from the Foreign Office. It was the Austrian note to Serbia. He had been reading or speaking for several minutes before I could disengage my mind from the tedious and bewildering debate which had just closed. We were all very tired, but gradually as the phrases and sentences followed one another, impressions of a wholly different character began to form in my mind. This note was clearly an ultimatum . . . such as had never been penned in modern times. As the reading proceeded it seemed absolutely impossible that any State in the world could accept it, or that any acceptance, however abject, would satisfy the aggressor. The parishes of Fermanagh and Tyrone faded back into the mists and squalls of Ireland, and a strange light began immediately, but by perceptible gradations, to fall and grow upon the map of Europe." [21]

I was returning from a walk in St. James's Park and coming in out of the sunlight of that radiant July evening I found the Cabinet dispersing in the cool dusk of the hall. My mind was full of the breakdown of the Conference when I met Winston, who was hurrying toward the staircase leading down to the garden. I was arrested by the expression of his face. It was not its gravity alone which struck me. I could see that he was in instant travail—yet he seemed far away. I said: "Is it so serious— the breakdown of the Conference? You never had great hopes of it? Now we must go through with the Amending Bill?" He looked at me as though I were a sleepwalker. "The Amending Bill?" he repeated as though he had never heard the words before. "There is a real danger that this Austrian ultimatum may mean war. I must get back to the Admiralty at once. . . ."

War? I knew nothing of the Austrian ultimatum and I felt stunned and bewildered. It was almost a month since the murder of the Archduke Franz Ferdinand at Sarajevo and though I knew of my father's deep anxiety about the European situation the Irish drama had obscured all other issues not only in the press and public mind but in my own—and apparently in that of leading politicians on both sides. Addressing the City bankers only a week or two before, Mr. Lloyd George had reiterated his appeal for economy on the Navy on the ground that the international sky had never been "more perfectly blue." On the very day the Austrian ultimatum was delivered he had told the House of Commons that our relations with Germany were better than they had been for years and that the next Budget ought to show economy on armaments. I took this with a pinch of salt—but the idea that the murder of an Archduke in the Balkans could involve us in a European war had never occurred to me. We had become inured to Balkan wars. They had raged intermittently since 1912. Two conferences to settle them had been held in London. The first broke up and fighting was resumed; the second, convened and presided over by Sir Edward Grey and attended by the five Great Powers, was a diplomatic triumph. Frontiers were finally agreed and peace secured. Surely this could be settled too?

I waited till Edward Grey had left my father in the Cabinet Room and then went in to see him. He was alone, pacing up and down, and his face was overcast. "Winston is talking about a danger of war—what does he mean?" I felt confident that he would smile, brush Winston's words aside and reassure me, but he replied that it was a very serious situation—the most serious in years. Serbia could not possibly accept the terms of the Austrian ultimatum. Russia must stand by her and this would involve France and Germany. "But the murder was the action of an individual, not a state. . . ." "That is what makes the Austrian motive so sinister and suspect." "Couldn't Edward Grey convene a conference as he did last time?" "A conference would be the way out—*if* they want to find one."

That night my father wrote in his diary: "We are within measurable distance of a real Armageddon."

Next day (Saturday, July 25th) we heard the news that Serbia had virtually accepted Austria's terms. This surely meant that Edward Grey could get to work on the conference—if indeed it was still necessary. Almost as reassuring to me was the news that Winston had gone off to join his family at Cromer. He would not have left the Admiralty unless he felt that things were blowing over. But on Sunday morning after a telephone conversation with Prince Louis, who reported to him rumors that Austria was not satisfied with Serbia's submission, he decided to return at once to London. Meanwhile he instructed Prince Louis not to allow the Fleets, now on their way to port after a test mobilization, to disperse. By a happy chance he had decided in the interests of economy to substitute a test mobilization of the Navy for the usual grand maneuvers in July. Thanks to this operation the First and Second Fleets were thus on a war footing and (in Winston's words) "complete in every way for battle" in this crucial hour.

On his return to London, after hearing from Prince Louis at the Admiralty that the situation was deteriorating, Winston called on Sir Edward Grey and found that he took a grave view of the position. Winston asked him whether it would be helpful or the reverse if we stated in public that "we were keeping the Fleet together." [22] Both Sir Edward Grey and Sir William Tyrrell, who was with him, were in favor of proclaiming it at the earliest possible moment, believing that it might have the effect of "sobering the Central Powers and steadying

Europe." Winston therefore drafted a communiqué which was issued next morning: "Orders have been given to the First Fleet, which is concentrated at Portland, not to disperse for manoeuvre leave for the present. All vessels of the Second Fleet are remaining at their home ports in proximity to their balance crews."

On July 27th Sir Edward Grey told the House of Commons that he had made a proposal to Germany, France and Italy to hold a conference with Great Britain, that France and Italy had accepted, but that no reply had been received from Germany. That evening the German Government rejected the proposal. Next day Austria declared war on Serbia. Yet there was still no public realization that we were approaching the edge of the precipice. The quarrel was still regarded as a Balkan scrap.

On Wednesday, July 29th, my father sent precautionary telegrams to every part of the Empire informing them that they must prepare for war. This emergency measure had been discussed for some time at the Committee of Imperial Defence but it had never been taken before. Next day (Thursday, July 30th) the second reading of the Amending Bill was to have been moved by my father, but that morning when he was preparing his speech he received an urgent message from Mr. Bonar Law asking whether he could see him and Sir Edward Carson at his house in Kensington and there they met. Mr. Bonar Law suggested that because of the gravity of the international situation the Government should postpone the debate on the Amending Bill. "To advertise our domestic dissensions at this moment would weaken our influence in the world for peace." My father welcomed their attitude and agreed.

When my stepmother and I went to the House of Commons that afternoon we found the Ladies' Gallery packed with expectant and excited women who gave us the usual chilly reception described by my stepmother as a "general withdrawal of skirts." There was a gasp of astonishment when my father rose and said that he did not propose to make the motion standing in his name and added: "I should like to give the reason. We meet today under conditions of gravity which are almost unparalleled in the experience of every one of us. The issues of peace and war are hanging in the balance and with them the risks of a catastrophe of which it is impossible to measure either the dimensions or the effects. In these circumstances it is of vital importance that this country should present a united front and be able to speak and act with the authority of an undivided nation. . . ." The Government therefore proposed to put off the consideration of the Amending Bill.

These words produced bewilderment in the Ladies' Gallery. Many of its occupants had been blithely and busily engaged in preparations for the impending civil war—attending Red Cross classes, rolling bandages and making splints and slings etc. One Ulster matron, Lady M. (whose figure was particularly well adapted for the purpose), was reputed to have smuggled rifles galore into Belfast under her petticoats. Even now the idea of real war did not penetrate their minds and we dispersed amid a volley of questions: "What did it mean? Doesn't the Government realize the dangers of delay? Fighting may break out any moment in Ireland. . . ." They did not know, and though I had not their excuse, I could not mobilize my imagination. I dared not think in personal terms of that which lay ahead. When I was with my father I felt, through him, the scale of the events we lived through hour by hour, their tragic implications, the inexorable decision he must make. In the rare moments that I shared with Winston I felt in him a sense of tense expectancy and exhilaration—as of an arrow in a bow waiting impatiently to be released.

During these days his thoughts and powers were concentrated on one absorbing task—the preparation and disposition of the Fleet for action. One crucial decision he could not take alone. As early as Tuesday, July 28th, he became convinced that the Fleet should go to its war station at Scapa Flow. He has recorded that he "feared to bring this matter before the Cabinet lest it should mistakenly be considered a provocative action and thus likely to damage the chances of peace." He therefore went to my father, who at once gave his approval. "To him alone," wrote Winston, "I confided the intention of moving the Fleet to its War Station on 30th July. He looked at me with a hard stare and gave a sort of grunt. I did not require anything else." [23]

Thus secretly the great Fleet sailed, passing the Straits of Dover in the hours of darkness, to its war station in the mists of Scapa Flow. I shall never forget the relief I read in Winston's eyes when this vital action was accomplished. I hardly saw him in these days but in a fleeting meeting in a hall or passage of Downing Street we exchanged shining glances of complicity. Mine meant "I know," his meant "I knew you knew," both meant "Thank Heaven it's done!"—then with a chuckle "And even the Cabinet doesn't know!" As he has written, "We were now in a position, whatever happened, to control events. . . . If war should come no one would know where to look for the British Fleet. Somewhere in that enormous waste of waters to the north of our islands, cruising now this way, now that, shrouded in storms and mists, dwelt this mighty organization. . . . The King's ships were at sea." [24]

And now the pace of events quickened from hour to hour. On Friday, July 31st, Austria and Russia ordered general mobilization and, though conversations were still proceeding in St. Petersburg between the Russian Foreign Minister and the Austrian Ambassador, Germany sent an ultimatum to the Russian Government demanding that they should countermand their mobilization within twelve hours. Next day (Saturday, August 1st) Sir William Tyrrell came to Downing Street late in the evening with a long message from Berlin complaining that the German Ambassador's efforts for peace had been suddenly frustrated by the Tsar's decree for a complete mobilization. My father at once set to work with Sir William Tyrrell, Maurice Bonham Carter (his principal private secretary and my future husband) and Sir Eric Drummond (his Foreign Office secretary) to draft a direct personal appeal from the King to the Tsar. He then called a taxi and drove to Buckingham Palace at 1:30 A.M. to see the King. An entry in his diary records that "The King was hauled out of his bed and one of my strangest experiences was sitting with him clad in a dressing-gown while I read the message and the proposed answer."

While the European struggle gathered momentum day by day, a daily and hourly struggle was taking place within the Cabinet itself. It was acutely divided. A majority of its members (Winston assessed them at three quarters) were determined that we should remain neutral unless we were ourselves attacked. The leaders of the neutralists were Lord Morley, John Burns and Sir John Simon, supported by Lewis Harcourt and Lord Beauchamp—and Mr. Lloyd George was on their side. Their horror of war, which was fully shared by all their colleagues, inclined them to blind wishful thinking. They argued that we were in no way committed to intervene on behalf of France, that we should not allow a "mistaken interpretation of the Entente" (John Morley's phrase) to force us into a European quarrel, that it was improbable that if Germany attacked France she would attack her through Belgium and unlikely that if she did so the Belgians would resist. Against these were ranged Sir Edward Grey, Winston, Lord Haldane and my father. He held his hand as was his wont, striving day in, day out, to hold the Cabinet together as he had so often done before. But this time it was not for party reasons but because a divided party meant a divided nation. Yet no one could have doubted where he stood. In his speech in the House of Lords after my father's death Edward Grey said that in the early days of the last week of July, 1914, "the Government were so deeply divided that the division was apparently irreconcilable. The House of Commons was divided. The country was divided. . . . It would be an error to suppose that Asquith in his own mind had not settled what the ultimate decision would be. But if the Prime Minister had precipitated a decision I believe the consequences would have been that at the moment of crisis we should have had a divided Government, a divided Parliament, a divided country."

And so the long Cabinets went on, assembling and reassembling from eleven in the morning onwards sometimes until late into the night, and silent, waiting, watching crowds began to gather in Downing Street.

The man who suffered the most cruel ordeal during these days was Edward Grey. His life's work was at stake. Germany was making bids for our neutrality, offering if England kept out to annex only the colonies of France "after the German victory," bargains which Edward Grey indignantly refused. France and Russia were asking insistently where we stood—what action we should take if they were attacked. He had to make Germany realize that we were a force to be reckoned with and at the same time to try to restrain France and Russia from precipitate or warlike action. He has been criticized for failing to prevent the Russian mobilization, but, as he himself has said, "After Germany refused the Conference I could not put pressure on Russia. She was far less prepared for war than Germany. If I had tried to hold back her military preparations, Sazonov would at once have said: 'Then will you help us if war comes?' " [25] To this question he could not answer "Yes," for neither the Cabinet nor the House of Commons would at that time have supported him in giving such an undertaking.

Grey believed, not only that we were bound in honor to stand by France, but that if we abandoned her to her fate and acquiesced in the German domination of Europe we were sealing our own doom.

On Saturday morning Winston had demanded mobilization of the Fleet and the Cabinet had refused its consent. That night we received the news that Germany had declared war on Russia. When it reached Winston at the Admiralty after dinner he hastened across the Horse Guards Parade to Downing Street where he found my father, Edward Grey, Lord Haldane and Lord Crewe in conclave. He then declared his intention of mobilizing the Fleet at once in spite of the Cabinet decision and said that he would take full responsibility for this step to the Cabinet next morning. My father, who felt himself bound to the Cabinet, said nothing, but Winston felt "clear from his look that he was quite content." (I am sure this was an understatement of his feelings.) When they broke up Edward Grey took Winston aside and said to him: "You should know that I have just done a very important thing. I have told Cambon * that we shall not allow the German fleet to come into the Channel." Winston went back to the Admiralty and gave the order to mobilize the fleet forthwith.

On Sunday morning, August 2nd, my father was having breakfast when Prince Lichnowsky † suddenly appeared. He looked distraught and said he must speak to him at once. My father told us afterward that Lichnowsky had implored him not to side with France, saying that Germany was far more likely to be crushed with her Army cut in two between France and Russia. He had finally broken down and wept. He was bitterly critical of the policy of his own Government in not restraining Austria and seemed quite heartbroken. Poor Lichnowsky—he had always wanted peace and worked for it, but he was the helpless dupe of his own Government.

The Cabinet sat almost continuously throughout Sunday. When they broke up for an interval at luncheon time all those I saw looked racked with anxiety and some stricken with grief. Winston alone was buoyant for he was where he loved best to be—in action and fully extended. He was also convinced that it was imperative and right that we should act without delay for Germany was now at war with France and Russia and had violated the neutrality of Luxembourg. He certainly believed that the Cabinet was on the verge of breaking up and went to see Mr. Balfour in the luncheon interval, no doubt with the possibility of coalition in his mind. He had been in touch with F. E. Smith since Thursday to find out where he and others in his party stood as he had received letters from one or two important Unionists protesting against our being drawn into war.

Although he did not know it, my father had already received from Mr. Bonar Law an assurance of Opposition support in any measures he might be obliged to take. John Burns had resigned that morning but was persuaded to hold on till the evening.

Evening brought the German ultimatum to Belgium. Would she resist? That very day the Belgian Foreign Minister had informed us that his Government had "no reason whatever to suspect Germany of an intention to violate her neutrality," and had not "considered the idea of an appeal to other guarantee Powers, nor of intervention should a violation

* The French Ambassador.
† The German Ambassador.

occur. They would rely upon their own armed force as sufficient to resist aggression, from whatever quarter it might come." [26] After dinner, Grey and Haldane, who were living together in Queen Anne's Gate, walked across to Downing Street to see my father. They all agreed that the Army must be mobilized and my father, who was still Secretary of State for War, gave Haldane written authority to give the necessary orders to the War Office.

Monday, August 3rd, was the day of decision. When the Cabinet met my father received the resignations of three colleagues—Lord Morley (who had tendered it the night before and been asked to "sleep on it"), Sir John Simon and Lord Beauchamp. The other members of the Peace Group held their hand. According to Lord Morley, Mr. Lloyd George had tried to dissuade him from resigning with the plea "But if you go, it will put us who don't go, in a great hole." Lord Morley remained unmoved by what he described as "this truly singular remark." [27] While the Cabinet was in session the news came through that Belgium had refused the German ultimatum and that King Albert had appealed to King George for intervention. The atmosphere was immediately transformed. All but a few now realized that we were in honor bound to go to war.

That afternoon Edward Grey made his historic speech to the House of Commons, the speech which brought us into war as a united nation—a speech described by Lord Hugh Cecil as "the greatest example of the art of persuasion" he had ever listened to. Yet art had played little part in it. He had had no time to prepare it. Lichnowsky had been with him until the last moment before he left for the House. "The words," he wrote, "had to look after themselves." He deliberately refused to make any appeal to passion or emotion. He made no attempt even to arouse indignation against Germany. He wished the nation's great decision to be made in cold blood, to be based on justice and reason alone.

When he rose about three o'clock, the House was crowded from floor to roof and one felt its tension and its dreadful expectancy, an apprehension which was not fear, but awe. Edward Grey has written of that moment: "I do not recall feeling nervous. At such a moment there could be neither hope of personal success nor fear of personal failure. In a great crisis a man who has to act stands bare and stripped of choice. He has to do what it is *in* him to do, . . . and he can do no other." [28] He dealt first with our obligations to France, telling the story of the Entente, the military conversations, our agreement in 1912 about the disposition of our two fleets, our promise (made the day before) to protect the Channel. We were in no way technically committed to France. How far our friendship entailed obligation "let every man look into his own heart, his own feelings and construe the extent of that obligation for himself."

When he turned to Belgium he seemed to have the whole House with him. For the first time he was cheered. He quoted the words of the treaty by which we were bound to defend her neutrality; he read the appeal from the King of the Belgians to King George. If Belgium fell, Holland and Denmark would follow. If France were beaten to her knees in a life-and-death struggle while we stood aside, if we allowed the whole of Western Europe opposite to us to fall under the domination of a single power, "if in a crisis like this we run away from those obligations of honour and interest . . . I doubt whether, whatever material force we might have at the end, it would be of very much value in face of the respect we should have lost." When he sat down amid cheers, it was clear that he had the overwhelming support of the House behind him.

The speech has often been described as a "personal triumph." But it was not a triumph. It was the culminating point of a poignant personal tragedy. In his public life Edward Grey had had one supreme purpose— to keep the peace of Europe—and it had failed.

Bonar Law said a few words and Redmond made a most moving speech assuring the Government that "they might tomorrow withdraw every one of their troops from Ireland" in confidence that the armed Nationalist Catholics in the South would be only too glad to join arms with the armed Protestant Ulstermen in the North "to defend her shores."

Before the House dispersed Edward Grey rose again to read a message he had just received from the Belgian Legation containing the terms of the German ultimatum and the Belgian reply. "The Belgians have answered that an attack on their neutrality would be a flagrant violation of the rights of nations and that to accept the German proposal would be to sacrifice the honour of a nation. Conscious of its duty Belgium is firmly resolved to repel aggression by all possible means."

When we drove back to Downing Street, our car was surrounded by large cheering crowds and the police were hard put to it to clear a way for us. I understood their wild excitement for I shared it, but why I wondered did they look so *happy*? They could not realize what "war" meant—and they were not alone in this. None of us realized, though some imagined more than others. My own imagination was still frozen and paralyzed. After the long-drawn-out days of suspense, divided counsels, threatened disruption, feared dishonor, I felt above all else a flood tide of relief for my father, for Edward Grey, for Winston, for us all, that the die was cast, that we were keeping faith with our friends and honoring our word.

"What do we do next?" I asked my father when I said good night to him in his bedroom. "We shall send an ultimatum to Germany to stop the invasion of Belgium tomorrow." It was not worth asking what their answer would be, for we both knew. Winston asked the same question of Edward Grey as they left the House of Commons together and received the same reply.

Next morning (August 4th) the news came that the Germans had invaded Belgium and announced that if necessary they would push their way through by force of arms. An ultimatum to Germany, to expire at midnight, was drafted by my father and Sir Edward Grey and dispatched.* It asked for an assurance that they should respect Belgian neutrality. In his daily notes my father wrote: "The whole thing fills me with sadness."

No one could have described Winston as "filled with sadness." He rose to this greatest of all adventures with glowing zest. (And who can blame him—though some did.) For three years he had devoted all his powers to preparing the Navy to meet the challenge of this hour and he knew that he had done it well. The hour had come. He hailed it with a cheer. He knew that our cause was a just one, worth living and dying for, and his heart was high.

My father once said that till the test came he had no idea how his colleagues differed from one another in character and temperament. He thus described them at an earlier stage: "Winston who has a pictorial mind brimming with ideas is in tearing spirits at the prospect of war, which to me shows lack of imagination. Crewe is wise and keeps an even keel; no one can force Grey's hand, he and I see eye to eye over the whole situation; Lloyd George is nervous; Haldane, Samuel and McKenna very sensible and loyal." It is true that the dark and tragic certainties to which Grey and my father were alive were hidden from Winston's eyes. Against this he was alive to things which others did not see. His power of concentrating on one aim to the exclusion of all else was at once his weakness and his strength.

* On the night when the ultimatum was due to expire the question suddenly arose in Downing Street and in the Foreign Office, whether the time-limit "midnight" applied to G.M.T. or to Continental time. The final ruling was for Continental time, i.e., 11 P.M. G.M.T.

Downing Street was again thronged with excited crowds who surrounded and escorted my father to and from the House of Commons cheering him all the way. My stepmother and I went to the Ladies' Gallery to hear him announce the ultimatum. He rose in a hushed House, which though deeply moved seemed calm and resolute, and began by reading some telegrams—from our Ambassador in Berlin, from our Minister in Brussels, from the Belgian Legation in London saying that the territory had been violated near Aix-la-Chapelle—and lastly a telegram from the German Foreign Secretary to the British Government promising to annex no Belgian territory and to respect the neutrality of Holland and explaining that "a French attack across Belgium was planned according to unimpeachable information. . . . Germany had consequently to disregard Belgian neutrality, it being for her a question of life and death to prevent the French advance." My father then paused and said: "I have to add on behalf of His Majesty's Government: We cannot regard this as in any sense a satisfactory communication. We have, in reply to it, repeated the request we made last week to the German Government that they should give us the same assurance in regard to Belgian neutrality as was given to us and to Belgium by France last week. We have asked that a reply to that request, and a satisfactory answer to the telegram of this morning—which I have read to the House—should be given before midnight."

There was a moment of breathless stillness which was suddenly broken by a great wave of cheering increasing to a tide as my father rose from his seat, walked slowly to the Bar and faced the Speaker. To him he then delivered "a message from His Majesty signed by His Majesty's own hand." It was a proclamation calling out the Army Reserves for permanent service, "embodying the Territorial Force and making such arrangements as may be proper for units and individuals whose services may be required in other than a military capacity."

"Units and individuals . . ." For the first time I saw the war in personal terms. I thought of my four brothers, of my uncounted friends.

That night we sat together in the Cabinet Room watching the sands of peace run out. Three friends watched with us—Edward Grey, Sir William Tyrrell and Winston Churchill—waiting to flash the order to the Fleet. Before Big Ben rang out the appointed hour he left us and returned to tell my father that the deed was done.

Chapter Twenty-One

AT WAR

IT IS NOT my purpose, nor would it be within my powers, to attempt to tell the story of the First World War. My theme is Winston Churchill. Thus far I have attempted to describe him as I saw and knew him in the thick of the political struggle which for thirteen years had been the context of his thought and action.

Now the scene changes and he must play his part upon a greater battlefield in which the combatants are nations and the stakes annihilation or survival. I must not allow the dust and din of conflict in this vast arena to engulf or to obscure the central figure of my story, but try to assess the measure of his influence on events and their impact on his character and fortunes.

My memories of the first few days of war, tossed in a tumult of emotions, defy chronology. Though we were living from hour to hour, moment to moment, there was a dreamlike sense of starting a new life in a new world in which there were no bearings. All landmarks seemed to be swept away. Human beings alone remained the same and, comfortingly, true to form.

One significant event and one great figure stand out in my remembrance of the fifth of August. The event was the Council of War convened by my father at 10 Downing Street that afternoon. The figure was that of Lord Kitchener, suddenly striding into No. 10. I had imagined him to be already far away on the high seas en route for Alexandria, but there he stood in the dim hall, larger than life. I remember the surprise, relief and almost joy I felt on finding him still in this country. "Then you're not gone?" "Your father stopped me—I was on the boat," he said. "And now you're going to stay with us? You must." "I don't know about that yet. I ought to get back." I had a strong feeling that he very much wanted to get back. The East was his happiest hunting ground, his spiritual home. He knew his place there—and other people's. He understood its tortuous politics. He gloried in his ignorance of ours and felt profound mistrust of them.

My father had shown prevision when on August 3rd he had had Lord Kitchener picked off a Channel steamer on which he had already embarked for Egypt and asked him to return at once to London. He had not then made up his mind to appoint him Secretary of State for War, but he felt that Lord Kitchener's presence at the War Council was essential. By the morning of the 5th he had decided to give up the War Office, to which it was clearly impossible for him to give the undivided time and thought it now demanded, and to install Lord Kitchener there as his successor. The appointment was greeted with universal acclamation. My father had responded, whether he knew it or not, to the unanimous desire of the nation.* Lord Kitchener was more than a national hero. He was a national institution. The word "popular" does not begin to describe his hold on the public imagination. He was an almost symbolic figure and what he symbolized, I think, was strength, decision and above all success. South Africa, Khartoum—everything that he touched "came off." There was a feeling that Kitchener could not fail. The psychological effect of his appointment, the tonic to public confidence were instantaneous and overwhelming. And he at once gave, in his own right, a national status to the Government.

Lord Kitchener accepted the War Office reluctantly and only because it was presented to him as a duty. My father recognized the appointment as a "hazardous experiment" but "the best in the circumstances." In one way I was delighted for I had always had a soft spot for this hard and enigmatic man. But I could not imagine him in this, or any other, Cabinet. What would he make of our lobster pot? And they of him? And how I wondered would his presence at the War Office affect Winston?

I remembered the history of their past relations—how Lord Kitchener had done everything in his power to prevent Winston from taking part in the River War. The fact that Winston had outwitted him and taken part in it in the dual role of Lancer and correspondent for the *Morning Post* had not placated him. When the war was over he had done his best

---

* The imperious orders for his appointment issued by the Northcliffe press (the *Times* and *Daily Mail*) appeared one day too late.

to exclude Winston from the Victory March by putting him in charge of a convoy of sick camels while they hobbled their weary way along the Nile to Cairo from Khartoum. Winston again defeated him, this time by the simple expedient of disobeying orders. He shed the camels, leaped on a boat and got back in time to ride triumphantly through London with the Lancers. Thereafter he proceeded to deal with Lord Kitchener's character and campaigns "in two bulky volumes conceived throughout in a faithful spirit of impartiality."

The great Commander-in-Chief and the rebellious and articulate subaltern met now on equal terms. Lord Kitchener was sixty-four; Winston was still only thirty-nine. Would Lord Kitchener's appointment conduce to harmony between the elements of land and water, the Admiralty and the War Office?

The same questions, as I know, occurred to Winston, though he welcomed the appointment wholeheartedly. "My relations with Lord Kitchener," he wrote, "had been limited. Our first meeting had been on the field of Omdurman. . . . He had disapproved of me severely in my youth, had endeavoured to prevent me from coming to the Soudan Campaign, and was indignant that I had succeeded in getting there. It was a case of dislike before first sight." It was twelve years before they met again at Army maneuvers in 1910 and were formally introduced to each other. But I think it was during our visit to Malta on the *Enchantress* in 1912 that a thaw in their relationship set in and that they began to know each other. "Thenceforward," wrote Winston, "we used to talk over Imperial Defence topics when from time to time we met. . . . I had found him much more affable than I had been led to expect. . . . I was glad when he was appointed Secretary of State for War, and in those early days we worked together on close and cordial terms. He consulted me constantly on the political aspects of his work, and increasingly gave me his confidence in military matters. Admiralty and War Office business were so interlaced that during the whole of the first ten months we were in almost daily personal consultation." [1]

Winston was incapable of rancor; Lord Kitchener was too big a man to harbor petty grudges. Each recognized the other's quality. (And there were sharper irritants in store for both of them.)

The first War Council (described by my father as "rather a motley gathering") was attended by Lord Roberts, Lord Kitchener, Sir John French, Sir Ian Hamilton, Sir Douglas Haig and their expert advisers and my father, Edward Grey, Winston and Lord Haldane. There was a school of thought within the Cabinet and outside it in both parties, who believed that we could fight this war by naval action alone and that our Army should not be sent overseas. There was, however, complete unanimity that the whole British Army should be sent immediately to France according to the Haldane plan. On behalf of the Admiralty Winston gave assurances that it would provide its transport and guarantee its crossing. He was also willing to waive the condition that two regular divisions should be kept here to guard against invasion. The Admiralty was prepared to take entire responsibility for the security of our shores in their absence. It was therefore decided to dispatch immediately the Expeditionary Force of six divisions under the command of Sir John French and this decision was accepted by the Cabinet next day with much less demur than my father had expected.

At this, the first Cabinet after the declaration of war, Winston has recorded that Lord Kitchener "in soldierly sentences . . . proclaimed a series of inspiring and prophetic truths." Of these the most surprising to his colleagues was his estimate of the probable duration of the war. There was a general assumption even among the experts that it would be a short one. Kitchener prophesied truly that the war would last for many years and that we must raise and put armies of millions into the field. He declared his intention of creating as a start a new Army of at least a million men pledged to serve for a provisional period of three years. Some of his colleagues were startled by this pronouncement; Edward Grey has admitted his own incredulity. It was nevertheless accepted "in silent assent"; and on the following day he made his first appeal for a hundred thousand volunteers. I shall always remember seeing in Trafalgar Square the first of those vast posters which were soon to cover the whole country, of Kitchener's face complete with piercing eye, bristling mustache, imperious forefinger outstretched and underneath the caption "Your Country Needs YOU."

Winston believed that if Lord Kitchener had there and then demanded universal National Service the Cabinet would have acquiesced. I doubt it and I am sure that he showed wisdom in refraining from making any such request. He was, however, unwise in refusing to use the Territorial Army as the framework of his new force. He was quite ignorant of the Territorials and despised them as amateurs. I had the temerity to ask him why he preferred raw recruits who would have to learn everything from scratch to volunteers who for years past had proved their ardor and sacrificed their leisure to regular part-time training. He replied: "I prefer men who know nothing to those who have been taught a smattering of the wrong thing." He had no reason to assume that the Territorials had been "taught the wrong thing" and they confuted him by their subsequent record. By this error of judgment he complicated his tremendous task. As recruits poured in by the hundred thousand there was no machinery to deal with their training or equipment. In vain Lord Haldane pleaded with him to use that of the County Associations which had been created for this very purpose. He would not touch them, and the birth of Kitchener's armies, by improvisation out of confusion, was a miracle.

The passage of the Army to France began on August 6th. Mobilization and transport went off without a hitch according to the timetable and in complete secrecy. For those of us who knew, sealed lips and poker faces were the order of the day. It was an order I was well inured to, but never before was it exposed to such a test. Close friends with sons and brothers in the Army made agonized inquiries day in, day out. I remember two, in particular, from the mothers of two midshipmen, aged fourteen, both serving in battleships, which had been ordered to sea. Surely these children were not going into action? There was here no question of discretion for it was common knowledge that the Navy had been mobilized and I wrote a note to Winston asking if I might set their minds at rest. It seemed to me unthinkable that these little boys should be plunged into the inferno of a naval battle. I shall always remember the gentleness and understanding of his immediate reply: "My dear, it is true. But you must remember and remind their mothers that they belong to a great Service. This ordeal is an honour of which they would not wish to be and should not be deprived. I know that it is harder to face these ordeals for others than for oneself. We shall both have many in the days to come. We must help each other. W."

Since August 3rd Winston had been enduring "the tortures of Tantalus" over the fate of the *Goeben,* the one German ship at large in the Mediterranean which outstripped in speed and power every vessel in the French Navy. Our battle cruisers, the *Indomitable* and the *Indefatigable,* which alone could compete with her in speed were ordered to shadow and hold her and during the hours before the expiry of the ultimatum we had her in our power. The Cabinet, however, felt that we were in honor bound to observe the rules of the game. Meanwhile, as my father has noted, "Winston's mouth watered for the Goeben." The chase went on and at five o'clock on August 4th Prince Louis observed that "there was still time to sink the Goeben before dark." [2] Bound by the Cabinet decision Winston was unable to give the word. The Italian declaration of neutrality hampered the hunters in their task, for our ships were ordered to respect it and not to infringe the six-mile limit off the Italian coasts. Under cover of darkness the *Goeben* gave her pursuers the slip. When she arrived at Messina her Commander received news that a treaty had been concluded between Germany and Turkey, with orders to proceed at once to Constantinople. Of this fateful treaty we knew nothing.

The *Goeben* and the light cruiser *Breslau* now spent thirty-six hours coaling from German colliers at Messina. The British Commander-in-Chief, Sir Berkeley Milne, when he located them set two battle cruisers to guard the northern exit from the Straits, but left the southern exit open and through this the *Goeben* and the *Breslau* made their escape.

In the Adriatic Rear-Admiral Troubridge who was commanding an armored cruiser squadron of four good ships and eight destroyers, acting on his own responsibility, decided to intercept the *Goeben,* reported his decision to the Commander-in-Chief and gave orders to his squadron to hasten southward at full steam. Having received no reply nor orders from Sir Berkeley Milne he became convinced that fighting in broad daylight and in the open seas the *Goeben* could sink his four ships one by one while keeping outside their range. He had been instructed not to engage "a superior force" and recognizing the *Goeben* as such he gave up the pursuit.

By six o'clock on the morning of August 7th she was clear away, her course set for the Dardanelles, "carrying with her for the peoples of the East and Middle East more slaughter, more misery and more ruin than has ever before been borne within the compass of a ship." [3]

These days of constantly frustrated hope were very hard for Winston to bear. The prize he longed for had eluded him through a chapter of accidents, miscalculations and mistakes. No wonder that he saw in its escape "the influence of that sinister fatality which at a later stage and on a far larger scale was to dog the enterprise against the Dardanelles. . . . The terrible 'Ifs' accumulate. . . . If we could have opened fire on the Goeben during the afternoon of 4th August; if we had been less solicitous for Italian neutrality; if Sir Berkeley Milne had sent the Indomitable to coal at Malta instead of Bizerta; if the Admiralty had sent him direct instructions when on the night of the 5th they learned where the Goeben was; if Rear-Admiral Troubridge in the small hours of 7th August had not changed his mind . . . the story of the Goeben would have ended here. There was, however, . . . one more chance of annulling the doom of which she was the bearer. That chance, remote though it was, the Fates were vigilant to destroy." [4] Of that one chance and its destruction there will be much to tell hereafter.

How often we plowed and replowed the arid ground of terrible "ifs"!

"It was all the Admirals' fault," I said. "I told you all about Admirals when I first saw them at Malta in 1912. Who but an Admiral would *not* have put a battle-cruiser at both ends of the Messina Straits, instead of putting two at one end and none at the other? And why did Sir Berkeley Milne not answer Troubridge's signal and say: 'Yes—go ahead hell for leather'? The Captains on the other hand both came out splendidly.* Take my advice and turn your Captains into Admirals like one o'clock."

The Board of Admiralty, however, did not share my irreverent view of Admirals. Rear-Admiral Troubridge was tried by court-martial in September and honorably acquitted of all blame and the First Sea Lord recorded the opinion "that Admiral Milne had taken the best measures with the force at his disposal, that his dispositions were the proper ones" etc., etc. On this pronouncement Winston records his "sole comment" (August 27th): "The explanation is satisfactory; the result unsatisfactory."

The Navy's first operation had been bungled. For some time Winston found it difficult to accept the accomplished fact and wished to send a torpedo flotilla through the Dardanelles to sink the *Goeben* and the *Breslau*. But this plan was strongly opposed both by Lord Kitchener and Lord Crewe lest it should stir up the Moslems in India and Egypt. My father agreed that we should not take the initiative against Turkey. She must be compelled to strike the first blow.

Meanwhile the Admiralty awaited in tense expectancy and sober confidence a German challenge to open battle in the North Sea. In Winston's words, "we expected it and we courted it." But nothing happened. "The Grand Fleet remained at sea; the German Fleet did not quit the shelter of its harbours." German cruisers in foreign waters vanished. German merchant ships sought refuge in neutral harbors while our Merchant Marine continued to carry on our sea-borne trade.

The first four divisions of the Expeditionary Force crossed to France between August 6th and 20th and the fifth and sixth followed at the beginning of September. No attempt was made to interfere with their passage. Not a ship was sunk, not a man was drowned. All this was a triumph for British sea power and for Winston, who had been its vigilant and militant trustee. My father wrote, on August 18th, when for the first time the passage of the Army was made public: "The curtain is

---

* The two brothers Kelly commanding the light cruisers *Dublin* and *Gloucester* had done everything in their power to intercept the *Goeben* and the *Gloucester* pursued her at great risk until called off by the Commander-in-Chief.

lifted today and people begin to realize what an extraordinary thing has been done in the last ten days. The poor old War Office, which has always been a by-word of inefficiency has proved itself more than up-to-date, for which the credit is mainly due to Haldane and the Committee of Imperial Defence. The Navy too has been admirable; not a single torpedo has slipped through either end of the Channel." On the following day he added: "Kitchener thinks the Germans are going in for a large enveloping movement which will enable them to have a dash at the French frontier between Lille and Maubeuge. If so the big battle will not begin for some days. He is very good at these things and predicted this a week ago when all the French officers here declared it to be impossible."

Lord Kitchener's prophetic instinct was again confirmed. The French who had taken the offensive by an advance into Lorraine were soon outflanked and in full retreat and our small army which had been hurried forward to Mons to shield their left was faced with four German Army corps and in grave danger of encirclement. Nevertheless when late on the evening of August 23rd Lord Kitchener discussed the situation with Winston he was still "darkly hopeful."

But on the following day he paid two early morning calls of sinister import, the first on Maurice Bonham Carter, who was then sleeping at No. 10, and who awoke to find the Field-Marshal's gigantic figure standing by his bed. "Bad news," he said and handed him a telegram from Sir John French which he asked him to convey immediately to the Prime Minister. Lord Kitchener then went on to the Admiralty where at seven o'clock he found Winston sitting up in bed at work upon his official boxes. Of this visit there is a vivid description in *The World Crisis:* "He paused in the doorway and I knew in a flash and before ever he spoke that the event had gone wrong. Though his manner was quite calm, his face was different. I had the subconscious feeling that it was distorted and discoloured as if it had been punched with a fist. His eyes rolled more than ever. His voice, too, was hoarse. He looked gigantic. 'Bad news,' he said heavily and laid the slip of paper on my bed. I read the telegram. It was from Sir John French.

" 'My troops have been engaged all day with the enemy on a line roughly East and West through Mons. I have just received a message from G.O.C. Fifth French Army that his troops have been driven back, that Namur has fallen, and that he is taking up a line from Maubeuge to Rocroi. I have therefore ordered a retirement to the line Valenciennes—Longueville—Maubeuge, which is being carried out now,

It will prove a difficult operation, if the enemy remains in contact. . . . I think that immediate attention should be directed to the defence of Havre.' " [5]

Three features of this message brought a chill to Winston's heart. First, the fall of Maubeuge, that strong fortress which had been the pivot of the turning movement we had planned, taken in a single day. Then the threat to the "naked Channel ports"—Dunkirk, Calais, Boulogne. "Fortify Havre," said Sir John French. And lastly the baleful sentence "It will prove a difficult operation, if the enemy remains in contact."

There followed the dark days of the retreat from Mons—unforgettable for those who lived through them and in my memory comparable only to those of the evacuation of Dunkirk in the Second World War. Was our splendid Army doomed to destruction? Could it be saved? Could anything be saved? The French Armies were being rapidly forced back. Would the tide ever turn? And what could turn it? And there was worse to come. On August 30th an alarming message was received from Sir John French. It contained the shattering news that he was about to withdraw his army from the fighting line and retire behind the Seine. My father, Lord Kitchener and the whole Cabinet were filled with consternation. They felt that such action would amount to "leaving our Allies in the lurch in the moment of their extreme need." It was indeed thus construed by the French Government, who fully shared the Cabinet's consternation and expressed it in a moving appeal. After an anxious day of inquiry my father held a midnight conference on August 31st with Lord Kitchener, Winston and a few other colleagues and decided to send Lord Kitchener out to France immediately to deal with the situation. Winston provided him with a destroyer which took him that night from Dover to Le Havre; he was in Paris next morning and in consultation with Sir John French at the British Embassy in the afternoon. That evening at seven thirty he was able to report to my father that "French's troops are now in the fighting-line, where he will remain, conforming to the movements of the French Army, though at the same time acting with caution to avoid being in any way unsupported by his flanks."

My father wrote in his diary on September 1st: "He [Kitchener] is a real sportsman when an emergency offers, and went straight home to change his clothes and started by special train from Charing Cross about 1.30 this morning." But, alas, he changed into the wrong clothes—with unfortunate results. "If," wrote Winston, "Lord Kitchener had gone in plain clothes no difficulty would have arisen, but his appearance in Paris in the uniform of a Field-Marshal senior to the Commander-in-Chief at that dark and critical moment, wounded and disconcerted Sir John French deeply and not unnaturally. I laboured my utmost to put this right and to make it clear that the Cabinet and not Lord Kitchener were responsible." [6]

No one could have done more to soothe Sir John French's ruffled feelings. French wrote to him: "As usual you have poured balm into my wounds"—a rare tribute for Winston to receive, for though he showered his friends with many precious gifts balm was not usually one of them. In spite of more balm from my father (who dispensed it of necessity at all times and in many quarters) the wound continued to rankle, and Sir John's doubts and suspicions about Lord Kitchener were fostered and exploited by mischief-makers. Apart from this incident I was always aware of a temperamental disharmony between them. Their relations were rather like those between a dog and a cat. Kitchener was the dog who did not bother about the cat until he had to do so, French was the cat which arched its back and spat.

The position in France had been straightened out by Kitchener's visit to Paris but at home acute anxiety pervaded every hour. The casualty lists were coming in. Thousands were missing. Stricken parents who had expected to see their sons back for Christmas mourned "the unreturning army which is youth." The news was bad and rumor even worse, the French were on the verge of moving out of Paris, a general sense of disaster prevailed.

Then suddenly and, as it seemed, miraculously the tide turned. The Russian Armies had invaded East Prussia and though they had been overwhelmingly defeated at Tannenberg the German High Command was sufficiently unnerved to withdraw two Army corps. Von Kluck exposed his flank. The days of retreat were over. On September 6th the French and British Armies (in Winston's words) "turned upon their pursuers and sprang at their throats." [7] They advanced together to win the victory of the Marne. The German attempt at a knockout blow in the West had failed.

During the last dark days of August Winston had been cheered by an audacious and brilliantly successful action in the Heligoland Bight planned by two Commodores, Tyrwhitt and Keyes, with the invaluable support of Admiral Beatty and his battle cruisers. Three enemy cruisers and a destroyer were sunk and three others crippled without loss or serious injury to a single British ship.

The Admiralty was now working at full stretch and strain. Winston's day began at nine and often went on till 2 A.M., broken for him (though not for his secretaries) by a siesta of an hour every afternoon. Early in August the Cabinet had drawn up a plan for the seizure of the German colonies in every part of the world. (My father had observed to his colleagues, "We look more like a gang of Elizabethan buccaneers than a meek collection of black-coated Liberal Ministers," [8] and Winston commented: "A month before, with what horror and disgust would most of those present have averted their minds from such ideas!" [9]) But it was essential to deny bases and harbors of refuge to German cruisers and thus safeguard our sea communications. The transport and convoying of troops from the Empire and Dominions laid another heavy burden on the Admiralty. The Canadian Army, the Australian and New Zealand Army corps, the five divisions from India and their replacement by Territorials—these were transported while all the enemy cruisers were still at large ranging the seas without mishap to any ship or the loss of a single life. Winston records that as many as twenty enterprises dependent entirely on sea power "were proceeding simultaneously in different parts of the globe." [10]

To secure and maintain the command of the seas throughout the world was a task which would have slaked the appetite and the capacity for work of most men. But Winston's dynamic versatility knew no limits and by the end of August he was operating in three elements, air, land and water. He had always been air-minded and believed from the earliest days of flying that the airplane had a great part to play in any future war. The senior stick-in-the-muds of the services were skeptical, but Jack Seely (then at the War Office) was keenly and actively co-operative and when in 1912 the Royal Flying Corps came into being it had a naval wing for coastal reconnaissance and hunting submarines, a realization of Winston's hopes at Malta. When war began he urged the creation of a ministry to control and develop a united air service, but there were not enough machines or men to justify it, so two separate, independent Air Forces continued to exist under the War Office and the Admiralty.

Lord Kitchener, whose planes were actively engaged in covering and supporting our retreating Armies in France, asked Winston to take over from the War Office the responsibility for aerial home defense. He accepted eagerly. It was a tough assignment for when the war began there were as yet no antiaircraft guns nor searchlights and radar was of course undreamed of. A purely defensive role was alien to his spirit.

The best form of defense was the attack. Instead of hanging about our coasts on the off chance that a Zeppelin might turn up our planes would seek out and scotch the Zeppelins in their hangars.

On August 27th a squadron of Royal Naval Air Service airplanes landed at Dunkirk under the command of Commander Samson. Air bases were set up there and at Calais from which (according to Sir Sefton Brancker) "with a handful of men, a few nondescript aeroplanes, and some commandeered cars with improvised armour, he was here, there and everywhere, terrorizing marauding Uhlans and inspiring French Territorials." [11] The Royal Naval Air Service made a series of daring and successful raids over Zeppelin sheds at Cologne, Cuxhaven, Düsseldorf and Friedrichshafen and within a year they claimed a bag of six Zeppelins, destroyed on the ground or in the air. But our air bases must themselves be defended. How?

In *The World Crisis* we are told how "the needs and activities of the naval aeroplanes at Dunkirk led directly to the development of the armoured car." All available Rolls-Royce cars were purchased by the Admiralty, clad in improvised armor and used for the protection of Commander Samson's air operations. The German cavalry retorted by digging trenches across roads and by the middle of October these trenches had reached the sea. Winston refused to accept defeat for the armored car. He drew the conclusion that if it could not move *around* the enemy's trenches some method must be devised which would enable it to pass over them. At his request Admiral Bacon designed a car carrying a bridge in front, which on arriving at a trench it could drop, pass over and then raise behind it. The Caterpillar Tractor and other designs were tested but none of them filled the bill until, in February, 1915, a vast "land battleship" was devised under the direction of the Landships Committee of the Admiralty which Winston had set up for the purpose. This was the prototype of the first tank used at the Battle of the Somme in 1916. He has written truly that "the air was the first cause that took us to Dunkirk. The armoured car was the child of the air; and the Tank its grandchild." [12]

His third iron in the fire was a diversionary force of marines at Ostend which originated as follows. I quote from my father's diary notes to prove that this much-maligned enterprise had the highest official backing: *"Aug. 26th*—When I came back from the House I had a long visit from Winston and Kitchener and we summoned Edward Grey into our councils. They were bitten by an idea of Hankey's to dispatch a brigade of Marines, about 3,000, conveyed and escorted by battleships to Ostend, to land there and take possession of the town and scout about in the neighbourhood. This would please the Belgians and annoy and harass the Germans who would certainly take it to be the pioneer of a larger force and it would further be quite a safe operation as the Marines could at any moment re-embark. Grey and I consented and the little force is probably at this moment disembarking at Ostend. Winston I need not say was full of ardour about his Marines. . . . *Aug. 27th*— Winston has been scoring some small but not unimportant points. His 3,000 Marines have 'taken' Ostend and are scouting about the country in the region and the Kaiser Wilhelm, a huge armed German liner, has been sunk by the Highflyer."

In order to publicize and magnify the operation Winston announced in the House that a British force had begun landing at Ostend. The German General Staff reacted as desired. The head of their Operations Branch recorded that: "One day countless British troops were said to have landed at Ostend and to be marching on Antwerp. At Ostend a great entrenched camp for the English was in preparation."

On September 16th Marshal Joffre telegraphed to Lord Kitchener asking whether a brigade of Marines could be sent to Dunkirk to reinforce the garrison and to confuse the Germans and alarm them about their lines of communication. Once more Lord Kitchener appealed to Winston, who agreed provided that a regiment of Yeomanry cavalry could be sent for their protection. Fifty motorbuses from the London streets went with them to make them at once mobile and conspicuous. Their aim was to be well advertised and ubiquitous, turning up where they were least expected, "ostentatiously displaying themselves in Ypres, Lille, Tournai and Douai." This was the famous Dunkirk Circus which became a target for the criticism and derision of Winston's ever-ready chorus of detractors. No casualties were incurred and an amusing time was had by all, including Winston himself. He often skipped over to France to superintend his Circus, his flying base and what my father called "his own little Army" at Dunkirk.

It is quite untrue to suggest as Lord Beaverbrook and others have done that my father felt irritation and impatience at these diversionary side shows, though it is true that he was sometimes obliged to discharge Winston's duties at the Admiralty in his absence. On one occasion only did he demand his immediate return from abroad. My father was on the contrary amused and fascinated by Winston's adventurous and fertile ingenuity and by the resources of a mind wholly unlike his own. He abhorred conventionality and staidness and turned with infinite relief to the original and the unexpected and these he never failed to find in Winston. During these weeks and months of grueling anxiety on the rare occasions when I saw him enjoy the *détente* of a private smile or chuckle and asked to share the cause of his amusement he invariably recounted to me some exploit or some phrase of Winston's and always with intense appreciation and delight. "Who else could have said that? Done that? No one in the world but Winston."

Others were often asking the same question, but with a very different inflection. The general reaction to his achievements was critical and even jaundiced. Though Winston inspired devotion in his personal friends and in those who served him he could not have been described as popular. I was constantly aware of the hostility he seemed to provoke quite unconsciously and unwittingly. Lord Beaverbrook has written that in the Conservative Party "he was hated, he was mistrusted, and he was feared." [13] Among certain sections of our own party he was an object of vague suspicion. His successes were grudgingly conceded while his failures were greeted with exultant *Schadenfreude*. Why was it? I wondered unceasingly. Most people recognized his genius. Were they jealous of it? Were they afraid of it? Or were they merely offended because they believed him to be insufficiently interested in themselves and their opinions? In this belief they were, incidentally, dead right. He was not interested. Nor did he seek to conceal his indifference by any softening subterfuge.* To save his life he could not have pretended to an interest that he did not feel, nor would he have thought it worth doing. He enjoyed the ovation of the crowd but he still ignored the necessity of having a personal following. The fact that he had no body-guard around him, while against him were arrayed the solid, bitter enmity of the Tory party and its press and a sprinkling of critics in all camps, made his position vulnerable when things went wrong.

He has written of himself (and there is pathos in his words): "Looking back with after-knowledge and increasing years, I seem to have been too ready to undertake tasks which were hazardous or even forlorn. Taking over responsibility for the air defence of Great Britain when resources were practically non-existent and formidable air attacks imminent, was from a personal point of view 'some love but little policy.' The same is true of the Dunkirk guerrilla. Still more is it true of the attempt to prolong the defence of Antwerp. . . . I could with perfect

---

* Though he would not I think have acted quite as ruthlessly as his father, Lord Randolph, who when buttonholed by a bore at a club rang the bell for a waiter and said: "Waiter—please listen to the end of Colonel B.'s story."

propriety, indeed with unanswerable reasons, have in every one of these cases left the burden to others." [14]

He might well have done so, but being himself he could not. He could not say "no" to opportunity. He could not turn his back on action. Prudence has been described by William Blake as an "ugly, old maid courted by Incapacity." She could never claim even a nodding acquaintance with Winston.

Chapter Twenty-Two

ANTWERP

I COME now to the part played by Winston in the defense of Antwerp. No event in his whole career, with the one exception of Gallipoli, did him greater and more undeserved damage. Once more that part was not of his own seeking. He responded to an appeal from Lord Kitchener.

The Battle of the Marne, which lasted four days and which Winston ranks as the greatest of the war, had been fought and won and the Germans had been hurled back to the Aisne. He has written that "the struggle of *armies* and *nations* having failed to reach a decision, *places* recovered their significance, and geography rather than psychology began to rule the lines of war. Paris now unattainable, the Channel Ports —Dunkirk, Calais and Boulogne—still naked, and lastly Antwerp, all re-appeared in the field of values like submerged rocks when the tidal wave recedes." [1]

Antwerp was, both for the Germans and ourselves, of the highest strategic value. Apart from its significance to the Belgian people it guarded the whole line of the Channel ports and it threatened the rear of the German Armies in France. On September 9th the Kaiser ordered the capture of the city whatever the cost. No serious assaults took place until September 28th, when the Germans began pounding the forts with heavy howitzers firing projectiles of over a ton. The Belgian Government became suddenly alarmed.

I had accompanied my father to the three great meetings he had addressed on our war aims in London, Edinburgh and Dublin and on October 2nd I went with him to the fourth at Cardiff. I recall his deep anxiety about the fate of Antwerp and his desire to find some means of saving it. We discussed the position in the train and I remember his saying that this would be no task for Winston's "little army," that only Regulars could do the job. The French had offered a division to fight under a British General and it might be possible to divert our Seventh Division which had been destined for France. When we got back from Cardiff the following day, we found alarming news awaiting us from our Minister in Antwerp, Sir Francis Villiers. The Belgian Government had decided to leave Antwerp for Ostend and the King and the Army would withdraw toward Ghent to protect the coastline. It was said that the town would hold out for five days but he doubted whether resistance would last as long once the Court and Government had gone.

Apart from receiving full information day by day, Winston had had no hand or voice in these events, so little indeed that on the evening of October 2nd he entrained as he had planned at Victoria Station for Dunkirk. At eleven o'clock that night when he was some twenty miles from London en route for Dover the train was suddenly stopped and returned to Victoria Station where he was met by an urgent summons from Lord Kitchener to come immediately to his house in Carlton Gardens. Here he found Sir Edward Grey, Prince Louis of Battenberg (the First Sea Lord) and Sir William Tyrrell who showed him the telegram. There was general consternation at the news, which was wholly unexpected. Till now the Belgians had been standing firm and resolute. That they should suddenly throw up the sponge when heavy guns and troops were coming to their aid was bewildering and seemed incomprehensible. What could and should be done? In Winston's words "there is always a strong case for doing nothing, especially for doing nothing yourself." But the small group of Ministers at their midnight conclave resolved that Antwerp could not be yielded up without a struggle. They sent a telegram to Sir Francis Villiers stressing the vital importance of its defense and promising to send a brigade of marines next day followed if possible by reinforcements from the main Army and adding: "We urge you to make one further struggle to hold out."

Realizing that they were taking upon themselves a heavy responsibility in urging the Belgians to reconsider their decision and this without full knowledge of the local situation, it was decided that someone in authority should go at once to Antwerp to assess the position and report upon it. Lord Kitchener expressed "a decided wish" that Winston should go. My father (who had not then returned from Cardiff) records that after the meeting "I fancy with Grey's rather reluctant consent, the intrepid Winston set off at midnight and ought to have reached Antwerp at about nine this morning. Sir John French is making preparations to send assistance by way of Lille. I have had a talk with Kitchener this morning and we are both rather anxiously awaiting Winston's report. I do not know how fluent he is in French, but, if he was able to do himself justice in a foreign tongue, the Belges will have listened to a discourse the like of which they have never heard before. I cannot but think that he will stiffen them up." [2]

And stiffen them up he did, for within two days my father notes that "Winston succeeded in bucking up the Belgians who gave up their idea of retreat to Ostend and are now going to hold Antwerp for as long as they can trusting upon our coming to their final assistance." An old friend, Jack Seely, who had arrived in Antwerp from Sir John French's headquarters, describes the dramatic transformation of the scene effected by Winston's presence. "From the moment I arrived it was apparent that the whole business was in Winston's hands. He dominated the whole place—the King, Ministers, soldiers, sailors. So great was his influence that I am convinced that with 20,000 British troops he could have held Antwerp against almost any onslaught." [3] Winston was able to inspire this conviction in others because he held it so strongly himself. He was not merely "deeply involved" in this "tremendous and highly critical local situation," he was possessed by it. The marines were already in the Antwerp trenches. The rest of the Naval Brigade had been ordered to follow. The Seventh Division was on its way. Sir Henry Rawlinson had been appointed by Lord Kitchener to command the whole force. If Antwerp could hold out till it arrived all might be saved. But every day that passed increased the danger to the Belgian Army of being cut off.

I prided myself on an intimate understanding of Winston and had usually been able to explain his actions to myself, though not always to others. But he now took a step which staggered me. On October 5th he telegraphed to my father offering to resign his office and "undertake the command of the relieving and defensive forces assigned to Antwerp. . . . 'I feel it my duty to offer my services because I am sure this arrangement will afford the best prospects of a victorious result to an enterprise in which I am deeply involved. . . . I wait your reply. Runciman would do Admiralty well.' "

My father, though equally astounded, was I think less deeply shaken. Perhaps he had lost the capacity to be surprised by the vagaries of his colleagues? He notes: "Of course, without consulting anybody I at once telegraphed to him warm appreciation of his mission and his offer, with a most decided negative saying we could not spare him at the Admiralty. I had not meant to read it at the Cabinet, but as everybody, including Kitchener, began to ask how soon he was going to return, I was obliged at last to do so." My father added: "Winston is an ex-lieutenant of Hussars, and would, if his proposal had been accepted, have been in command of two distinguished Major-Generals, not to mention Brigadiers, Colonels, etc." [4]

That such an appointment would have outraged the military hierarchy did not worry me nor apparently Lord Kitchener, who expressed his willingness to make him a Major-General if my father gave him the command. What amazed and shook me was the sense of proportion (or lack of it) revealed by Winston's choice. His desire to exchange the Admiralty, in which for years he had invested all his treasure and which was now faced with its first test and greatest opportunity, for the command of a mere Major-General, one of many, in the field seemed to me to be hardly adult. It was the choice of a romantic child. In terms of scope and power the two jobs were not comparable. He would be abdicating his part in the grand strategy of the war, which he had always seen in world-wide terms, in order to play a personal part in a small patch of it. On the great issues of war aims and peace terms he would have no say. He would be exiled from the inner councils of the nation in the greatest crisis of its history. Had he imagined life without his telegrams and boxes, his access to the heart of things? He had always found action at close range irresistible and at a lesser moment in a narrower sphere I could imagine his preferring action in a limited and visible field to greater power at a desk. But *now* . . . ? I could not reconcile his wish with his dramatic sense or his imaginative range.

Nor was it a momentary aberration. My father has a note (undated) after the fall of Antwerp: "Since I came back I have had a long call from Winston, who, after dilating in great detail on the actual situation, became suddenly very confidential and implored me not to take a conventional view of his future. Having, as he says, tasted blood these last few days, he is beginning, like a tiger, to raven for more, and begs that sooner or later—and the sooner the better—he may be relieved of his present office and put in some kind of military command. I told him that he could not be spared from the Admiralty, but he scoffs at that, alleging that the naval part of the business is practically over, as our superiority will grow greater and greater every month. His mouth waters at the sight and thought of Kitchener's new armies. Are these 'glittering commands' to be entrusted to 'dug-out trash' bred on the obsolete tactics of twenty-five years ago, 'mediocrities who have led a sheltered life mouldering in military routine', etc. etc.? For about a quarter of an hour he poured forth a ceaseless cataract of invective and appeal, and I much regretted that there was no shorthand writer within hearing, as some of his unpremeditated phrases were quite priceless. He was, however, three parts serious." [5]

To return to Antwerp: on October 5th, the day Winston had telegraphed to my father asking to be relieved of the Admiralty, he sent the following telegram to Lord Kitchener: "It is my duty to remain here and continue my direction of affairs unless relieved by some person of consequence in view of the situation and developing German attack." Lord Kitchener replied that General Rawlinson would reach Antwerp that day. My father was by now becoming somewhat restive at Winston's absence. He writes on the following day (October 6th): "Winston persists in remaining there, which leaves the Admiralty here without a head, and I have had to tell them to submit all decisions to me. I think that Winston ought to return now that a capable general is arriving. He has done good service." [6] Some twenty thousand troops were now on their way and the two Naval Brigades had arrived. When in the evening Winston went to meet them and place them under the command of General Paris at his headquarters on the Lierre road he was under heavy fire. While they discussed plans around a cottage table "the whole house thudded and shook from minute to minute with the near explosions of shells whose flashes lit the windowpanes." He was in one of his many elements and at the moment it made a more imperious appeal to him than any other. The London war correspondent of the *Giornale d'Italia* who was reporting the siege of Antwerp describes him thus: "In the battle line near Lierre in the midst of a group of officers stood a man enveloped in a cloak and wearing a yachting cap. He was tranquilly smoking a large cigar and looked at the progress of the battle under a rain of shrapnel which I can only call fearful. It was Mr. Churchill who had come to view the situation for himself. It must be confessed that it is not easy to find in all Europe a Minister who would be capable of smoking peacefully under that shell-fire. He smiled and looked quite satisfied."

Here I should perhaps explain the origin and composition of the Naval Brigades who had their baptism of fire at Antwerp, because one of the many subsequent strictures passed on Winston—and perhaps the least undeserved—was the use of these untrained and ill-equipped men in the front line. In 1913 Winston had begun to form the Royal Naval Division, consisting of three brigades: the Marines, the Naval Volunteer Reserve and the Fleet Reserve. The Marines, as highly skilled as any Regulars, were already in existence; the Naval Volunteers were men who had hoped to serve afloat but who loyally accepted land service as a duty though a second best. When war broke out many recruits who had no naval antecedents but were attracted by the naval background of the force joined the Royal Naval Volunteer Reserve, among them my third brother, Arthur Asquith ("Oc"), my beloved friend Rupert Brooke, a gifted young musician, Denis Browne, and the heroic "Salamander of the British Empire," Bernard Freyberg (then an unknown New Zealander). They had only begun their military training at Betteshanger in Kent at the end of September. I could therefore hardly believe my ears when I heard that they had been sent into the line at Antwerp.

My brother told me that they had just had their antityphoid inoculation and in consequence were feeling rather feverish and muzzy when at five o'clock in the morning of October 4th they were roused from sleep and told that at nine they were to march to Dover with their full equipment. He thought it was an exercise, a kind of fire practice for which a better moment might well have been chosen. At Dover they were embarked for Dunkirk, where Rupert Brooke imagined they would spend a month "quietly training." On arrival they were informed that they were going straight to Antwerp and that their train would probably be attacked. My brother rushed out to a chemist to buy some first-aid appliances for his platoon. They had no bandages or medical stores. The officers had no revolver ammunition and many of the men had never fired a rifle or dug a trench. About a quarter of them were Reservists, the rest were raw recruits who had barely started their training. After a march through the streets of Antwerp, where they were greeted with enthusiasm, cheered and kissed, they had a few hours' sleep in the deserted garden of a château, thus described in a letter by Rupert Brooke: "On the rather dirty and wild-looking sailors trudged, over lawns, through orchards and across pleasaunces. Little pools glimmered through the trees and deserted fountains, and round corners one saw, faintly, occasional Cupids and Venuses—a scattered company of rather bad statues—gleaming quietly. The sailors dug their latrines in the various rose-gardens and lay down to sleep—but it was bitter cold—under the shrubs. By two the shells had got unpleasantly near and some message came. So up we got—frozen and sleepy—and toiled off through the night. By dawn we got into trenches—very good ones and relieved Belgians." Green, raw, untutored as they were this strange amalgam of stokers, sailors, scholars and musicians acquitted themselves valiantly. They played a vital part in covering the retreat of the Belgian Army and were among the last to leave the doomed and burning city.

For Antwerp was doomed to fall. On the evening of General Rawlinson's arrival a Council of War was held, presided over by the King. General Rawlinson was prepared to carry on the fight. Both he and Winston stressed our readiness and ability to throw into it the forces we had promised. But alas, it was now too late. The Belgians believed, not without reason, that their communications were in such immediate peril that they must at once move their Army across the Scheldt as they had originally planned to do. They might thus be able to join up with our relieving forces. This decision had to be accepted and in Winston's opinion it was vindicated by events. He left Antwerp with General Rawlinson that night, and after "an anxious drive over roads luckily infested with nothing worse than rumour," [7] arrived in London the next day.

The Naval Division held on to the last and then stole away by night— a thirty-mile march through the deserted, blazing city, over the Scheldt on a pontoon bridge, the sky alight with burning villages, the rivers seas of burning petrol. Rupert Brooke has written: "Antwerp that night was like several different kinds of Hell—the broken houses and dead horses lit by an infernal glare. The refugees were the worst sight. The German policy of frightfulness had succeeded so well that out of that city of half a million, when it was decided to surrender, not ten thousand would stay. . . . I'll never forget that white-faced endless procession in the night, pressed aside to let the military—us—pass, crawling forward at some hundred yards an hour, quite hopeless, the old men crying and the women with hard drawn faces. What a crime!" Most of the Naval Division got home safely, but in the darkness and confusion two battalions strayed over the Dutch border and were interned.

Now came the inquest. A savage and venomous campaign was unleashed against Winston in the Conservative press. The *Morning Post* asked the Government on whose authority "this adventure was arranged and conducted? Was it military or was it naval? If it was military were the plans approved by General French and Lord Kitchener? If it was naval was it a scheme arranged and approved by the whole Board of Admiralty? Is it not true that the energies of Mr. Winston Churchill have been directed upon this eccentric expedition and that he has been using the resources of the Admiralty as if he were personally responsible for naval operations? It is not right and proper that Mr. Churchill should use his position of civil authority to press his tactical and strategic fancies on unwilling experts. . . . We understand that Mr. Churchill has been once at the British Headquarters in France, once in Dunkirk and once in Antwerp within the last month. . . . His place is at the Admiralty day and night. We suggest to Mr. Churchill's colleagues that they should quite firmly and definitely tell the First Lord that on no account are the military and naval operations to be conducted or directed by him." [8] The *Times* replied in a fair leader rightly placing the responsibility on the shoulders of the Government as a whole and especially on those of the Prime Minister and the Secretary of State for War.[9] My father fully accepted his own responsibility and never doubted that the attempt to save Antwerp, though it had failed, was justified and had achieved a useful purpose. He wrote on October 10th: "Winston has just been in to talk over the situation. We both agree with Hankey— who is a good influence—that this last week, which has delayed the fall of Antwerp by at least seven days and has prevented the Germans from linking up their forces, has not been thrown away." [10] Except on the use of the untrained recruits in the Naval Brigade I never heard my father say a critical word of Winston's action in this enterprise and I heard from him many words of admiration and sympathy. He came back terribly depressed, feeling that his mission had been in vain. The performance of the Naval Brigades in which he felt a personal pride and satisfaction was one of the few bright spots and I tried to dwell on this when we discussed it. He was haunted and harrowed by might-have-beens but felt no reproach toward anyone but Fate.

Looking back on it in perspective two years later Winston wrote: "It is idle to pretend that Lord Kitchener or anyone else foresaw all the consequences good or bad which flowed from the decision of 4th October. The event was very different from both hopes and expectations. But never in the Great War have more important results been achieved by forces so limited and for losses so small as those which rewarded this almost forlorn enterprise." [11]

We find an impressive vindication of the enterprise in the impartial verdict of the British *Official History of the War*: "The British effort to save Antwerp had failed. Nevertheless it had a lasting influence on the operations. Until Antwerp had fallen the troops of the investing force were not available to move forward on Ypres and the coast, and though when they did they secured Zeebrugge and Ostend without a struggle, they were too late to secure Nieuport and Dunkirk and turn the northern flank of the Allies as was intended. Further the whole general movement of the German forces in the north was affected. The advantages of a day, nay even of a few hours, in the advance of the Germans on Ypres or an equal delay in the arrival of the French and British reinforcements might have tipped the scale to the enemy's side. Had events turned out more favourably for the main Allied armies in the first week of October the defence of Antwerp might have been decisive."

I was not disturbed by the outcry against Winston over Antwerp for I knew he had not suffered from it in the eyes of colleagues or of the High Commands. But two anxieties, one private and one public, did disturb me. My private worry was his request to exchange the Admiralty for a command in the field. The Admiralty had been the realization of his highest ambition. For two years it had been his vocation, his romance, his obsession. He had served it with the passion of a lover and the dedication of a friar. Every power he possessed had been devoted to preparing it—for what? To face this very hour. Now that the hour had struck, when the war was barely two months old he sought impatiently for other hands to take it over. ("Runciman would do Admiralty well"—the incredible concluding words of his telegram to my father!) For the first time I was inwardly shaken. I had so often and so fiercely combated the critics who complained that they "could not take him seriously." I could not take *this* seriously. And yet there is no doubt that it was seriously meant and that the desire to take a military command persisted, for a time at least, after the curtain had fallen on Antwerp.

My other worry was that, owing to a run of bad luck, his public position was, at least temporarily, impaired. Just before Antwerp the Navy suffered a misfortune for which he was most unjustly blamed by those who did not know the facts. Three British cruisers, the *Aboukir,* the *Hogue* and the *Cressy,* were sunk while patrolling the Dutch coast. While visiting the Grand Fleet he had chanced to hear these three old cruisers referred to as a "live-bait squadron" and had ordered their instant withdrawal, but there was a fatal delay in carrying out his order. It was doubly unfortunate that on the very day before this disaster occurred he had made an unwise speech which jarred on public opinion. "So far as the Navy is concerned," he said, "we cannot fight while the enemy remains in port. . . . If they do not come out and fight they will be dug out like rats from a hole." To many these words seemed to be asking for trouble and when disaster swiftly followed it was felt, irrationally, that Winston by his *hubris* had invited it. Then, on October 27th, came another cruel misfortune. The *Audacious,* one of our newest Super-Dreadnoughts, was sunk by mine or torpedo. The Admiralty was insistent that the loss should be kept secret and to this the Cabinet reluctantly agreed after a long and heated discussion.

There is no doubt that Winston felt oppressed by the "constant, gnawing anxieties about the safety of the Fleet from submarine attack" and also by the unfair criticism to which he was subjected and to which it was often impossible to reply. He has written that "in spite of being accustomed to years of abuse, I could not but feel the adverse and hostile currents that flowed about me." [12] What he minded most was the question, often heard: "What's the Navy doing?" How could he tell them? It was guarding our shores, protecting our trade throughout the world, safeguarding the passage of our troops and supplies to France. The public had expected a great sea battle in which the German Fleet would be annihilated. But the Army seemed to be doing all the fighting. The Fleet was neither seen nor heard of, except when some loss occurred.

An ugly symptom of this frustration was the cruel campaign which now began against Prince Louis of Battenberg. At the outbreak of war, when the Admiralty was being acclaimed on all sides for its instant mobilization and the transport of the Expeditionary Force, no objection to his German parentage was heard from any quarter. But now he became the victim of a disgraceful witch hunt. Assailed in the press and by a flood of abusive letters, both anonymous and signed, he felt that he could not continue to bear his heavy load of responsibility without the support of public confidence. He resigned his office in a letter of great dignity, and in accepting his decision Winston expressed to him his deep indebtedness and his profound respect and assured him that "the Navy of today and still more the Navy of tomorrow will bear the imprint of your work." It was a painful decision for Winston and I shall never forget my father's disgust at having to comply with it, but they both felt it to be inevitable.

When my father mentioned to me the problem of filling his post I told him that I had not a shadow of doubt that Winston would wish to appoint Lord Fisher as his successor. There was a magnetic mutual attraction between these two and they could not keep away from one another for long. Fisher had paid frequent visits to the Admiralty since the beginning of the war and Winston records that on these occasions he "watched him narrowly to judge his physical strength and mental alertness"—for he was now seventy-four. But he appears to have emerged

triumphantly from these observations and Winston was particularly reassured when on one occasion "he became so convulsed with fury that it
seemed that every nerve and blood-vessel in his body would be ruptured"—but they stood the strain magnificently. Winston has written
that he was "never in the least afraid of working with him, and I thought
I knew him so well . . . that we could come through any difficulty together." [13] He assured my father that he could work with no one else.
When he talked to me he was full of happiness and excitement at the
prospect of their reunion and there was no more talk or thought of leaving the Admiralty. Fisher had reinvested it with romance. I said: "No
one knows his weather better than you do—and you are no doubt prepared for squalls ahead." Winston replied: "I know him—and I know
that I can manage him." (Fisher no doubt felt the same confidence
about his ability to manage Winston.)

Winston was, however, well aware that he was making a controversial appointment. One voice was raised against it in emphatic protest—that of the King. He has recorded in his diary that when Winston
came to see him to propose that Fisher should succeed Prince Louis as
First Sea Lord: "I did all I could to prevent it and told him he was not
trusted by the Navy and they had no confidence in him personally. I
think it is a great mistake and he is seventy-four. At the end I had to
give in with great reluctance." [14] "So in the end," wrote Winston, "for
good or ill I had my way." Alas, it was for ill.

Yet at the outset all went swimmingly. A pact was sealed between
the First Lord and the First Sea Lord that neither of them should take
any important action without consulting the other. Because of Lord
Fisher's age and habit of life the rhythm of their working hours at the
Admiralty was readjusted. Lord Fisher would go to bed at eight o'clock
and wake up between 4 and 5 A.M. or even earlier. It was in these early
morning hours that his dynamic working power was at its peak. Winston
records that "as the afternoon approached the formidable energy of
the morning gradually declined, and with the shades of night the old
Admiral's giant strength was often visibly exhausted." [15] Winston altered his own timetable to fit in with Lord Fisher's. He was called at
eight instead of seven and took his usual hour's siesta, whenever possible, after luncheon. He was thus enabled to work until two o'clock in
the morning without fatigue. Between them this "unsleeping watch" was
kept throughout the day and night. Winston's minutes were written in
red with Fisher's in green. In Winston's words: "As long as the port
and starboard lights shone together all went well."

Lord Fisher, whom I had not seen since Malta, came to luncheon with us at No. 10 soon after his appointment and was, as my stepmother put it, "at his gayest and coarsest." Although the shades of afternoon were approaching he was bubbling with vitality and anecdotes. He told us that the whole German Fleet had left the Kiel Canal. We knew that on November 15th the War Office had sent an order to the Territorial camps that they were to start at 3 A.M. for the east coast and many of our friends had dashed off in high excitement to meet the great "German raid" which never took place. We asked Lord Fisher why it had been expected. "A dark new moon, high tide, long nights and weather which will only get worse. This is the time—it is now or never. And a full dress rehearsal is a very useful thing." He rambled on about the Navy. "You remember, Prime Minister, when I changed all that? What was the good of a fleet under a blue sky on blue water—white decks, white tops to their caps etc.? No—no—no—that's not the place for a fleet! It should be in an atmosphere of pea-soup fog with two feet of icicle aboard. . . . In war you should think in oceans and shoot at short range. When Nelson (or was it Napoleon?) was asked what he considered was the secret of his success he said: 'I was always fifteen minutes before the other fellow.' " And thus he went on. He produced from his pocket some scarlet sticky labels with the word RUSH printed on them in large black capital letters. "I stick these on every loiterer I find in and out of the Admiralty." His conversation (if so it can be called) was torrential. I tried to imagine a tête-à-tête between him and Winston and wondered which of them did the listening. And I reminded myself that he was the greatest sailor since Nelson.

He gave immediate proof of his mettle. Within twenty-four hours of his arrival at the Admiralty we suffered the tragic naval defeat of Coronel. Admiral von Spee had been for some time at large in the Pacific with two powerful armored cruisers, the *Scharnhorst* and the *Gneisenau,* and three light cruisers, *Leipzig, Dresden* and *Nürnberg,* seeking whom he might destroy. His whereabouts and his destination were unknown. Great anxiety was naturally felt at the Admiralty about the danger he presented to our merchant shipping and to the New Zealand and Australian convoys. After much uncertainty and speculation it was (rightly) surmised that he was on his way to the South American coast and Rear-Admiral Cradock was advised to concentrate his forces in the Magellan Straits or near the Falklands. The *Canopus,* an elderly thirteen-knot ship,* was sent to reinforce him. Lord Fisher at once

* In *The World Crisis, 1911-1914,* Churchill puts the speed of the *Canopus* at 15½ knots.

ordered the *Defence,* then on the east coast of South America under
the command of Admiral Stoddart, to follow. But it was too late. Action
had already been joined by Admiral Cradock off Coronel. In an un-
equal battle lasting less than an hour in a high sea the British ships were
silhouetted against a sunset sky while the Germans were hardly visible
against the background of the Chilean coast. The *Good Hope* and the
Monmouth were set on fire and sunk and their crews perished to a man.
The little *Glasgow,* which by a miracle remained afloat and continued
firing until "she was left alone in darkness on the stormy seas," described the battle in her log as "the saddest naval action of the war." The
Germans suffered no loss of life. The Admiralty was blamed for its
failure to reinforce Cradock with a swifter and more powerful ship
than the *Canopus.**

Fisher acted immediately. He took two battle cruisers, the *Invincible*
and the *Inflexible,* from the Grand Fleet and ordered them to leave
within three days for the Falkland Islands. The dockyard protested that
the brick bridges of the *Invincible*'s boilers could not be finished before
midnight on November 13th. The reply was that bricklayers and material were to sail in the *Invincible* if the bridges were not completed
by the appointed date. The battle cruisers sailed with workmen on
board—and they sailed just in time. The glorious story of the Falkland
Islands is wonderfully told in *The World Crisis.* By a dramatic chance
von Spee ran into the British force which was coaling in the harbor of
the Falklands. When the Germans saw the "fatal tripods" of the Dreadnoughts rising from behind the promontory they fled. But there was no
chance of escape. Every ship of that dread squadron went to the bottom
and von Spee, who in the *Gneisenau* fought to the very end, was killed
with his two sons. Coronel was avenged.

The victory was acclaimed as Fisher's work. Winston wrote him a
generous letter:

My dear,
    This was your show and your luck. I should only have sent one *Grey-
hound* and *Defence.* This would have done the trick. But it was a great *coup.*
Your *flair* was quite true. Let us have some more victories together and
confound all our foes abroad—and (don't forget) at home.[16]

No victory can have brought him greater peace of mind, for now
"no German ships of war remained on any of the oceans of the world." [17]
Four months of war had sufficed to sweep the seas for British trade and

* Churchill gives the case for the Admiralty in *The World Crisis, 1911-1914,*
pp. 423-26.

convoys. Here was a vindication of the record of the Admiralty under Winston's leadership, with or without Fisher.

Occasional ups and downs soon began to occur between them, but looking back on these and on the earthquakes which were to follow Winston still felt able to write in after years: "He was far more often right than wrong and his drive and life-force made the Admiralty quiver like one of his great ships at its highest speed."

To be told a secret is an exciting privilege. It is a proof of trust, a tribute to discretion and—now and then—a sop to curiosity. I enjoyed knowing and keeping secrets. But there was one secret that I wish I had never known. So much depended on it that the knowledge tortured me. I was sometimes haunted by the insane fear which grips one on the giddy edge of cliffs and tempts one to jump over—the fear that I might go mad and shriek it from the housetops.

This secret was our possession of the German naval code. After the wreck of the *Magdeburg* in the Baltic the body of a drowned German *Unteroffizier* was picked up by the Russians. In death he still held clasped in an iron grip the cipher and signal books of the German Navy. In September the Russian Naval Attaché called on Winston and told him that because we were the greatest naval power of the Alliance his Government felt that the British Admiralty should have these books. A ship was sent to bring them and the officers in charge to England and the "sea-stained priceless documents" were handed over to Winston and Prince Louis. Our Naval Intelligence officers worked on the cipher and gradually succeeded in decoding German naval messages so that the enemy's plans and movements in the Heligoland Bight became known to us.

Nothing of importance came through until December 14th when Sir Arthur Wilson reported the probability of an impending movement of battle cruisers which might have "an offensive character against our coasts." Orders were given for the battle cruisers and the Second Battle Squadron with light cruisers and a flotilla of destroyers to put to sea with a view to interception next morning. For thirty-six hours the Admiralty held its breath and awaited events in expectancy and doubt—but nothing happened. On the morning of the sixteenth, when Winston (as on the day of Sidney Street) was in his bath, an officer hurried in with a naval signal which Winston "grasped with dripping hand": "German battle cruisers bombarding Hartlepool." He leaped from the bath, pulled on his clothes "over a damp body" and ran to the War Room where Lord Fisher had just arrived. He has confessed that "sympathy for Hartlepool was mingled with what Mr. George Wyndham once called 'the anodyne of contemplated retaliation' " [18] (and I have no doubt about the proportions in which these elements were mingled). The war map showed the German battle cruisers within gunshot of the Yorkshire coast, while between them and Germany, cutting their line of retreat, were "four British battle cruisers and six of the most powerful battleships in the world. . . . Only one thing could enable the Germans to escape annihilation. . . . The word 'visibility' assumed a sinister significance." [19] And while messages of distress poured in by telephone and telegram from Scarborough, Whitby and Hartlepool where homes had been destroyed and children killed, while the War Committee asked "how such a thing was possible," "What was the Navy doing? And what were they going to do?" [20] the veil of mist over the North Sea became a curtain. The ships reported only two thousand yards' visibility. Though Admirals Beatty and Warrender steamed ahead in hot pursuit the invisible enemy eluded them and so escaped their doom. "Thus ended this heart-shaking game of Blind Man's Buff," [21] wrote Winston.

Five hundred civilians had been killed and wounded in the bombarded towns. Public indignation naturally vented itself in criticism of the Admiralty for its failure to protect our shores from enemy attack or to avenge the victims. The Admiralty could not defend itself. To do so would have involved revealing the prompt pre-emptive measures they had taken on information whose source must at all costs be kept secret. So they endured indictment and reproach in silence, taking comfort from the fact that the secret source had proved reliable, that it would be available another day and that on that day there might not be a fog.

These hopes were realized when on January 22nd Sir Arthur Wilson burst into Winston's room with thrilling news: "First Lord, these fellows are coming out again!" "When?" "Tonight." And come they did. The battle of the Dogger Bank was fought—a victory which would have been even greater had not Admiral Beatty's flagship, the *Lion,* been severely damaged and obliged to drop out of the line. But the *Blücher* was sunk and two German battle cruisers were knocked out. At home we rejoiced; the neutral world was impressed; confidence in the Admiralty was restored and carping ceased. The German Navy did not venture out again for fifteen months.

But I must keep step with events. The first month of the new year was to hold decisions fateful to Winston's fortunes, to those of the Government and of the war itself.

Chapter Twenty-Three

GALLIPOLI

THE EPIC STORY of Gallipoli with which this chapter is concerned is one that I cannot hope to tell dispassionately. I lived, through others, at its core. I saw it through the eyes and felt it through the heart of Winston, who conceived it, of my brother and close friends who fought on the Peninsula from first to last, of my father who believed in and supported it throughout. I shared with them its glories and its setbacks, its high hopes and the heartbreak of its final failure. Personal emotion may have blurred my vision. But I saw it then and see it still as the most imaginative conception of the First World War and one which might, had all gone well, have proved the shortest cut to victory. Not only so, but in the light of what has happened since it is now recognized by many that it might have changed the course of history. For had we forced the Dardanelles in 1915 or 1916 we could have got arms through to Russia. She might not have signed a separate peace and the Russian Revolution might not have happened as and when it did. Though ultimately inevitable it might have taken a different form.

This tragedy of wasted opportunity was born of divided counsels, military and naval, and exploited by political prejudice. Winston no doubt made tactical mistakes, owing to impatience and to his imperviousness to the state of other people's minds. But his instinct was throughout a true one and he never swerved from it.

For me the story began on December 29th when my father told me he had received two very interesting memoranda, written quite independently, one from Winston and one from Hankey. Both were seeking to find a way around the deadlock of trench warfare in the West which, apart from its futility, was exacting a deadly toll in lives. We had had a million casualties in the first three months of war. Why should the new armies, in Winston's phrase, be sent to "chew barbed wire"? Much to my surprise Winston had put forward Lord Fisher's plan that we should seize Borkum and invade Schleswig-Holstein. Our domination of the Baltic would enable Russia to land troops near Berlin. Hankey's plan was the one I should have expected from Winston, i.e., to attack Turkey. From the outset of the war Winston's imagination had been fired by the idea of forcing the Dardanelles and after reading Hankey's paper he wrote to my father: "We are substantially in agreement, and our conclusions are not incompatible. I wanted Gallipoli attacked on the declaration of war." [1] Meanwhile Lloyd George was pressing for an expedition to Salonika.

Within two days Lord Kitchener, who had always taken the Army view that there should be no division of forces, received an urgent message from the Grand Duke Nicholas. He said that the Turks were threatening the Russian forces in the Caucasus and appealed to Lord Kitchener to make some demonstration, naval or military, elsewhere and thus draw off Turkish forces and ease the Russian position. Lord Kitchener could not ignore this appeal. The Russians had suffered terrible casualties and were short of rifles and ammunition. He discussed the matter with Winston and wrote to him next day: "The only place that a demonstration might have some effect in stopping reinforcements going East would be the Dardanelles. Particularly if, as the Grand Duke says, reports could be spread at the same time that Constantinople was threatened." [2] On the same day he sent a telegram to the Grand Duke promising that "steps will be taken to make a demonstration against the Turks." We were therefore pledged to action. The plan which originated with Hankey was now, quite independently and for different reasons, adopted by Kitchener.

Next morning Lord Fisher, who had studied all the Cabinet papers and been fully informed of Winston's conversation with Lord Kitchener, wrote to Winston (in capital letters): "I consider Turkey holds the field —but *only* if it's immediate." However, he went on to suggest the dispatch of an expeditionary force of seventy-five thousand "seasoned troops" under Sir William Robertson, which, as Winston knew, was crying for the moon. He also made the practical suggestion that old battleships should be used to force the Dardanelles. Winston immediately telegraphed to Vice-Admiral Carden, who was in command there: "Do you consider the forcing of the Dardanelles by ships alone a practicable operation? . . . Importance of results would justify severe loss." Carden replied: "I do not consider Dardanelles can be rushed. They might be forced by extended operations with large number of ships." [3]

The War Council met that afternoon (January 5th) and again on the 8th. Lord Kitchener once more expressed his preference for the Dardanelles as an objective. He estimated that one hundred and fifty thousand men would be sufficient for the capture of the Peninsula but made it clear that no troops were available. Admiral Carden had sent a plan of operations which was approved by Lord Fisher and Admiral Oliver. The War Staff of the Admiralty suggested that the *Queen Elizabeth,* which had just been armed with 15-inch guns and was going to fire her gunnery trials in the Mediterranean, should use the Turkish forts as targets. Here was an unexpected windfall.

On the thirteenth Admiral Carden's plan was submitted to the War Council. Sir Maurice Hankey minuted: "The Admiralty were studying the question and believed that a plan could be made for systematically reducing all the forts within a few weeks. Once the forts were reduced the minefields would be cleared, and the Fleet would proceed up to Constantinople and destroy the Goeben. . . . Lord Kitchener thought the plan worth trying. *We could leave off the bombardment if it did not prove effective."* (My italics.)

This postscript is significant for it clearly expresses Lord Kitchener's view that if the bombardment failed we could treat the operation as a feint and break off the attack. I do not know whether this argument was in fact used to persuade hesitant members of the War Council, but I know from subsequent conversations that it was in the minds of some of them. The decision of the Council was unanimous: "That the Admiralty should prepare for a naval expedition in February to bombard and take the Gallipoli Peninsula * with Constantinople as its objective." [4] Lord Fisher and Sir Arthur Wilson were both present but neither of them spoke. Their silence could only be interpreted as assent, for the Carden plan had been approved at the highest level in the Admiralty and he had now been ordered to proceed with it and told that "the sooner we can begin the better." Winston's assertion that "right or wrong it was a Service plan" is incontrovertible. It is equally true that, as he added, "I seized upon it and set it on the path to action." And what else are plans for?

* It seems strange that no one should have questioned the decision to "take the Gallipoli Peninsula" without troops when Lord Kitchener had estimated that one hundred and fifty thousand would be sufficient for that purpose and had made it clear that no troops were available.

And now the die was cast. I have rarely seen Winston more completely happy and fulfilled. He was wholly pervaded by the plan and
talked of little else. Its possibilities seemed limitless and he unrolled
them before my dazzled eyes. Once the fleet had broken through the
Straits into the Sea of Marmara the Greeks and the Bulgarians, hungry
for spoils, might join us in attacking Turkey; Italy might be weaned
from her neutrality; Rumania would not stand aside alone. The Balkan
States might form a united front to sweep the Turks from Europe. But
what mattered most was to help Russia in her desperate need. When
Constantinople fell we could release her shipping bottled up in the
Black Sea. She could export her grain to us and we could send her arms
and ammunition. He painted with a master brush upon his glowing
canvas a vision of the Fleet appearing at the Golden Horn. I accepted his
assumption that the sight alone of these great ships would take the city.
Turkey had proved herself susceptible to ships!

Then suddenly, within a fortnight, a storm blew up. Lord Fisher
had had second thoughts. He wrote to Winston: "First Lord: I have no
desire to continue a useless resistance in the War Council to plans I
cannot concur in but I would ask that enclosed may be printed and
circulated to members before the next meeting. F."

The paper opposed the Dardanelles plan and made a plea for a purely
passive and defensive strategy. "Being already in possession of all that
a powerful Fleet can give a country we should continue quietly to enjoy
the advantage without dissipating our strength in operations that cannot improve the position." [5] Such a naval policy would, in Winston's
words, have condemned us to complete inactivity.

My father notes on January 28th: "A personal matter which rather
worries me is the growing friction between Winston and Fisher. They
both came to see me . . . before the War Council and gave tongue to
their mutual grievances. I tried to compose these differences by a compromise, under which Winston was to give up for the present his bombardment of Zeebrugge, Fisher withdrawing his opposition to the operation against the Dardanelles." [6] At the War Council (of which Lord
Fisher has left his own record), after Winston had made his report on
the preparations for the Dardanelles operation Lord Fisher said he
understood that this question was not to be raised at this meeting. The
Prime Minister knew his views on the subject. The Prime Minister said
that in view of what had already been done the question could not be
left in abeyance. Thereupon Lord Fisher rose and left the Council table.
Lord Kitchener followed him and asked him what he meant to do. Lord
Fisher replied that he would not return to the Council table and would

resign his office as First Sea Lord. He finally yielded to Lord Kitchener's appeals to do his duty to his country and was persuaded to return to the Council table.

This incident is worthy of record because it illustrates the unpredictability of Fisher's "weather." That morning he had appeared to accept the compromise suggested by my father. Yet within an hour he was trying to resign on it. On the same afternoon he veered again, for after a long and friendly talk with Winston, who urged him not to "go back" on the Dardanelles plan, he "definitely consented to undertake it." "When I finally decided to go in," he said before the Dardanelles Commission, "I went in the whole hog, totus porcus."

It was not a hog that I would ever have undertaken to drive to market. I said both to my father and to Winston—once more confident and happy under blue skies—that though I did not doubt Lord Fisher's genius I thought him dangerous because I believed him to be mad. Who but a madman would have seriously proposed, as he did earlier in the month, to shoot all German prisoners here as a reprisal for the Zeppelin raids? (On this too he had resigned.) And on this very day (January 28th) he had changed his mind about the Dardanelles four times.

Yet though it is difficult to forgive the part he played it is just possible to understand his plight. He lived by instincts, hunches, flashes which he was unable to justify or sustain in argument. Though words poured from his lips and from his pen he was no match for Winston as a dialectician. In trying to defend his own position he trumped up reasons and pretexts of no substance which Winston easily demolished. "He out-argues me," he once complained pathetically to Hankey. His personal intimacy with Winston and affection for him increased his sense of helplessness in standing up to him. "I am in no way concealing the great and continuous pressure which I put upon the old Admiral," [7] wrote Winston. And on this occasion Winston had behind him an overwhelming body of opinion—the decision of the War Council, the personal support of Lord Kitchener, the authority of the Prime Minister. Lord Fisher himself admitted afterward that naval opinion was unanimous. "I was the only rebel." Under this pressure Fisher's outer defenses collapsed but the inner citadel of his instinctive judgment remained unshaken. Thus he committed himself to undertake an enterprise in which he did not in his heart believe.

Ought Winston to have guessed his state of mind? He never spent much time in guessing what other people might be thinking. He be-

With his second-in-command, Major Sir Archibald Sinclair,
in France, 1916

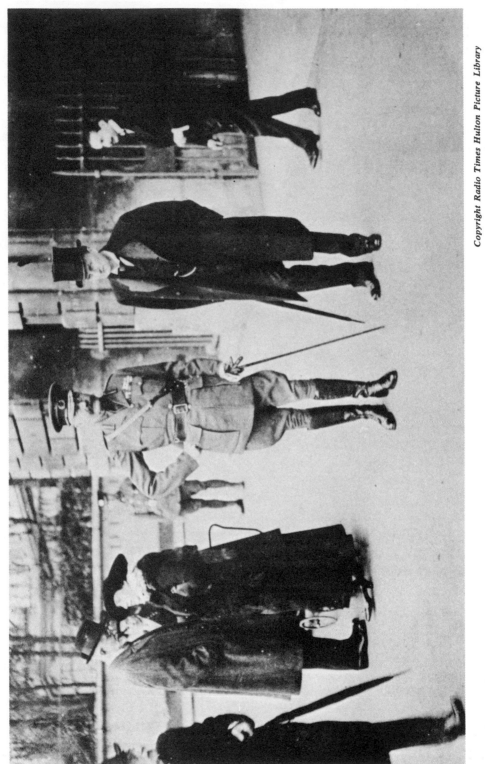

Lord Kitchener and Sir Edward Grey, in Paris, about 1915

BELOW:

On his return from the trenches, March 1916

Portrait of the author
by Sir William Orpen, 1916

lieved, not without reason, that he had the power to carry others with him. When he attended the afternoon War Council meeting he was able to announce on behalf of the Admiralty, and with the agreement of Lord Fisher, that they had decided to undertake the task with which the War Council had charged them so urgently. "This," he wrote, "I took as the point of final decision. After it, I never looked back. We had left the region of discussion and consultation, of balancings and misgivings. The matter had passed into the domain of action." [8]

At the meeting of the War Council on January 18th it had been accepted by all present that the attack on the Dardanelles should be a purely naval operation. Lord Kitchener had made it clear that he had no troops to spare. But the Council was seriously concerned by the impending military collapse of Russia and by the need to influence the political situation in the Balkans. It was suggested that if one or two divisions (including the 29th Division) now destined for France could be deflected from the West and offered to Greece we might persuade Mr. Venizelos and the Greek King to come in on our side and go to the aid of Serbia. Winston was asked by the Council to go to Headquarters in France and put the case before Sir John French.

I have a vivid recollection of his return from this mission. My father and I were at Walmer Castle. This historic house, where Pitt had lived and Wellington had died, stands on a rock overlooking the English Channel. It was within earshot of the guns in France and my father used it as a convenient place for secret rendezvous at week ends between the front and home. Winston arrived on the morning of January 31st traveling, as my father said, "in his usual regal fashion," having crossed the Channel in a Scout and keeping a special train waiting while he spent the morning with us. He was in the highest spirits after his two days at the front, where he was recognized everywhere and greeted as "Good old Winston." His negotiations with Sir John French though tough had been persuasive and successful. In return for a promise of the divisions Sir John had asked for in order to take over the French lines between our forces and the sea, he had undertaken to let us have two of them back in time to send them to the Balkans toward the end of March.

While agreeing with the soldiers that in theory it is a mistake to divide your forces both my father and Winston were of one mind that at this moment policy should override strategy. If by helping Serbia we could bring in Greece and Rumania we could add some eight hundred thousand men to the Allied strength. Although the Dardanelles had played no part in Winston's mission it was directly relevant to its aim, for it was an integral part of the great turning movement which might sweep Eastern Europe into the Allied net and end the bloody stalemate on the Western front. It was clear that it held first place in Winston's mind and imagination. Rarely, if ever, have I seen him so wholly possessed by an idea. I needed no conversion, but once again he made it shine for me with the romance of a crusade. My father listened, half moved, half amused, but without astringent comment. After all as a plan of action it had been endorsed by his own dispassionate judgment, that of Edward Grey and even that of cool skeptic Arthur Balfour, the enemy of enthusiasm, who had said in Council: "It would be difficult to imagine a more helpful operation."

Next day Delcassé came over and my father, Winston and Lord Kitchener lunched with Sir Edward Grey to meet him. My father noted that "Winston was very eloquent in the worst French anyone has ever heard. 'S'ils savent que nous sommes gens qu'ils peuvent conter sur' was one of his flowers of speech." [9] The urgent need of helping Serbia was agreed on by all and at the War Council on the following day, attended by Sir John French, it was agreed to offer Greece the 29th Division together with a French division if she would join us. The price was not high enough and the offer was turned down by Venizelos. He agreed, however, to allow us to use the island of Lemnos with its great harbor of Moudros as a naval base for the attack upon the Dardanelles, and two battalions of Marines were sent there.

Now that it had become apparent that troops were after all available for the Middle East Lord Fisher and Sir Henry Jackson began once more to demand them for the Dardanelles. Colonel Hankey expressed to my father his strong view that naval operations should be supported by a military force. Winston did not join his voice to these demands but abided loyally by his agreement with Lord Kitchener for a purely naval plan. But he and others saw great advantages in concentrating such forces as were available on a Middle Eastern base, Egypt or Lemnos, ready to strike where opportunity might offer. Such a force might seize the Isthmus of Bulair after the Fleet had passed the Straits or occupy Constantinople. On February 16th, which Winston has called "a Day of Resolve," [10] it was duly agreed by the War Council that the 29th Division should be sent to Lemnos and this decision he claims to be "the foundation of the military attack upon the Dardanelles."

But it was not, alas, adhered to by Lord Kitchener. Our strategy was bedeviled by two conflicting schools of thought—the "Western" and the

"Eastern" policies—and he was torn in half between them. The official military view both in the British and French High Command was that victory could be achieved only by concentrating every resource that we possessed, in man power, gun power, shell power, on the Western front and hurling it against the German lines. Only by killing Germans at a greater rate than they killed us could we get through. The War Council could not accept this doctrine and its members sought for a way around the barbed wire and the trenches (now stretching from the North Sea to the Alps) by an outflanking movement in the East. Lord Kitchener, steeped in his long experience and intimate knowledge of the East, was naturally drawn in this direction. But he was a high priest of the orthodox military hierarchy whose gospel was the indivisibility of forces, and as such a prey to constant pressure by his French and English colleagues. He was pulled this way and that and on February 20th ("a Day of Recoil") went back upon his promise to send the 29th Division and seemed opposed to the idea he had supported of a concentration of forces in the East. Yet on the twenty-fourth he said that "if the Fleet could not get through the Straits unaided the Army ought to see the business through. The effect of a defeat in the Orient would be very serious. There could be no going back." [11] He ordered General Birdwood, Commander of the Australasian Corps, an officer he knew and trusted, to go from Egypt to the Dardanelles to report on the possibilities of military action. But when, at the War Council on the twenty-sixth, both my father and Winston appealed to him to send at least one Regular Division, the 29th, to the East he was adamant in his refusal. Who could have suspected that behind that iron jaw and massive breast there lurked such palsied indecision and infirmity of purpose? Perhaps he too, like Fisher, was a hunchmonger whose judgment acted on no rational or calculable process? His shilly-shallying over the 29th Division, which he ultimately sent to Lemnos on March 29th, wasted three precious months.

From us the secrets of the future were mercifully hidden. Filled with high hopes we awaited day by day the Fleet's assault upon the Dardanelles, while Admiral Carden waited for the weather. On the morning of the 19th Eddie Marsh telephoned to me that "it has begun." We held our breath. But the weather was bad and for the next five days high seas made further action impossible. No news of the attack was given until the 22nd when, rather to my surprise, the Admiralty issued the following communiqué:

Yesterday (Friday) at 8 A.M. the British Fleet of battleships and battle cruisers, accompanied by flotillas and aided by a strong French squadron, the whole under the command of Vice-Admiral Carden began an attack upon the forts at the entrance to the Dardanelles.

The forts of Cape Helles and Kum Kaleh were bombarded with deliberate long range fire. Considerable effect was produced on two of the forts. Two others were frequently hit, but being open earthworks it was difficult to estimate the damage. The forts, being outranged, were not able to reply to the fire. . . .

At 2.45 P.M. a portion of the battleship force was ordered to close and engage the forts at closer range with secondary armaments. The forts on both sides of the entrance then opened fire and were engaged at moderate ranges by *Vengeance, Cornwallis, Triumph, Suffren, Gaulois, Bouvet*, supported by *Inflexible* and *Agamemnon* at long range. The forts on the European side were apparently silenced. One fort on the Asiatic side was still firing when the operation was broken off owing to failing light.

No ships of the Allied Line were hit. . . .

As I had feared, some murmurings were aroused by this communiqué. In the War Council Lord Kitchener had twice used the argument that we could "leave off the bombardment if it were ineffective." This announcement appeared to commit us to a major operation from which it would be difficult to retreat. In fact I think we were committed, but it gave rise to some criticism of Winston for having rushed the Government and cut off any possible retreat. The press certainly treated it as the first move in a major operation. The *Times* stressed that "bombardment from the sea will not carry such a project very far unless it is combined with troops. . . . No greater mistake could be committed in such a case than to give the Fleet insufficient military support. . . . The one thing the Allies dare not risk in a persistent attack on the Dardanelles is failure." [12] The general note was one of hope and welcome to the enterprise.

Bad weather followed but on the 25th the storm subsided and the attack was resumed and this time with complete success. All the outer forts were silenced and the four long-range guns defending the mouth of the Straits were destroyed and the Turkish and German gunners retreated to the north. On the following day parties of marines and sailors were landed on both sides of the Straits and blew up what was left of the guns and the forts. No ship was lost or damaged and the casualties were three men killed and seven wounded. By March 2nd the outer defenses of the Dardenelles had fallen. When Winston telegraphed to Admiral Carden asking him how many fine days he would need to get through he replied "Fourteen." At home everyone smiled, including Lord Fisher and Lord Kitchener. Everyone was now a supporter of the Dardanelles and most people claimed to have had a hand in it.

Here I must interrupt the story of the attack upon the Straits by a personal parenthesis which bears upon its later stages. Knowing Winston's strong (and legitimate) addiction to amphibious operations it had occurred to me that the Naval Division, in which I had so many stakes, might well be used in this one. On the day of the announcement of the first attack I chanced to hear that a friend in the *Hood* Battalion of the Naval Division, Patrick Shaw Stewart, on "laryngitis leave" in London, had been ordered back at once to their headquarters at Blandford.

That night I dined with Winston and Clemmie at the Admiralty and he confirmed my expectation that they were going. I quote the following extract from my diary: "He [Winston] was in the throes of a 'low' Influenza, rather piano and dressed in dark green plush—but thrilled at the prospect of the military expedition and full of plans for landing them in Gallipoli when the teeth of the situation had been drawn by the ships and marching them into Constantinople. 'That will make them sit up—the swine who snarled at the Naval Division!' This reflection seemed to afford him even more satisfaction than the prospect of the impending downfall of the Ottoman Empire! He was in very good and characteristic form at dinner, patches of purest nonsense and crudest fun alternating with really 'purple' breaks of speech and thought. Very amusing about K's psychology and the way he had jockeyed Lord Curzon out of India. 'I would *never* have resigned. I would have abandoned my policy if people at home were against it—I would have waived everything—I would have been studiously uncivil to him in public—but resign—*never*. I would have waited my time and fought him on some other issue and beaten him. Never resign.' [Was he perhaps remembering Lord Randolph?]

"He discussed every aspect of the strategy, naval and military, with tremendous zest and then breaking off he said to me with sudden gravity: 'I think a curse should rest on me because I am so happy. I know this war is smashing and shattering the lives of thousands every moment, and yet—I cannot help it—I enjoy every second I live.' He expressed a thought which is constantly in my own mind—that when one watches the arbitrary and haphazard way in which death and destruction are meted out by Providence with no guiding principle of justice or expediency apparently at work one feels more than ever convinced of the unimportance of life. It cannot matter as much as one thinks it does whether one is alive or dead. The absolute planlessness here makes one suspect a bigger plan elsewhere. I asked him if I might tell Oc * and Rupert † where they were going and he said yes, but *no one* else must know. He told me I must come down to Blandford on Thursday and see them reviewed by the King before sailing."

I have a note on the following day: "Oc came up from Blandford. I met him at the station and told him and we spent the afternoon buying maps and compasses and tinder-lighters and Baedekers of Constantinople (rather sanguine this!) which were only to be found in German." I told him to tell Rupert, who wrote to me in an ecstasy of joy. "Oh Violet—it's too wonderful for belief! I had not imagined Fate could be so benign. I almost suspect her. Perhaps we shall be held in reserve out of sight, on a choppy sea, for two months. . . . Yet even that! . . . But I'm filled with confident and glorious hopes. I've been looking at the maps. Do you think *perhaps* the fort on the Asiatic corner will want quelling, and we'll land and come at it from behind, and they'll make a sortie and meet us on the plains of Troy? It seems to me strategically so possible. Shall we have a Hospital Base (and won't you manage it?) on Lemnos? Will Hero's Tower crumble under the 15-inch guns? Will the sea be polyphloisbic and wine-dark and unvintageable? Shall I loot mosaics from St. Sophia and Turkish Delight and carpets? Shall we be a Turning Point in History? Oh God! I've never been quite so happy in my life I think. Not quite so pervasively happy; like a stream flowing entirely to one end. I suddenly realize that the ambition of my life has been—since I was two—to go on a military expedition against Constantinople. And when I thought I was hungry or sleepy or aching to write a poem—*that* was what I really, blindly wanted. This is nonsense. Good-night. . . . I'm very tired with equipping my platoon."

This was Rupert's response to the great adventure which lay ahead. I saw it shining in his eyes when I found him and Oc awaiting my arrival in the deep mud of Blandford Camp. I quote again from my diary: *"Thursday, 25th February, 1915.* A brilliant sun sparkling on frost—air like crystal. We started early for the Review. Clemmie and I

* My brother Arthur Asquith.
† Rupert Brooke.

were on horseback and we cantered down the lines. They were drawn up in battalions on a lovely sweep of downland. . . . When Winston and that mystic body 'the Board' had gone by the formations melted out of their military pattern and we talked to them—literally du haut en bas—I feeling very high up and 'high-horse' and conscious of the superiority of cavalry over infantry. . . . We cantered about till the King came. Then there was the formal march past . . . Winston glowing with pride in his troops."

When the others left for London I stayed behind to spend the last two days near them and see them off. Most of the time they were on duty packing up and all I could do was to buy a few things for them like "Fox's special puttees" and Keatings powder for the men. Visiting the camp in late afternoon twilight I found it in a state of chaos—"500 marvellous mules as big as hunters dragging helpless, baffled stokers in all directions while equally non-plussed officers bellowed directions at them. Deep ruts in which transport waggons were sticking in holes like graves—Oc giving out sun-helmets to his men. Dined at the Crown at Blandford then back to camp where Rupert produced a glorious frowst in Oc's 'bedroom' (a small box made of deal boards) and we sat and talked and talked. . . . *Sat. 27th February*—I came up for the last time. The camp had disintegrated overnight. Great waggons packed with blankets lay across the road becalmed in a sea of mud. Mules still rioted, stokers tore about, officers whistled, formations of men stood here and there being counted and equipped. We had a table in Oc's little deal box and lunched together. Rupert joined us later, very tired; the bubble of excitement had momentarily gone off him. He had had his hair cut very short—by order—and his sun-helmet was too small for him and wouldn't go on. He complained bitterly that Kelly had got hold of his sonnets and was spreading them among his mess-mates. He gave me all his things to take back with me—books, papers, futurist curtains. I also took Oc's and Patrick's. Saw Freyberg for a moment who said to me pathetically that as all the others had had their photographs taken he had done so too. 'I have got 6 Cabinet photogravures 12 x 8 and I don't know a single woman in England to give one to. I *was introduced* to the Duchess of Marlborough, but . . .' (hastily) 'would you like one?' Of course I leapt at it and carried back a huge military portrait inscribed 'Kia Ora'.

"*Sunday 28th February*. I started at 7.30 for Avonmouth, driving through lovely sleepy Thomas Hardy country, stone villages overgrown with moss and lichen, narrow lanes with high, wild tangled hedges.

Bristol by mid-day. Drove through and out the other side—by the Severn winding between steep banks. Then a little town began, built round the Docks. Showed my Pass, a great door opened and let me through and I saw huge watery pens in which great ships were moored and alongside on the quays a confusion of soldiers, trucks, mules, packing-cases and gangways. I made my way past many ships before I reached the Grantully Castle. I watched and waited for a Hood cap and then asked for Oc. He was on board shaving. . . . Denis Browne came and took charge of me and said he would go for Oc. Rupert appeared. He had 'failli', had to stay on board but had just managed to exchange his watch with Kelly and was free till 4. Oc joined us and we went off to an hotel recommended by Edwin Montagu, surrounded by sham rockeries. It was not *quite* all our fancy had pictured but not too bad for all that. They seemed quite happy about their food which was the main thing. There was a long discussion about what their last drink should be and Burgundy was finally decided on. After luncheon Rupert's chief desire was, as usual, to get as warm as possible and we coiled ourselves almost *in* the fireplace till it was time to go. . . . Rupert showed me a lovely little new poem beginning 'When colour is gone home into the eyes'. He said in his usual, intensely quiet modest-eyed way, 'I think the first line perfectly divine'.

"We went back to the ship. . . . On arrival at the Quay we found to our dismay that the ship had moved and was lying in the mouth of the harbour! . . . I went on board the Transport with them. It was a not-bad Union Castle boat and they were only two in a cabin. I went in to see poor Patrick who was lying in his bunk among cough mixtures and bandages looking as green as grass and very septic. I lingered on with Oc and Rupert with a terrible pre-operation feeling. The suspended knife seemed just above us all. Then the dull muffled siren booms began, charged with finality, and we knew that it was falling. Rupert walked with me along the narrow crowded decks, down the plank stairs. I said goodbye to him. I saw in his eyes that he felt sure we should never see each other again.

"Oc took me over the gangway and we talked for a few moments feverishly—'I shall come back' he said 'I may be wounded but I shall come back.' Another imperious hoot and he had to hurry back. The gangway was raised and the ship moved slowly out, the Hood trumpeters playing a salute on their silver trumpets as it passed the mouth of the harbour. The decks were densely crowded with young, splendid figures, happy, resolute and confident—and the thought of the Athenian expedition against Syracuse flashed irresistibly through my mind. . . ."

Lord Kitchener was now prepared to use an army in the Dardanelles operation. Of what size it would be and on what date it would be assembled at Lemnos nobody knew. I find an entry in my diary (undated). "There is still a tug-of-war going on between W. and K. about sending out the 29th Division—a necessity from the very first. . . . K. is like a screw who feels economical so long as he is spending money slowly. He doesn't like parting. . . . He has used the bad Russian knock in the East as a reason for holding back the 29th Division. But the surest way to help Russia is to use it here and now at the Dardanelles. This is the main object of the operation.

"Talking to him last night after dinner I said 'If the Dardanelles comes off W. will deserve full and almost sole credit. He has shown such courage and consistency in taking the responsibility throughout all the vacillations of Fisher and others.' Lord K. replied indignantly: 'Not at all—I was always strongly in favour of it. No one who has seen as much of the East as I have could fail to appreciate its importance.' I said I was glad to hear it as if it went wrong he would be there to support and stand by Winston.*

"W. speaks sanguinely of the whole thing being a picnic and Oc writes afraid that they will get there too late, but Hankey thinks it will be a tough job. He has maintained from the first that it couldn't be done without men. *Tuesday* [undated]. I talked to Ian Hamilton after dinner. I knew that he was to be sent in full command and I felt in a difficult position, not knowing how much he knew or guessed as he talked round it the whole time. He has a real crusading fervour about carrying the Cross to Stamboul. He said (was it a douceur?) that one of the first things he would do if sent was to offer Rupert a place on his Staff. (This from a sense of literary free-masonry!)" He dined with us a week later when he knew of his appointment and I noted: "He was in ecstasy. I think he probably has just the right dash of irregularity for the job."

Winston welcomed the appointment of his old friend wholeheartedly. He felt relief that what he called "a concerted military plan" was be-

---

* When long afterward I quoted this to Winston and told him I had a contemporary note of it, he asked me whether I would submit it in evidence before the Dardanelles Commission. I said that I would but when the time came Lord Kitchener was dead.

ginning to emerge. He asked my father to arrange an interview between Lord Kitchener and himself in his presence. He then asked Lord Kitchener whether he took full responsibility for the military operations and the strength of the forces needed "to achieve success." Lord Kitchener at once replied that he did and the Royal Naval Division was handed over to his command. On March 10th the 29th Division was at last ordered to Lemnos.

The success of the first bombardment of the Straits reverberated through Europe and beyond. In Constantinople the break-through of the Allied Fleet was expected and plans were made for the Sultan and the Court to flee to Asia Minor; on the Chicago Stock Exchange wheat prices fell steeply. A more awkward result was the demand by Russia for a declaration that, in the event of an Allied victory, she should annex Constantinople. It was a difficult decision. To consent would rouse misgivings in many quarters, but could we afford to refuse? Russia was (in Winston's words) "reeling under the German cannonade." To keep her in line we must encourage and sustain her by every means within our power. Then a further question arose: Had the present Government the right to pledge its successors to this course of action? If, as was possible, the Opposition were called upon to honor these commitments ought they not first to be consulted?

Whether this point was originally raised by Winston I do not know. That it was welcomed by him with enthusiasm I can vouch for. It is a curious fact that although no one had fought the party battle with greater zest and fervor, although no one was more bitterly hated by the Opposition he had always been drawn to coalition. He had hoped and worked for it during the Home Rule crisis of 1912; he had tried to prepare the way for it on the outbreak of war and he had hankered after it off and on ever since. Lord Beaverbrook writes truly that he had "a curious passion for bringing the Tories, who were fundamentally hostile to him, into the Ministry." [13] He often talked to me about this desirable possibility. "Do try and persuade your Papa to consider it." I invariably returned a dusty answer. "What should we gain? Whose counsel among the lot of them would you value? Bonar Law's? Sir Edward Carson's? Walter Long's? Would they add to our stockpot of wisdom? They would merely add to our dissensions—of which we've got quite enough already. We've got Arthur Balfour, who is the pick of the bunch, on the War Council. Our people would hate it—and you cannot pretend the Tories are fond of us—or *even* of you." But Winston continued, in his own words, to view "with great disquiet the spectacle

of this powerful Conservative Party . . . brooding morosely outside
. . ." [14] and it was his dearest hope that the meeting of the War
Council to which Lord Lansdowne and Mr. Bonar Law had been
invited to discuss Constantinople might prize open the door to coalition.

In fact it did nothing of the kind. He has himself recorded that "the
Council did not march satisfactorily although a united decision was
reached. And on the whole, as a result, a chilling impression of domestic
politics was, I think, sustained by the Prime Minister." [15]

In *Politicians and the War* Lord Beaverbrook describes the meeting
as "a trap." He writes that "Bonar Law had no knowledge at all that
he was being invited tacitly to step into a Coalition Government. None
the less, with his customary acuteness, he suspected that something lay
behind the invitation, and he behaved at the meeting with even more
than his habitual caution." [16] This caution was unnecessary. Whatever
hopes Winston may have entertained, nothing was further from my father's mind than to use the meeting as a "trap" or "tacit" invitation to
coalition. Any such invitation from him would have been explicit and
direct. Even Lord Beaverbrook admits that he was "not in the least
forthcoming."

The upshot of the meeting was that the Russians were informed that
Great Britain and France agreed to the annexation of Constantinople
by Russia as a part of a "victorious peace" and this fact was publicly announced on March 12th. I was surprised that the decision was taken
and accepted with so much equanimity. I could see no reason to feel
confidence in the postwar policy of the Russian Government, which we
knew to be a tyranny and as such both vulnerable and incalculable.
But she was our ally, we were fighting for our lives and the desperate
exigencies of war demanded that at all costs we should sustain her
(the same considerations which dictated our concessions at Yalta, though
these were exacted not by Russian weakness but by Russian strength).

Meanwhile Balkan reactions to our attack on the Dardanelles had
realized all our hopes. Reports reached us from our Mission in Sofia
that the Bulgarian Army might move against Turkey, Russia began to
assemble an Army corps at Batum, Rumania became interested and
friendly and the Rumanian Prime Minister told our Minister in Bucharest
that he was convinced that "Italy would move soon." The Italian Minister was apparently already counting the spoils. He spoke of "acquisi-
tions on the Adriatic coast" and "a share in the eventual partition of
Turkey. . . ." Within a month Italy could mobilize an army of
1,800,000 men.

But the most dramatic event of all was still to come. One evening in the first week of March I was sitting with Clemmie at the Admiralty when Winston came in in a state of wild excitement and joy. He showed us, under many pledges of secrecy, a telegram from Venizelos promising help from the Greeks, both naval and military—an Army corps of three divisions for Gallipoli! Our joy knew no bounds. "Is the King 'sound'?" I asked. (He had a German wife and German sympathies.) "Yes, our Minister said Venizelos had already approached the King and he was in favor of war." Winston totted up our combined forces. . . . In the background Bulgaria, Rumania and Italy were waiting—ready to pounce —all determined to play a part in the fall of Constantinople. All these tremendous consequences had flowed from our united naval enterprise.

I went back across the Horse Guards treading on air. Turkey, encircled by a host of enemies, was doomed, the German flank was turned, the Balkans for once united and on our side, the war shortened perhaps by years and Winston's vision and persistence vindicated. When I went to bed that night I indulged in romantic daydreams. Constantinople had fallen. The Naval Division, Oc, Rupert, stokers, mules and all were marching through its streets to the sound of silver trumpets— peace was almost in sight.

Within a day Fate intervened and all our hopes lay shattered in the dust. M. Sazonov informed us that the Tsar "could not in any circumstances consent to Greek co-operation in the Dardanelles." In Athens, where Venizelos was receiving great popular ovations, the Russian Minister intimated to the King that "in no circumstances would he be allowed to enter Constantinople with his troops." It was in vain that we represented through our Ministers the incalculable advantages of Greek intervention both to Serbia and to Russia herself—the co-operation of Bulgaria and Rumania, the possibility of gaining Corfu as a French naval base for the Adriatic.

For Winston these were cruel hours to live through. It was a tragic irony that Russia, retreating before the German onslaught, starved of munitions, cut off from her friends, should yet be capable of inflicting this wanton injury upon our fortunes and perhaps sealing her own doom. In his acute distress Winston wrote late at night to Edward Grey: "I beseech you at this crisis not to make a mistake in falling below the level of events. Half-hearted measures will ruin all, and a million men will die through the prolongation of the war. You must be bold and violent. You have a right to be. Our Fleet is forcing the Dardanelles. No armies can reach Constantinople but those which we invite, yet we seek nothing here but the victory of the common cause. Tell the Russians that we will meet them in a generous and sympathetic spirit about Constantinople. But no impediment must be placed in the way of Greek co-operation. We must have Greece and Bulgaria, if they will come. I am so afraid of your losing Greece, and yet paying all the future into Russian hands. If Russia prevents Greece helping, I will do my utmost to oppose her having Constantinople. She is a broken Power but for our aid, and has no resource open but to turn traitor—and this she cannot do. If you don't back up *this* Greece—the Greece of Venizelos—you will have another which will cleave to Germany." [17]

Alas, the hour for diplomatic "boldness" or "violence" had already passed. Next morning, before the letter had been sent, a telegram arrived from Athens: "The King having refused to agree to M. Venizelos' proposals, the Cabinet have resigned."

Despite this heavy blow no one either at the Admiralty or in the Cabinet or War Council suggested breaking off the operation. In Winston's words: "The vision of victory had lighted the mental scene. The immense significance of the Dardanelles and of the city which lay beyond had possessed all minds. The whole combination which had been dispersed by Russia on March 6th was still latent. . . . Everyone's blood was up. There was a virile readiness to do and dare. . . ." [18] I can vouch for the truth of these words. Never from any quarter, even among the most fainthearted, did I hear a suggestion that the enterprise should be abandoned.

Meanwhile Admiral Carden, who had seemed hesitant about renewing the attack, declared his intention of taking the first favorable opportunity of doing so. Then, suddenly, he suffered a nervous breakdown. He was succeeded by Admiral de Robeck, who expressed his full agreement with the plan of operations.

On March 18th in brilliant sunshine on a calm sea the whole Allied Fleet of fourteen British and four French battleships advanced to the assault upon the Narrows. The attack began with a terrific bombardment of the forts and by the early afternoon their fire had almost ceased. Admiral de Robeck reported that "at 4 P.M. the forts of the Narrows were practically silenced; the batteries guarding the minefields were put to flight and the situation appeared to be most favourable for clearing the minefields." The mine sweepers were ordered to go forward and exploded some six mines on their way. The ships now advanced to engage the Narrows, confident in their mastery of the forts and expecting to steam through the Straits with little loss.

And now disaster intervened. They struck a line of unsuspected mines. Three battleships were sunk and one French and one English battleship severely damaged and put out of action. Admiral de Robeck, mystified, disturbed, and disconcerted by these losses, of which he did not know the cause, broke off the action. When night began to fall the gallant Commander Roger Keyes asked de Robeck for permission to go back in a destroyer to try to salvage or torpedo the *Irresistible* and the *Ocean* (two of our damaged battleships). He has described in his memoirs the eerie stillness and silence of the battlefield on which no sign of life survived except the Turkish searchlights which still swept to and fro across the water. "I had," he wrote, "a most indelible impression that we were in the presence of a beaten foe. I thought he was beaten at 4 P.M. and at midnight I knew with still greater certainty that he was absolutely beaten; and it only remained for us to organize a proper sweeping force and devise some means of dealing with drifting mines to reap the fruits of our efforts." Keyes' faith in the enterprise was as firm and as unshaken as Winston's and had he then been the Admiral in command I have no doubt whatever that the Navy would have forced the Straits. It was certainly his conviction. In his memoirs published in 1934 he has written: "I wish to place on record that I had no doubt then, and have none now—and nothing will ever shake my opinion— that from the 4th April, 1915, onwards, the Fleet could have forced the Straits, and, with losses trifling in comparison with those the Army suffered, could have entered the Marmora with sufficient force to destroy the Turco-German Fleet." [19]

His instinct was a true one. As we now know the forts had fired away half of their ammunition (the heavy guns which alone could harm the fleet had only twenty rounds apiece) and there was no possibility of replacing it. The Turks were so short of mines that they had been collecting those that the Russians had been floating down the Bosporus from the Black Sea and shipping them to the Dardanelles. Victory would have cost us at most a few outdated battleships. Enver Pasha is quoted as having said during the war: "If the English had only had the courage to rush more ships through the Dardanelles they could have got to Constantinople; but their delay enabled us thoroughly to fortify the Peninsula and in six weeks' time we had taken there over two hundred Skoda guns."

Winston was in no way disheartened by the action of March 18th. The three old battleships which had been sunk were due for scrap and in the whole British Fleet only sixty-one men were killed and wounded. He regarded the news only as "the results of the first day's fighting." Lord Fisher and Sir Arthur Wilson were of the same mind. The War Council which met that morning authorized Winston to "inform Vice-Admiral de Robeck that he could continue the naval operations against the Dardanelles if he thought fit." [20] And de Robeck replied that he hoped to commence operations in two or three days.

We now know that de Robeck, distressed and alarmed by the loss of his ships, had feared dismissal after the failure of the attack. But his morale had been completely restored by Keyes and by the reassuring and sympathetic telegram he had received from Winston. He had since been promised four more battleships to replace his losses, destroyers were being equipped with sweeping apparatus to deal with the mines, and a squadron of aircraft led by Air Commodore Samson were arriving to spot the enemy guns. He wrote to General Hamilton: "We are all getting ready for another go and not in the least beaten or down-hearted."

It was therefore with amazement and "consternation" that within two days of writing this letter (on March 23rd) Winston received from him a telegram which indicated a complete *volte-face*. He was unwilling to move without the Army and as the Army would not be ready to act until April 14th he proposed to delay the next attack for another three weeks. Winston immediately drafted a reply in which he pointed out the dangers of delay through submarine attack and the heavy cost of the military operation, and ordered him to make all preparations to renew the attack at the first favorable opportunity. Then summoning a meeting of Lord Fisher and the War Staff at the Admiralty he placed the telegram before them.

But now he records that he encountered "insuperable resistance." The Chief of Staff alone was ready to order the renewal of the attack. Lord Fisher, Sir Arthur Wilson and Sir Henry Jackson refused to do so. They had been willing to support the naval operation so long as it was recommended by the Admiral on the spot, but now that de Robeck and General Hamilton had recommended a joint operation they could not overrule their judgment. Winston saw clearly the "vista of terrible consequences behind this infirm relaxation of purpose. For the first time since the war began, high words were used around the octagonal table." [21] He was supported by the Chief of Staff, Commodore de

Bartolomé, but he was the youngest there and the old sea-dogs remained obdurate.

Winston then took the draft of his telegram to my father, who agreed with it wholeheartedly,* as did Mr. Balfour. Winston entreated my father to intervene and impose his view upon Lord Fisher and the Admirals. But, as my father said to me, how could he override and over-rule the opinion not only of Lord Fisher and his Admiralty colleagues but also that of the Admiral in command and order him to undertake an operation which he thought dangerous and undesirable? All his instincts and his judgment were for renewing the attack, but as a lay-man he was incapable of assessing the danger of the mines, the techni-cal difficulties of dealing with them and the resources de Robeck had at his disposal for doing so.

Winston was, rightly, convinced that a fatal decision had been taken. With difficulty he got another telegram to de Robeck, passed by Fisher, giving him a strong lead but no direct order. It failed to spur him to action. Fisher wrote to Winston that he was "very wrong to worry and excite himself. Do remember that we are the ten lost tribes of Israel. We are sure to win! ! !" Winston knew better. He com-mented: "It is right to feel the things that matter; and to feel them while time remains." [22]

What had happened to produce the sudden change which took place in de Robeck's mind between March 21st and 23rd? On the 22nd he had taken the *Queen Elizabeth* to Lemnos for a conference with Sir Ian Hamilton. The others present were Generals Birdwood and Braithwaite and Admiral Wemyss. There are divergent versions of what took place in the discussion which ensued. Sir Ian Hamilton gives the following account: "The moment we sat down de Robeck told us *he was now quite clear he could not get through without the help of all my troops.* Before ever we went aboard Braithwaite, Birdwood and I had agreed that, whatever we landsmen might think, we must leave the seamen to settle their own job, saying nothing for or against land operations or amphibious operations until the sailors themselves turned to us and said they had abandoned the idea of forcing the passage by naval operations alone. They have done so. . . . So there was no discussion. At once we turned our faces to the land scheme." [23]

* My father noted in his diary on March 23rd: "I agree with Winston and K. that the Navy ought to make another big push so soon as the weather clears. If they wait and wait until the Army is fully prepared they may fall into a spell of bad weather or find that submarines, Austrian or German, have arrived on the scene."

According to Sir Ian Hamilton therefore it was de Robeck who took the initiative in suggesting the abandonment of the naval attack in favor of a joint operation. Yet he had given Roger Keyes a wholly different impression of his views before the meeting. And even after the meeting he had written in a message to London: "I do not hold the check on the 18th as decisive but having met General Hamilton on 22nd and heard his proposals I now consider a joint operation essential to obtain great results and object of campaign . . . to attack Narrows now with Fleet would be a mistake as it would jeopardize the execution of a better and bigger scheme." Here he clearly attributes his new strategic approach to Sir Ian Hamilton's proposals. Whatever the reasons may have been Admiral de Robeck had now changed his mind. Convinced that to delay and wait for the Army would be fatal Keyes pleaded with him in vain on his return to reverse his decision. He remained un- moved and immovable. There is perhaps something to be said for my father's simple explanation—i.e., that "the Admiral seems to be in rather a funk."

At home Winston was obliged to tell the War Council "with grief" of the refusal of the Admiralty to continue the naval attack. "Lord Kitch- ener," he writes, "was always splendid when things went wrong. Con- fident, commanding, magnanimous, he made no reproaches. In a few brief sentences he assumed the burden and declared he would carry the operations through by military force." [24] Had these "brief sentences" been spoken three months earlier, what a different prospect would have faced us. If the 29th Division had been sent in February, as originally intended, the landing of troops would have taken place immediately, before the Turks had time to pour in reinforcements and cover the Peninsula with a network of entrenchments. But it was still far away upon the seas and General Hamilton decided that the Army at Lemnos which had arrived ill organized and ill equipped should return to Alex- andria to prepare for the attack.

Lord Kitchener expressed the hope that naval pressure, the bombard- ment of the forts and attempts by ships to force the Narrows would be kept up and Winston urged these measures on de Robeck. But they were not undertaken. Both in the Admiral and the Admiralty the will to act seemed frozen. "Henceforward," wrote Winston, "the defences of the Dardanelles were to be reinforced by an insurmountable mental barrier. A wall of crystal, utterly immovable, began to tower up in the Narrows and against this wall of inhibition no weapon could be em- ployed. . . . 'No' had settled down for ever on our councils, crushing with its deadening weight what I shall ever believe was the hope of the world." [25]

The Admiralty lay frost-bound by a spell which Winston's fire and faith were powerless to exorcise. That spell was cast by the "No" principle incarnate in Lord Fisher.

These were dark days to live through but mercifully the darker ones which lay ahead were hidden from our eyes. We could not guess that never again would our great ships renew the attack upon the Narrows. Never would they sail through and seize the victory which lay beyond.

Those who could see and were prepared to do and dare were impotent. Timidity and blindness had their way. "Not to persevere— that was the crime." [26]

Chapter Twenty-Four

A TURNING POINT IN
HISTORY—MISSED

DURING the next weeks we awaited in tense expectancy the landing of the Army in Gallipoli. I felt that Winston was weighed down by heavy anxiety. He was haunted by the certainty that every day that passed the Turks were digging, that their numbers were increasing, that the danger of German submarines arriving in the Aegean became more imminent. He realized, as Lord Kitchener did not seem to do, that the military risks to which we were now committed far outweighed the naval risks we had refused to take.

And he had other grave anxieties. In February the Germans had started their campaign of submarine attacks upon our merchant ships and it was later extended to neutral shipping. In the end this proved to be a blessing in disguise. The sinking of the *Lusitania* shocked the conscience of the world and prepared the way for American intervention.

But Gallipoli held the first place in his heart and mind. When he thought of the fleet lying idle at anchor, compelled to abdicate the decisive part it could have played, the iron entered into his soul. "What should we have risked?" he asked again and again. "Far fewer lives than we throw away day in, day out in France to take a trench which is retaken next day. And *what* a stake we stood to win. . . ." I tried sometimes to distract and cheer him by reminding him of his land force, the Naval Division, who were about to play their part.

I was receiving eager, happy, excited letters from some of them dated "4 days out," "7 days out," then "Lemnos" and finally "Port Said." Reading Rupert's letters I was continually reminded of the lines:

> And by the vision splendid
> Is on his way attended.

That vision shone for him until the end. He did not live to see it "fade away and melt into the light of common day." On "Cairo leave" from Port Said he, Oc and Patrick visited the Sphinx by moonlight, rode on camels, shopped in the bazaars, and I received strange jewels which Cartier would not have passed as such. When Ian Hamilton reviewed the division at Port Said he was as good as his word to me at dinner and offered Rupert a post on his staff. Rupert refused it as I knew he would. He was laid low with a "touch of the sun" for some days and wrote to me: "But while I shall be well I think for our first thrust into the fray I shall be able to give my Turk, at the utmost, a kitten's tap. A diet of arrow-root doesn't build up violence. I am as weak as a pacifist." They sailed from Egypt on April 9th and on the 19th my brother wrote to me describing the island of Skyros where they had landed: "It is like one great rock-garden of white and pink-white marble, with small red poppies and every kind of wild-flower; in the gorges ilex, dwarf holly and occasional groups of olives—and everywhere the smell of thyme (or is it sage? or wild mint?). Our men kill adders or have fun with great tortoises. The water near the shore where the bottom is white marble is more beautifully green and blue than I have ever seen it anywhere." The ordeal by fire which lay ahead appeared to cast no shadow on their happiness.

At the Admiralty Winston was enduring ordeal by obstruction. He was obliged to fight for "every officer, every man, every ship, every round of ammunition required for the Dardanelles." Lord Fisher's "weather" had rarely been more turbulent and unpredictable. Though Winston has written that their relations remained "pleasant, intimate and always frank" he records explosive hiccoughs in Lord Fisher's letters such as (April 2nd): *"We cannot send another rope yarn even to de Robeck. We have gone to THE VERY LIMIT!!!"* (April 5th): "You are just simply eaten up with the Dardanelles and cannot think of anything else! Damn the Dardanelles! They will be our grave!" [1] Against this when notice was given of a Parliamentary question asking whether the First Sea Lord had agreed to the attack on March 18th he wrote across the draft answer: "If Lord Fisher had not approved of this operation he would not now be First Sea Lord." * Thus he continued to blow hot and cold. I was of course ignorant of these violent changes of temperature and when I occasionally asked Winston for a bulletin of Lord Fisher's mood he usually replied reassuringly: "Changeable— but I can manage him."

* The question eventually was **not put.**

Other storms were raging on all sides—between Lord Kitchener and Lloyd George over the new Committee on Munitions which had been set up to deal with the shortage of high explosives, between Lloyd George and McKenna; there was also continuous friction between Lord Kitchener and Sir John French and between Sir John French and General Joffre, Sir John complaining that Joffre was apt to treat him as a corporal.

Meanwhile great efforts were being made to bring Italy into the war on the side of the Allies and she was hovering on the brink of a decision. Russia was again obstructive, but this time we were determined that she should not be allowed to impose a veto as she had done so disastrously in the case of Greece. Edward Grey, who had been warned just before the outbreak of war that his eyesight was threatened, remained heroically at his post, counting but facing the cost. He was in dire need of a rest, and at the beginning of April my father (who seemed impervious to fatigue) took over the Foreign Office for a fortnight and with it the negotiations with Italy which had reached a crucial point.

Although my father "looked on tempests and was never shaken," his inner calm and equilibrium were disturbed by malice, pettiness, intrigue and talebearing. One morning Massingham came to see him with a tale that Winston was "intriguing hard" to oust Edward Grey from the Foreign Office and replace him by Arthur Balfour. My father did not believe it, and the revulsion and disgust he felt was against Massingham, not Winston. Unfortunately Lloyd George followed on Massingham's heels, and when my father, still hot from the impact of the story, mentioned it to him Lloyd George assured him that he believed it to be true. Knowing the close intimacy that existed between them my father was, not unnaturally, shaken and unhappy. He had a real and deep affection for Winston and hated to think ill of him. When he told me about it I begged him not to believe a word of it and said that I could vouch for Winston's loyalty to Grey. I was indignant with Lloyd George for having fostered such suspicions. But though I longed to ask for a direct denial from Winston I felt I could not do so without provoking yet another row—this time between himself and Lloyd George. This incident confirmed my conviction, based on intimate experience, that in their close yet curious relationship loyalty existed on one side only.

On April 22nd I went over to Ireland to spend a few nights at the Chief Secretary's lodge. The thought of the landing in Gallipoli, which I knew to be imminent, filled my mind, but I was in no immediate anxiety as I knew that it was timed to take place between April 25th and

28th. On arriving in the early morning after a broken night and choppy crossing I went to bed for a few hours, fell fast asleep and had a very vivid dream in which I had a conversation with Rupert Brooke—just the sort of talk we should have had if we had happened to be together. There was nothing sad or sinister about it, no hint of doom, finality or farewell. While dressing for dinner that night I was called to take a message from the Admiralty. It was from Eddie Marsh: "There is bad news of Rupert, he is ill with blood-poisoning on French hospital ship. Condition grave. I am hoping and will wire you directly I hear more." After the dinner party as I was going up to bed I heard the telephone ring again and stood waiting on the stairs with the certainty that it was for me. My dear friend Sir Matthew Nathan (the Permanent Under-Secretary) had gone to take the message and I read it in his eyes. Rupert was dead. I returned to London on the following day.

The story of the death of Rupert Brooke has been told by his friend Denis Browne in the Memoir by Eddie Marsh published with his *Collected Poems*. He was buried at night under a clouded moon on the island of Skyros by his comrades—my brother Oc, Bernard Freyberg, Charles Lister, Patrick Shaw Stewart and Cleg Kelly. Denis Browne describes his grave "in an olive grove where he had sat with us on Tuesday—one of the loveliest places on this earth, with grey-green olives round him, one weeping above his head; the ground covered with flowering sage, bluish-grey and smelling more delicious than any flower I know. . . . We lined his grave with all the flowers we could find and Quilter set a wreath of olive on the coffin." My brother wrote to me: "The moon thinly veiled, a man carrying a plain wooden cross and a lantern leading the way; other lanterns glimmering, the scent of wild thyme, a dim group of French and English officers, the three volleys—the Last Post."

Next morning at six the *Grantully Castle* sailed for Gallipoli.

Winston had only met Rupert Brooke once or twice, and once only, after dinner at the Admiralty, had there been any real interchange between them. But his imagination was caught by Rupert's eagerness and beauty and by his romantic sense of dedication. He was the incarnate symbol of the spirit of 1914—a spirit so alien to that of the youth of later years that they have found it difficult even to believe in. That spirit is epitomized in Winston's tribute in the *Times* of April 26th:

Rupert Brooke is dead. A telegram from the Admiral at Lemnos tells us that this life has closed at the moment when it seemed to have reached its springtime. A voice had become audible, a note had been struck, more true, more thrilling, more able to do justice to the nobility of our youth in arms engaged in this present war, than any other—more able to express their thoughts of self-surrender, and with a power to carry comfort to those who watched them so intently from afar. The voice has been swiftly stilled. Only the echoes and the memory remain; but they will linger. . . .

When I got back to Downing Street on Monday, the twenty-sixth, I found an enormous luncheon party impending, and not feeling in the mood for it I lunched instead with Edwin Montagu and Maurice Bonham Carter, who were living together in Queen Anne's Gate. I find a note in my diary: "As we walked back together across St. James's Park we saw the Italian Ambassador's large black car standing by the Downing Street steps. B.* said to me: 'Italy has signed.'" This was a triumph for my father, who, in Winston's words, "for ten days grasped the Italian business in his own hands with downright vigour." [2]

The landings in Gallipoli began at daybreak on April 25th and the news was not released until two days later. Night and day I thought of little else, but we knew little of what was happening. The newspapers were full of accounts of the first use of poison gas by the Germans in France which aroused a storm of indignation, and of reports of a terrible reverse, amounting almost to a collapse, suffered by the Russians in Galicia. There was only one war correspondent in Gallipoli—Ashmead Bartlett, who narrowly escaped being shot as a spy by the Australians.

Ian Hamilton's first dispatches to Lord Kitchener which announced the landing of twenty-nine thousand men were written in terms of such rosy optimism that no one could have guessed the nature of the events which they recorded. On April 26th he wrote: "Thanks to God who calmed the seas and to the Royal Navy who rowed our fellows ashore as coolly as if at a Regatta, thanks also to the dauntless spirit shown by all ranks of both Services we have landed 29,000 upon 6 beaches in the face of desperate resistance." On the following day he added: "Thanks to the weather and the wonderfully fine spirit of our troops all continues to go well." Lord Kitchener was naturally relieved and pleased.

Next day came the news of our heavy losses. And on the seventh we read Ashmead Bartlett's first report, describing the epic Battle of the Beaches—the Anzacs at Gaba Tepe, the 29th Division followed by the Naval Division at Cape Helles. I shall not attempt to retell the immortal story of heroism and horror at Sedd el Bahr which I heard from the lips of a few survivors. It should be read in Alan Moorehead's master-

* Maurice Bonham Carter.

piece *Gallipoli*. The bare facts are as follows: the landing was preceded by a terrific naval bombardment to which there was no reply. After an hour it was assumed that this unnatural stillness meant that the Turks were either dead or absent. The *River Clyde* with two thousand men on board, surrounded by some twenty smaller boats, approached the shore in early morning daylight on calm seas. When they grounded within a few yards of the beach the Turks leaping from their trenches poured a devastating fire at close range into the densely crowded mass of men packed shoulder to shoulder in the boats—and there they died in hundreds and boatloads full of dead and dying "drifted helplessly away." Some plunged into the sea and swam to the shore—to be mown down upon the beach or hung on the barbed wire. Two hundred reached the cliffs and crouched beneath their shelter. "This was the beach," wrote Alan Moorehead, "on which the Marines walked in perfect safety two months before."

Air Commodore Samson, flying over Sedd el Bahr and looking down, saw that "the calm blue sea was absolutely red with blood for a distance of 50 yards from the shore—a horrible sight to see." At last night came as a friend. Under cover of darkness the *River Clyde* was able to land her remaining men. Others crept from their hiding places and cut their way through the barbed wire. The naval guns thundered again and food and water and new troops began to reach the shore. At daybreak the shattered force was able to advance under cover of fire from the ships, capture the position on the heights and go forward for some miles unopposed. Here and elsewhere we had gained, at immense cost, a precarious foothold on the southern tip of the Peninsula.

Winston did not share Kitchener's complacency. He was, rightly, disturbed by our tremendous losses and took Lord Fisher with him to the War Office where they both entreated Lord Kitchener to send immediate reinforcements from Egypt. Lord Kitchener began by doubting whether these were needed, but he yielded in the end and ordered an Indian brigade and a Territorial division to be sent from Egypt to the Dardanelles. Had they been made available before the landing they would have been ready to follow up the advance on the 28th—when the Turks, exhausted and discouraged, were retreating. Now Ian Hamilton was obliged to wait until the 6th of May to start his new offensive. By then opportunity had passed. Though we threw in all our forces we gained only a few hundred yards. Trench warfare had begun.

On May 8th we received a telegram from Ian Hamilton saying that my brother had been wounded, shot through the knee—"no loss to life or limb." It came almost as a relief to me for I had been dreading worse news. Since the first day of the war I had been haunted by a guilty feeling that I ought to be nursing in a hospital. I did not pretend to a vocation but nursing appealed to me as a form of direct and personal service and, in addition, as a mortification of the flesh. Though debarred from sharing danger one could at least endure some measure of discomfort to salve one's restive conscience. But this step was strongly opposed both by my father and by Winston. My father gave no reasons for his opposition. Winston gave his with eloquence. "No, my dear— on no account. *This* is your war station and you must not desert it. You must remain here at your father's side—and mine. Those of us who are held behind the lines need sustenance, solicitous attention, distraction, delectation—and we cannot be deprived of them. We, who are directing these immense and complicated operations (on which the fate of humanity may well depend), are staggering under terrific burdens. We need every comfort, care and cosseting. *Ours* is the heartbeat you should listen to—our lightest scratch should be your care and your concern. *We* are your duty. This is your war station—by your father. I command you to remain here," etc.

In spite of these behests I had been planning to join a hospital in France and was on the point of going over to visit it. But now I resolved to go out to Alexandria instead and look after my brother. Apart from my longing to spend what might be our last weeks together I had the "Gallipoli fever." I wanted to be near Gallipoli. My father consented to my going and was in no way shaken by official warnings that the Mediterranean was now "submarine-infested." Winston too gave his blessing and to my joy entrusted me with a job of work after my own heart—i.e. to set up in Alexandria an Admiralty information service for reporting to their next of kin the arrival of R.N. and R.N.D. wounded, their condition and their progress. This task was performed by the Red Cross for the Army, but the Navy insisted on having its own organization.

I made immediate plans to sail within a week from Marseilles on a Japanese ship, was inoculated against typhoid, studied the technique of card indexes and hunted for a shady hat. Then, just two days before I was due to start, I found on going to bed a note left on my pillow by my father. It said: "Don't go from me now—I need you"—nothing more. I still don't know what prescience prompted it. He could not have foreseen the events the coming week would hold. Yet to write thus he must have felt hard-pressed by acute stresses and anxieties, for he never asked for anything for himself. I canceled all my plans at once. I little guessed how thankful I should be that I had done so.

Lloyd George spent the week end with us at the Wharf * and I had long talks with him alone both nights after dinner while others played bridge. Though bad news was coming in from all the fronts, France, Russia and the Dardanelles, I note in my diary that he was at the very top of his form. There was much speculation whether the sinking of the *Lusitania* would lead to America's coming in and the benefits this might bring us were assessed. It was agreed that she could organize munitions making on a huge scale and have a large army ready for next year. Lloyd George's estimate of the duration of the war was "more than one year more." I cannot remember any mention of the Admiralty. No one foresaw the gathering storms which were to break over our heads during the coming week.

First came a letter from de Robeck offering to renew the naval attack upon the Straits. The offer was put forward in a reasoned letter with a careful balance-sheet of pros and cons. Lord Fisher was resolutely opposed to any action by the Fleet until the Army had effectively occupied the shores of the Narrows. De Robeck's offer was refused.

On the night of May 12th the *Goliath* was torpedoed in the Dardanelles by a Turkish destroyer. Lord Fisher thereupon demanded the immediate recall of the *Queen Elizabeth*. Winston did not demur to this, provided that other vessels were sent out to replace her. But he was painfully aware that Fisher "wished at all costs to cut the loss and come away from the hated scene," while he himself felt "bound, not only by every conviction, but by every call of honour, to press the enterprise and sustain our struggling Army to the full." [3]

Lord Kitchener was, for once, furious and at a stormy meeting at the Admiralty protested at this desertion of the Army in their hour of need. Lord Fisher flew into an even greater fury. "The *Queen Elizabeth* would come home; she would come home at once; she would come home that night, or he would walk out of the Admiralty then and there." Winston did his best to placate Lord Kitchener.

On Friday, May 14th—the last day but one of this fateful week—a War Council was held which Winston has described as "sulphurous." Lord Kitchener complained that he had been persuaded to undertake the Dardanelles operations on his assurance that the Navy would force the Straits. Not only had they abandoned the attempt but they had now withdrawn the *Queen Elizabeth* when his army was fighting for its life

* Our little house at Sutton Courtney on the Thames.

with its back to the sea. Winston records, "Lord Fisher at this point interjected that he had been against the Dardanelles operations from the beginning, and that the Prime Minister and Lord Kitchener knew this fact well. This remarkable interruption was received in silence." [4]

Lord Kitchener's report upon the various fronts was steeped in gloom. Increasing Russian weakness might enable the Germans to switch troops to the West for a renewed offensive; in France shells were being expended at an alarming rate. And who could say that at any moment an invasion of our shores might not take place? Winston did his best to restore a sense of proportion. He said that the Dardanelles operations had never depended on the *Queen Elizabeth* and that naval support for the Army would be in no way affected by her withdrawal. The Admiralty had no fear of invasion. It had never believed that a landing in force could be effected or sustained. We should stop the vain and costly offensives on the Western front until we had adequate superiority in men, guns and ammunition and meanwhile concentrate our available forces on the Dardanelles and give them "such ammunition as was necessary to reach a decision there at the earliest moment." This wise comment was well received.

When Winston got back to the Admiralty he sat down and wrote a letter to my father. (Of the many letters I have quoted from, this is the only one I remember reading directly after its delivery.) "I must ask you to take note of Fisher's statement today that 'he was against the Dardanelles and had been all along. . . .' The First Sea Lord has agreed in writing to every executive telegram on which the operations have been conducted; and had they been immediately successful, the credit would have been his. But I make no complaint of that. I am attached to the old boy and it is a great pleasure to me to work with him. I think he reciprocates these feelings. My point is that a moment will probably arise in these operations when the Admiral and General on the spot will wish and require to run a risk with the Fleet for a great and decisive effort. If I agree with them, I shall sanction it, and I cannot undertake to be paralysed by the veto of a friend who, whatever the result, will certainly say, 'I was always against the Dardanelles.' You will see that in a matter of this kind *someone* has to take the responsibility. I will do so—provided that my decision is the one that rules—and not otherwise."

A paragraph follows about the incalculable mental processes which led Lord Kitchener to give or to withhold reinforcements. "Kitchener will punish the Admiralty by docking Hamilton of his division because we have withdrawn the *Queen Elizabeth,* and Fisher will have the *Queen Elizabeth* home if he is to stay." Then came a sentence which impressed me by its courage, serenity and unconquerable hope and resolution. "Through all this with patience and determination we can make our way to one of the great events in the history of the world." [5] That was the faith and aim from which he never swerved.

After writing to my father he applied himself to planning and minuting the naval reinforcements and convoys for the Dardanelles. He took the precaution of visiting Lord Fisher in his room and showing him these proposals before they parted for the night and he records that their conversation was quite friendly. Winston said to him that it was not fair to obstruct the necessary steps at the Dardanelles and then, if there was a failure, to turn around and say: "I told you so, I was always against it." "He looked at me in an odd way and said, 'I think you are right—it isn't fair'." He accepted the minutes and "we parted amicably." [6] Next day (Saturday, May 15th) I went with my father to the marriage of our friend Geoffrey Howard * to Kitty Methuen in Henry VII's Chapel, Westminster Abbey. There was hardly time for a word to be exchanged between us during the two minutes' drive from Downing Street to the Abbey. I read in my diary: "When he had signed the register and we got back he called me into the Cabinet Room and told me a most astonishing piece of news in these words: 'Fisher has levanted.' He had simply *run away* from the Admiralty, deserting his post and work, had pulled down all the blinds in his own house and left a red-herring trail in the direction of Scotland. Masterton[-Smith] expected him to be making for France and was out after him scouring the Continental railway stations and expresses, Lloyd George was out following another scent, Bongie † on a third. Father had armed the beagles with a paper to serve on him saying: 'Lord Fisher—In the name of the King I command you to return to your post'. We were to have driven down to the Wharf that afternoon and we sat (through hours of glorious sunshine!) waiting. . . . Finally he was found, caught, carried in a retriever's mouth and dropped—bloodshot and panting—at the door of the Cabinet Room. Father spent about an hour with him—which to me seemed eternity. He told me that Fisher had been very friendly and mellow but complained that he found W. quite impossible to work with. He was always doing things without consulting him (Fisher),

* The Hon. Geoffrey Howard, M.P., a Liberal Whip.
† Maurice Bonham Carter.

was overbearing, etc. etc. Father told him that if he wished to resign he must do so in the proper way and state his reasons for doing so in writing. This I have no doubt will tax him severely. Personally I suspect him of inspiring the recent poisonous press campaign against Winston and giving the impression right and left that he had always been opposed to the Dardanelles, had fought it tooth and nail and been over-ridden. The truth being that though he was never 'keen' about it he did not lift up his voice against it in the War Council, signed every order for it with his own hand—and if it had 'come off' at the start would have claimed his full share of the credit. It would then have been 'the Fisher touch.' I consider that he has behaved in a lower, meaner and more unworthy way than any Englishman since war began. He may have found W. exasperating to work with but he had no right to desert him at this juncture. He ran away from his post of duty through sheer funk." (Thus I exploded.)

When at last we drove down to the country together that evening my father showed me the undated letter he had received from Fisher that morning.

My dear Prime Minister,

As I find it increasingly difficult to adjust myself to the increasing policy of the First Lord in regard to the Dardanelles I have been reluctantly compelled to inform him this day that I am unable to remain as his colleague— and I am leaving at once for Scotland so as not to be embarrassed or embarrass you by any explanations with anyone.

Your admiring Master of Balliol * said "Never explain"—but I am sure you will understand my position.

Yours truly,
FISHER.

I enclose a copy of my resignation to the First Lord.

In his letter of resignation to Winston, dated that morning (May 15th), Fisher wrote:

First Lord,

After further anxious reflection I have come to the regretted conclusion that I am unable to remain any longer your colleague. It is undesirable in the public interest to go into details—Jowett said "Never explain"—but I find it increasingly difficult to adjust myself to the increasing daily requirements of the Dardanelles to meet your views—as you truly said yesterday I am in the position of continually vetoing your proposals.

* Benjamin Jowett.

This is not fair to you besides being increasingly distasteful to me.
I am off to Scotland at once to avoid all questionings.

Yours truly,
FISHER.

When Winston received this letter he did not take it very seriously. He had had several others like it in the past and he felt sure that a friendly talk would smooth the old Admiral's rumpled feathers as it had often done before. But he was disturbed when he got back to the Admiralty to find that Fisher had disappeared. He then came over to see my father and report the facts.

My father thought that he had "shaken" Fisher in his resolve to resign but he felt no certainty about it. He had at least prevented him from leaving London. He hoped that Winston would be able to patch things up with him once more. I was so angry with Fisher that I protested. Why should he be wheedled and persuaded to come back? Surely he had much better go. How can a man who runs away and plays a game of hide-and-seek at such a moment be left in a responsible position? Supposing the German Fleet had come out this morning, where should we have been? My father agreed that he had behaved quite indefensibly—but at this moment, with Italy coming in, our Army in Gallipoli in full battle and the Opposition out for Winston's blood (as they had always been), it would create a very difficult situation if there was a public breach between him and Fisher.

My diary continues: "Our Sunday was mouvementé in the extreme. B.* came down after luncheon having spent the morning with the King (in a low blue turned-down collar and golfing clothes!). The King had been very anxious to discuss War Office affairs which aren't going too smoothly either. The King is a strong Kitchenerite and would like him to be made Commander-in-Chief and have military authority over French. Then McKenna telephoned that he was driving down and arriving at 4.30, so we were in rather a pother when Masterton rang up to say that Winston wanted to come and was then starting. We didn't much want them to coincide and told Masterton to try and delay him a little by hook or crook. Went for a short walk with B. along the river towards Abingdon and picked armfuls of marsh-marigolds. When I got back I found McKenna closeted with Father and Prince Paul of Serbia loose in the garden! I had a longish talk with him and gathered that they (the Serbians) dreaded being absorbed by Russia more than anything and hoped to goodness we should keep Constantinople

* Maurice Bonham Carter.

if we got it. Also that the Grand Duke Nicholas was an awful old toper and debauchee and that he had constantly carried him home dead-drunk at night! (This last strained my credulity—Prince Paul couldn't carry a fly—let alone a dead-drunk Grand Duke!)

"Mr. McKenna was tucked up in his motor and speeded off. (Relief! that he and W. hadn't overlapped.) Went out with Edgar * in a boat for half an hour's relaxation after this and when we returned Winston was standing at the bottom of the lawn on the river's brink looking like Napoleon at St. Helena. I walked up and down the garden with him in my dressing-gown while all the others were dressing for dinner (it was the only way to get a quiet talk). He was *very* low I thought. I ached for him. I asked him if he had no inkling that he was on the edge of a volcano in his relations with Fisher. He said—'No'—they had always got on well—differed on no principle—he had always supposed him to be perfectly loyal, etc. Poor darling W.—there is a naïve and utterly disarming trustfulness about him. He is quite impervious to the climatic conditions of other people. He makes his own climate and lives in it and those who love him share it. In an odd way there was something like love between him and Fisher—a kind of magnetic attraction which often went into reverse. Theirs was a curiously emotional relationship—but as in many such they could neither live with, nor without, each other. I said to W. that the dynamite must have been piling up and asked what spark he thought had fired the explosion? He said he thought it was a visit by the Italian Naval Attaché who came to see him at midnight at the Admiralty (after Fisher had gone to bed)."

Winston had been over to Paris the week before negotiating with the Italians and, when the balance seemed to waver, had (in his own words) "thrown in the Trident." When naval co-operation was discussed he had promised to send four light cruisers to reinforce the Italian Fleet in the Adriatic. Fisher had agreed to all the terms of the Naval Convention including the dispatch of the four cruisers. The Italian Government had now resigned as a result of opposition to Italy entering the war. Their Naval Attaché, who was with the Allies heart and soul, assured Winston that the arrival of the cruisers might be a decisive factor and begged him to hasten their departure. If they could arrive by the morning of the sixteenth (instead of on the eighteenth as promised), naval co-operation between ourselves and Italy would be a *fait accompli*. Winston therefore agreed to send the cruisers forty-eight hours earlier than was originally intended, telegraphed the necessary

---

* Viscount D'Abernon, later our Ambassador in Berlin.

orders for them to proceed at once and wrote: "First Sea Lord to see after action." This was in Winston's view "the spark that fired the train." * In justice to Winston it must be added that a covering note was attached to the minute: "My dear Fisher, I send this to you before marking it to others in order that if any point arises we can discuss it. I hope you will agree. Yrs ever, W."

Whatever the reason Winston was now convinced, after an interchange of letters with Fisher and Fisher's obdurate refusal to see him, that the resignation must be accepted as final. He had had a talk that morning with Sir Arthur Wilson, who had told the Sea Lords that it was their duty to remain at their posts. He had asked Sir Arthur whether he would be willing to accept the position of First Sea Lord and he had consented. All this Winston had told my father, at the same time offering to go himself if my father wished to make a change. My father had replied that he did not wish it—which I knew to be true.

Clemmie was naturally very upset and as ever very brave. We had quite a happy dinner and they both drove away in better spirits. In *The World Crisis* Winston writes that my father's secretary mentioned to him in conversation that "the Prime Minister thought the Unionist leaders would have to be consulted on the steps to be taken." My father had told me that he would have to tell Bonar Law what had happened and to this I attributed no baleful significance. In view of the beans Fisher would inevitably spill and scatter broadcast I thought it both natural and necessary. I went to bed thankful that Winston had got Sir Arthur Wilson and his Board.

Early next morning I drove up to London with my father. He saw

---

* Lord Fisher's biographer, Admiral Sir R. H. Bacon, refutes this explanation on the ground that Lord Fisher had no knowledge of the telegram until after he had resigned. He adds, however: "But when he did see it, the unusual and unfortunate marking . . . 'First Sea Lord to see after action', hardened his resolve to have no further relations with Mr. Churchill." Admiral Bacon attributes the resignation to the fact that Winston had added to the minute of reinforcements for the Dardanelles (which had been previously agreed) two more E-class submarines. Admiral Bacon quotes Captain Crease, Lord Fisher's secretary, as having warned Masterton-Smith who gave him the minute that he "had no doubt whatever Lord Fisher would resign instantly if he received it. . . . Masterton-Smith said he would tell the First Lord my opinion before . . . handing me the minute to pass on. After some delay . . . he came back with the dispatch-box and said it must be sent on, for the First Lord was certain that Lord Fisher would not object to the proposals . . . *and that, in any case, it was necessary that they should be made*. I repeated my warning . . . and then arranged for the dispatch-box to be delivered early in the morning to Lord Fisher."

(*Lord Fisher* by Admiral Bacon, Vol. II, pp. 247, 254-55.)

Bonar Law before luncheon and I did not see him for the rest of the day. That evening I went out early to a play with Edgar D'Abernon and my brother Cys, on "London leave" from the Queen's Westminsters in which he was serving. I quote from my diary: "When I got back I found a message that Father wanted to speak to me directly I came in. I went into the Cabinet Room. He was sitting at the table writing with a heavy look of unhappiness I had rarely seen on his face. Open on the table beside him was a letter from Haldane. As I stood beside him and our eyes met I had a sudden flash of realization. 'Father—is it a Coalition?'—'I'm afraid so.' We both sat there in despair. 'All this butchery I have got to do. . . .'—'*Must* poor Haldane go?'—'Yes—it is a *shameful* sacrifice to have to make—but they insist on it. I feel strongly tempted to go myself but that would mean a complete break-up. I've had the utmost difficulty in persuading Edward Grey to stay. He is— rightly—outraged.'—'Was there no other way out?'—'No—we couldn't have had a public brawl between Fisher and Winston at this moment —with Italy on the brink of coming in. Things aren't very happy at the War Office either. K. and French can't get on.' We sat on and talked and talked. . . . When at last we parted and said good-night to each other he said: 'This has been the unhappiest week of my life.' I believe it has."

Winston had not been mentioned between us (except in my father's allusion to his quarrel with Fisher) and I felt no anxiety about him. Whether the Conservative leaders had already demanded his head or not I do not know. Had they done so I think my father must have mentioned it to me. But the grief and shame of sacrificing Haldane seemed to obliterate all else that night. Haldane had been the friend of his youth. Together they had started work at the Bar and shared the long and weary wait for briefs. Together they had resolved to stand for Parliament as Liberals and been returned for Scottish seats. Success had come to both and they had worked together in three Cabinets. No colleague had given more selfless, single-minded and efficient service to the nation. It was thanks to Haldane that the Army had been re-created and reorganized and that the Expeditionary Force was equipped and ready for its task at the outbreak of war. This shining record availed him nothing against the squalid clamor of the gutter press, led by Lord Northcliffe and Lord Beaverbrook. At the very moment when he was writing to my father to advise Lord Kitchener's appointment as Secretary of State for War he was accused of trying to worm his way back into the War Office. He was accused of being a friend of Germany, of having opposed the mobilization of the Army and the dispatch of the Expeditionary Force. Anonymous letters poured in upon him. "On one day," he wrote, "in response to an appeal in the Daily Express, there arrived at the House of Lords no less than 2600 letters of protest against my supposed disloyalty to the interests of the nation. These letters were sent over to my house in sacks, and I entrusted the opening and disposal of their contents to the kitchenmaid." [7]

A word from Bonar Law could have put a stop to this infamous witch hunt. But it was not spoken. To their lasting discredit the Conservative leaders aligned themselves behind this vile and ignorant campaign of lies and demanded his dismissal. To be obliged to bow to such humiliating necessity was a deep wound to my father's sense of honor and decency.

When I went to bed on the night of Monday, May 17, 1915, all I knew of the events of that crucial day (in addition to the short diary entry I have quoted) is that my father had that morning received the following letter from Mr. Bonar Law:

Dear Mr. Asquith,

Lord Lansdowne and I have learnt with dismay that Lord Fisher has resigned, and we have come to the conclusion that we cannot allow the House to adjourn until this fact has been made known and discussed.

We think that the time has come when we ought to have a clear statement from you as to the policy which the Government intend to pursue. In our opinion things cannot go on as they are, and some change in the constitution of the Government seems to us inevitable if it is to retain a sufficient measure of public confidence to conduct the War to a successful conclusion.

The situation in Italy makes it particularly undesirable to have anything in the nature of a controversial discussion in the House of Commons at present, and if you are prepared to take the necessary steps to secure the object which I have indicated, and if Lord Fisher's resignation is in the meantime postponed, we shall be ready to keep silence now. Otherwise I must to-day ask you whether Lord Fisher has resigned, and press for a day to discuss the situation arising out of his resignation.

Yours very truly,

A. BONAR LAW

My father had drafted a reply to Bonar Law inviting him to enter a coalition Government in which he intended to ask the Irish and Labour leaders to take part. He told me that, quite apart from Bonar Law's communication, he had reached the conclusion that the Government must be reconstructed. Nothing could be more disastrous than a heated public controversy in the House of Commons at this moment, when Italy was on the verge of throwing in her lot with the Allies. But leaving aside the exigencies of the immediate crisis he was convinced that this kind of situation, in one form or another, was certain to recur. He had therefore written to all his Cabinet colleagues asking them "with sincere reluctance and regret" to put their resignations in his hands. Winston was not mentioned between us and it never occurred to me that his position could be affected now that Fisher had gone.

What meanwhile was taking place within the Tory party has been revealed by Lord Beaverbrook in his book *Politicians and the War*. He tells us that "just as Opposition members were aware of the Shell trouble between Lord French and Lord Kitchener, so many of them were intimately informed of the progress of the conflict between Lord Fisher and Mr. Churchill at the Admiralty. Lord Fisher had seen to that. . . . Bonar Law knew quite well . . . that the resignation of Lord Fisher would be the signal for an outbreak of hostility to the Government which he would be quite unable to control. On the Shell scandal Bonar Law had his followers well in hand. . . . On the Admiralty crisis he had not.—And here in the main he sympathized with his own followers. He believed that a Shell scandal might keep Italy from coming into the war on our side. He thought . . . the dismissal of Churchill from the Admiralty might actually encourage Italy—for he had no belief in Churchill as a responsible administrator. One thing he knew for certain. If Churchill came down to the Commons on Monday, 17th May, with a new and tame Board of Admiralty in his pocket, the Tory party would revolt instantly. The Truce of God between the Liberal and Conservative parties would come to an abrupt end." [8] Bonar Law was well aware that in this event the Conservative Party, in a minority both in the House of Commons and the country, could not form or support an alternative Government. Coalition was the only way out.

He had refused to see Fisher, who had sought an interview with him through an intermediary, and "he was annoyed with Fisher for the method chosen for imparting the news of the resignation to various members of the Opposition." [9] In his own case it took the form of a marked cutting from the *Pall Mall Gazette* enclosed in an envelope addressed in Lord Fisher's hand reporting that "Lord Fisher was received in audience of the King, and remained there about half an hour." Bonar Law guessed rightly that Lord Fisher had resigned . . . "and it was clear that soon after the House met on Monday the storm would break." [10] After communicating with Lord Lansdowne he wrote his letter to my father and then went to see Lloyd George, who confirmed that Fisher's resignation was "an accomplished fact." Bonar Law then pointed out to Lloyd George that "Fisher was the darling of the Tory party, Churchill had become its bugbear. Was the first to go and the second to stay? The rank and file of the Opposition would not tolerate it. When the House met again on Monday the new list of the Admiralty Board would have to be read out. Then the tempest would break with uncontrollable violence, and the Opposition would once again begin to oppose. Bonar Law finally told Lloyd George plainly that of his own personal knowledge . . . he could not hold his followers back, even if he wished to." [11] Faced with the alternative between coalition and open rupture Lloyd George replied: "Of course we must have a Coalition, for the alternative is impossible." A conversation then took place between Mr. Bonar Law and my father after which Bonar Law summoned his Tory colleagues to a meeting at Lansdowne House and informed them of Fisher's resignation and of the decisions which had ensued.

Such is Lord Beaverbrook's account of the events within the Tory party which led to the fall of the Liberal Government and the birth of the first coalition. I am of course unable either to challenge or to confirm its accuracy (though there are some inaccuracies in his previous record of events, as, for instance, that "Lord Fisher departed for Scotland" [p. 103] which in fact my father prevented him from doing). On one point I am in complete agreement with Lord Beaverbrook—i.e. that it was on the crisis in the Admiralty and not on the shell shortage that the Government fell.

Winston's own record of this fateful day, May 17, 1915, is to be found in *The World Crisis.* [12] "On Monday morning I asked Mr. Balfour to come to the Admiralty. I told him Lord Fisher had resigned, and that I understood from the Prime Minister that he would approve the reconstruction of the Board of Admiralty with Sir Arthur Wilson as First Sea Lord. . . . Mr. Balfour was indignant at Lord Fisher's resignation. He said that it would greatly disturb his Unionist friends and that he would himself go and prepare them for it and steady their opinion. Nothing could exceed the kindness and firmness of his attitude. I spent the rest of the morning preparing my statement for Parliament, expecting a severe challenge but also to be successful. I still had no knowledge whatever of the violent political convulsions which were proceeding around me and beneath me."

That afternoon he went down to the House of Commons with the list of his new Board complete, and armed to the teeth for the debate. On his way to my father's room he looked in on Mr. Lloyd George, who told him that Fisher's resignation had "created a political crisis," that he was convinced that it could only be met by the creation of a national coalition Government and that he himself would resign unless such a Government were formed at once. Winston replied that he had always been in favor of coalition and had pressed it on every possible opportunity but that he hoped now that it might be deferred until his Board was reconstituted and in the saddle at the Admiralty. Lloyd George said that "action must be immediate." Winston then went on to see my father. "He received me with great consideration. I presented him with the list of the new Board. He said, 'No, this will not do. I have decided to form a National Government by a coalition with the Unionists, and a very much larger reconstruction will be required.' He told me that Lord Kitchener was to leave the War Office, and then added, after some complimentary remarks, 'What are we to do for you?' I saw at once that it was decided I should leave the Admiralty, and I replied that Mr. Balfour could succeed me there with the least break in continuity. . . . The Prime Minister seemed deeply gratified at this suggestion, and I saw that he already had it in his mind. He reverted to the personal question. 'Would I take office in the new Government or would I prefer a command in France?' At this moment Mr. Lloyd George entered the room. The Prime Minister turned to him. Mr. Lloyd George replied, 'Why do you not send him to the Colonial Office? There is great work to be done there.' I did not accept this suggestion,* and the discussion was about to continue when . . . a secretary entered with the following message for me: 'Masterton-Smith is on the telephone. Very important news of the kind that never fails has just come in. You must come back to the Admiralty at once.' "

Within five minutes he was at the Admiralty. There he learned that the whole German Fleet was coming out and that the message from the German C.I.C. to the fleet contained the words: "Intend to attack by day." The moment he had watched, hoped, waited, lived for was at hand. "The political crisis and my own fate in it passed almost completely out of my mind." The truth of these words is beyond doubt to those who knew him. He had no First Sea Lord but with the Chief of Staff, Admiral Oliver, and the Second Sea Lord, Sir Frederick Hamilton, to help him he sent orders to the Grand Fleet and all other available forces to put to sea. "I was determined that our whole power should be

* Lord Beaverbrook alleges that he did. *Politicians and the War*, Vol. I, p. 122.

engaged if battle were joined, and that the enemy's retreat should be intercepted." [13] To the Commander-in-Chief he sent a message: "It is not impossible that tomorrow may be The Day. All good fortune attend you."

It was in this turmoil of emotions that he received late that evening a red box from my father containing the note which asked all Ministers to place their resignations in his hand. In his reply he wrote: "So far as I am concerned, if you find it necessary to make a change here I should be glad—assuming it was thought fitting—to be *offered* a position in the new Government. But I will not *take* any office except a military department, and if that is not convenient I hope I may be found employment in the field.

"I am strongly in favour of a National Government, and no personal claims or interests should stand in its way at the present crisis. I should be sorry to leave the Admiralty, where I have borne the brunt, but should always rely on you to vindicate my work here." [14]

Writing these words it must inevitably have crossed his mind that if that night the British Navy were to annihilate the German Fleet his work would need no vindication, his enemies would be scattered and his tenure of the Admiralty secure.

He went to bed and slept a little. "With the earliest daylight" he went down to the War Room. It then appeared that the enemy had altered course and at last, at about ten thirty, it became clear that the German Fleet was on its way home. "The episode was over. All our fleets, squadrons and flotillas turned morosely away to resume their long-drawn, unrelenting watch, and I awoke again to the political crisis. But my hour had passed. . . ." [15]

I did not see Winston on Tuesday and barely saw my father, who was immersed in the painful task of re-forming the Government, in his own words, "the most uncongenial task that has ever come my way." It meant parting with many of his old and faithful friends and colleagues. Everyone behaved with admirable dignity and selflessness but there was naturally a feeling of resentment against those who had brought about the crisis. Lord Kitchener was not removed from the War Office. (I had never heard that this was suggested and my father had certainly never desired it.) The Northcliffe press campaign against him had begun but it did not get into its full stride until Friday the twenty-first when a violent attack aroused great public indignation and the *Daily Mail* was burned upon the Stock Exchange. I learned from B. of Winston's impending move from the Admiralty and of the false dawn of the German Fleet's sortie and felt heartbroken for him. B. assured me that it was useless to intercede with my father on his behalf. "He has done his damnedest but the Tories won't have Winston at any price. It is after all their hatred of Winston and their blind belief in Fisher which has brought about this crisis. Bonar Law has never liked Winston, as we know. I hear that Arthur Balfour did his best for him but he cuts no ice at all with his own party. The worst of it all from a national point of view is that with this balancing of personal claims and party quotas the new Government may well be a less efficient instrument for carrying on the war than its predecessor. Differences will be multiplied and decisions still harder and slower to arrive at."

I was sailing for Alexandria on Thursday (May 20th). My journey had already been postponed once and I had received a telegram from my brother Oc, "Wound healing, sands running out, come soon." I could not delay longer or I might miss seeing him—perhaps for the last time. I spent all Tuesday shopping and making my last traveling arrangements. I had a short talk with my sad and harassed father late that night. He was about to issue a statement that Edward Grey, Lord Kitchener and he himself would retain their present offices. He hoped to get Arthur Henderson (as a representative of Labour) and John Redmond to join the Government. He was intensely unhappy about the exclusion of Haldane and full of sorrow for and sympathy with Winston, for whom he had a deep affection, whose policies he had supported wholeheartedly and for whose record at the Admiralty he had the greatest admiration. "It is a tragedy," he said to me (not for the first time), "that he seems to provoke so much prejudice and hostility. Among the Tories A.J.B. and F.E. are his only friends and advocates and neither of them carry any weight with their party. But even among our own men, as you know, he isn't exactly popular. . . ." He went on to say that he feared the Tories were going to press for the inclusion of Carson and that this would create great difficulties with our people and might prove an obstacle to Redmond coming in. He added that Bonar was a difficult man to place. Lloyd George wanted to go, at least for a time, to the new Ministry of Munitions which was to be created. The Exchequer would seem to be the obvious place for Bonar but it would be impossible to have a whole-hogging Tariff Reformer there. I spent part of the rest of the night talking, first to Edwin Montagu and then to B. Both were steeped in gloom.

Next day (Wednesday, May 19th) I went with my father in the early afternoon to a patriotic meeting at the Guildhall at which he, Bonar

Law and most of the High Commissioners spoke. My diary records that "We slipped away before it ended to the House, where, after some talk with Lloyd George and Gulland,* Father made a statement about Coalition. It was received in black and angry gloom by the supporters of both sides. I left the Gallery when he sat down and met Winston in the passage. He took me into his room and sat down on a chair—silent, despairing—as I have never seen him. He seemed to have no rebellion or even anger left. He did not even abuse Fisher, but simply said, 'I'm finished'. I poured out contradictions, protestations—but he waved them aside. 'No—I'm done. What I want above all things is to take some active part in beating the Germans. But I can't—It's been taken from me. I'd go out to the Front at once—but these soldiers are so stuffy—they wouldn't like my being given anything of a command. No—I'm finished.' I did not know that I was crying but I suddenly felt hot tears rolling down my cheeks, and there were tears in his eyes too. I tried vainly to convince him that in spite of this cruel and unjust reverse vindication *must* come—and with it opportunity. There was a future which belonged to him as surely as a birthright—no one could take it from him so long as he kept faith with himself, and in himself. My faith in him and in his fortunes was absolute.

"At one moment in our talk he said to me very gently and not really reproachfully, 'I think your father might perhaps have stuck to me—with Wilson and the Board—*if* there was going to be a Coalition. If there wasn't, it was another matter. Party capital might have been made. But with a Coalition I think he might have done it.'—'But don't you see,' I said, 'that *this* is part of the price of Coalition? Your head and Haldane's? Can you imagine my father parting with either of you while he remained the master of his own house? *This* is what Coalition means —the sacrifice of one's friends to the blind prejudice of their enemies— what is called "the principle of give and take"—irrespective of quality or justice or even expediency. Yet you have always longed for it and worked for it.'—'Ah—I wanted it in a different way. I wanted us to go to the Tories when we were strong—not in misfortune to be made an honest woman of.' I asked him how he thought my father could have met this particular crisis otherwise. 'He should have held a Secret Session and put the whole case before Parliament. If he had challenged it with a vote of confidence he would have been supported by a great majority. He could then have made his own terms with the Opposition.' He added that he thought the Coalition was 'in a dangerous condition

* William Gulland, Liberal Chief Whip.

now as the Tories are trying to make the Cabinet a political vantage-
ground and not a non-political perfect war-machine. . . . My plans—
that's what I'm anxious about—my plans—that they should be carried
out if I go.' This was a theme he recurred to pathetically again and
again. My heart was wrung for him and I felt miserable at going away
to-morrow.—Hurried home to a large dinner-party (invited before the
crisis)—Lord K., John Morley, Dr. Jim (Jamieson), Mark Lockwood,
Crewes and many others—Went in to see Father afterwards who told
me with emotion of a wonderful scene in a Committee Room of the
House that afternoon. After his statement he was told that all the
'cream' of our party were meeting in a room upstairs—were in open
revolt against the Coalition, wouldn't stand it at any price and were
passing hot resolutions against it, saying that it was the two Tories in
the Cabinet—W. and K.—who had brought us to ruin. He went up and
made a personal appeal to them to support him in this course which he
disliked as much as any of them. He said, 'I can only ask you to trust
me, to believe me when I say that this course was an absolutely necessary one. I can only appeal to you to stand by me as you have always
done in the past.' He said that many of them were in tears. They cheered
him to the echo and backed him to the last man. It was a wonderful
personal triumph and he was deeply moved by it.—I told him of my
tragic talk with W. and begged him to give him a job in which he would
find some scope. He said: 'I'll do my best. Ll.G. suggested the Colonial
Office but the Tories are averse to his going there and I shall be hard
put to it to find places for their men. In any case I shall insist on keeping
him in the War Council.' I also mentioned to him W.'s suggestion that
he should have laid all the facts before the House in a Secret Session."

The arguments for this course of action are set forth by Winston in
The World Crisis (p. 373). "The impressive recital of all that the War
Office had achieved under Lord Kitchener would greatly have mitigated
the complaints on what had been neglected. I am sure I could have
vindicated the Admiralty policy. Moreover on May 23rd, towering over
domestic matters, came the Italian declaration of war against Austria.
The Prime Minister's personal share in this event was a tremendous
fact. I am certain that had he fought, he would have won; and had he
won, he could then with dignity and with real authority have invited the
Opposition to come not to his rescue but to his aid."

My father had two objections to Winston's attractive proposal. First,
he doubted whether the secrecy of a Secret Session would be effective.
(It is true that it was respected in the Second World War, but Winston

did not then have to contend, as my father did, with two powerful press machines bent on the destruction of his Government, nor with Cabinet colleagues who supplied them with ammunition to achieve their purpose.) His second objection was that a hotly contentious debate, even though it ended in a victory for the Government, would not be a persuasive prelude to a future coalition, or conduce to its harmony. In spite of these arguments my sympathy was with Winston. I would have preferred to take the risk of a secret session, give Parliament the facts and challenge the issue on the floor of the House of Commons. Like Winston, I felt confident that we should have won. Bitterness might well have ensued but in the long run it is better for a Government to create bitterness than to show weakness. One question, however, I cannot answer. Would a leak exploited by a hostile press have deterred Italy from declaring war? This consideration weighed with my father above all others. I note in my diary: "He came into my bedroom later on and talked to me till three about every aspect of the situation and other things. . . . I feel a terrible wrench at leaving him."

I left next morning with a heavy heart and on arrival at Marseilles I was aghast to find my ship was held up by a strike. It was an irony to be becalmed between England and Egypt, in both of which I longed to be. I sent a despairing telegram home and received two in return from my father and from B., one suggesting conditional and the other unconditional return. But I had burned my boats, strike-bound or not. The delay enabled me to receive a letter from B. about Cabinet making just before I sailed: "At first the Tories would have been content with about six members of the Cabinet but now they have stiffened in their demands and ask for their numerical proportion at least. This I have no doubt is the result of agitation from their back benches where there is a feeling that they are losing a good deal by giving up their right of criticism. So now it looks as though we should have eight or nine of them in the Cabinet. . . . I am not sure whether Carson will be in or not. Our Irish have definitely refused which is a great disappointment to your father, but I gather it would at once have made Redmond suspect. Haldane I fear goes—the Tories insist on this. Grey minds his exclusion bitterly. So does the King who takes a very right view of his merits. . . . Winston of course, poor devil, has been struggling hard to keep his office but once he received the final decision accepted it really well and wrote to say he would take any office that might be offered to him. . . . Of course he is without an inkling of what the party feels towards him. . . . As you know they loathe Coalition and

regard the crisis as being due to the action of the two Tory members—
W. and K. Your father, Ll.G., Crewe and McKenna had a discussion
with B.L. and A.J.B. on the composition of the Cabinet. It is gradually
taking shape and *much* you will dislike it—viz" (here follows a list
of names and offices). . . . "The chief interest of these discussions has,
I gather, been the attitude of the Tories to one another. . . . B.L.
has no illusions about his own position in the party, frankly recognizing
that he is a compromise."

I was surprised to hear that Winston was still clinging to the hope
of keeping the Admiralty and struggling to remain there. When I said
good-by to him I had felt in his despair an acceptance of finality. I
found it even more difficult to understand that he should have addressed
his appeals to the leader of the Tory party for (as Lord Beaverbrook
has written truly) "it was precisely the Tory backing of Lord Fisher
that had thrown him down." [16] His letter to Mr. Bonar Law, written
as late as Friday, May 21st (of which I knew nothing until its publication many years later), in which he asks to be "judged justly, deliberately and with knowledge" reveals a curious imperviousness to the
Tory party's inveterate dislike of him and all his ways. That he could
have brought himself to plead for mercy from his bitterest enemies
would have seemed to me a lapse from pride—and realism—wholly out
of character, had I known it at the time.

I did not know it. Looking back I can explain it only by his desperate
desire to salvage and to safeguard (what he called) his "plans." And
those plans meant the enterprise on which he had staked his heart—
Gallipoli.

I sailed at last. My ship was painted a dark, murky gray in imitation
of a battleship (the Captain's bright idea of protective coloring). He
naïvely confessed to me: "We're trying to look as much like a man-of-
war as possible to frighten the submarines away. I've even got a sham
gun to rig up!" From this uncalled-for ruse I begged him to desist.

But it was not of submarines I thought through the long days gliding
over summer seas, but of my father and of Winston. Italy had declared
war, which must bring my father much relief and should bring him deserved credit. What balm was there for Winston's wound—the sharp-
est and the deepest wound (I still believe) he suffered in his whole career
—I wondered helplessly and endlessly, until there came a morning when
I woke at dawn and through my porthole saw on the horizon the long,
low, yellow line which is Port Said.

Chapter Twenty-Five

RESIGNATION AND RETURN
TO ARMS

MY FOUR WEEKS in Alexandria, spent among the wounded of the Naval Division, made me so intimately familiar with Gallipoli—its discomforts, trials, triumphs, setbacks—that I almost felt that I had been there and shared them. Cape Helles, Achi Baba, Sari Bair, were no longer names on a map—I could see them. And I visualized the heroism and the horror of the landings as never before.

Oc had telegraphed that he would meet me at Sidi Gaber and (I find in my diary) "sure enough, when I put my head out of the train-window, there he was—hopping down the platform on crutches in the white glare like a lame jackdaw." In the inexpressible joy of our reunion we forgot all else. But I found him and his companions in the R.N.D. bewildered and distraught by the news that Winston had left the Admiralty and been relegated to the Duchy of Lancaster—a Cabinet wastepaper basket. How had it happened? What could it mean? They feared its dire effect on their own fortunes and those of their enterprise. Winston was their creator and preserver; he could be trusted to fight for them and to meet their every need. And he believed in what they were fighting for, in driving the Turks from the Peninsula and forcing the Straits. Their crusade was his policy. Was the Government wavering in its purpose? One and all they felt orphaned.

In the *Hood* Battalion this sense of loss was especially acute, for they had had three "private wires" with the powers that be. They could reach Winston through Eddie Marsh, my father through Oc, and both Winston and my father through me. Now two of the three wires were cut. Arthur Balfour was a remote, impersonal figure of whom they knew nothing. I did my best to reassure them. At least I could tell them with my hand on my heart that he was and always had been a firm believer in the Gallipoli operation and had supported it throughout. But I could not honestly pretend that he resembled Winston in any other respect whatever.

I began to receive letters from home and B.'s contained press comments which he knew I should want to see, about Winston's fall from the Admiralty. The *Times* naval correspondent wrote: "The news that Mr. Churchill is leaving the Admiralty has been received with a feeling of relief in the Service both afloat and ashore." [1] From the *Morning Post:* "Our constitutional theory has no place for a civilian Minister who usurps the functions of his Board, takes the wheel out of the sailor's hand and launches ships upon a naval operation. In this great war which is a matter of life and death for the British Empire we dare not take such risks." [2] The *Times* even opposed his inclusion in the Cabinet. But on the following day it accepted the *fait accompli* as a personal whimsy of my father's which must be humored: "Perhaps the most interesting single item of news to-day is that Mr. Churchill is to remain in the Cabinet. He has always been regarded as one of Mr. Asquith's special protégés and the Prime Minister while accepting his resignation of the post of First Lord of the Admiralty declined to part altogether with his masterful energy and driving-power." [3]

I spent much of my time in the various hospitals, setting up my Admiralty Information Bureau. I wrote: "The wounded are a pathetic sight lying in long rows in the stifling heat with the flies crawling over them. In Oc's room there is a poor Australian Colonel paralyzed from the waist downwards by a bullet which hit him in the spine before he even disembarked from the boats in the landing. I have interviewed several Generals, who are all very co-operative, and secured a palatial office in the National Bank of Egypt, and better still the services of the cream of its staff (all male). They are all dressed in white linen and highly competent. It is such a comfort to be working with hard-headed, busy, professional men instead of soft-hearted, idle, fuddled women. I sat down to write my report to Winston—and suddenly woke up again to the fact that he is no longer at the Admiralty to report to. I *cannot* realize or accept it."

I had long talks with Rupert's doctor—Schlesinger—and heard from him more details of his illness and death. We shopped in the bazaars with Ronald Storrs, an old friend, who was then Oriental Secretary, and saw a lot of Ego Charteris * and Oc's brother officers, among them

---

* Lord Elcho, son of Lord and Lady Wemyss, whose sister Cynthia had married my second brother. He was killed.

Bernard Freyberg, with whom I made great friends. I liked his direct and almost primitive simplicity, his singleheartedness and candid ambition. He bathed with us daily at Stanley Bay, a little inlet of the Mediterranean "containing (alas!) all Alexandria but also the biggest waves I have ever seen—terrifying to my water-cowardice. Freyberg takes me in—*right in*—and as they arch their necks and tower high and dark above us he lifts me right off my feet and we are borne over them together in a swirl of foaming surf. Water is his element and when unhampered by me he goes shooting and bounding through the centre of the waves like a porpoise. All this with an abdominal wound which has not yet healed!"

Of the Australians I write: "Their spirits and *élan vital* know no bounds and their physique and appearance are magnificent. Men like young gods, bare to the waist, burnt brown by the sun, wearing broad-brimmed hats (in which the New Zealanders stick a wild bunch of emu feathers)—riding, usually at full gallop on an iron road with beautiful seats—(of the Wild West rather than the Leicestershire type!). They are unpopular with δι πολλοι * for their wealth, insolence and lack of discipline and manners. Ego told me that the very most their officers could do was to ring up the Colonels of other regiments and say: 'I think it is my duty to warn you that my men are going to raid you to-night!' They are said to dig up graveyards and tear off women's yashmaks. Any act of 'unsittlichkeit' is immediately explained away by the word 'Australian'. But in Gallipoli they fight with heroic dash and courage, advancing irresistibly (so it is said) without any order like a football scrum."

We occasionally dined with Sir Henry McMahon, Lord K.'s somewhat incongruous successor, a slight, tenuous man rather like a cricket with an excellent sense of humor and no proconsular vices. He had come from India and was interesting about Lord Curzon, whom he had seen with unblurred eyes. He had met Edwin Montagu in India and diagnosed his ambition, i.e., to become its future Viceroy. I asked him how on earth he had guessed this? He said: "I noticed a glint in his eye which I have learnt to recognize." It was at the Residency that I met Lord Edward Cecil, whom his mother, Lady Salisbury, was said to have described as "the stupidest and the cleanest of my sons." Her interlocutor replied that in any other family he would have been regarded as "very clever and rather dirty." Apart from Generals, we had no other official contacts.

* Hoi polloi.

On the eve of Freyberg's return to Gallipoli, we had a farewell dinner with him at the Savoy, which we were all determined to make a gay one. Halfway through it, Schlesinger came in, very excited and overwrought, bringing us terribly bad news of the R.N.D. The artillery had shelled a dummy trench and they were then told to advance and take it. They found it to be a dummy and went on to the next, which was quite intact. This they captured with great gallantry and terrible losses, taking six machine guns. They were then shelled both by the Turkish artillery and our own, heavily counterattacked and had to retire, leaving their guns, the officers being practically wiped out in the retreat. *Howe, Hood* and the new *Collingwood* battalions had all suffered cruelly. Denis Browne was wounded and missing and the C.O.'s, who all (with the exception of Collins of the *Hood*) led their battalions in the charge, were killed or wounded to a man. Freyberg, whose brother had just joined the *Collingwood,* said he didn't want to ask or know anything more about it as this was his last evening and he wanted to enjoy it. I could see that he was very upset and feared that his brother was dead. We went on to a place called Le Jardin de Rosette where we tried to lasso objects with rings and watched a rather bad performance from a box. But all our hearts were chilled with fear.

Freyberg asked me to go for a drive with him next day before he sailed and called for me in the morning in a *goz*. We drove to the Nasser Gardens, green and lovely, full of gazelles and strange birds wandering in groves of hibiscus and golden mimosa. As we drove around and around, he told me all about his life. He had been wandering since he was fifteen and knew the South Sea Islands well. It was partly through his love and understanding of them that he had felt so close to Rupert. Just before the war he had gone to Mexico where civil war was raging and offered his services first to Huerta and then to Villa, who accepted them. He was fighting as a mercenary for Villa when he heard of the outbreak of war in Europe. He deserted with a blood price on his head, walked and hitch-hiked some three hundred miles across America, arrived penniless in San Francisco, won a swimming competition he saw advertised, sold his cup and got home on the proceeds. Here he offered himself to the Naval Division and got his commission.* He dropped me at my office in the Bank of Egypt and went to find out about his sailing time. When he came back he said to me: "I need you very badly. My

* I asked Winston in December, 1960, through whom Freyberg made contact with the R.N.D. and he told me that Freyberg had accosted him one day on the Horse Guards Parade and asked if he might apply to serve in it, which Winston encouraged him to do.

brother is killed." His brother, who had come out with the new battalion, had only landed on the Peninsula two days before his death. Freyberg looked dazed and stunned and said to me again and again: "It's odd—I've never cared for people before. I've never had any real friends—and now I do care for the first time in my life they're all getting killed." We sat together on the crowded beach until his sailing time. He showed me a little talisman around his neck and said it would be sent to me if he got killed. But mercifully it did its work.

And now Oc's sailing time approached and with it mine. I was thankful that my ship sailed first. I did not want to *see* him go back to what I knew awaited him. He remained calm and steadfast until the end. But I knew that his confidence in the conduct of the campaign was shaken. Again and again when an advance was made at heavy cost there were no reserves behind to follow up the thrust and push it through. At best they were halted in their tracks, at worst driven back over dearly gained ground. This gave the Turks a breathing space to reform and reinforce themselves and strengthen their positions. The Gallipoli campaign had already become a tragic example of giving too little and too late. As Winston wrote: "We have always sent two-thirds of what was necessary a month too late. . . ." [4]

Within a week of my return to England at the end of June, I became engaged to be married to Maurice Bonham Carter. To my intense relief and joy my father accepted the situation with far more than equanimity or resignation (the best that I had hoped for) but with unqualified happiness. He was devoted to B., who had become an indispensable part of his life—as he had of mine—and he knew that this marriage would separate us less than any other. My brothers all rejoiced and so did most of my friends. For ten frenzied days letters and telegrams poured in, crowds of photographers and pressmen invaded Downing Street, cameras clicked, telephones rang, my stepmother took me from shop to shop to choose and buy clothes, an occupation for which she had both passion and genius. "Such nonsense all this talk about not having a trousseau in wartime. Whether it's war or peace, you can't be married without a rag to your back!"

Why was it that I saw the lovely models who defiled before me—opened my presents—read my letters—through a strange haze of headache? She assured me: "It's being engaged. Nothing in the world makes one feel so ill. When I was engaged to your father I felt like death and lost two stone." This depressed me. Was it really "being engaged" that made me feel as I was feeling now? It was almost a relief to discover that this was not the cause. Our family doctor, Sir Thomas Parkinson, summoned to dissipate my headache before a dinner party, told me that I had typhoid fever. My father was appalled, incredulous, and (for once) angry. The word "typhoid" held for him fatal implications, for my mother had died of it. He denounced this irresponsible, alarmist and slapdash diagnosis as—what in fact it was—a guess made at a glance. But it was none the less a true one.

My wedding, which was to have taken place at the end of July, was put off. For two months I lay in bed in the big, shadowed room over the front door facing the Foreign Office, hearing the echoes of life and seeing it through a mist. I was visited by several of my father's colleagues—by Edward Grey, Lloyd George, Augustine Birrell, and of course by Winston.

The first time he came into my room and sat down by my bed, he seemed consternated by my weak and supine state and assured me with emotion: "But you will recover, you will arise again in all your . . ." (here followed a series of glittering qualities only used in epitaphs and which I had never, even in rudest health, possessed). I had no doubt whatever that I should recover, but his touching reassurance made me wonder whether he thought that I might be dying? A moment later, however, he got into his normal stride and told me all about everything. I was too ill to read or write so I have no record of our conversations but I remember my impressions of his state of mind.

First, as he had prophesied, the new Government was proving a worse instrument for making war than its predecessor. There were more divided counsels and consequent delays. The new Ministers had to be educated, and informed not only about the facts of the present situation but of the past events which had led to it, and this took time. Where four or five Ministers had taken decisions in the past a dozen had to be consulted now. The Cabinet had decided that a smaller body was necessay to deal with the actual conduct of the war. But the Dardanelles Committee which they appointed (and which took the place of the old War Council) consisted of no less than eleven members,* not counting the experts. He himself had been treated considerately and well. He was asked to write and circulate papers on the strategic situation.† In

---

* I.e., the Prime Minister, Secretary for War, Minister of Munitions, First Lord of the Admiralty, Mr. Churchill, Sir Edward Carson, Mr. Bonar Law, Lord Lansdowne, Lord Crewe, Lord Curzon and Lord Selborne.

† These masterly documents are to be found in *The World Crisis, 1915,* from p. 385 onward.

the first he had urged that we should try to obtain a decision in Gallipoli, where a comparatively small reinforcement might make all the difference, and "wind up the enterprise in a satisfactory manner as soon as possible." We had neither the men nor the ammunition to take decisive action in France. He told me that Kitchener, after many oscillations, had come around to this view. But I could see that he was not happy. The mere process of changing over from one Government to another had caused serious delays at a moment when quick decisions were imperative and the Dardanelles campaign had suffered seriously in consequence. After considerable controversy, three divisions had been sent there at the beginning of June and two more had followed at the end of the month. But the old paralyzing tug-of-war between Easterners and Westerners went on.

Coalition had not added to the speed, wisdom or unity of our counsels. New currents of hostility and mutual distrust were flowing in all directions. He spoke almost nostalgically of our Liberal divisions in the past which "swirled over a bedrock of solidarity." He was not critical of my father, realizing that his difficulties had been increased tenfold. (He has written: "Had the Prime Minister possessed or been able to acquire plenary authority, and had he been permitted to exercise it during May and June without distraction or interruption, . . . he would have taken the measures which even at this stage would have resulted in securing a decisive victory." [5] But such authority was now more than ever before outside my father's grasp.) When I told Winston of the grief of the Naval Division at losing him, there were tears in his eyes.

I was cheered and delighted when my father, after adjuring me to the strictest secrecy, told me an exciting bit of news. Winston was going out to Gallipoli to see the position there with his own eyes and report on it. Only two other colleagues, Grey and Kitchener, knew of his mission. I felt this might well be the turning point in the campaign. Winston's mere presence among the tired and discouraged troops, who often felt themselves to be forgotten men, would lift up their hearts. It would certainly give a lift to Ian Hamilton's. It might even spur de Robeck into action. A new offensive would take place when the five new divisions arrived. He would be able to discuss strategy and commands with Ian Hamilton and come home prepared to further and support their agreed plans. My father told me that Winston was leaving almost immediately.

Two days later, when I imagined him to be already on his way, I was appalled to hear that his visit had been vetoed, at the last moment, by his Conservative opponents in the Cabinet. This is the story as he himself told it to me. He was to start on the following day (I cannot remember the exact date). Ian Hamilton had been advised of his coming and everything was prepared. A Cabinet was held on the evening before. It had dispersed into the hall, but he lingered on in the Cabinet Room to say good-by to my father, Edward Grey and Lord K. and have a last word with them. He was in the act of taking leave of them when Lord Curzon suddenly came back into the Cabinet Room, saw them shake hands and heard words of farewell. He immediately asked where Winston was going. There was nothing for it but to tell him, though he was the last confidant they would have chosen. He then went straight to his Conservative colleagues and stirred up such a hornet's nest of trouble and opposition that Bonar Law intervened and after a row royal Winston was, at the last moment, prevented from going. Colonel Hankey was sent to Gallipoli in his place.

It was one of the bitterest disappointments of Winston's life. He went over it with me again one day in the autumn of 1956 and I realized that the passage of over forty years had not blunted its sharpness. The results for the coming offensive and the campaign which followed were incalculable. His presence must have helped to shape the Suvla operation and thus averted its ultimate disaster.

In a memorandum for the Cabinet dated June 18th, Winston wrote: "There can be no doubt that we now possess the means and the power to take Constantinople before the end of the summer if we act with decision and with a due sense of proportion. . . . It will multiply the resources and open the channel for the re-equipment of the Russian armies. It will dominate the Balkan situation and cover Italy. It will resound through Asia. Here is the prize, and the only prize, which lies within reach this year. It can certainly be won without unreasonable expense and within a comparatively short time. But we must act now, and on a scale which makes speedy success certain." [6]

Action had at last been taken in sending out large reinforcements, but alas, it proved once more to be delayed action. The date of the next great offensive on the Peninsula "was governed by two factors— the arrival of the new army, and to a lesser extent by the state of the moon. . . . If the dark period of July was missed, the operation . . . must stand over till the similar period in August." [7] The Dardanelles Committee had expected the attack to take place in the second week of July, believing that the new divisions would have arrived by then. But they did not arrive until the end of July and thus a whole month was lost. During that month, ten new Turkish divisions reached the Peninsula and thus, wrote Winston, "our new divisions . . . were equated and cancelled out before they got to the spot." [8]

He was not at the time aware how far the War Office performance had lagged behind its schedule and when, at the end of the first week of July, Lord Kitchener added two more Territorial divisions to the reinforcements already bound for the Dardanelles, he wrote in a joyful letter to Sir Ian Hamilton: "And now that you are equipped with all that you have asked for, and more, the next great effort can be made." And he added: "I never look beyond a battle. . . . It is a culminating event, and like a brick-wall bars all further vision. But the chances seem favourable, and the reward of success will be astonishing." [9]

Yet he certainly looked beyond the battle, as indeed we all did, to the prize which lay within our reach "and could certainly be won."

The assault was to take place on August 6th. The plans had long been laid and the most extreme precautions had been taken to keep them secret. The five new divisions had passed through the Mediterranean without the loss of a single man and they disembarked in darkness on the islands. Suvla Bay had been chosen as the place for the new landing.

The tragic story of the battle which ensued is told in *The World Crisis* and in Alan Moorehead's *Gallipoli*. I will only quote Winston's epitaph: "The long and varied annals of the British Army contain no more heart-breaking episode than the Battle of Suvla Bay. . . ." [10] He has written of "the extremes of valiant skill and of incompetence, of effort and inertia, which were equally presented," of "the malevolent fortune which played about the field." Two errors stand out from all the rest: the choice of the General who was to have command of the new landings at Suvla and that of the troops who were to make them. For the first, and fatal, choice Ian Hamilton cannot be blamed. He had asked for General Sir Julian Byng or General Sir Henry Rawlinson, but Lord Kitchener replied that he could not spare either of them in France. He appointed instead General Sir Frederick Stopford, aged sixty-one, who had not been in action since the eighties and had never commanded troops in war. When it was too late, General Byng and other capable and experienced leaders were sent out from France—to retrieve the irretrievable.

But for the second mistake Ian Hamilton was responsible. He had originally thought of entrusting the first landing at Suvla to the well-tried and seasoned 29th Division (then at Helles). But he changed his mind and decided that it should be made by the new divisions which

were coming out from England. Alan Moorehead has written of the
officers commanding the five new divisions: "Many of them, generals
and colonels alike, were men who were well over fifty and who had been
in retirement when the war broke out. . . . It was a curious position;
while the generals were old Regular Army soldiers, their troops were
civilians and very young; and all of them, generals as well as soldiers,
were wholly unused to the rough and individual kind of campaigning
upon which they were now to be engaged." [11]

Even so the landings at Suvla were successfully accomplished but
owing to General Stopford's almost paralytic inertia they were not
followed up. Forty-eight precious hours were lost on the beaches.

Winston has recorded that this was "the largest action fought upon
the Peninsula, and it was destined to be the last." [12] Our losses ex-
ceeded forty-five thousand and those of the Turks were estimated at
not less than forty thousand. We were defeated by the time factor.
"Force and time in this kind of operation amount to almost the same
thing. . . . A week lost was about the same as a division. Three divisions in February could have occupied the Gallipoli Peninsula with little
fighting. Five could have captured it after March 18th. Seven were insufficient at the end of April, but nine might just have done it. Eleven
might have sufficed at the beginning of July. Fourteen were to prove insufficient on August 7th. . . ." [13]

Lying in bed, feverish and muddleheaded, I knew little of the errors,
blunders, might-have-beens of the battle of Suvla Bay. I knew only that
victory had again eluded us. What I do remember vividly is my father's
overwhelming disappointment. He had built high hopes on it and his
biographer records that "if there was any moment in which he lost
his habitual composure it was when the news came that it had failed." [14]
I suffered for him, for Winston and for our men on the Peninsula who,
after all they had endured and sacrificed and hoped, were now cheated
of the victory they dreamed of and consigned again to trench warfare.
I received sad letters from my friends in the Dardanelles where ammunition was short and illness was rife. They were mourning the loss of
comrades and facing a winter without hope. I also feared that we should
soon hear pleas for evacuation from those who had always been against
the enterprise. These were to come but not yet.

The loss of the battle of Suvla Bay had far-reaching and disastrous
repercussions. We had been trying to win Bulgaria's support and urging
Serbia and Greece to make concessions to her. Serbia was obdurate in
her refusal and thus sowed the seeds of her own doom. Venizelos would

have been willing, but he had his King to contend with. All these three nations were watching our fortunes in Gallipoli. Bulgaria was awaiting the outcome of the battle of Suvla Bay and there is no doubt that its result was the factor which decided her to throw in her lot against us.

Another untoward consequence was the renewed pressure of the Westerners. My father with Lord Kitchener and Mr. Balfour had held a conference with the French at Calais early in July and strongly opposed a new offensive in the West in 1915. The French had then agreed without demur to an "active-defensive" strategy. After our failure at Suvla, Lord Kitchener on his return from a visit to French Headquarters summoned Winston and told him "with appreciable hesitation" that he had agreed with the French to a major offensive on the Western front: "if it succeeded it would restore everything, including of course the Dardanelles." [15] Winston received this news with despair. He knew that there was no chance of success and he said so. They drove together to the War Committee where Lord Kitchener informed his colleagues that owing to the desperate situation in Russia he felt unable to abide by the Calais agreement to postpone the offensive until the Allies were ready. He said that he himself had urged this course on General Joffre. Winston protested that we had neither the men nor the ammunition to justify such an operation; that it could not take place in time to relieve Russia; that it would "rupture fatally" our plans for opening the Dardanelles and that it could only lead to "useless slaughter on a gigantic scale." He was strongly supported by many of his colleagues. Lord Kitchener himself could hold out no promise or even likelihood of a "decisive success." But it was said that the French would march in any case and "if we did not march too, the Alliance would be destroyed." [16] Even Winston had to concede that if the French persisted in their action we should be obliged to fall into line. Sir John French, who was questioned by the Cabinet and with whom Winston also had a private interview, was no more optimistic than Lord Kitchener. He stressed the necessity of "acting in harmony with the French" and informed Winston that Joffre meant to employ no less than forty divisions in the French sector. This was to be an operation on a greater scale than any we had before attempted. Yet Winston left him with the conviction "that we were confronted with the ruin of the campaign alike in the East and in the West." [17]

Then came a sudden dazzling break in the dark skies. The French Government announced its intention of sending an army of six divisions to the Dardanelles under the command of General Sarrail. They were to land on the Asiatic side of the Straits and attack the forts of Chanak. They asked us to help in the transport of this force. Needless to say, our Government, astonished, leaped at the proposal and transport was assembled. Alas, it was a false dawn. Within a few weeks the Easterners in France persuaded their Government to deflect the expedition to Salonika in an attempt to save Serbia, now threatened by a renewed Austro-Hungarian attack and by Bulgaria's imminent entry into war. In response to an appeal from Venizelos we were ourselves obliged to transfer the 10th Division from the Dardanelles to Salonika. And there was worse to come. While the troops we had taken from the Dardanelles were on their way to Salonika, King Constantine of Greece dismissed Venizelos on whose invitation they had come. "The Allies," wrote Winston, "therefore found themselves confronted with a pro-German Greece determined to repudiate its treaty obligations to Serbia. Thus the object of the expedition to Salonika had entirely disappeared." [18]

In his Cabinet letter to the King on September 22nd, my father wrote: "Thus ends one of the impotent chapters in the history of diplomacy. The discredit for the result must be divided between Russia, but for whom Bulgaria would probably have been brought in months ago, and Serbia whose obstinacy and cupidity have now brought her to the verge of disaster." [19]

Winston continued to point to the Dardanelles as "the master key to the problem" and to a naval assault on the Straits as "the sole chance of changing the action of Bulgaria and averting the destruction of Serbia." [20] He appealed to Mr. Balfour in vain; de Robeck and the First Sea Lord, Sir Henry Jackson, were not willing to make the attempt and he did not feel justified in overriding them. Of my father's attitude, Winston has written: "He was, in my opinion, throughout unwavering in his intention to persevere at the Dardanelles, and he used every resource of patience and tact to guide and carry opinion in that direction and to secure the necessary decisions at the earliest possible moment. A more vigorous course would probably have broken up the Government." [21]

Meanwhile the great offensive in France had resulted only in slight advances at the expense of huge casualties. Our offer to sign a military convention with Rumania and Greece met with no response. The Bulgarians invaded Serbia, captured Monastir and routed her Army which they were soon to destroy. Sir Edward Carson resigned because we had failed to save her. He told the House of Commons that "the Dardanelles operations hang like a millstone round our necks and have brought upon us the most vast disaster that has happened in the course of the war."

I had been too ill to follow the course of these events in the newspapers but in the isolation of my sickroom I heard their echoes and felt the dull thud of catastrophe. I did not see Winston during September and for the first time in my life I did not want to see him. I knew too well the agony that he was living through but I did not feel strong enough to witness it. I was obsessed by one gnawing dread—the evacuation of Gallipoli.

In October it began to cast its shadow. Lord Kitchener asked Sir Ian Hamilton for his estimate of the probable casualties such a course would entail, while making it clear that no decision to evacuate had yet been taken. Sir Ian replied that "it would not be wise to reckon on getting out of Gallipoli with less loss than that of half the total force." [22]

On October 14th, Sir Ian was recalled and replaced by General Monro—a Westerner to the core. Winston has written of him that "he belonged to that school whose supreme conception of Great War strategy was 'killing Germans'. Anything that killed Germans was right. Anything that did not kill Germans was useless, even if it made other people kill them, and kill more of them, or terminated their power to kill us. To such minds the capture of Constantinople was an idle trophy, and the destruction of Turkey as a military factor, or the rallying of the Balkan States to the Allies, mere politics, which every military man should hold in proper scorn." And he adds the significant words: "The special outlook of General Monro was not known to the Cabinet." [23] General Monro was now asked to give his opinion on whether the Gallipoli Peninsula should be evacuated or another attempt made to carry it; on the number of troops that would be needed, (1) to carry the Peninsula, (2) to keep the Straits open, and (3) to take Constantinople.

The General came to a quick decision. He spent just six hours on the Peninsula and on the following day sent a telegram recommending total evacuation and the abandonment of the campaign.

Lord Kitchener reacted to this advice with creditable violence. He telegraphed at once to General Birdwood who had been left temporarily in command of the Dardanelles Army: "I shall come out to you; am leaving tomorrow night. I have seen Captain Keyes and I believe the Admiralty will agree to making naval attempt to force the passage of the Straits. We must do what we can to assist them." He then proceeded to suggest the steps that might be taken. "All the best fighting men that could be spared, including your boys from Anzac and everyone I can

sweep up in Egypt, might be concentrated at Mudros ready for this enterprise." He offered Birdwood the command of the whole force, adding
that Monro would be appointed to the command in Salonika, and he
ended with the words: "We must do it right this time. I absolutely refuse
to sign orders for evacuation, which I think would be the gravest disaster
and would condemn a large percentage of our men to death or imprisonment."

"Here," wrote Winston, "was the true Kitchener. Here in this flaming
telegram . . . was the Man the British Empire believed him to be
. . . resolute, self-reliant, creative, lion-hearted."

Yet the next day Lord Kitchener sent a further message: "I am
coming as arranged. . . . I fear the Navy may not play up. . . . The
more I look at the problem the less I see my way through, so you had
better work out very quietly and secretly any scheme for getting the
troops off the Peninsula." [24] What had shaken his purpose?

The indomitable Roger Keyes had come home to lay before the
Admiralty a daring plan he had devised for forcing the Straits. It had
the strong support of Admiral Wemyss, who held the post of Second
in Command, though not of Admiral de Robeck. Arthur Balfour was
much attracted by the plan. "It is not often that when one examines a
hazardous enterprise," he told Keyes, "—and you will admit it has
its hazards—the more one considers it the better one likes it." [25]
Naval reinforcements were ordered to the Dardanelles and the First
Lord wrote a tactful letter to de Robeck suggesting that he should
come home on leave for a rest. Kitchener grasped at the plan like a lifeline and urged Keyes to get the Admiralty to consent to it.

All seemed to be going well till, on the eve of Kitchener's departure,
a Cabinet was held at which the old division between the supporters of
Gallipoli and those of Salonika flared up again. Bonar Law, who had
always been an opponent of the Dardanelles, threatened to resign unless evacuation of the Peninsula took place. Arthur Balfour, a staunch
believer in Gallipoli, asked for an assurance of military support, which
Kitchener was unable to give. Hence his change of mood, though not of
heart.

In Paris where Kitchener spent a night en route he was cheered at
finding that the French Government was strongly opposed to evacuation.
They even promised him the help of six old battleships. He telegraphed
to Keyes to join him at Marseilles and sail with him so that they might
discuss plans on the voyage. Had Keyes received his message, caught
the ship, concerted with him their joint strategy during the journey,

been at his side when he arrived to meet de Robeck and Monro, they might together have saved the day. But the evil Fate which dogged the fortunes of the Dardanelles from start to finish played its last card. By a mischance the message never reached him. Lord Kitchener was confronted on arrival, not only by de Robeck and Monro, but by General Maxwell, the Commander-in-Chief in Egypt, and Sir Henry McMahon, the High Commissioner—all solid for evacuation. "Before this phalanx his native hue of resolution paled. Though his inspection of our forces and the defenses had convinced him that the troops could hold their own, he was persuaded to abandon the idea of an attempt to force the Straits and to recommend instead a new landing on the Asiatic coast of Turkey at Ayas Bay. (This plan was turned down by the General Staff at home.) But on evacuation he still held his hand. Roger Keyes arrived too late to repair the damage done though he and Admiral Wemyss fought hard to do so.

And others fought at home—Winston, my father, even Lord Curzon. Colonel Hankey wrote a powerful memorandum stressing the danger of freeing Turkish forces for an attack on Russia and urging that the troops sent to Salonika should be transported to Gallipoli.

But for Monro the sailors might have won. He remained obdurate and immovable. He is the only man of whom I have ever heard Winston speak vindictively. "I should like him to starve," he said to me, "to starve without a pension in a suburban hovel facing a red-brick wall." "You don't *mean* that," I said. "Yes, I do mean it—that is how I want him to live to the end of his days—staring into a blank wall."

The final die for evacuation was not yet cast but I felt a leaden certainty that it must come.

Meanwhile another tragedy in Winston's fortunes was taking place at home. My father had felt for some time that the Dardanelles Committee was proving itself to be a most unsatisfactory instrument for waging war. It was far too large, its discussions ranged over too wide a field and the Cabinet often insisted on covering the same ground over again. He had suggested cutting down its numbers by splitting it into two small committees, one to deal with the conduct of the war and the other with economic and domestic matters. This plan met with little support as everyone wanted to serve and many nominated their friends as well. The Cabinet finally decided that the War Committee should consist of the Prime Minister, Mr. Balfour, Lord Kitchener, Sir Edward Grey and Mr. Lloyd George. This meant the exclusion of Winston. True, he was one of many who shared the same fate—among whom was Lord

Curzon, who expressed his bitter disappointment, and Mr. Bonar Law (who was added later as a result of Conservative protest and pressure). Winston's sole reason for accepting the Duchy of Lancaster as an office was the knowledge that with a seat on the War Council he would have a voice and a hand in the direction of the war and that he would be able to support and sustain the Dardanelles enterprise. He now felt powerless to do so. He knew that "in the teeth of the opinions which were now prevailing" [26] it was a lost cause and that even if he had been accorded a seat on the War Committee he could not have saved it. He was convinced that as a result of the course which had been followed evacuation must take place. He therefore resigned from the Government. My father broke the news to me. I felt stunned, for somehow I had been blind to such a possibility. Winston out of the Government—in war? In what other element was it possible for him to breathe and act and live? And then, even as I asked myself, I knew that there was one, and only one, other element for him. "He will go to the front." And my father replied: "That is what I believe he intends to do." And he added: "It is a terrible waste. I think he has more understanding of war than any of my colleagues. Unfortunately few, if any, of them share my view." He then told me that Winston had wanted to resign a few weeks ago, but that he had refused to accept his resignation and had hoped that he had persuaded him to stay. He said that for months he had been trying to cut down the size of the War Council which had proved to be an impossible body. Now that the Cabinet had at last agreed to take drastic action he must support its decision regardless of personal preferences.

In his final letter of resignation to my father (dated November 11th) Winston wrote: "Knowing what I do about the present situation and the instrument of executive power, I could not accept a position of general responsibility for war policy without any share in its guidance and control. . . . Nor do I feel able in times like this to remain in well-paid inactivity. I therefore ask you to submit my resignation to the King. I am an officer and I place myself unreservedly at the disposal of the Military authorities, observing that my regiment is in France.

"I have a clear conscience, which enables me to bear my responsibility for past events with composure."

My father replied regretting that he had felt unable to reconsider his decision to resign, and praising his services in council and administration. He ended his letter: "I am sure that you will continue to take an active and effective part in the prosecution of the war. As you know well, on personal grounds I feel acutely the severance of our long association."

The letters were published in the *Times* on Saturday, November 13th. I saw Winston for a moment on the day before. I was grief-stricken, he was serene and calm. He told me that he was going to make his resignation speech in the House of Commons on Monday (November 15th) and intended to cover the whole ground of his Admiralty record, including Antwerp, and that I must be there to hear it. He asked me to luncheon on the day after (Tuesday) and said that he expected to leave for France before the end of the week.

Press comments on his resignation were on the whole friendly. The *Times* Parliamentary correspondent wrote: "He was an eager and active member of the old War Committee and it was obvious that his exclusion from the new Committee vitally affected his position. It seems that Mr. Asquith wished to find a place for him in the new Committee. Circumstances proved too strong for him. . . . The House of Commons will undoubtedly approve Mr. Churchill's wish to join his regiment in France much as it will regret the passing of his brilliant personality. Nobody imagines that his disappearance from the political arena will be more than temporary." [27] The *Manchester Guardian* mourned his going "as a great national loss, for in our opinion—though we dare say there are few who now share it—he had the best strategic sense in the Government. . . . There have been two opportunities of winning the war. One was last October before the fall of Antwerp, the other was this spring when a great effort by land and sea would have won through to Constantinople and saved us all our troubles in the East now. Mr. Churchill saw them both at the time and though his ideas were adopted, neither in Flanders nor in the East did they have anything like a fair chance. . . ." [28]

On Monday I went to the House to hear his farewell speech. When he rose from a back bench he was received with sympathy rather than enthusiasm but the House rapidly warmed toward him and he was soon getting cheers from all directions. It was a masterly and deeply moving speech—an unanswerable vindication of his record at the Admiralty, starting with Coronel and the Falkland Islands, going on to Antwerp and ending with the Dardanelles. He showed great restraint, for there were still some facts he could not reveal. He told the truth about Fisher, while paying him a generous tribute. He made it clear to the House beyond a doubt that the naval attack on the Dardanelles "was a naval plan, made by naval authorities on the spot, approved by naval experts in the Admiralty, assented to by the First Sea Lord, and executed on the spot by Admirals who at every stage believed in the operations. . . . I will not have it said that this was a civilian plan, foisted by a political amateur upon reluctant officers and experts."

He ended his speech with a prophetic passage: "There is no reason to be discouraged about the progress of the War. We are passing through a bad time now, and it will probably be worse before it is better, but that it will be better, if we only endure and persevere, I have no doubt whatever. Sir, the old wars were decided by their episodes rather than by their tendencies. In this war the tendencies are far more important than the episodes. Without winning any sensational victories, we may win this war. We may win it even during a continuance of extremely disappointing and vexatious events.

"It is not necessary for us to win the war to push the German lines back over all the territory they have absorbed, or to pierce them. While the German lines extend far beyond their frontiers, while their flag flies over conquered capitals and subjugated provinces, while all the appearances of military successes attend their arms, Germany may be defeated more fatally in the second or third year of the War than if the Allied Armies had entered Berlin in the first." [20] These words could have been spoken with equal truth about the Second World War.

Winston received an ovation from the whole House when he sat down. Then my father rose and paid tribute to him: "I desire to say to him and of him, that having been associated with him now for ten years in close and daily intimacy, in positions of great responsibility and in situations varied and of extreme difficulty and delicacy, I have always found him a wise counsellor, a brilliant colleague, and a faithful friend."

I met Winston for a fleeting moment before leaving the House. The afterglow of his speech shone in his eyes and was reflected in every feature. For the moment the triumph of his performance had blotted out past and future. I poured out my libation of praise and relief. "Thank God at last you've said it. Now they *know*." He said: "I think it went well. And, as *we* know, there was more to say I didn't say, but as your father said it must and will be said someday." I asked how some of his bitterest critics had *looked* at close range. (I could not see their faces through the gallery grille.) "Foolish—sheepish—oafish—blank" were his descriptions of a few of them. Seeing him so happy and triumphant, here in the House, his normal and inevitable context, I could not make myself believe that in a fortnight he might well be in the trenches. So to test reality I said it: "In a fortnight you may be under fire in France—*can* it be true?" "Yes—and in a fortnight you will be married—that's just as strange and just as true." Then came a purple passage about Fate's whirligig, the wheel on which our lives revolved, which I can't reproduce. I remember saying that there was a needle in our inner compass which no wheel could deflect or move. The compass took him to the stars and how on different nights in different latitudes the heavens' kaleidoscope is shaken and familiar lights are scattered and displaced in the celestial skyscape and, for a time, seem lost to our eyes. Yet if we search we find the constellations that we know in new positions but true to their unchanging pattern. "And some-where in that heavenly hurly-burly is your star—the one that led you in South Africa. Don't forget you've got a star." "I shan't forget it—I may see rather more of it than I shall like during the coming months. . . ." We parted, and again I tried to visualize him huddled in a trench, up to his knees in mud and water under the cold skies. And, worse than any physical discomforts, the sudden exile from the heart of things, the blotting out of the world-wide perspective he had lived with, in exchange for a few miles of front. Did he realize it? Could he endure it?

Next day I went to a farewell luncheon with him and Clemmie at Goonie Churchill's house in Cromwell Road. It was pervaded by the earthquake of his imminent departure, baggage and other military im-pedimenta piled in the hall and stacked on landings. Margot came with me. The other members of the party were Goonie, Eddie Marsh and Clemmie's sister, Nellie Hozier. Clemmie was admirably calm and brave, poor Eddie blinking back his tears, the rest of us trying to "play up" and hide our leaden hearts. Winston alone was at his gayest and his best and he and Margot held the table between them. They had always been an uneasy combination, as neither of them really enjoyed the other's society and she could not forbear from rubbing in the evils which had followed in the wake of coalition and reminding him that he had always wanted one. He made his stock reply, that we should have sought one, not in our hour of weakness but at a time of strength. Margot retorted that "if we had been full of strength we should never have asked the second- and third-rate men that we've got from the other side today to come and help us—X (charming, courtly, elderly, barren), Y (provincial, ignorant, unreliable), Z (sticky and correct)," etc., etc. This was fortunately a moment when strictures on his Conservative colleagues did not annoy him!

When our last good-bys were said and we had left, she said to me that "somehow it was not a great success," for once a wild understatement. For most of us it was a kind of wake. My heart ached for Clemmie, and Eddie was very pathetic. Winston was not unmindful of his plight and had asked my father to take him on as an extra private secretary as he could not bear to think of poor Eddie being plunged back into the bowels of the Colonial Office, sans personal function, sans friends, sans anything. So he was coming to us at No. 10 to be put in charge of Civil List pensions which we hoped would make him feel a little less of a motherless child.

I had no interchange with Winston. Only the implicit passed between us. The one thing that cheered me was that he still seemed to be infused with excitement and exhilaration. Once more he heard the call of danger and adventure, the call he had never failed throughout his life to "greet with a cheer." Two days later, as Major Churchill of the Oxfordshire Yeomanry, he sailed for France.

Within a fortnight I had crossed the stormy Channel on a troopship en route for my honeymoon at La Mortola in northern Italy. For the first time for many years I lost touch with his fortunes and with the day-to-day and hour-to-hour events of politics and war.

I was married on November 30th at St. Margaret's, Westminster. I remember as in a dream the drive there with my father through the crowds in Parliament Square, the misty vision through my veil and my emotion of that loveliest of churches filled by a vast faceless throng, of the Archbishop in his splendor at the end of the long aisle waiting to marry us. . . . It was over and we went behind into the vestry to sign the register, to find my father, Margot, father-in-law awaiting us with open arms. After family embraces I turned to greet the other signatories—Arthur Balfour, Edward Grey, Lord Haldane and (was I dreaming still?) the gigantic figure of Lord Kitchener whom we all believed to be still far away across the seas. I heard afterward that he had unexpectedly returned that morning and that his appearance created what is known as a "sensation" when he strode into the church. To those colleagues who were seeking to displace him and who had counted on a longer absence to attain their end the "sensation" was disturbing.

What advice had he brought with him? I did not know before leaving England. The news reached me abroad that he had agreed to the abandonment of Suvla and of Anzac though he still wished us to retain Cape Helles. I knew this to be the beginning of the end of all our hopes.

And yet, in Winston's words, "hope flared up" once again for those at home. The Navy, led by Admiral Wemyss, fought on to force the Straits and was supported by the Cabinet. But General Munro once more won his battle against both. By mid-December the decision was reached to evacuate the whole Peninsula.

Sitting in sunshine in a paradisal garden by the sea, I was haunted by forebodings. The official estimate of the casualties had been not less than 30 per cent and probably more than 50 per cent. Even Lord Kitchener's iron nerves were shaken and he told my father that he "paced his room by night seeing the boats fired at and capsizing and the drowning men." My heart was flooded by a great tide of relief and thankfulness when I received a letter from my father in which he told me that Suvla and Anzac had been evacuated without the loss of a single life. The last fortnight had been a nightmare to him. But now the incredible had happened—a miracle even greater than the miracle of Dunkirk.

And like Dunkirk many acclaimed it as a victory. I could not do so, even when the men at Helles who had held their ground alone on the Peninsula for twenty days pushed off unscathed from the same beaches they had won. Nor did the men. They too had had their "vision splendid," their dream of victory, which shone throughout their long ordeal of sacrifice and suffering, and now they saw it fading in retreat. Alan Moorehead tells how "they came to their officers in hundreds and asked to be the last to leave the shore."

Thus the greatest opportunity of the First World War was thrown away by men of little faith. It might have been as Rupert Brooke believed "a turning point in history." Through blindness and timidity we failed to grasp and turn the vital hinge. History has not yet forgiven us.

----◄◄ ►►----

Chapter Twenty-Six

FRONT LINE TO BACK BENCHES

WHEN we returned from our honeymoon to 10 Downing Street in the last days of December, 1915, we found my father wrestling with an acute Cabinet crisis. The Derby national recruiting campaign had failed to produce the men necessary to maintain in the field the seventy divisions demanded by the General Staff. The issue of compulsory military service which had been smoldering for some time flared up and the Cabinet was divided. To my father compulsion in wartime was a pure question of practical expediency. Once necessity was proved he was ready to act. His main anxiety was to enlist the greatest possible measure of "general consent" and he has recorded that "I have never had a harder task in public life than to secure the fulfilment of that condition." [1] Lord Kitchener had always supported the voluntary system and "so long as sufficient men came in, it was not my duty to ask for special means of obtaining them," he said at a meeting of members of the House of Commons before leaving on his last journey to Russia in June, 1916. But in view of the urgent need of man power it had been agreed that the Derby recruiting scheme should be accepted as the final test of voluntary enlistment. It had failed, and the Cabinet decided that it was necessary to go forward with compulsion. Within a week my father received the resignation of three colleagues—Sir John Simon, who objected to conscription on principle, Mr. McKenna, who held it to be impossible on financial grounds, and Mr. Runciman, who said it would drain our essential industries of man power.

This was enough to tax even my father's powers of endurance. But the worst was still to come. He received a letter from Sir Edward Grey, his closest and most deeply valued friend and colleague, saying that if the other three went he too must go—though for different reasons. He recalled the injustice done to Haldane when the Coalition was formed. Though tempted to resign then, he had forborne from doing so in what he believed to be the national interest. Now he felt that his presence at the Foreign Office was no longer indispensable either at home or abroad. My father could not have received a more wounding blow from a more unexpected quarter. He ascribed it, rightly, to Edward Grey's state of health. He wrote him a firm letter appealing to him to stand by him and to act as a conciliator with the other three. Edward Grey responded; McKenna and Runciman put their case to the Cabinet; my father, Austen Chamberlain and McKenna were asked to confer immediately with the Treasury and the General Staff, and report to their colleagues. In the end all resignations were withdrawn except that of Sir John Simon.

During this week of storm and stress I felt the great void, political and personal, of Winston's absence. For ten years my first impulse in any crisis had been to find out his attitude to what was happening. Next to my father's his was the mind whose reaction to events I awaited most eagerly. He was not the compass by which I steered my course, but he was the searchlight which illumined it. I had no doubt whatever where he would have stood on this issue. He had been pressing for conscription ever since the Coalition came into being though, to my mind, he underrated the obstacles which stood in its way, for instance, the importance of "general consent" and the fact that organized labor was against it root and branch.

I wondered anxiously how he was faring in France. He was never a correspondent. Letters were not his natural medium of communication and his own do not reflect or reveal him. (Those I have received from him fall into two categories: [1] short, heartfelt expressions of sympathy, gratitude, congratulation, affection, elicited by some event or utterance; [2] argumentative dissertations on some issue on which we disagreed.) Yet no one was more meticulous in acknowledging the letters he received. I never wrote to him on any subject, private or public, without receiving a reply, usually by telegram, within twenty-four or, at the latest, fortyeight hours. And his telegrams were not laconic but lavish, prodigal, regardless of expense.

Apart from one or two brief notes from France my news of him had been mostly secondhand, through Eddie Marsh who kept in constant touch with him. It was from Eddie that I heard that when Winston had arrived at Boulogne with the Oxfordshire Yeomanry Sir John French had sent a car to meet him and bring him immediately to his headquarters. They had been close friends for years and Winston had helped French by his sympathy and understanding in many difficult moments, throughout the war. French knew that his own position was highly precarious and this no doubt gave him a strong fellow feeling for Winston in his present plight.

Winston has recorded that that night they dined together and discussed the general war situation. "It was not until the next morning that he said to me, 'What would you like to do?' I said that I would do whatever I was told. He said, 'My power is no longer what it was. I am, as it were, riding at single anchor. But it still counts for something. Will you take a Brigade?' I answered that of course I should be proud to do so, but that before I could undertake any such responsibility, I must learn first-hand the special conditions of trench warfare." [2] The Commander-in-Chief agreed and it was arranged that he should be attached to "the best school of all"—the Guards. Lord Cavan, who commanded the Guards Division, was summoned and promised to send him to one of the best Colonels he had. He invited Winston to luncheon at his headquarters, gave him a warm welcome and drove him to the Grenadier Battalion he was to join as a Major under instruction. Winston has given a most amusing account of his feelings when Lord Cavan, having introduced and handed him over to the Colonel and his staff, "got into his car and drove off leaving me very like a new boy at school in charge of the Headmaster, the monitors and the senior scholars." [3] The companies had already started on their march to the trenches. The Colonel and Winston were to ride and overtake them about a mile ahead. "It was a dull November afternoon and an icy drizzle fell over a darkening plain. . . . We paced onwards for about half an hour without a word being spoken on either side. Then the Colonel: 'I think I ought to tell you that we were not at all consulted in the matter of your coming to join us.' I replied respectfully that I had had no idea myself which battalion I was to be sent to, but that I dared say it would be all right. Anyhow we must make the best of it.

"There was another prolonged silence. Then the Adjutant: 'I am afraid we have had to cut down your kit rather, Major. . . . We have found a servant for you, who is carrying a spare pair of socks and your shaving gear. We have had to leave the rest behind.' I said that it was quite all right and that I was sure I should be very comfortable." [4] After three and a half hours of progress in "the same sombre silence" they reached the headquarters of the battalion, "a pulverized ruin called

Ebenezer Farm," where they had some food and "strong tea with condensed milk" (not Winston's idea of nectar). He was asked where he would like to sleep and offered the choice between a signal office eight feet square and stiflingly hot "occupied by four busy Morse signallers" and a dugout two hundred yards away. Having "surveyed" the signal office Winston said he would like to see the dugout. They walked out into the sleet and after a quarter of an hour's search in pitch darkness they found it. It turned out to be "a sort of pit four feet deep containing about one foot of water. I thanked the Second-in-Command for the trouble he had taken in finding me this resting place, and said that on the whole I thought I should do better in the signal office. . . . The bullets, skimming over the front line, whistled drearily as we walked back to Ebenezer Farm. Such was my welcome in the Grenadier Guards." [5]

It is immensely to Winston's credit that in spite of this frosty reception from his military superiors in the battalion he succeeded within forty-eight hours in thawing them. "I was infinitely amused at the elaborate pains they took to put me in my place and to make me realize that nothing counted at the front except military rank and behaviour." [6] He asked the Colonel whether he might accompany him on his rounds of the trenches and thereafter they "slid or splashed or plodded together through snow or mud . . . for two or three hours at a time each day and night; and bit by bit he forgot that I was a 'politician' and that he 'had not been consulted in the matter of my coming to his battalion.'" [7] In fact so high did he rise in the Colonel's esteem that when the Second-in-Command went on leave Winston was invited to undertake his duties during his absence—"one of the greatest honours I had ever received." He then suggested to the Colonel that he would learn more of the conditions in the trenches if he lived with the companies in the line, instead of at the battalion headquarters. "The Colonel considered this a praiseworthy suggestion. . . . I must confess . . . that I was prompted by what many will think a somewhat inadequate motive. Battalion Headquarters when in the line was strictly 'dry'. Nothing but the strong tea with the condensed milk, a very unpleasant beverage, ever appeared there. The Companies' messes in the trenches were, however, allowed more latitude. And as I have always believed in the moderate and regular use of alcohol, especially under conditions of winter war, I gladly moved my handful of belongings . . . to a Company in the line." [8]

No dramatic military action took place during Winston's sojourn with the Grenadiers but danger and discomfort were his constant companions. He has written that "cannonade and fusillade were unceasing" and that "no one was ever dry or warm."

One incident is, however, worth recording for it seems to afford further proof that his life was miraculously protected and preserved to fulfill some hidden purpose. As he has written: "Chance, Fortune, Luck, Destiny, Fate, Providence seem to me only different ways of expressing the same thing, to wit, that a man's own contribution to his life story is continually dominated by an external superior power." [9]

After he had spent about a week in the line he received a field telegram informing him that the Corps Commander wished to see him at four o'clock at Merville and that a car would be waiting at the Rouge Croix Crossroads at three fifteen. He did not relish the prospect of "trapesing across three miles of muddy fields, the greater part under the observation of the enemy by daylight, and then toiling back all the way in the evening" but he had no option but to obey orders. He and his soldier servant were scarcely two hundred yards away from the trenches when they heard "the shriek of approaching shells." Turning around he saw four or five of them bursting over the trenches they had left. He gave no thought to them but "toiled and sweated on" until at last he reached the rendezvous, only to hear, after a long wait, that there had been a mistake, the car had gone to the wrong place and it was now too late for him to see the General. Winston inquired what was the nature of the business which caused the General to bring him out of the line? "Oh," said the Staff Officer airily, "it was nothing in particular. He thought as he was coming up this way he would like to have a talk with you." Winston was not unnaturally indignant as he now began "another long, sliding, slippery, splashing waddle back to the trenches. . . . The sedentary life of a Cabinet Minister which I had quitted scarcely a month before, had not left me much opportunity to keep fit. Tired out and very thirsty, I put my head into the nearest Company Mess for a drink. 'Hello,' they said, 'you're in luck to-day.' 'I haven't seen much of it,' I replied. 'I've been made a fool of.' 'Well, you're in luck all the same,' said the Grenadier Officers." [10] Their allusions to his luck were lost on him until, when he approached his own shelter, he was met and intercepted by his sergeant: " 'We have shifted your kit to Mr. ——'s dug-out Sir.' 'Why?' I asked. 'Yours has been blown up Sir.' 'Any harm done?' 'Your kit's all right Sir, but —— was killed. Better not go in there, Sir, it's in an awful mess.' . . . 'When did it happen?' I asked. 'About five minutes after you left, Sir. A whizzbang came in through the roof and blew his head off.'

"Suddenly," wrote Winston, "I felt my irritation against General —— pass completely from my mind. All sense of grievance departed in a flash. . . . How thoughtful it had been of him to wish to see me again, and to show courtesy to a subordinate. . . . And then upon these quaint reflections there came the strong sensation that a hand had been stretched out to move me in the nick of time from a fatal spot." [11]

That hand had been stretched before. It had a longer reach than the General's.

And now an incident occurred of which I knew nothing at the time but which later caused me much distress. My father, who had taken over Lord Kitchener's duties at the War Office during his absence abroad, had settled many contentious matters between the War Office and the Ministry of Munitions. But the most serious problem which occupied his mind was that of bringing about a change in the Command-in-Chief in the field. He was convinced that such a change should now be made. In his own words, "I had for some time past felt fears and growing doubts as to Sir John French's capacity to stand the strain of his task with its ever-increasing and unforeseeable responsibilities." [12] He had of course talked the matter over with Lord Kitchener who shared his misgivings but was not inclined himself to make a change. My father had no doubt that Sir Douglas Haig was the right man to succeed Sir John French as Commander-in-Chief. He entrusted to Lord Esher, an old and intimate friend of Sir John French (then on service in Paris), the delicate task of seeing Sir John and telling him the decision he had reached. Lord Esher carried out his mission with consummate tact. Sir John wrote to my father in generous terms, thanking him for all his personal kindness, accepting his decision without question and suggesting that he should come over to London to discuss matters. He arrived after I had left for abroad so that though I knew the object of his visit I heard nothing of their conversations, in the course of which he mentioned to my father his intention of giving Winston the command of a brigade. To this my father demurred, pointing out that such an appointment given to a politician who, despite his military genius, had never held a command in the field would be certain to unleash a flood of criticism, *sotto voce* in the Army and outspoken in the House of Commons.

These predictions were verified all too soon. Rumors that Winston was to be given a brigade soon got about and in due course reached the House of Commons. His many enemies in the Tory party whose vindictive spleen remained unslaked even by his fall from office put down questions. On December 16th Sir C. Hunter asked the Under-Secretary of State for War whether Major Winston Churchill had been promised the command of an infantry brigade; whether this officer had ever commanded a battalion of infantry; and for how many weeks he had served at the front as an infantry officer. The Under-Secretary of State for War, Mr. Tennant, replied, "I have no knowledge myself and have not been able to obtain any, of a promise of command of an infantry brigade having been made to my right honourable and gallant Friend referred to in the question. On the second point I have consulted books of reference and other authentic sources of information, and the result of my investigations is that my right honourable and gallant Friend has never commanded a battalion of infantry. No report has been made to the War Office of the movements of Major the Right Honourable Winston L. S. Churchill since he proceeded to France on the 19th November. If he has been serving as an infantry officer between that date and to-day, the answer to the last part of the question would be about four weeks." (Laughter.)

Sir C. Hunter: "Will my right honourable Friend let me know if he is promised a command of an infantry battalion?" (Cries of "Why not?") Sir C. Scott Robertson: "Is not the question absurd on the face of it, Major Winston Churchill being under 60 years of age?" (Laughter.) Mr. E. Cecil: "Is the right honourable Gentleman aware that if his appointment were made it would be thought by very many persons both inside and outside this House a grave scandal?" (Cries of "Oh.") [13]

This passage of arms at question time in the House of Commons reveals the malignity with which Winston was still pursued by his enemies and also the fact that he still had many friends.

When within a month Sir John French was succeeded as Commander-in-Chief by Sir Douglas Haig the matter was still in abeyance and Haig offered Winston the command of a battalion of the 6th Royal Scots Fusiliers. This was no doubt a keen disappointment to Winston and (though he never mentioned it to me) he is said to have deeply resented my father's opposition to French's suggestion. This caused me great distress, for no shadow had fallen between them when he left the Admiralty. He understood only too well that my father was acting against all his personal inclination under the duress of a shotgun Coalition caused by Lord Fisher's desertion. Again when Winston resigned from the Government on losing his seat on the War Council my father had begged him to stay on and play his part in the Cabinet. On this occasion he felt that the appointment would make Winston once more the target of attacks and would be difficult to defend on military grounds. In *Politicians and the War* Lord Beaverbrook describes him as being "apparently frightened." [14] My father's only fears were on Winston's behalf.

I agree nevertheless with Lord Beaverbrook in thinking that Winston would have made "an invaluable adviser to any Commander-in-Chief," and for such a post had it been offered my father would have whole-heartedly supported him. Lord Beaverbrook has written that "Bonar Law was very strongly pressed to help Churchill to an appointment of this kind. He responded with an unswerving antagonism to Churchill. He thought that to give Churchill an influence on the conduct of affairs in France would be a disaster. Lloyd George would not give any countenance to projects for Churchill's preferment." [15] There is no doubt in my mind that Sir John French would have welcomed him in this capacity. Whether Sir Douglas Haig would have done so I cannot say. But that his genius and dynamic power in thought and action should have been wasted at such a moment on the command of a battalion seemed to me to be sheer tragedy.

Yet he flung himself into the task with the zest and concentration with which he invested the smallest as well as the greatest things in life. Nothing that he touched was ever done by halves.

A small paper-back (published in 1924) called *With Winston Churchill at the Front* by Captain Gibb gives an amusing account of the impression he made on his new command. The regiment was born in 1678 and the battalion, which was one of the "First Hundred Thousand," had won laurels at the Battle of Loos. The men were mostly Lowland Scots, many of them miners from the Ayrshire coal fields. When Captain Gibb was told by a Transport Officer with whom he was "exchanging rumours" that Winston Churchill was coming to take over the battalion he determined not to be outdone and retorted that Lord Curzon had been made Transport Officer of the adjoining battalion and was already in a position to "teach him." When, however, it turned out that the rumor was not a leg-pull but the sober truth Captain Gibb records that as the news spread "a mutinous spirit grew. Everybody liked the old C.O. and nobody could see why any prominent outsider should come in and usurp his place so easily." [16]

Battalion headquarters were in a tumble-down and "more than usually dirty farm," inhabited by "more than usually dirty and unprepossessing farm people." It was only one thousand yards from the sector of the front line called "Plugstreet" (Ploegsteert) and according to Winston, it therefore made little difference whether they were in or out of the trenches as they lost about the same number of men through shell-fire. Three hundred yards separated their front-line trenches from those of the Germans.

Whatever the feelings of the battalion Winston's advent produced a flutter among the dirty farm ladies who "rose up to the accompaniment of loud whispers of 'Monsieur le ministre!' . . . 'Ah, c'est lui?' 'C'est votre ministre?' and in this way imparted to the proceedings at once an irregular air of friendliness and international colour." [17] Winston immediately set about knowing his officers, scrutinizing them "silently and intently from head to foot." He then proceeded to address them: " 'War is declared, gentlemen,' he began, 'on the lice. . . .' With these words did the great scion of the house of Marlborough first address his Scottish Captains assembled in council." [18] He then delivered a masterly biography of the louse as a factor in wars ancient and modern and called for concerted measures for the "utter extermination of all the lice in the battalion." After four days of unsavory toil with hot irons and other lethal instruments a triumphant victory was won. The 6th Royal Scots Fusiliers became a liceless battalion.

He made other innovations. One of them was singing on the march, a practice which halves fatigue but which he found it hard to inculcate because the knowledge of words to sing was "at a premium." He had his own ideas on the laying of sandbags and bricks, the building of parapets and traverses and parados, the devising of shelters and scarps and counterscarps and dugouts and half-moons and ravelins. (How he must have enjoyed rolling out these romantic names—suggesting as they did Shakespearean stratagems, the glorious conceits of heraldry and not just digging in the mud!)

We read that "early and late he was in the line. . . . Just as the enemy field guns began, the Colonel came along to our trench and suggested a view over the parapet. As we stood up on the fire-step we felt the wind and swish of several whizzbangs flying past our heads, which, as it always did, horrified me. Then I heard Winston say in a dreamy, far-away voice: 'Do you like War?' The only thing to do was to pretend not to hear him. At that moment I profoundly hated war. But at that and every moment I believe Winston Churchill revelled in it. There was no such thing as fear in him. . . . No commanding officer ever was more interested in or more attentive to his wounded. On the one hand he was utterly impervious to all feelings of aversion from the unpleasant sights of war and I have seen him . . . sitting calmly discussing questions of state with 'Archie' in blood-saturated surroundings: but on the other he was always first on the scene of misfortune and did all in his power to help and comfort and cheer." [19]

"Archie" was Winston's close and dear friend Sir Archibald Sinclair *

* Now Viscount Thurso.

whom he had somehow managed to extract from the 2nd Life Guards and attach to the Royal Scots Fusiliers as his Second-in-Command. They had first met at Maxine Elliott's house near Maidenhead and were immediately attracted to one another. Both were passionate polo players and both loved talking. Some years before the war Winston had persuaded Archie to go into politics and to stand for Parliament as a Liberal at the next election. He was a romantic figure, gay, gallant and good-looking, the owner of one hundred thousand acres of Caithness in the northernmost tip of Scotland. Archie was in every sense the king of that wild and beautiful domain—great tracts of hill and moorland, spangled with lochs, through which the Thurso River runs from its source to the sea. It was not only his heritage but he was its Lord-Lieutenant and was to become its representative in Parliament. Here with tireless activity and skill he fished for salmon and walked for miles across the heather in pursuit of stags and grouse. In 1916 few could have foreseen that he was destined, in the thirties, to become the Leader of the Liberal Party, to fight the battle against Appeasement with a courage second to none and hold the office of Secretary of State for Air in the National Government, from 1940 onward throughout the Second World War. Winston was his political godfather and remained his constant friend though their political paths occasionally diverged. They delighted in one another's society even when both poured out a Niagara of words, as often happened, simultaneously. I had a very slight acquaintance with Archie before the First World War (though in after years he was to become one of my dearest friends) and for this reason I can only remember one characteristic story he told me of his days with Winston in the Royal Scots Fusiliers. On one occasion a very pompous and unpopular military bigwig—in rank a Brigadier—visited their battalion headquarters after it had been badly damaged by shelling. He sent for Winston and told him that *this really would not do,* that he ought to get something more effective done for the protection of the men, in short that he must make it *safe.* He ended up with the words, "You know it's dangerous—it's positively *dangerous.*" "Yes Sir," replied Winston, "but you know this is a very dangerous war."

Captain Gibb ends his account with a tribute to the "complete conquest" achieved by Winston in two or three short months over "men of a race not easily moved and won over." Those months were the author's most treasured "war memory." He quotes Winston's words of encouragement in difficult moments. "War is a game to be played with a smiling face." "And never," he adds, "was precept more consistently practised than this." [20]

His smile was not a mask. He still loved "the bright eyes of danger," action and adventure. But these no longer sufficed to meet the needs of his whole being. He was homesick for the bigger battlefield he had left behind. His mind was seething with ideas and starved of outlet. Already in November he had written, at Sir John French's request, a memorandum entitled "Variants of the Offensive" dealing among other things with the use of tanks (then known as Caterpillars) "used in large numbers by surprise with smoke and other devices." He had sent a copy to the Committee of Imperial Defence. Would it be heeded or pigeon-holed? He wanted once more to influence great events from the center of power. He felt remote, forgotten, ineffectual.

My two elder brothers were both in France, Raymond in the Grenadiers, Beb * in the Artillery. To our great joy my brother Oc came home on his first leave in the spring. My father had not seen him since he sailed for the Dardanelles and I not since we parted in Alexandria in June. He gave a memorable and moving account of the last months in Gallipoli and of the final evacuation from Cape Helles. The Naval Division was among the last to leave. I said how I wished that Winston were not away in France and could be with us to hear it. My father then told us that he had just heard that Winston was back on a week's leave, that he intended to speak on the Navy Estimates on the seventh and that he and Margot had been invited to meet him at dinner on the sixth. When they returned from this dinner party Margot, who had sat next to him, told me that she had said to him that she was sorry he was going to speak in the debate and that he had replied "with a glare in his eye" that he had "a good deal of importance to say about the Navy." She said that she then told him what a "fine exit" he had made, giving up money and position, taking his place with his fellows and risking his life for his country, and added, "Don't go and spoil it all." Later he asked her whether she thought a proper Opposition in the House of Commons would be a good, or a bad, thing for the country. She said she could not see the elements of a good Opposition in Dalziel, Markham, Mond, Carson, etc., and added that she could not see him co-operating with the Simon group. I cannot vouch for the accuracy of Margot's reports of conversations but this one struck me as having an alarming degree of plausibility. She was convinced that Win-

* Herbert Asquith.

ston was "dreaming of an amazing Opposition which he was to lead." My father told me that he had had a short private talk with Winston after dinner and feared that he was going to make a most unwise speech which could do him nothing but harm. He had done his best to dissuade him from it but evidently felt that he had failed. I said that I was surprised at not having had a word or a sign from him since he got back. My father replied, "That doesn't surprise me in the least in view of his intentions."

I felt deep misgivings as we set out for the House of Commons next day—my father, Margot, Oc and myself. The debate lives in my memory as one of the most painful I have ever listened to. Arthur Balfour opened by introducing the Navy Estimates and Winston followed him. In his opening sentences he gave notice to the House that in his remarks that afternoon "I shall have to strike a jarring note, a note not of reproach, nor of censure, nor of panic, but a note in some respects of warning." He then paid tribute to Sir John Jellicoe, Sir Doveton Sturdee and Sir David Beatty and made it clear that it was not the men responsible for maneuvering and handling the fleet but the forces at their disposal in relation to the forces of the enemy which were causing him anxiety.

Were the programs of construction which the present First Lord had inherited from himself, Prince Louis and Lord Fisher being executed "at full blast"—were they being executed punctually?

He had received from sources on which he must to some extent rely impressions of a less completely satisfactory and reassuring kind than would be derived from the statement of the Minister responsible. . . . "We do not know what Germany has done, an impenetrable veil . . . has fallen for eighteen months over the German dockyards, naval and commercial. . . . We are bound to assume that Germany has completed every vessel begun before the War. . . . If, therefore, the German ships have been completed and ours have not been so completed, then I say that serious and solid reasons must be required in the case of each vessel to justify and explain its postponement or delay. . . . A shortage in naval material . . . would give no chance of future recovery. . . . I say advisedly that . . . the Admiralty must not think the battle over. They must forthwith hurl themselves with renewed energy into their task, and press it forward without the loss of a day. . . . A strategic policy for the Navy, purely negative in character, by no means necessarily implies that the path of greatest prudence is being followed. I wish to place on record that the late Board would certainly not have been content with an attitude of pure passivity during the whole of the year 1916. . . . I cannot understand myself why all these many months, with resources far greater than those which Lord Fisher and I ever possessed, it has not been found possible to carry on the policy of raiding" [21] (i.e., Zeppelin sheds).

All this was calculated to shake the confidence of the House in the energy, initiative and determination of the present Board of Admiralty and to arouse fears that Germany was secretly outbuilding us. Some listeners wondered anxiously what conclusions Germany might draw from this frank expression by our late First Lord of his misgivings about the present state of our Navy. But there was worse to come. "I have not spoken to-day," he said, "without intending to lead up to a conclusion." What was that conclusion? I could not believe my ears when I heard Winston's own voice demanding as a necessary condition of our national salvation—the recall of Lord Fisher to the Admiralty. He recalled that "when in November, 1914, Prince Louis of Battenberg . . . felt it his duty to retire . . . I was certain that there was only one man who could succeed him. . . . I was sure that there was no one who possessed the power, the insight, and energy of Lord Fisher. I therefore made it plain that I would work with no other Sea Lord. In this way the oppositions, naval and otherwise, which have always, perhaps not unnaturally, obstructed Lord Fisher's faithful footsteps, were overcome. . . . I did not believe it possible that our very cordial and intimate association would be ruptured, but the stress and shocks of this war are tremendous. . . . We parted on a great enterprise upon which the Government had decided . . . and in which the fortunes of a struggling and ill-supported Army were already involved. It stood between us as a barrier. I therefore should have resisted, on public grounds, the return of Lord Fisher to the Admiralty—and I have on several occasions expressed this opinion in the strongest terms to the Prime Minister and the First Lord of the Admiralty. We have now reached an entirely different situation. . . . The existence of our country and of our cause depend upon the Fleet. . . . No personal consideration must stand between the country and those who can serve her best. I feel that there is in the present Admiralty administration, for all their competence, loyalty and zeal, a lack of driving force and mental energy which cannot be allowed to continue, which must be rectified while time remains and before evil results, and can only be rectified in one way. I am sure the nation and the Navy expect that the necessary step will be taken. . . . I urge the First Lord of the Admiralty without delay to fortify himself, to vitalize and animate his Board of Admiralty by recalling Lord Fisher to his post as First Sea Lord. . . ."

Had I gone mad? Had Winston? He had spoken in calm and measured terms, without excitement and with the utmost deliberation. His speech, as always, had been most carefully prepared. What possessed him? I remembered long talks in which he had poured out his heart to me about Fisher, his vacillations, his constant resignations (my father and I once counted up nine), his desertion. Fisher was responsible for the forced Coalition, for Winston's exile from the office he loved so dearly, in part at least for the failure of the Dardanelles. He had dealt with him faithfully in his resignation speech. Could he possibly believe in the course which he was advocating? It would be unlike him to swerve from his convictions. Yet, if he believed in it he must surely be deranged?

I left the gallery when he sat down feeling unable to face what was to follow. I followed Margot to my husband's room. He was speechless. Eddie Marsh (who never attempted to pass judgment on any speech, even Winston's, saying that he did not know a good speech from a bad one) had tears in his eyes and said to Margot tremulously, "Do you think he has done for himself?" For once she tempered the wind to the shorn lamb and replied, "He is young—and if he goes back and fights like a hero it will all be forgotten."

Rumors began to circulate as to how it all arose. It was said that when Winston returned on leave on March 2nd he did not even know the Naval Estimates were to be debated on the 7th; that he had dined with his mother who had invited Garvin (Editor of the *Observer*), to meet him. Other guests were mentioned, whose names I will not quote, as I feel quite sure that one of them at least, F. E. Smith, would never have advised Winston so unwisely. They were said to have told Winston he was the *homme nécessaire* who alone could save a rapidly deteriorating situation and urged him to take action and lead an Opposition in Parliament. C. P. Scott, Editor of the *Manchester Guardian* and one of Winston's most faithful and fervent supporters, was said to have been summoned by telegram. All this was said. I cannot say if all or any of it is accurate, though I think there is no doubt that Garvin played a leading part and that C. P. Scott's support was sought and enlisted. F. E. Smith told Margot later that he had been present at a luncheon in Cromwell Road at which Fisher was Winston's guest. I knew what agony this must have been to Clemmie, who had no illusions about Fisher or the ruin he had brought to Winston's fortunes. According to F. E. she had said to Fisher at luncheon, "Keep your hands off my husband. You have all but ruined him once. Leave him alone now." I only record this (which is hearsay at second hand) because I feel sure that whether she said it or not it expressed her feelings. There is certainly evidence that a plot or plan of some kind was being hatched and that Winston was its chosen instrument or tool. I remember as we left the House after the debate noticing a small group of sandwich-men parading between boards on which the words "We want Jacky back" were inscribed. This demonstration coincided suspiciously with the burden of Winston's unfortunate and, to me, inexplicable speech.

I longed, yet hesitated, to get in touch with him. That he had made no sign of any kind did not surprise me now. He knew exactly what I should have felt and said. I asked my father's advice the day after the debate. He told me that he had had a visit that morning from Lord Kitchener who informed him that Winston had just sent in his resignation from the Army. He had "asked to be relieved of his command in order to grapple with the political situation at home." My father felt that this would be a disastrous step for Winston to take at this moment ("suicidal" was the word he used to me), and he asked Lord Kitchener not to answer Winston's letter until he (my father) had seen him. He was obviously deeply anxious and unhappy about Winston and said to me that anyone who cared about his future should see him and urge him to go back to the front. We left for the House with heavy hearts to hear the end of the debate and I sent down a note to Winston suggesting that we should meet either at Downing Street or elsewhere.

Arthur Balfour made a devastating reply to Winston's speech which he described as "very unfortunate both in form and in substance. . . . In the first part he strove to arouse the doubts, misgivings, and suspicions about the strength of the Fleet and the energy of the present Board of Admiralty in dealing with national interests; and in the second part . . . he suggested a remedy that would, he thought, put an end to a condition of things which, if it existed, everybody would admit would be lamentable." In refuting Winston's charges with chapter and verse Mr. Balfour said, "Of course, there are degrees of crime. It is a much better and a much less serious attack upon public policy to suggest suspicions which really on examination have no foundation at all than to suggest suspicions, fears, and misgivings which have a foundation. It is one of the cases in which the greater the truth the greater the injury to the public, and, therefore, I admit that in the charges which my right honourable Friend has levelled against the present Board of Admiralty he has not done nearly the same injury to the public interest as he would have done supposing his charges had been well-founded." All this was effective and convincing defense. When he came to the remedy proposed by Winston for these imaginary ills, he went into the attack. "I do not imagine that there was a single person who heard my right honourable Friend's speech who did not listen to this latter part of it with profound stupefaction. My right honourable Friend has often astonished the House, but I do not think he ever astonished it so much as when he came down to explain that the remedy for all our ills, so far as the Navy is concerned, is to get rid of Sir Henry Jackson and to put in his place Lord Fisher. My right honourable Friend has never made the smallest concealment, either in public or in private, of what he thought of Lord Fisher. . . . What did he say when he made what at the time he thought was his farewell speech, when he exchanged a political for a military career? He told us that the First Sea Lord, Lord Fisher, did not give him, when he was serving in the same Admiralty with him, either the clear guidance before the event or the firm support after it which he was entitled to expect. . . . My right honourable Friend had six months in which to meditate over his relations with Lord Fisher before he made that considered judgement, and anybody who knows my right honourable Friend is aware that when he makes one of these great speeches they are not the unpremeditated effusions of a hasty moment. . . ."

Arthur Balfour then quoted the words Winston had used the day before in the debate, "that he would have resisted on public grounds the return of Lord Fisher to the Admiralty and had on several occasions expressed this opinion in the strongest terms to the Prime Minister and the First Lord of the Admiralty. . . . I do not know what Lord Fisher thought of that apology. I know that if a friend of mine had made it about me I should regard it as the deepest insult that could be offered. It means that because Lord Fisher . . . disapproved of the expedition to Gallipoli, therefore, in the opinion of my right honourable Friend, although the Army was involved, he could not be trusted to carry out effectively and vigorously the measures necessary in order to support the Army. If that were true, it is almost high treason. I do not believe for a moment that it is true. 'But,' says the right honourable Gentleman, 'that is all over.' . . . Who ever got up in this House and commended to a Government the acceptance of the services of a great public servant in a great position of public responsibility on the ground that he could not be adequately trusted to do his work when he disapproved of the policy of the Government, but that he could be trusted to carry it out when he approved of it?" . . . Then followed a well-deserved eulogy of Sir Henry Jackson. "When the right honourable Gentleman comes down to this House, and, without a tittle of evidence . . . suggests to the Government that this great public servant should be turned adrift in order to introduce in his place a man . . . who, according to the right honourable Gentleman himself, has not done that which is his first duty to do, namely, to give guidance and advice to the First Lord and his colleagues in the Cabinet, [this] seems to me the most amazing proposition that has ever been laid before the House of Commons. I should regard myself as contemptible beyond the power of expression if I were to yield an inch to a demand of such a kind, made in such a way." [22]

He sat down in a storm of cheering and Winston made a short and (inevitably) lame reply, calling Arthur Balfour "a master of Parliamentary sword-play, and of every dialectical art" and making him "a present of all the rhetorical and debating retorts" which he could derive from the "fertile field" of his relations with Lord Fisher.

But there was really nothing to be said or done. Even Admiral Sir Hedworth Meux, an old and faithful friend, had spoken against him, both in sorrow and in anger, the day before, accusing him of "intrigue" ("That is the meaning of this intrigue—to turn out the Government, nothing else") and ending with the words, "We all wish him a great deal of success in France, and we hope that he will stay there." [23]

Winston sent me a note asking me to meet him at his mother's house in Mayfair. I found him alone there. He looked pale, defiant, on the defensive. I shall never forget the pain of the talk which followed. I knew better than to criticize, reproach or even ask the question that gnawed at me—"What possessed you? *Why* did you do it?" I saw at once that, whatever his motive, he realized that he had hopelessly failed to accomplish what he set out to do. His lance was broken. What he had conceived as a great gesture of magnanimity—the forgiveness of the wrongs Fisher had done to him for the sake of a greater aim, our naval supremacy—had not been interpreted as such. It was regarded instead as a clumsy gambler's throw for his own ends. It was thus expressed by the *Morning Post* in its political notes. " 'What is he after?' is the question members asked each other in the Lobby after Colonel Churchill had spoken. A very general impression of the intention of the speaker was thus summarized by one legislator of epigrammatic turn, 'See what a fine First Lord you had and what a First Lord you have.' " [24] Just or unjust this was, I fear, the general consensus.

I had not seen him since our farewell luncheon at Cromwell Road in November, two days before he left for the front. My first words were of the joy of his safe return, the miracle of the evacuation of Gallipoli, of his own experience since—but I knew that his attention was perfunctory and his mind elsewhere. After a pause he said, "I suppose you are against me like the rest of them." I said that he knew well that I could never be against him, but that I was strongly against reinvesting Fisher with any sort of authority as he had proved himself quite unfit for it. I could never trust him again and I was amazed that Winston could bring himself to do so. "You may forgive what he has done to you. You have not the right to forgive the ruin he has brought on others and on the Dardanelles campaign." He sheered off the Dardanelles and said that he knew from private sources that things were going badly at the Admiralty; that Fisher's fire and drive could pull it out of the rut, reanimate it, speed it forward, etc., etc. "Arthur's never been exactly a dynamo at the best of times." I did not pursue the argument but after a time asked what his plans were. Was it true, as my father had told me, that he thought of resigning from the Army, here and now, and not returning to France? He said it was. He had come to the conclusion that it was right for him to remain here and exercise what influence he had at the heart of affairs. Many others thought so too. He had many friends and supporters (this rather militantly) including the *Manchester Guardian*. Had I read it that morning?

He had had a bad press as was only to be expected and the *Manchester Guardian* alone had given him wholehearted support. "The defect of this Government, has been the lack of weighty, instructed, responsible opposition. . . . We believe that Mr. Churchill can best serve his country in his old character of a Parliamentarian. Fresh blood is wanted, fresh life with criticism, originality and driving-power in administration. Mr. Churchill's speech reminds us how much poorer we have been in such qualities since he left us." [25] I said that I had read it and of course I agreed that he could give greater service in Parliament than in the field. It was for this reason that my father had begged him to remain a member of the Cabinet and play his part there when he lost his seat on the War Council. Then followed the heartbreaking task of trying to persuade him—for his own sake, for the sake of his future power to influence events—to return to France. It was a difficult and agonizing endeavor, because I did not want to enhance his sense of failure by stressing the fact that he had fatally weakened his own position by his speech, and that by leaving the Army now he would injure it still further. But far worse was the dreadful thought that if my words had any effect at all I might be urging him to go back to his death. I told myself that I could not possibly influence or move him by an inch from his resolve, that he had shown no signs of being moved from it. . . . Yet when I left him I was haunted by this nightmare possibility and wondered weakly *what* I really wanted him to do?

Next day he came to see my father at 10 Downing Street. I found my father deeply moved after their talk and asked him what had passed between them. He told me that he had reminded Winston how his father, Lord Randolph (to whom my father was devoted), had committed political suicide through one impulsive action. He had said, "If I can, I want to save you from doing the same thing. You will know that nothing but affection prompts me. It is because I care for you that I shall save you." He said that Winston had tears in his eyes when they parted and that he was sure that he would go back to France. He added that it was strange how little Winston knew of the attitude of others toward himself. He had spoken to my father, as he did to me, of the many ardent supporters who looked to him for leadership and my father had said to him, "At the moment you have none who count at all." One of the things which saddened my father most about this episode was that he was always watching and hoping for an opportunity when the climate of opinion in the Tory party would change and enable him to bring Winston back into the Government. Alas, "at this moment he has few political friends inside it or outside, nor is there a single office he could be given." I said the wheel must turn. "He will, he *must,* come back some day. If only he isn't killed. . . . Supposing that he were killed—what should *we* feel, those of us who have urged him to go back?" My father said, "I could only advise him to do what I am sure is right—right above all for his own sake." Next day Winston wrote to my father that he had decided to go back to France.

But it was not to be for long. Early in May it had been decided to amalgamate the 6th and 7th battalions of the Royal Scots Fusiliers and as Winston was the Junior Colonel he lost his command. He would then no doubt have been eligible for a brigade, but he no longer wanted one. He wanted above all things to be back on his old battlefield in Parliament. Duty and desire both tugged in the same direction (and who can say which pulled the harder?). He wrote to Lord Kitchener asking to be released from the Army. Lord Kitchener, knowing that he faced criticism whatever his reply, accepted Winston's resignation on condition that he undertook not to apply for military service again during the war.

In the meantime many fateful events had taken place and these, though Winston played no part in them, cannot go unrecorded.

At the end of March my father visited Italy at the invitation of the King, accompanied by my husband, Colonel Hankey and Mr. Hugh O'Beirne, a diplomatist of great charm and ability. Though Italy had declared war on Austria she was not yet at war with Germany and it was thought desirable to establish closer links with her and draw her into the heart of the Alliance. They spent three useful days in Rome and then went north to the fighting fronts of the Isonzo and the Julian Alps. Here my father found the King living in a small farm in a single room which served him both as bedroom and study. They had long talks and drove around the mountain fronts together. The Italians were on the offensive and there was not an Austrian soldier on Italian soil. Lord Hankey has written that "the visit was not without influence in determining Italy to declare war on Germany, which she did on August 28th." [26]

On his return on April 6th my father had to face another Cabinet crisis. His colleagues were once more rent with dissension on the issue of compulsory military service. The Act passed in January had failed to produce the necessary number of recruits. On that measure he had received the resignation of four Liberal colleagues, of Mr. Arthur Henderson, the Labour member of the Cabinet, and of the two other Labour Ministers. Now compulsion must be extended. The Conservative Party had always believed in conscription and hankered after it even in peacetime; to most Liberals and to Labour it was anathema and only accepted as a dire necessity in war. Ministers would have found it easier to reach agreement had they felt confident that they could carry their parties with them. This was especially true of Mr. Bonar Law who was always looking over his shoulder to see if he was being followed. "I believe," he wrote to my father, "that it is easier for you to obtain the consent of your party to general compulsion than for me to obtain the consent of my party to its not being adopted"—a plea which reveals the inherent weakness of a coalition. As Conservative Leader Mr. Bonar Law felt himself to be answerable first and foremost to his party, whereas my father as Leader of the Government owed an equal duty to all parties. On this occasion he was convinced that it was essential in the national interest to retain the support of Labour both in Parliament and in the country.

The breakup of the Government was narrowly averted by the skill and infinite patience with which he held it together. After two days of secret session an agreement was finally reached and a Bill was passed conscripting all men between the ages of eighteen and twenty-one.

The Government had not yet weathered this storm when another burst upon them. During the night of April 20th a German auxiliary, disguised as a neutral merchant ship and carrying arms and ammunition, was intercepted and sunk off the coast of Ireland. Her German crew was captured. On the following day Sir Roger Casement was landed in Kerry by a German submarine, recognized by a coast guard and taken prisoner.* On Easter Monday, April 24th, a body of Sinn Fein Volunteers seized the Post Office and other public buildings in Dublin, looted, set fire to houses, and murdered British soldiers in the streets. Reinforcements were rushed to Dublin from England and Belfast, Sir John Maxwell was placed in command and after six days of fighting the Rebellion was suppressed and its leaders arrested. Fifteen of these were tried by court-martial and executed and two thousand of their followers were interned in England. Our dear friend Augustine Birrell, the Chief Secretary for Ireland, resigned and my father accepted his resignation "with infinite regret."

My father realized only too well that though the Rebellion was crushed Sinn Fein remained, and that the rebels who had been executed would be hallowed as martyrs while the Irish civilians they had killed might well be forgotten.† He told the House of Commons that he felt it was his immediate duty to go to Ireland and consult with the civil and military authorities and within a few hours he and my husband left for Dublin. He was more than ever determined to seek and find a solution in conciliation and to resist those who were urging the barren expedient of coercion. He conferred with General Maxwell, Lord Wimborne (the Viceroy), the Attorney General and others, visited the wounded soldiers in hospital and the Sinn Fein prisoners (many of whom had taken no part in the rising and ought not to have been arrested). He returned convinced that immediate action must be taken to prevent a landslide of the Nationalist movement to Sinn Fein.

He succeeded in persuading his Unionist colleagues to consent to negotiations with the Irish leaders with a view to bringing the Home Rule Act into operation straightaway. It seemed a heaven-sent miracle

---

* Sir Roger Casement, born in Dublin (1864), entered the British Consular Service and made his name by his remarkable report on the Belgian atrocities in the Congo. After his retirement in 1912 he devoted his life to the cause of Irish Independence. After his arrest on April 21, 1916, he was tried for treason in London and executed on August 3rd.

† The civilian casualties were 180 killed and 614 wounded.

when an agreed plan was arrived at by Mr. Lloyd George, Mr. Redmond and Sir Edward Carson and accepted both by the Nationalists and by the Ulster Unionists. But in spite of Mr. Balfour's strong and unqualified support it was vehemently opposed by some Unionist members of the Cabinet, headed by Lord Lansdowne and Mr. Walter Long. In the end the settlement was deliberately wrecked by Lord Lansdowne's speech in the House of Lords which Mr. Redmond described as "a gross insult to Ireland." He reminded the House of Commons that 150,-000 Irishmen were serving in the armed forces and that "England was wasting another, and possibly her last, opportunity." [27] Once more the blind prevailed over those who had eyes to see.

Within a week of the Irish Rebellion the Battle of Jutland took place —our greatest sea battle since the days of Nelson. On the evening of May 30th the Admiralty knew that the German Fleet was preparing to put to sea. This knowledge reached them through the "usual channels." "Without the cryptographers' department," wrote Winston Churchill, "there would have been no Battle of Jutland. But for that department, the whole course of the naval war would have been different." [28] My first suspicions were aroused when, late in the afternoon of the following day, B. telephoned to say that Maurice Hankey would like to spend the night with us at Dorset House (our new home to which we had now moved from Downing Street). I knew from experience that a visit from Maurice Hankey meant that some critical event was impending, and I waited in suspense for B.'s return. He flashed back for a few minutes before dinner and told me in closest secrecy that Maurice Hankey had come from the Admiralty to the House of Commons with a secret message from Arthur Balfour to my father that a Fleet action was "imminent." He then went back to the Admiralty to await events. When he returned with Maurice Hankey well after midnight they feared the action might be broken off.

This was, however, not the case. All through the next day (June 1st) the fighting was going on and driblets of news were coming through from the Admiralty, mostly, alas, of our heavy losses, though we tried to take comfort in the hope that the German casualties might be heavier than our own. But by the evening of the following day (June 2nd) we were shattered to hear that we had lost three battle cruisers, three armored cruisers and certainly eight destroyers (possibly more) against one German battleship, a problematical second battleship and some light cruisers and destroyers (this though our superiority in battle cruisers was two to one). Nothing had been made public so far and my poker mask weighed heavily on me. It was only on the following morning (June 3rd) that the Admiralty communiqué, drafted the night before, was published in the press.

It was a disastrous document giving the impression that we had suffered a major naval defeat. The *Times* presented it under banner headlines:

GREAT NAVAL BATTLE

HEAVY LOSSES

6 BRITISH CRUISERS SUNK

8 DESTROYERS LOST

Although the official communiqué said that "the enemy's losses were serious" it was unable to assess their extent. Everyone was steeped in gloom. The Germans announced a triumphant victory over the British Fleet, both to their own people and to America. Meanwhile news of the German losses began to filter in from secret sources and present a more balanced picture of the battle. In Government circles there was indignant criticism and condemnation of the Admiralty's original communiqué. (I remember my stepmother exclaiming that she would like to strangle the man responsible for it. That man, alas, was Arthur Balfour.)

Winston, who had now returned from France, issued a reassuring statement to the press in which he declared that our margin of superiority was "in no way impaired" and that "the hazy weather, the fall of night and the retreat of the enemy alone frustrated the persevering effort of our brilliant Commanders Sir John Jellicoe and Sir David Beatty to reach a final decision." Those who would have given him good marks for this attempt to put things in perspective and restore public morale were still so incensed by his speech on the Navy Estimates that their only comment was "Comes well from *him*."

He has given a dramatic and detailed account of the battle in *The World Crisis, 1916-1918*,[29] in which he claims that he has "tried to steer a faithful and impartial passage." He writes truly that "there was no victory for anyone." [30] But he is clearly critical of Sir John Jellicoe for erring on the side of caution and gives as examples three crucial moments when, in his view, "the chance of an annihilating victory had perhaps been offered" [31]—adding, "Three times is a lot." Yet he admits: "The standpoint of the Commander-in-Chief of the British Grand Fleet was unique. . . . It might fall to him as to no other man—Sovereign, Statesman, Admiral or General—to issue orders which in the space of *two or three hours* might nakedly decide who won the war. The destruction of the British Battle Fleet was final. Jellicoe was the only man on either side who could lose the war in an afternoon." [32] No one realized his awful responsibility more deeply than Jellicoe himself.

The British people had dreamed of a Trafalgar. In Jutland they experienced perhaps their bitterest disappointment of the war. Yet Lord Hankey is right when he records that "From the point of view of the grand strategy, however . . . Jutland was as sweeping a success as Trafalgar." [33] For never again did the German Navy attempt to challenge us to battle on the high seas. The North Sea remained inviolate until the day when the German Fleet sailed to its final surrender at Scapa Flow.

Three days after the Battle of Jutland the nation was stunned by the news of the death of Lord Kitchener—drowned in the North Sea off Scapa Flow where he had embarked on a mission to Russia. Within two hours of sailing the ship had struck a mine and sunk.

My father was moved to tears when he told us this tragic news. Alone among his colleagues he had loved Lord Kitchener. Alone he had inspired his trust. To the nation, to whom Kitchener was a legend, it was as though Nelson's Column had suddenly fallen at their feet. For years there were many who refused to believe in his death, invented strange myths to explain his disappearance and clung to the hope of his return. In their imagination he had been deified and gods cannot die.

The mission had been a closely guarded secret. For some time the Government had been feeling deep disquiet and anxiety about the state of affairs in Russia. She was suffering from an acute shortage of armaments and of credit and it was feared that she was contemplating a new offensive. It was decided that a member of the Government whose personality and prestige would commend him to the Russian Government should be sent to make a firsthand report on the situation. My father suggested that Mr. Lloyd George should go and he was eager to do so, provided that he were accompanied by a military expert. It then transpired that Lord Kitchener would like to go. (I remember wondering with amusement whether they would have found each other more congenial as fellow travelers than they were as colleagues.) While the question was still in the balance Mr. Lloyd George was put in charge of the negotiations which followed the Irish Rebellion and Lord Kitchener received from the Tsar an invitation to visit Russia which he accepted on May 27th.

My father records that "the last week of his life was a busy one and to him the happiest he had spent since the first day of the war." Despite his critics who "had said their worst" he received a vote of confidence from the House of Commons, which was carried by a sweeping majority. "On June 2nd, 1916 at his own suggestion, he attended a large private meeting of members of Parliament, addressed to them a memorable speech in vindication of his administration, and submitted himself to cross-examination. He completely carried his audience with him, and the meeting ended with a unanimous resolution of gratitude and admiration. On the evening of the same day he came to see me to say goodbye. He was in the highest spirits and described with gusto and humour some of his passages of arms with his hecklers at the House. He left the room gay, alert, elastic, sanguine. I never saw him again." [34]

Lord Kitchener left London on the evening of the fourth of June with the members of his mission, which included his devoted military secretary, Colonel Fitzgerald ("K.'s Fitz"), and Hugh O'Beirne, one of our most successful diplomatists in Russia, Paris and Sofia. Through an error O'Beirne went to Euston Station instead of to King's Cross and thus missed the train. He chartered a special train and managed to rejoin the others in time to share their doom. After lunching with Lord Jellicoe on his flagship, the *Iron Duke,* Lord Kitchener went on board the *Hampshire* * which was to take them to Archangel. A strong gale was blowing and the weather was so bad that Jellicoe asked him to delay his journey but Lord Kitchener refused. The *Hampshire* sailed at five and was escorted by two destroyers for the first two hours. The Captain then sent them back because the very heavy seas made it impossible for them to keep pace with the *Hampshire.* Soon afterward the ship struck a mine and sank within a quarter of an hour. All on board were drowned except a few members of the crew who managed to reach a nearby island. The faithful Fitzgerald's body alone was washed ashore.

Of Lord Kitchener's death Winston has written: "The sudden onrush of the night, the deep waters of the North, were destined to preserve him and his renown from the shallows." [35]

Except for brief glimpses in crowded rooms I had not seen Winston since he returned from France. Our first real interchange was in mid-June during a long and (to me) unforgettable week end we spent together in Sussex.

* The same cruiser on which he had come from Alexandria to meet us at Malta in 1912.

A strange eccentric figure, Claude Lowther by name, who possessed an inspired flair for recognizing and acquiring beautiful objects of all kinds, invited us to spend Friday to Monday with him at Herstmonceux, a fifteenth-century brick castle which, when he bought it in 1913, was hardly more than a ruined shell. He had salvaged and rebuilt it, repairing its broken walls and battlements and towers with the old bricks from the ruins. He had often described to me his work of re-creation and said how much he wished to show it to me. He now urged us to come and spend a Sunday there, telling me as an inducement (though I needed none) that I should find Winston and Clemmie in a house in the Park which he had either let or lent to them. My husband and I managed to scrape up just enough of our (strictly rationed) petrol to drive down on Friday evening and I shall never forget our first glimpse of this enchanted castle. It burst upon us suddenly as we came over the crest of a high ridge and looked down on a deep green bowl, overgrown with bracken and old oak trees. . . . There, below us, we saw rising a cluster of rose-colored towers, turning to gold and silver in the light of the setting sun—a castle in a dream which must surely dissolve and vanish at our approach? But it stood firm, even when we crossed the drawbridge over a grassy moat and passed through the great archway of a double gatehouse—to be greeted by Claude Lowther dressed in black knee breeches, black silk stockings and buckled shoes as though for a Court Ball. "But—is there a *party*?" I stammered breathlessly (not liking to ask point-blank whether the *King* was expected). "No— we are alone, except for Mrs. Cornwallis West who hasn't yet arrived. . . . Come and see a few of the rooms before dinner." And as we followed him through twilit medieval halls and galleries glowing with the glory of the Renaissance and libraries adorned with Grinling Gibbons carvings, I agreed with Horace Walpole who, when he visited the castle in 1752, had found it "as perfect as the first day."

When I came down to dinner I was startled by the sight of a vast ram, with muddy hoofs and clotted pelt, roaming at large among the priceless furniture and *objets d'art*. It broke into a sudden canter and nearly knocked down Mrs. West who screamed, "What *is* this animal doing here?" Our host replied, "This animal, as you call him, is my beloved Peter—the mascot of my Territorial Battalion, 'Lowther's Lambs.' He has the freedom of the castle and comes and goes when and where he chooses." He fortunately did not choose to come to dinner. Winston and Clemmie came. At the first glance I saw that he was overcast, not one whit happier than he had been on his last leave.

The talk was general, Mrs. West chattering briskly. Winston took little part in it and for me the evening was shadowed by his gloom. When we said good night he told me he was coming up next morning to paint in the garden and I said I would join him there.

I awoke to a burning June day and wandered through a postern gate over a bridge up to the garden—a green pleasance where herbaceous borders flowed in torrents of color against a background of old brick walls. Winston had not yet arrived there. His coming was heralded by a procession of gardeners bearing an easel, a large canvas, a chair, a box of paints and a bristling bundle of brushes—the whole armory of his new art. He followed in their wake clad in a white coat and hat and, having observed the light, chosen his site, deployed his man power and his apparatus, set to work. It was the first time I had ever seen him paint—an occupation he had started the year before after his fall from the Admiralty.

In *Painting as a Pastime* (one of his most enchanting and self-revealing books) he has described how painting came to his rescue in that dark moment of his life and the solace that it brought to him. "When I left the Admiralty at the end of May 1915 I still remained a member of the War Cabinet and the War Council. In this position I knew everything and could do nothing. The change from the intense executive activities of each day's work to the narrowly measured duties of a counsellor, left me gasping. Like a sea-beast fished up from the depths, or a diver too suddenly hoisted my veins threatened to burst from the fall in pressure. I had great anxiety and no means of relieving it; I had vehement convictions and small power to give effect to them. . . . I had long hours of utterly unwanted leisure in which to contemplate the frightful unfolding of war. At a moment when every fibre of my being was inflamed to action, I was forced to remain a spectator of the tragedy, placed cruelly in a front seat. And then it was that the Muse of Painting came to my rescue—out of charity and out of chivalry, because after all she had nothing to do with me—and said 'Are these toys any good to you? They amuse some people.'" [36] As I watched him with "these toys" I realized what a precious talisman she had put into his hands. She had endowed him with a new creative act and given him new tools to work with. As he painted his tensions relaxed, his frustration evaporated. He was as happy as a child with his new toys. "Just to paint is great fun. The colours are lovely to look at and delicious to squeeze out." (The squeezing obviously gave him a voluptuous kick.) He enjoyed every moment of it. He had been transported into "a wonderful new world of thought and craft, a sunlit garden gleaming with light and colour" in which he found "the old harmonies and symmetries in an entirely different language . . . an unceasing voyage of entrancing discovery . . ." and one in which "the first quality that is needed is Audacity." [37] And in his painting as in his life he has always loved bright colors, "rejoiced with the brilliant ones" and had little use for the "poor browns." Although in Heaven he hoped for a still gayer palette, on which orange and vermilion will be the "darkest, dullest colours," [38] he made good use of both on earth. I remember once in his early painting days when we were both staying in a country house, set in a monochrome of dull, flat, uneventful country, I went out to watch him paint, half wondering what he would make of it. Looking over his shoulder I saw depicted on his canvas range upon range of mountains rising dramatically behind the actual foreground. I searched the skies for a mirage and then inquired where they had come from, and he replied, "Well—I couldn't leave it quite as dull as all that." No landscape and no age in which he lived could ever be consigned to dullness. And in his age at least there was no need to snatch the brush out of the hands of Fate.

Watching him paint for the first time on that June morning I became suddenly aware that it was the only occupation I had ever seen him practice in silence. When golfing, bathing, rock climbing, building sand castles on the beach, even when playing bezique or bridge he talked— and thus enhanced for all the drama and excitement of these pastimes. But he painted silently, rapt in intense appraisal, observation, assessment of the scene he meant to capture and to transfer to his canvas. He has (characteristically) compared painting a picture to fighting a battle. "It is, if anything, more exciting than fighting it successfully. . . . It is the same kind of problem as unfolding a long, sustained, interlocked argument. . . . It is a proposition which, whether of few or numberless parts, is commanded by a single unity of conception. . . ." [39] Painting challenged his intellect, appealed to his sense of beauty and proportion, unleashed his creative impulse, and it was because he was thus once more wholly engaged that painting brought him peace. I felt that I was witnessing a miracle and poured out gratitude to Fate for bringing it about.

The spell was only broken once that day by the dull distant thunder of the cannonade in France. He broke off then, laid down his brush and spoke with bitterness of his position; of the unfair attacks upon him for the failure in Gallipoli, of his desire for a public inquiry, in which he could have the chance of vindicating himself, of the Government's duty to lay the relevant papers before Parliament; of his sense of unjust exclusion from the great world struggle in which he knew that he could play an essential part, of all the ideas he could pour into it—now running to waste in the sand. "They don't want to listen to me, or use me. They only want to keep me out." What could I say? I knew that it was true of the Conservative Ministers and of their rank and file. I knew that it was not true of my father. But (though I could not say it) I knew also that the Fisher speech had made it far more difficult for him to find an opening for Winston and to impose him on unwilling colleagues. I could not see the turn of the wheel which was going to bring him back although I knew that sometime, somehow it *must* come. I tried to say as much but the words rang hollow to us both and I was thankful when he turned back to his canvas and tension eased and the clouds lifted.

Thus passed two sunlit days in this strange, magic setting. I had throughout the sense of unreality I had experienced in my first glimpse of the glittering towers rising from the bracken-filled valley—that it must vanish and dissolve and leave us facing the stark world we lived in. And when on Sunday night we said good-by and drove back through the dark I saw ahead of me a parting of the ways between myself and Winston. As friends there was not, and could never be, a rift between us. But as an ally I was now useless to him. He felt himself to be an enemy of the Government from which he was an exile. (That he had freely chosen to leave it was irrelevant to his emotions.) My father was the Leader of that Government and my loyalty to him must range me in the enemy camp. Therefore, however fast our friendship, I could no longer be his militant accomplice, nor his confidante. In all that mattered most to him in life he felt I could no longer be "on his side." No words that passed between us bore this implication. I am quite sure that he himself was unaware of it. Yet with deep sorrow I realized and accepted it. And understanding him I understood it.

In the years that followed, though we never lost our way into each other's minds, and though at moments nothing counted but the unbroken human bond between us, there were times when our passionate disagreement was vehemently expressed; others when our differences seemed too deep to be bridged by words and silence fell between us— times of incomprehension and bewilderment. Until at last a day came when the paths that for so long had parted us suddenly met. And as they brought us face to face we knew that we were once more side by side.

SOME SIGNIFICANT DATES IN THE LIFE OF
WINSTON CHURCHILL

◄ ►

Born: November 30, 1874

1888   Entered Harrow

1893   Entered the Royal Military College at Sandhurst

1895   Entered Army. With Spanish forces in Cuba

1897   With Malakand Field Force

1898   With Tirah Expeditionary Force, Nile Expeditionary Force. At Battle of Omdurman. Published *The Story of the Malakand Field Force*

1899   Contested, and lost, his first election for the House of Commons. Published *The River War*

1899-1900   With the South African Light Horse in Boer War; correspondent for the *Morning Post.*

1900   Published *Savrola, London to Ladysmith via Pretoria,* and *Ian Hamilton's March*

1901   Entered House of Commons

1903   Published *Mr. Broderick's Army*

1906   Published *Lord Randolph Churchill*

1906-1908   Under Secretary of State for the Colonies

1908   Married Clementine Hozier. Published *My African Journey*

1908-1910   President of the Board of Trade

1910-1911   Home Secretary

1911-1915   First Lord of the Admiralty

1915   Chancellor of the Duchy of Lancaster

1916   Lieutenant-Colonel in France. Retired from Army

1917   Minister of Munitions

1918-1921   Secretary of State for War and Air

1921   Secretary of State for Air and the Colonies

1922   Secretary of State for the Colonies

1923-1929   Published *The World Crisis,* four volumes

1924-1929   Chancellor of the Exchequer

1930   Published *My Early Life*

1931   Published *The Eastern Front*

1932   Published *Thoughts and Adventures*

1933-1938   Published *Marlborough: His Life and Times,* four volumes

1937   Published *Great Contemporaries*

1938   Published *Arms and the Covenant*

1939   Published *Step by Step*

1939-1940   First Lord of the Admiralty

1940-1945   Prime Minister, First Lord of the Treasury, Minister of Defence

1941   Published *Into Battle*

1942   Published *The Unrelenting Struggle*

1943   Published *The End of the Beginning*

1944   Published *Onwards to Victory*

1945   Published *The Dawn of Liberation*

1945-1951   Leader of the Opposition

1946   Received Order of Merit. Published *Victory* and *Secret Session Speeches*

1948   Published *The Sinews of Peace, Painting as a Pastime,* and *The Gathering Storm* (Volume I of *The Second World War*)

1949   Published *Their Finest Hour* (Volume II of *The Second World War*)

1950   Published *Europe Unite* and *The Grand Alliance* (Volume III of *The Second World War*)

1951   Published *In the Balance* and *The Hinge of Fate* (Volume IV of *The Second World War*)

1951-1955   Prime Minister

1952   Published *Closing the Ring* (Volume V of *The Second World War*)

1953   Made Knight of the Garter. Awarded Nobel Prize for Literature. Published *Stemming the Tide*

1954   Published *Triumph and Tragedy* (Volume VI of *The Second World War*)

1956   Published *The Birth of Britain* and *The New World* (Volumes I and II of *A History of the English-Speaking Peoples*)

1957   Published *The Age of Revolution* (Volume III of *A History of the English-Speaking Peoples*)

1958   Published *The Great Democracies* (Volume IV of *A History of the English-Speaking Peoples*)

1959   Won election, his last, to the House of Commons

1963   Made honorary citizen of the United States

Died: January 24, 1965

LIST OF PRINTED SOURCES

Asquith, the Earl of Oxford and: *Memories and Reflections, 1852-1927,* 2
    vols. (Cassell, 1928)
                            Fifty Years of Parliament (Cassell, 1926)
Atkins, J. B.: *Incidents and Reflections* (Christophers, 1947)
Bacon, Admiral Sir R. H.: *The Life of Lord Fisher of Kilverstone,* 2 vols.
    (Hodder & Stoughton, 1929)
Baring, Maurice: *The Puppet Show of Memory* (Heinemann, 1922)
Beaverbrook, Lord: *Politicians and the War, 1914-1916,* 2 vols. (Thornton
    Butterworth, 1928)
Birkenhead, 2nd Earl of: *F.E., The Life of F. E. Smith, First Earl of Birken-
    head* (Eyre & Spottiswoode, 1959)
Blunt, Wilfrid S.: *My Diaries,* 2 vols. (Martin Secker, 1919)
Callwell, C. E.: *Field-Marshal Sir Henry Wilson,* 2 vols. (Cassell, 1927)
Churchill, W. S.: *The River War,* 2 vols. (Longmans, Green, 1899)
            London to Ladysmith (Longmans, Green, 1900)
            Lord Randolph Churchill, 2 vols. (Macmillan, 1906)
            My African Journey (Hodder & Stoughton, 1908)
            Liberalism and the Social Problem (Hodder & Stoughton,
                1909)
            The World Crisis, Vol. I, *1911-1914;* Vol. II, *1915;* Vol. III,
                1916-1918 (Thornton Butterworth, 1923-31)
            My Early Life (Odhams, 1930)
            Thoughts and Adventures (Odhams, 1932)
            Great Contemporaries (Thornton Butterworth, 1937)
            Painting as a Pastime (Odhams & Benn, 1948)
Dugdale, B. E. C.: *Arthur James Balfour, K.G., O.M., F.R.S.,* 2 vols. (Hutch-
    inson, 1930)
Ensor, R. C. K.: *England 1870-1914* (O.U.P., 1936)
Fitzroy, Sir Almeric: *Memoirs,* 2 vols. (Hutchinson, 1926)
Gardiner, A. G.: *Pillars of Society* (James Nisbet, 1913)
Gibb, Captain A. D.: *With Winston Churchill at the Front* (Gowans & Gray,
    1924)
Grey of Fallodon, Viscount: *Twenty-Five Years, 1892-1916* (Hodder &
    Stoughton, 1925)
Haldane, General Sir Aylmer: *A Soldier's Saga* (Blackwood, 1948)
Haldane, R. B.: *An Autobiography* (Hodder & Stoughton, 1929)
Halévy, E.: *The Rule of Democracy,* 2 vols. (Benn, 1932)

Hamilton, Sir Ian: *Gallipoli Diary*, 2 vols. (Arnold, 1920)

Hankey, Lord: *The Supreme Command, 1914-18* (Allen & Unwin, 1961)

Hansard (H.M.S.O.)

Hendrick, B. J.: *Life and Letters of Walter H. Page*, 3 vols. (Heinemann, 1923)

Holland, Bernard: *Life of the Duke of Devonshire, 1833-1908*, 2 vols. (Longmans, Green, 1911)

Jenkins, Roy: *Mr. Balfour's Poodle* (Heinemann, 1954)

Keyes, Admiral Sir Roger: *Naval Memoirs* (Thornton Butterworth, 1934)

Lloyd George, David: *War Memoirs*, 6 vols. (Nicholson & Watson, 1933)

MacCallum, Scott: *W. S. Churchill*

Macmillan, Norman: *Sir Sefton Brancker* (Heinemann, 1935)

Macready, General Sir Nevil: *Annals of an Active Life*, 2 vols. (Hutchinson, 1924)

Magnus, Philip: *Kitchener* (Murray, 1958)

Marder, Arthur J. (ed.): *Fear God and Dread Nought*, 2 vols. (Cape, 1956)

Marsh, Sir Edward: *A Number of People* (Hamish Hamilton and Heinemann, 1939)

Masterman, Lucy: *C. F. G. Masterman* (Nicholson & Watson, 1939)

Maurice, Sir F.: *Haldane, 1856-1915*, 2 vols. (Faber, 1937)

Moorehead, Alan: *Gallipoli* (Hamish Hamilton, 1956)

Morley, Lord: *Recollections*, 2 vols. (Macmillan, 1918)

              Memorandum on Resignation, August 1914 (Macmillan, 1928)

Murray, Lt.-Col. Hon. A. C.: *Master and Brother* (Murray, 1945)

Nicolson, Harold: *King George the Fifth, His Life and Reign* (Constable, 1952)

Petrie, Sir Charles: *Life and Letters of the Rt. Hon. Sir Austen Chamberlain, K.G., P.C., M.P.*, 2 vols. (Cassell, 1940)

Raymond, E. T.: *Mr. Lloyd George, a Biography* (Collins, 1922)

Riddell, Lord: *More Pages from My Diary, 1908-14* (Country Life, 1934)

Ronaldshay, Earl of: *Life of Lord Curzon*, 3 vols. (Benn, 1928)

Seely, Major-Gen. J. E. B. (Lord Mottistone): *Adventure* (Heinemann, 1930)

Smuts, J. C.: *Jan Christian Smuts* (Cassell, 1952)

Somervell, D. C.: *British Politics since 1900* (Dakers, 1953)

Spender, J. A.: *Life of Sir Henry Campbell-Bannerman*, G.C.B., 2 vols. (Hodder & Stoughton, 1923)

Spender, J. A. and Asquith, Cyril: *Life of Herbert Henry Asquith, Lord Oxford and Asquith*, 2 vols. (Hutchinson, 1932)

Taylor, H. A.: *Jix, Viscount Brentford* (Stanley Paul, 1933)

Trevelyan, G. M.: *Grey of Fallodon* (Longmans, Green, 1940)

British Documents on the Origins of the War, 1898-1914 (H.M.S.O.)

ACKNOWLEDGMENTS

I would like to thank my friend Colin Coote, but for whom I would never have attempted to write this book, and whose help and advice have been invaluable to me throughout. I also wish to thank the following for permission to quote excerpts from the sources indicated: Heinemann & Co., Ltd., and the Literary Executrix of Maurice Baring (*The Puppet Show of Memory* by Maurice Baring); the Beaverbrook Canadian Foundation (*Politicians and the War* by Lord Beaverbrook); Jonathan Cape Ltd. (*Fear God and Dread Nought* by A. J. Marder); The Public Trustee, as administrator of the estate of Lord Riddell (*More Pages from My Diary* by Lord Riddell); the *Daily Mail* (items in the *Daily News* and the *Daily Mail*); the *Daily Telegraph & Morning Post* (items in the *Morning Post*); Eyre & Spottiswoode (Publishers) Ltd. (*F.E., The Life of F. E. Smith, 1st Earl of Birkenhead* by his son the 2nd Earl of Birkenhead; and *The River War* by Winston S. Churchill); Miss D. C. Bacon and Hodder & Stoughton Ltd. (*The Life of Lord Fisher of Kilverstone* by Admiral Bacon); Hutchinson & Co. (Publishers) Ltd. (*Arthur James Balfour, 1st Earl of Balfour, K.S., O.M., F.R.S.* by B. E. C. Dugdale; and *Life of Lord Oxford and Asquith* by J. A. Spender and Cyril Asquith); Sir Geoffrey Keynes (letters from Rupert Brooke); Macmillan & Co. Ltd. (*Recollections* by Lord Morley); Mrs. C. F. G. Masterman (*C. F. G. Masterman* by Mrs. Masterman); John Murray (Publishers) Ltd. (*Mr. Churchill in 1940* by Isaiah Berlin); Odhams Books Ltd. (*London to Ladysmith; Life of Lord Randolph Churchill; My African Journey; Great Contemporaries; Painting as a Pastime,* by Winston S. Churchill); The Syndics of the Fitzwilliam Museum, Cambridge (*My Diaries* by Wilfrid Blunt); The Times Publishing Company (items in *The Times*).

NOTES TO REFERENCES

Page references are to British editions of works cited.

CHAPTER TWO

1 Winston Spencer Churchill, *My Early Life* (1947), p. 5.
2 *Ibid.*, pp. 72-73.
3 *Ibid.*, pp. 109-10.
4 *Ibid.*, pp. 19-20.
5 Winston Spencer Churchill, *Thoughts and Adventures* (1948), pp. 31-32.
6 Winston Spencer Churchill, *My Early Life*, p. 46.
7 *Ibid.*, p. 38.
8 *Ibid.*, p. 15.
9 *Ibid.*, pp. 20-21.
10 *Ibid.*, p. 26.
11 *Ibid.*, p. 36.
12 *Ibid.*, p. 59.

CHAPTER THREE

1 Winston Spencer Churchill, *My Early Life*, p. 46.
2 *Ibid.*, p. 75.
3 *Ibid.*, p. 77.
4 *Ibid.*, p. 82.
5 *Ibid.*, pp. 107-8.
6 *Ibid.*, pp. 113-14.
7 *Ibid.*, pp. 153-54.
8 *Ibid.*, p. 165.
9 *Ibid.*, p. 169.

CHAPTER FOUR

1   Winston Spencer Churchill, *My Early Life*, p. 190.
2   *Ibid.*, p. 209.
3   *Ibid.*, p. 209.
4   *Ibid.*, p. 208.
5   Winston Spencer Churchill, *The River War* (1900), Vol. II, p. 162.
6   *Ibid.*, p. 377.
7   *Ibid.*, pp. 211-12.
8   *Ibid.*, pp. 214-15.
9   *Ibid.*, p. 143.
10   *Ibid.*, pp. 221-22.
11   *Ibid.*, pp. 224-25.
12   *Ibid.*, p. 226.

CHAPTER FIVE

1   Winston Spencer Churchill, *My Early Life*, pp. 197-200.
2   *Ibid.*, p. 201.
3   *Ibid.*, p. 204.
4   *Ibid.*, pp. 220-21.
5   *Ibid.*, pp. 222-23.
6   *Ibid.*, p. 224.
7   *Ibid.*, p. 225.

CHAPTER SIX

1   Winston Spencer Churchill, *My Early Life*, p. 228.
2   *Ibid.*, p. 230.
3   J. B. Atkins, *Incidents and Reflections*, p. 122.
4   Winston Spencer Churchill, *op. cit.*, p. 232.
5   *Ibid.*, pp. 233-34.
6   J. B. Atkins, *op. cit.*, pp. 124-25.
7   *Ibid.*, p. 126.
8   Winston Spencer Churchill, *op. cit.*, p. 240.
9   *Ibid.*, p. 240.
10   *Ibid.*, p. 241.
11   J. B. Atkins, *op. cit.*, pp. 127-28.
12   General Sir Aylmer Haldane, *A Soldier's Saga* (1948), p. 142.
13   Winston Spencer Churchill, *op. cit.*, pp. 243-44.
14   *Ibid.*, p. 249.
15   Winston Spencer Churchill, *From London to Ladysmith*, p. 96.
16   Winston Spencer Churchill, *My Early Life*, p. 249.
17   *Ibid.*, p. 250.
18   *Ibid.*, p. 256.
19   Winston Spencer Churchill, *From London to Ladysmith*, p. 98.

20   *Ibid.,* pp. 133-36.
21   Winston Spencer Churchill, *My Early Life,* pp. 256-57.

CHAPTER SEVEN

1   Winston Spencer Churchill, *My Early Life,* p. 266.
2   *Ibid.,* p. 271.
3   *Ibid.,* p. 271.
4   *Ibid.,* pp. 272-73.
5   *Ibid.,* p. 277.
6   *Ibid.,* pp. 278-80.
7   *Ibid.,* pp. 288-90.
8   *Ibid.,* p. 292.
9   *Ibid.,* pp. 293-94, 299.
10   *Ibid.,* p. 298.
11   *Ibid.,* p. 302.
12   *Ibid.,* p. 347.
13   *Ibid.,* p. 349.

CHAPTER EIGHT

1   Winston Spencer Churchill, *My Early Life,* pp. 351-52.
2   *Morning Post,* July 26, 1900.
3   *Ibid.,* August 20, 1900.
4   Winston Spencer Churchill, *My Early Life,* p. 352.
5   J. A. Spender, *Life of Sir Henry Campbell-Bannerman,* Vol. I, pp. 291-92.
6   *Daily News,* September 26, 1900.
7   Winston Spencer Churchill, *op. cit.,* pp. 352-53.
8   *Ibid.,* pp. 355-56.

CHAPTER NINE

1   Winston Spencer Churchill, *My Early Life,* p. 360.
2   *Ibid.,* p. 360.
3   *Ibid.,* p. 359.
4   *Ibid.,* p. 361.
5   *Ibid.,* p. 361.
6   Hansard, *Official Record of Parliamentary Debates,* February 18, 1901.
7   *Morning Post,* February 19, 1901.
8   *Daily News,* February 19, 1901.
9   Winston Spencer Churchill, *op. cit.,* pp. 361-62.
10   *Ibid.,* p. 362.
11   *Ibid.,* p. 362.
12   *Daily News,* March 13, 1901.
13   Winston Spencer Churchill, *op. cit.,* pp. 363-64.

14   *Ibid.,* p. 364.
15   Hansard, May 13, 1901.
16   *Times,* May 14, 1901.
17   *Daily News,* May 14, 1901.
18   Winston Spencer Churchill, *Thoughts and Adventures* (1948), p. 35.
19   *Ibid.,* pp. 35-36.
20   Hansard, April 14, 1902.
21   Winston Spencer Churchill, *My Early Life,* pp. 366-67.

CHAPTER TEN

1   Winston Spencer Churchill, *The World Crisis, 1911-15* (1923), p. 26.
2   Winston Spencer Churchill, *Thoughts and Adventures* (1948), pp. 5-6.
3   *Ibid.,* p. 34.
4   *Times,* May 22, 1903.
5   Hansard, *Parliamentary Debates,* June 22, 1903.
6   *Times,* July 16, 1903.
7   *Ibid.,* September 21, 1903.
8   Winston Spencer Churchill, *The World Crisis,* Vol. I, pp. 28-29.
9   Bernard Holland, *Life of the Duke of Devonshire,* Vol. II, p. 320.
10   *Times,* October 7, 1903 (Mr. Chamberlain's speech at Greenock).
11   *Ibid.,* November 12, 1903.
12   *Ibid.,* November 12, 1903.
13   J. A. Spender, *Life of Sir Henry Campbell-Bannerman,* Vol. II, p. 128.
14   *Manchester Guardian,* August 1, 1903.
15   *Daily News,* November 12, 1903.
16   *Ibid.,* November 26, 1903.
17   A. MacCallum Scott, *Winston Spencer Churchill* (1905), p. 202.
18   *Halifax Courier,* December 24, 1903.

CHAPTER ELEVEN

1   Hansard, *Parliamentary Debates,* March 29, 1904.
2   Winston Spencer Churchill, *The World Crisis,* Vol. I, p. 29.
3   A. MacCallum Scott, *Winston Spencer Churchill.*
4   Hansard, March 24, 1904.
5   *Ibid.,* March 29, 1904.
6   *Daily News,* March 30, 1904.
7   *Manchester Guardian,* March 16, 1904.
8   *Ibid.,* May 14, 1904.
9   Hansard, April 22, 1904.
10   *Daily Mail,* April 23, 1904.
11   Hansard, May 16, 1904.
12   *Daily News,* June 6, 1904.

CHAPTER TWELVE

1   Hansard, July 4, 1904.
2   Winston Spencer Churchill, *The World Crisis,* Vol. I, p. 28.
3   *Times,* December 6, 1904.
4   *Ibid.,* January 28, 1905.
5   Hansard, February 20, 1905.
6   *Manchester Guardian,* March 9, 1905.
7   Hansard, March 8, 1905.
8   *Ibid.,* March 28, 1905.
9   *Ibid.,* March 29, 1905.
10 *Ibid.,* July 24, 1905.
11 *Ibid.,* July 24, 1905.
12 *Times,* November 25, 1905.

CHAPTER THIRTEEN

1   *Manchester Guardian,* January 9, 1906.
2   *Daily Mail,* January 5, 1906.
3   H. A. Taylor, *Jix, Viscount Brentford,* pp. 61-62.
4   *Manchester Guardian,* January 5, 1906.
5   *Daily Mail,* January 13, 1906.
6   Winston Spencer Churchill, *Thoughts and Adventures,* p. 156.

CHAPTER FOURTEEN

1   "Mr. Churchill and F. D. R.," in *Cornhill,* Winter 1949/50.
2   Hansard, *Parliamentary Debates,* March 21, 1906.
3   *Ibid.,* July 30, 1906.
4   *Times,* August 7, 1906, Wimborne.
5   Hansard, June 25, 1907.
6   Winston Spencer Churchill, *Life of Lord Randolph Churchill,* Vol. I.
7   Elie Halevy, *The Rule of Democracy,* Vol. I, pp. 92-93.
8   Winston Spencer Churchill, *Great Contemporaries,* pp. 130, 132.
9   Sir Edward Marsh, *A Number of People,* p. 171.
10 Winston Spencer Churchill, *My African Journey,* p. 155.
11 Winston Spencer Churchill, *Thoughts and Adventures,* p. 157.
12 *Ibid.,* p. 158.
13 *Pall Mall Gazette,* April 25, 1908.
14 *Daily Express,* April 25, 1908.
15 *Daily Mail,* April 25, 1908.
16 Winston Spencer Churchill, *op. cit.,* p. 158.
17 Winston Spencer Churchill, *Liberalism and the Social Problem,* pp. 155, 163-68.

CHAPTER FIFTEEN

1   Lucy Masterman, *C. F. G. Masterman*, p. 97.
2   Lord Riddell, *More Pages from My Diary*, p. 1.
3   Hon. Arthur Murray, *Master and Brother*, p. 88.
4   Viscount Grey of Fallodon, *Twenty-five Years*, pp. 192-93.
5   E. T. Raymond, *Lloyd George*, p. 106.
6   *Times*, January 22, 1909.
7   A. J. Marder, ed., *Fear God and Dread Nought*, Vol. II, pp. 226-27.
8   Winston Spencer Churchill, *The World Crisis*, Vol. I, pp. 34, 36-38.

CHAPTER SIXTEEN

1   Winston Spencer Churchill, *Liberalism and the Social Problem*, pp. 354-55.
2   Lucy Masterman, *op. cit.*, p. 140.
3   *Ibid.*, p. 133.
4   J. A. Spender and Cyril Asquith, *Life of Lord Oxford and Asquith* Vol. I, p. 271; Vol. II, p. 350.
5   Hansard, *Parliamentary Debates*, April 14, 1910.
6   The Earl of Oxford and Asquith, *Fifty Years of Parliament*, Vol. II, pp. 86-88.
7   Sir Harold Nicolson, *Life and Reign of King George V*, p. 131.
8   *Times*, March 20, 1930.
9   David Lloyd George, *War Memoirs*, Vol. I, p. 36.
10 Mrs. Edgar Dugdale, *A. J. Balfour*, Vol. II, p. 77.
11 Spender and Asquith, *op. cit.*, Vol. I, p. 287.
12 *Ibid.*
13 Sir Harold Nicolson, *op. cit.*, p. 138.
14 Roy Jenkins, *Mr. Balfour's Poodle*, p. 129.
15 Hansard, May 15, 1911.
16 Lord Ronaldshay, *The Life of Lord Curzon*, Vol. III, p. 56.
17 Mrs. Edgar Dugdale, *op. cit.*, Vol. II, pp. 66-67.
18 *Ibid.*, Vol. II, p. 70.
19 *Times*, July 25, 1911.
20 *Daily Telegraph*, July 25, 1911.
21 *Evening Standard*, July 25, 1911.
22 Hansard, August 7, 1911.
23 *Ibid.*, August 7, 1911.
24 Sir Almeric Fitzroy, *Memoirs*, Vol. II, pp. 458-59.
25 Hansard, Lords, August 9, 1911.

CHAPTER SEVENTEEN

1   W. S. Blunt, *My Diaries*.
2   *Times*, November 9, 1910.

3   General Sir Nevil Macready, *Annals of an Active Life,* Vol. I, p. 155.
4   *Daily Express,* November 9, 1910.
5   Hansard, *Parliamentary Debates,* February 7, 1911.
6   Winston Spencer Churchill, *Thoughts and Adventures,* pp. 44, 45, 46, 47.
7   *Daily News,* January 4, 1911.
8   A. G. Gardiner, *Pillars of Society,* p. 58.
9   J. A. Spender and Cyril Asquith, *Life of Lord Oxford and Asquith,* Vol. I, p. 350.
10 Hansard, August 22, 1911.
11 Lucy Masterman, *C. F. G. Masterman,* p. 205.
12 Winston Spencer Churchill, *The World Crisis, 1911-1914,* p. 47.
13 *Ibid.,* pp. 49-50.
14 *Ibid.,* p. 52.
15 *Ibid.,* p. 51.
16 *Ibid.,* p. 60.
17 Richard Burdon Haldane, *Autobiography,* p. 236.
18 Winston Spencer Churchill, *op. cit.,* p. 65.
19 Richard Burdon Haldane, *op. cit.,* p. 230.
20 Winston Spencer Churchill, *op. cit.,* p. 68.
21 *Ibid.,* pp. 68-69.

CHAPTER EIGHTEEN
1   Winston Spencer Churchill, *The World Crisis, 1911-1914,* p. 70.
2   *Ibid.,* p. 72.
3   *Ibid.,* p. 77.
4   *Ibid.,* pp. 73, 74.
5   *Ibid.,* pp. 77-78.
6   *Ibid.,* pp. 78-79.
7   Sir Frederick Maurice, *Life of Lord Haldane,* Vol. I, p. 287.
8   Arthur Marder, *Fear God and Dread Nought, 1904-1914,* Vol. II, p. 416.
9   *Ibid.,* p. 430.
10 Winston Spencer Churchill, *ibid.,* pp. 119-20.
11 *Times,* February 10, 1912.
12 *Daily News,* February 10, 1912.
13 *Times,* February 10, 1912.
14 Hansard, *Parliamentary Debates,* March 18, 1912.
15 A. MacCallum Scott, *Winston Churchill in Peace and War,* p. 35.
16 Winston Spencer Churchill, *ibid.,* pp. 112-13.
17 *Ibid.,* p. 122.
18 *Ibid.,* p. 123.
19 Hansard, March 17, 1914.

20   Winston Spencer Churchill, *ibid.*, pp. 140-41.
21   *Ibid.*, pp. 126-27.
22   *Ibid.*, pp. 130-31.
23   Admiral Sir Reginald Bacon, *The Life of Lord Fisher of Kilverstone*, Vol. II, p. 148.
24   *Ibid.*, Vol. II, p. 153.
25   *Ibid.*, Vol. II, pp. 157-58.
26   Lucy Masterman, *Life of C. F. G. Masterman*, p. 234.
27   Lord Riddell, *More Pages from My Diary, 1908-14*, p. 78.
28   Hansard, December 11, 1912.
29   Winston Spencer Churchill, *ibid.*, pp. 172-73.
30   *Ibid.*, p. 178.

CHAPTER TWENTY

1   Hansard, *Parliamentary Debates*, April 11, 1912.
2   *Ibid.*, April 30, 1912.
3   *Ibid.*, April 11, 1912.
4   *Ibid.*, April 11, 1912.
5   Winston Spencer Churchill, *My Early Life*, p. 2.
6   *Times*, January 24, 1912.
7   *Ibid.*, September 14, 1912.
8   D. C. Somervell, *British Policies Since 1900*, p. 95.
9   The Earl of Oxford and Asquith, *Fifty Years of Parliament*, Vol. II, pp. 140-42.
10   Burton Jesse Hendrick, *Life and Letters of Walter H. Page*, Vol. I, pp. 138, 170-71.
11   J. A. Spender and Cyril Asquith, *Life of Lord Oxford and Asquith*, Vol. II, p. 31.
12   The Earl of Oxford and Asquith, *Memories and Reflections*, Vol. I, pp. 205-6.
13   Spender and Asquith, *op. cit.*, Vol. II, p. 36.
14   Winston Spencer Churchill, *The World Crisis, 1911-1914*, p. 182.
15   Spender and Asquith, *op. cit.*, Vol. II, p. 40.
16   Major-General C. E. Callwell, K.C.B., *Field-Marshal Sir Henry Wilson*, Vol. I, p. 131.
17   Winston Spencer Churchill, *ibid.*, p. 184.
18   R. C. K. Ensor, *England 1870-1914*, p. 479.
19   Hansard, April 28, 1914.
20   Winston Spencer Churchill, *ibid.*, p. 186.
21   *Ibid.*, p. 193.
22   *Ibid.*, p. 198.
23   Winston Spencer Churchill, *Great Contemporaries*, p. 148.
24   Winston Spencer Churchill, *The World Crisis, 1911-1914*, p. 213.

25 G. M. Trevelyan, *Grey of Fallodon*, p. 253.
26 Dr. G. P. Gooch and Sir Harold Temperley, *British Documents on the Origins of the War*, Vol. XI, p. 271.
27 Lord Morley, *Memorandum on Resignation*, p. 23.
28 Lord Grey of Fallodon, *Twenty-five Years, 1892-1916*, Vol. II, p. 14.

CHAPTER TWENTY-ONE

1   Winston Spencer Churchill, *The World Crisis, 1911-1914*, p. 234.
2   *Ibid.*, p. 227.
3   *Ibid.*, p. 252.
4   *Ibid.*, p. 255.
5   *Ibid.*, p. 268.
6   *Ibid.*, p. 277.
7   *Ibid.*, p. 277.
8   The Earl of Oxford and Asquith, *Memories and Reflections*, Vol. II, p. 25.
9   Winston Spencer Churchill, *ibid.*, p. 283.
10 *Ibid.*, p. 284.
11 Norman Macmillan, *Sefton Brancker*, p. 77.
12 Winston Spencer Churchill, *ibid.*, p. 320.
13 Lord Beaverbrook, *Politicians and the War*, Vol. I, p. 31.
14 Winston Spencer Churchill, *ibid.*, p. 322.

CHAPTER TWENTY-TWO

1   Winston Spencer Churchill, *The World Crisis, 1911-1914*, p. 331.
2   The Earl of Oxford and Asquith, *Memories and Reflections*, Vol. II, p. 41.
3   Major-General J. E. B. Seely, *Adventure*, p. 139.
4   The Earl of Oxford and Asquith, *op. cit.*, Vol. II, p. 42.
5   *Ibid.*, Vol. II, pp. 45-46.
6   *Ibid.*, p. 42.
7   Winston Spencer Churchill, *ibid.*, pp. 357-58.
8   *Morning Post*, October 13, 1914.
9   *Times*, October 14, 1914.
10 The Earl of Oxford and Asquith, *op. cit.*, Vol. II, pp. 44-45.
11 *Sunday Pictorial*, November, 1916.
12 Winston Spencer Churchill, *ibid.*, p. 398.
13 *Ibid.*, p. 402.
14 Sir Harold Nicolson, *King George V*, p. 251.
15 Winston Spencer Churchill, *ibid.*, p. 405.
16 Admiral Sir Reginald Bacon, *The Life of Lord Fisher of Kilverstone*, Vol. II, p. 178.
17 Winston Spencer Churchill, *ibid.*, p. 438.

18   *Ibid.,* p. 466.
19   *Ibid.,* p. 467.
20   *Ibid.,* p. 468.
21   *Ibid.,* p. 476.

CHAPTER TWENTY-THREE

1   Winston Spencer Churchill, *The World Crisis, 1915,* p. 92.
2   *Ibid.,* p. 94.
3   *Ibid.,* pp. 97, 98.
4   *Ibid.,* pp. 110, 111.
5   *Ibid.,* p. 157.
6   The Earl of Oxford and Asquith, *Memories and Reflections,* Vol. II, p. 59. Minutes of this meeting of the War Council are printed as an addendum.
7   Winston Spencer Churchill, *ibid.,* p. 165.
8   *Ibid.,* p. 165.
9   The Earl of Oxford and Asquith, *ibid.,* Vol. II, p. 61.
10   Winston Spencer Churchill, *ibid.,* p. 180.
11   *Ibid.,* p. 183.
12   *Times* (first leader), February 22, 1915.
13   Lord Beaverbrook, *Politicians and the War,* Vol. I, p. 58.
14   Winston Spencer Churchill, *ibid.,* p. 198.
15   *Ibid.,* p. 199.
16   Lord Beaverbrook, *ibid.,* Vol. I, p. 60.
17   Winston Spencer Churchill, *ibid.,* pp. 203, 204.
18   *Ibid.,* p. 217.
19   Admiral Sir Roger Keyes, *Naval Memoirs 1910-1915,* p. 186.
20   Winston Spencer Churchill, *ibid.,* pp. 230, 231.
21   *Ibid.,* pp. 234-35.
22   *Ibid.,* p. 237.
23   General Sir Ian Hamilton, *Gallipoli Diary,* Vol. I, pp. 41-42.
24   Winston Spencer Churchill, *ibid.,* p. 249.
25   *Ibid.,* p. 252.
26   *Ibid.,* p. 169.

CHAPTER TWENTY-FOUR

1   Winston Spencer Churchill, *The World Crisis, 1915,* p. 303.
2   *Ibid.,* p. 330.
3   *Ibid.,* p. 346.
4   *Ibid.,* p. 351.
5   *Ibid.,* pp. 353-54.
6   *Ibid.,* p. 357.

7   R. B. Haldane, *Autobiography*, p. 283.
8   Lord Beaverbrook, *Politicians and the War*. Vol. I, pp. 109-10.
9   *Ibid.*, p. 111.
10   *Ibid.*, p. 112.
11   *Ibid.*
12   Winston Spencer Churchill, *ibid.*, p. 365.
13   *Ibid.*, p. 366.
14   *Ibid.*, p. 369.
15   *Ibid.*, p. 370.
16   Lord Beaverbrook, *ibid.*, p. 124.

CHAPTER TWENTY-FIVE

1   *Times*, May 22, 1915.
2   *Morning Post*, April 23, 1915.
3   *Times*, May 25, 1915.
4   Winston Spencer Churchill, *The World Crisis, 1915*, p. 424.
5   *Ibid.*, p. 393.
6   *Ibid.*, pp. 407-8.
7   *Ibid.*, p. 394.
8   *Ibid.*, p. 395.
9   *Ibid.*, p. 428.
10   *Ibid.*, p. 432.
11   Alan Moorehead, *Gallipoli*, p. 243.
12   Winston Spencer Churchill, *ibid.*, p. 451.
13   *Ibid.*, p. 394.
14   J. A. Spender and Cyril Asquith, *Life of Lord Oxford and Asquith*, Vol. II, p. 181.
15   Winston Spencer Churchill, *ibid.*, p. 463.
16   *Ibid.*, p. 465.
17   *Ibid.*, p. 465.
18   *Ibid.*, p. 474.
19   J. A. Spender and Cyril Asquith, *op. cit.*, Vol. II, p. 185.
20   Winston Spencer Churchill, *ibid.*, p. 475.
21   *Ibid.*, p. 477.
22   General Sir Ian Hamilton, *Gallipoli Diary*, Vol. II, p. 253.
23   Winston Spencer Churchill, *ibid.*, p. 489.
24   *Ibid.*, pp. 490, 491.
25   Admiral of the Fleet Sir Roger Keyes, *Naval Memoirs*, Vol. I, p. 449.
26   Winston Spencer Churchill, *ibid.*, p. 499.
27   *Times*, November 13, 1915.
28   *Manchester Guardian*, November 13, 1915.
29   Hansard, *Parliamentary Debates*, November 15, 1915.

CHAPTER TWENTY-SIX

1 The Earl of Oxford and Asquith, *Memories and Reflections*, Vol. II, pp. 123-24.
2 Winston Spencer Churchill, *Thoughts and Adventures*, pp. 67, 68.
3 *Ibid.*, p. 69.
4 *Ibid.*, p. 69.
5 *Ibid.*, pp. 70, 71.
6 *Ibid.*, p. 71.
7 *Ibid.*, pp. 71-72.
8 *Ibid.*, p. 72.
9 *Ibid.*, p. 73.
10 *Ibid.*, pp. 76, 77.
11 *Ibid.*, pp. 77, 78.
12 The Earl of Oxford and Asquith, *op. cit.*, Vol. II, p. 114.
13 Hansard, *Parliamentary Debates*, December 16, 1915.
14 Lord Beaverbrook, *Politicians and the War, 1914-1916*, Vol. II, p. 75.
15 *Ibid.*, p. 76.
16 Captain Gibb, *With Winston Churchill at the Front*, pp. 10, 18.
17 *Ibid.*, p. 19.
18 *Ibid.*, pp. 21-22.
19 *Ibid.*, pp. 59, 68, 69, 73.
20 *Ibid.*, p. 110.
21 Hansard, March 7, 1916.
22 *Ibid.*, March 8, 1916.
23 *Ibid.*, March 7, 1916.
24 *Morning Post*, March 8, 1916.
25 *Manchester Guardian*, March 8, 1916.
26 Lord Hankey, *The Supreme Command*, Vol. II, p. 487.
27 Hansard, July 31, 1916.
28 Winston Spencer Churchill, *The World Crisis, 1916-1918*, Part I, p. 118.
29 *Ibid.*, pp. 108-61.
30 *Ibid.*, p. 161.
31 *Ibid.*, p. 161.
32 *Ibid.*, p. 112.
33 Lord Hankey, *op. cit.*, Vol. II, p. 493.
34 The Earl of Oxford and Asquith, *op. cit.*, Vol. II, p. 84.
35 Winston Spencer Churchill, *ibid.*, Part I, p. 35.
36 Winston Spencer Churchill, *Painting as a Pastime*, p. 16.
37 *Ibid.*, pp. 14, 15.
38 *Ibid.*, p. 24.
39 *Ibid.*, p. 19.

INDEX